A Global Ethic for
Global Politics and
Economics

A Global Ethic for Global Politics and Economics

Hans Küng

New York   Oxford
Oxford University Press
1998

Oxford University Press

Oxford New York
Athens Auckland Bangkok Bogotá Bombay
Buenos Aires Calcutta Cape Town Dar es Salaam
Delhi Florence Hong Kong Istanbul Karachi
Kuala Lumpur Madras Madrid Melbourne
Mexico City Nairobi Paris Singapore
Taipei Tokyo Toronto Warsaw

and associated companies in
Berlin Ibadan

Published by Oxford University Press, Inc.,
198 Madison Avenue, New York, New York 10016

Translated by John Bowden from the German
Weltethos für Weltpolitik und Weltwirtschaft
published 1997 by Piper Verlag GmbH Munich.

English translation first published 1997 by SCM Press Ltd., London.

Library of Congress Cataloging in Publication Data
Küng, Hans, 1928–
[Weltethos für Weltpolitik und Weltwirtschaft. English]
A global ethic for global politics and economics / Hans Küng;
[translated by John Bowden from the German].
p. cm.
Includes bibliographical references and index.
ISBN 0-19-512228-3 (cloth)
1. Ethics. 2. World politics—1989–
3. International economic relations.
4. International economic relations—Religious aspects.
5. Religion and international affairs. I. Title.
BJ1125.K8713 1998
170—dc21 97-30562

1 3 5 7 9 8 6 4 2
Printed in the United States of America
on acid-free paper

Dedicated in gratitude to
Count and Countess von der Groeben,
the founders of the
Global Ethic Foundation

Contents

Contents

Wanted – A Vision

No one has a vision today. No one can say what should happen or what the long-term future should bring. A sense of helplessness pervades cultural life, and there is an oppressive void. That is the complaint of one of the most prominent liberal commentators of our time, Marion Countess Dönhoff,[1] and she adds – with a reference to the utopias of Aldous Huxley in *Brave New World* (1922) and George Orwell in *1984* (1949) – that today there is also no one to give 'oracles' about the direction our civilization will take. (Though would another black utopia and terrifying picture of the future really help us, where hope can at best be recognized indirectly?)

I agree with her. On all sides we lack a realistic vision of the future. Moreover, such a vision is hardly to be expected from representatives of those great ideologies which in the last two centuries have served as 'scientific' total explanations and attractive pseudo-religions for our millennium now drawing to an end. These ideologies are now clearly bankrupt. Wherever one looks, whether to left or to right, there is nothing doing.

The revolutionary wave of 1989 and the collapse of the Communist systems in Europe have literally left speechless all those who, not only in the East but also in the West, fell in all too uncritically with the revolutionary ideology of progress propagated by real socialism. The intellectuals, an eloquent opposition in the 1960s and 1970s, have fallen amazingly silent in the face of the questions which keep thronging in.

Nor do all those who for a long time have believed in the ideology of the evolutionary and technological progress of the West have a constructive vision of the future today as they are confronted with the threat of ecological, economic and social collapse. All too often politicians and the great men of action in business and finance have simply muddled through and postponed the urgent problems. But problems continue to press in and the pressure is becoming greater, since today not only questions of national destiny but global questions, even that of the very survival of humankind, are on the political agenda, especially for Europeans and Americans. The 'Europe' of the cabinets is fixating itself on the uncertain future of the 'Euro', which is already having its genes manipulated politically on all sides, when it should be developing and putting into practice guidelines and aims for a 'common' foreign policy from which it has been distracted, and a financial and social policy which sometimes seems chaotic. After the Gulf War, the US President George Bush announced a 'new world order', but did not give the slightest indication of what he meant by this. In any case, visions were not his thing; when driven into a corner by questioners, he spoke quite disparagingly about 'the vision thing'. Yet a concrete vision of a new world order is being called for, particularly in and by America.

In this epoch-making paradigm shift in which the world, its politics, economy and culture are caught up, do we not need urgently to strive for at least **basic orientation** for the present in the light of the future, referring to the spiritual and cultural foundations of humankind? But who is in a position to offer such orientation? It is no small undertaking for an individual; a team could offer more specialist knowledge, but usually at the expense of the internal unity of the conception. It is a great undertaking if one is not on the one hand to give enigmatic oracles or prophecies, and to speak in dark suggestions and hints, yet on the other hand does not want simply to extrapolate particular data and statistical trends in order to give a supposedly certain prognosis of the future. Perhaps it is too great an undertaking, unless one simply wants to extol a 'utopia' (a 'nowhere') of the kind that in past centuries has so often led people astray and with its promises of a 'whole world' has robbed them of the power to make decisions. What I shall attempt here will be quite the opposite: no noble ideas without any earthing, no cleverly devised plans which are impossible to realize, no enthusiastic notions of the future with no real reference to the present, no programmes for the doctrinaire and the dreamers, saviours of the world and moral preachers who are so prone to indignation. But what can be done?

To put it plainly: this book aims to rediscovery and reassess **ethics** in politics and economics. It is **all for morality** (in the positive sense). But at the same time it is **against moralism** (morality in the negative sense). For moralism and moralizing overvalue morality and ask too much of it. Why? Moralists make morality the sole criterion for human action and ignore the relative independence of various spheres of life like economics, law and politics. As a result they tend to absolutize intrinsically justified norms and values (peace, justice, environment, life, love) and also to exploit them for the particular interests of an institution (state, party, church, interest group). Moralism manifests itself in a one-sided and penetrating insistence on particular moral positions (for example, in questions of sexual behaviour) which makes a rational dialogue with those of other convictions impossible.

In the face of the crisis of social orientation at the turn of the millennium, this book ventures a basic orientation, in a dialogue with politics and economics. It offers a **realistic vision or overall view**, seeking to explore the outlines of a more peaceful, just and humane world, in a dialogue which is very ready to learn. No central principle – the state, the market or the church – will regulate everything like a visible or invisible 'hand'. Nor will an account of existing conditions be caught up in a conceptual net of an ideology constrained by economics or exploited for party-political ends, which increases the problems it pretends to solve. What I shall attempt to give here is a viable **outline of the future** which takes historical experiences into account, comes to grips with present social reality and at the same time transcends it in search of a (relatively) better world order. Granted, in a world perspective we face unprecedented problems. But these must not be complained about as insuperable obstacles which barricade the way to the future: we have enough prophets of doom. Rather, the problems should be taken seriously as a great challenge which the younger generation – not so burdened as the generations of the First World War, the dictatorships, the Second World War or the post-war period – is called on to cope with. Often what has seemed impossible in the short term has become possible in the long term, through patience and persistence.

The vision sketched out here will not simply be proclaimed, announced or preached, but backed up with arguments. It represents an **ethically orientated overall view developed step by step through arguments**, which will be characterized
– by diachronic and synchronic thought in broad historical contexts,
– by unprejudiced criticism of conditions which really exist,
– by constructive alternatives which are rationally comprehensible,
– by concrete stimuli towards realizing it which are open to discussion.

Such a vision (without simplistic suggestions for a solution or cheap recipes) may prompt the experts and authorities in various areas to develop and work out those necessary **long-term strategies** which would be far beyond the author's competence. Or is that being too theoretical? On the contrary, even at the level of everyday business practice it could be helpful to decide on strategies and tactics in the light of an overall view. I feel that my approach has been confirmed by a number of conversations with leading figures not only in politics and economics, but also particularly in business. As one example out of many I might mention Reinhold Würth of the South German firm Künzelsau, who in the last forty years has turned a three-man business into a world-wide concern with more than 15,000 employees and a turnover of many billion DM per year. He explains in detail 'why successful businessmen are great visionaries':

> Visions are spiritual high flights between past and future. Visions are more than dreams, since they can be supported with arguments. Nevertheless they are less than strategic plans, because visions go beyond the time-scale of the latter. Learning from the experiences of the past but at the same time detaching himself from them, the successful visionary attempts to anticipate the future in his thoughts as boldly and as realistically as he can. If he succeeds in formulating this future in a way which is to some extent valid, i.e. credible and viable for a business, a successful visionary can become a successful businessman.[2]

A small note for possible **reviewers**, about whom I truly have no complaints (apart from a couple of notoriously prejudiced papers on the right wing and on the left). This book begins with diplomacy, but it is anything but a diplomatic book. It does not just describe, but also takes a firm position; it speaks bluntly and clearly. Since it is not obligated to any party or interest group, it is open to attack from all sides. However, its approach should be attributed less to my origin in the country of William Tell than to my advanced age, on the threshold of my eighth decade: I feel no pleasure in taking a concern which has long been with me to some extent 'into the grave'.

Anyone who ventures to judge current events from a political and ethical perspective must expect two charges:

– **'Political naivety'** ('How could a theologian take it upon himself to pass judgment on . . . ?'). But wait a minute . . . Anyone who from the age of ten (to be precise, after the shock of 12 March 1938) has not only been reading newspapers every day but has attempted to inform himself in every possible way may sometimes also allow himself some political judgments, even if he is not a politician or a political scientist (nor a 'political theologian');

– **'Moral arrogance'** ('He wants to teach us our business'). Anyone who speaks on moral questions and argues for an ethic need not think himself better than anyone else. And anyone who keeps engaging in self-criticism, time and again, may also allow himself, in all fallibility, some ethically motivated judgments, although he is not a saint or a zealot, but knows himself responsible to another authority. Therefore here, too, I would like to quote one of my favourite Latin sayings: *'Dixi, et salvavi animam meam'*, 'I have said it and have saved my soul.'

So, perhaps boldly and, I hope (following the example of Max Weber, who deliberately broke through the fences surrounding disciplines), in an awareness of history yet keeping close to the present, at the same time I want to continue the **project of a global ethic,** utilizing all that I have been allowed to learn in the course of half a century in the constant study of others, whose number is incalculable (I can mention only a few of them in my word of thanks at the end). Supported above all by my comprehensive investigations of *Judaism* (1991, English 1992) and *Christianity* (1994, English 1995), in which many of the ideas expressed here are already echoed (I hope that the volume on *Islam* will follow soon), I hope to demonstrate how the global ethic can be brought to bear concretely on global politics and global economics. Specialists in the various areas who know infinitely more than I do on individual points will understand better than others that, given the vast amount of material and the literature which extends endlessly in every direction, time and again I have had to be selective in my approach.

Nevertheless, precisely because the problems are pressing and a new millennium is dawning – what will it bring? – I shall attempt to sketch out this vision. It has not been written specially for this turning point, but has matured over long years. Despite all the manifest scepticism I feel strengthened by a document on the ethics of world peace by that passionate advocate of reason and undeterred visionary, Immanuel Kant, which has been much discussed on the occasion of its bicentenary and is still as topical as ever. Kant ends his last section 'On the Unanimity of Politics with Morality' with the sentence: 'Thus the **eternal peace** which follows the peace treaties (really cease-fires) falsely so-called is no empty idea but a task which, accomplished little by little (because the time in which the same progress takes place will hopefully become shorter and shorter), is steadily coming closer.'

Tübingen, January 1997   Hans Küng

A. Global Politics between Real Politics and Ideal Politics

I

The Old Real Politics Again?

Will perhaps the twenty-first century finally create that **new world order** which was beyond the capability of the twentieth century, at the beginning of which the crisis of modernity became visible? One could doubt it, if one reflects on world politics and the world order: three missed opportunities in a century:
– after the First World War, instead of a new world order and a real 'league of nations', there was unprecedented **world chaos**;
– after the Second World War, instead of a new world order and truly 'united nations', there was unprecedented **world division**;
– after the collapse of Soviet Communism, instead of a new world order and a common 'house of Europe', there was new **world disorder**.

To echo Heinrich Heine, the nineteenth-century Jewish German poet, if one thinks of Europe in the night, one is robbed of sleep. There is Bosnia, and also Chechnya: again wars simply for the preservation and extension of national power, with thousands of dead, mass rapes of women, senseless destruction of cities and villages. And in the face of this tragedy the UNO has been powerless, NATO for a long time inactive, the EC without a plan, the CSCE ineffective. People talk so much about the 'community of nations', 'world community'. But is there such a thing? Is there not still, as before, simply an association of sovereign states who pursue their old nationalistic interests behind the torrent of internationalist rhetoric?

In retrospect, the European revolutions of 1989 look like 'catching up revolutions',[1] which revealed no fundamentally new vision of a coming world order. Here the first question on the tips of some people's tongues is: **will world politics continue in the same style?** After this twentieth century, with all its terrors, are we simply to go on in the same way in the twenty-first? Clearly, anyone who does not learn from history is condemned to repeat it.

1. Global politics in the old style: Kissinger

Are we then to continue in the style of that European power politics of sovereign states which has dominated the whole of the modern age since it was successfully demonstrated in advance, 300 years ago, by **Cardinal Richelieu**, with success both immediately and in the medium term?[2] Reasons of state (*'raison d'état'*) are put above all moral principles. As one of Richelieu's present-day admirers, according to whom Richelieu 'achieved vast successes by ignoring, and indeed transcending, the essential pieties of his age', remarks: 'In the world inaugurated by Richelieu, states were no longer restrained by the pretence of a moral code.' Here I am quoting **Henry Kissinger**, and his masterpiece of almost 1000 pages, *Diplomacy*,[3] his legacy and his defence, which appeared in 1994. It is worth beginning our analysis of the problem with him, as a significant politician and political theorist both in theory and in practice, in order to get to the bottom of this 'real politics' by grappling with its great ancestors, above all Richelieu and Bismarck – not, to be sure, out of primarily historical interest, but with a view to the present day, in order to make historical experience useful for the future.

(a) The power-play of diplomacy

'Nations have pursued self-interest more frequently than high-minded principle' and 'have combated more than they have co-operated', and this will presumably continue to be the case: 'There is little evidence to suggest that this age-old mode of behaviour has changed, or that it is likely to change, in the decades ahead.'[4] That is what Henry Kissinger tells us. He was born in 1923 in Fürth in Franconia, and in 1938 emigrated with his parents to America, where from 1957 he taught political sciences at Harvard University. From 1969 to 1975 he was Security Adviser and from 1973 to 1977 Secretary of State to Presidents Nixon and Ford, and in those posts exercised a decisive influence on American foreign policy. The main aim of foreign policy could **not** be **peace and justice**. Statesmen, with the help of diplomacy, should want to strive **only for stability and security through a balance of power**, so that the world, which in any case is marked by tragedy, becomes somewhat more stable and secure through the establishment of a stable equilibrium of forces and is thus indirectly brought closer to peace: by containing crises and as far as possible avoiding wars, step by step, 'peace in fragments'.

In his theory about the nature and history of international politics

Kissinger wants to argue for stability and security through a balance of power, and as a politician he put this into practice. And regardless of how one regards some of his actions, it has to be conceded that he achieved both with a bravura that one misses in most women and men in science and politics: with a sharp intellect and a quick wit, he also showed courage in standing up for his convictions, and in addition showed the resolve to act on them with tenacity and persistence if the opportunity was offered him. This was the case even when initially he stood alone, or thought that he had to act alone.

It is the great achievement of the statesman Henry Kissinger that he achieved an intellectual reorientation of American foreign policy in the face of the hardened ideological fronts of the Cold War. And no one can deny him **three historical successes** in the first phase of his foreign policy:
– Détente with the Soviet Union through arms control (SALT 1) in 1969 and the Four-Power Agreement over Berlin in 1971;
– The opening up of the USA towards China with his bold secret mission to Peking in 1971;
– Diplomatic mediation between Israel and the Arabs during and after the Yom Kippur War in October 1973 and the troop disengagement agreement between Israel and both Egypt and Syria in 1974, the presupposition for the peace treaty between Israel and Egypt in 1979.

Kissinger, a person with an autocratic and mistrustful temperament, certainly could not have aimed at these successes had he not acted **alone and partially in secret**. He had to outplay the ponderous, immovable giant bureaucracy of the State Department ('Foggy Bottom'), which according to him provides only bureaucratic models of decision, namely the strategy to be pursued on each occasion, bracketed in by two absurd alternatives. Kissinger arrived at real alternatives for himself only within the framework of small committees for particular problems which he himself formed and led (for SALT, for crisis management, for Vietnam . . .) and in which the new solutions were talked through.

So for a time Kissinger acted like a **second Chancellor Metternich**, on whose allegedly model rational policy (in fact orientated less on the peace of Europe than on the preservation of Habsburg power!) he had already done academic work at an early stage.[5] Like Metternich in the Europe of the nineteenth century, so now in the world of the twentieth century Kissinger wanted to achieve a new global balance of power, above all between the superpowers of the USA, the USSR and the People's Republic of China (thus in fact ensuring above all that the USA maintained its power!). One cannot hold against Kissinger the fact that here Europe, whose statesmen still liked to keep presenting themselves as masters of the world, although they could not agree on basic questions of foreign policy, was cast somewhat into the shade in the shuttle diplomacy of the Secretary of State between Washington and Moscow. But one can criticize his neglect of Latin America and Africa and above all the United Nations (though, granted, its authority and power were weak), which he first of all largely ignored as a 'caricature of reality' and then, when put on the defensive, attacked because of the 'tyranny of the majority'.

But all this is connected with Kissinger's overall conception of foreign policy which he had developed, as far as America was concerned, in a comprehensive monograph while he was still a political theorist at Harvard,[6] and which he now presents again in his most recent work in a global perspective, by means of the great figures of world history, with a sovereign control of the encyclopaedic subject-matter. In his *magnum opus* he is concerned less with the techniques and tactics of diplomacy than with the **mechanics of power:** with the play of diplomacy between the great powers, which thirty years earlier Professor Kissinger made his students imitate as exercises in his Harvard Seminar. There they had to represent the great powers before the First World War and in their 'geopolitical' reflections and dodges deceptions, manipulations, intrigues and treachery were the order of the day: 'To survive this game one needed those characteristics which he also praises in his new book,' writes one of those who played the game at the time, the Englishman Simon Schama: 'a clear-sighted and unsentimental sense of the national interest, mistrust of agreements for collective security which presuppose a unanimous verdict or agreement; a preference for clear alliances which are based on particular interests instead of on pious talk about peace and freedom; and above all the sober assumption that in relations between states as between individuals conflict, rather than harmony, is the norm.'

Schama, since 1980 himself Professor of History at Harvard, adds: 'No wonder that the United States found no place in this game; the skills needed were precisely those cynical ploys of the old world against which the Republic was founded and Woodrow Wilson's Fourteen Points were drafted.'[7] No wonder, too, that in this game of old-style world politics there was no room for ethics: it would doubtless have forced a change in the rules of the game.

(b) Power politics as 'geopolitics'

As a brilliant analyst of modern and contemporary politics, Kissinger is too intelligent simply to set out openly as a principle that **'real politics'** which he himself practised massively as President Nixon's Security Adviser and Secretary of State. 'Real politics', *Realpolitik*, one of those ominous German terms which has unfortunately also been taken into English, is proscribed in America as a European perversion of politics. Even **'power politics'**, similarly an un-American term, is avoided by Kissinger as far as possible, although he regards such 'power politics' (also practised all too often by the USA) as natural and necessary. At the latest as Secretary of State, however, because of the increasingly negative reactions of public opinion to his policy, he had to recognize that simply because 'a country with America's idealistic tradition cannot base its policy on the balance of power as the sole criterion for a new world order',[8] at least America, this 'first society in history to have been explicitly created in the name of freedom', 'must take into account the core values' in 'any association with *Realpolitik*'.[9] These are those basic moral values (freedom, human rights), to which the United States owes its foundation. Within specific limits Kissinger's thought seeks also to integrate the ideal dimension of the 'American dream', which intrinsically is also completely focussed on power.

However, only very superficial European readers will read a synthesis of the European tradition of real politics and the American idealistic tradition out of this book and such concessions. Looked at more closely, Kissinger's book, which is both narrative and argumentative from beginning to end, is an eloquent and seductive **plea against** an **American 'idealism'** which is evidently ineradicable, and at the same time a **plea for a power politics orientated on European statesmen of the past**, though in his view this is not to be an unrestrained politics of force.

Some political scientists might see Kissinger simply as a legalist thinking in European terms, who like Metternich would like to fit the system of nation states with some rigidity into a structure of norms. But Kissinger and politicians of his stamp are concerned not only with a politics of right but also with a politics of power, which attempts to calculate and impose national interests coolly, unhindered by 'moral feelings', and which therefore can easily take on inhumane features. Sir Michael Howard, Regius Professor of Modern History at Oxford and later Professor of Military and Marine History at Yale, remarks that the book should really have been entitled 'Power Politics', and that this is simply concealed by the term **'geopolitics'** which Kissinger constantly uses, though he completely transforms its meaning (it originally denoted the science of the effect of geographical factors on politics).[10]

For **language** alone already **betrays the power politician**: when in Kissinger's analysis of history it is necessary to speak of moral values (since these keep on playing a role even in American foreign policy), the term is consequently qualified by words like 'feelings', 'emotions', 'pieties', 'rhetorical', 'missionary', 'messianic', 'crusading' and 'proselytizing', or intended as biting irony. Usually the politicians who use moral arguments appear in Kissinger's work as the stupid and the unsuccessful, and those engaged in calculating power politics as the wise and the successful. But at best the basic problem of ethics in politics is presented in a negative light – in order to conjure it away.

Here it would have been very interesting to know what universal ethical values and norms the secularized Jew and Euro-American Kissinger, open to a variety of traditions, accepts for foreign policy, if he accepts that there are any universal norms at all, and on what he bases them. However, words like 'ethic' (or 'ethos', the basic inner moral attitude), 'ethics' (the theory), or indeed 'morals' or 'morality' do not appear in the far more than 2,500 entries in the index. Moreover, important names in contemporary politics are also absent: not only Dag Hammarskjøld, almost certainly the most significant Secretary General of the United Nations so far (1953–1961), but also Mahatma Gandhi and Martin Luther King, all three of whom in their political actions and influence proved to be far more realistic than their opponents, who practised 'pure real politics'. Even Lech Walesa and Václav Havel are mentioned only in a sentence on the periphery. One asks oneself what **Kissinger's models** are, since he sees foreign policy above all as a history of great men and events, largely independent of all social and historical developments.

(c) Politics without 'moral feelings'

Even leaving aside Gandhi and King, Walesa and Havel, there can be no doubt that Kissinger admires not so much American politicians like Jefferson, Madison and Franklin, who were concerned to achieve a balance of ideals and interests, as European **power politicians of the stamp of Richelieu, Metternich, Palmerston, Disraeli and Bismarck.** Even Stalin (whose tremendous crimes are, of course, mentioned) comes off better with his cool and calculating foreign policy than an 'idealistic' American president like Franklin D.Roosevelt (though his strategic errors over Stalin, 'Uncle Joe', cannot be disputed).

However, Kissinger's great American hero, who 'commands a unique historical position in America's approach to international relations', is **President Theodore ('Teddy') Roosevelt** at the beginning of our century: 'No other president defined America's world role so completely in terms of national interest, or identified the national interest so comprehensively with the balance of power . . . In his perception of the nature of the world order, he was much closer to Palmerston or Disraeli than to Thomas Jefferson.'[11] For Teddy Roosevelt, international life meant a struggle, 'and Darwin's theory of the survival of the fittest was a better guide to history than personal morality'.[12] With admiration Kissinger calls Teddy Roosevelt the 'warrior statesman',[13] who concentrated on the world in which we live.

In contrast to Roosevelt, his rival, successor and opposite, **Woodrow Wilson** as **'priest–prophet'** comes off badly in Kissinger and is constantly presented to us as a political innocent who believed in an *a priori* harmony of the nations and had no inkling of their opposing interests. Wilson is said to have occupied himself too much with that 'real' world which politicians like him wanted 'to bring into being'.[14] According to Kissinger, Roosevelt certainly had the better arguments, but unfortunately in America down to the present day Wilson has the greater following.

Roosevelt, who is known to us as an unrestrained exponent of an American policy of expansion and intervention ('big stick policy') in Panama, in the Dominican Republic and the Philippines, in Cuba, Nicaragua, Mexico and Haiti, was, just like Bismarck, 'in favour of a policy of blood and iron'.[15] By contrast, Woodrow Wilson argued that 'binding arbitration, not force, should become the method for resolving international disputes'.[16] Granted, Teddy Roosevelt won the Nobel Peace Prize for his mediation in the the Russo–Japanese war of 1906. But the First World War gave Wilson the extraordinary opportunity to promote on a large scale a new and better approach to international affairs on the basis of America's belief in values which were higher than a 'balance of power'.[17] For Wilson, the war already had 'a moral foundation, whose primary objective was a new and more just international order'.[18]

But the **'realist' Kissinger,** who throughout his book both explicitly and implicitly engages in polemic **against 'Wilsonianism'** as the dominant ideology of American foreign policy from Jefferson to Clinton, will have nothing of this new 'approach'. He will not see that Wilson's allegedly typically American policy was first put forward by the British liberals, above all by the English Prime Minister, William Gladstone. Gladstone was steeped in a Christian humanitarian statesmanship and abhorred any political Machiavellianism. Kissinger presents him simply as a moralizing counterpart to the powerful real politician Disraeli; but 'Gladstone was the voice of the future, and his opponent that of the past'.[19]

At what, one asks does the real politician Kissinger take offence? One could understand it if he only took offence at America's 'special mission' ('exceptionalism') to be a 'beacon of freedom' to the rest of humankind and to rate the foreign policy of the democracies morally higher. But he takes offence above all at one thing: the view that foreign policy 'should reflect the same moral standards as personal ethics'.[20]

No less a figure than President **Thomas Jefferson** had required that the same ethical standard should apply to the state as to individuals, and not Machiavellian reasons of state: there is 'but one system of ethics for men and for nations – to be grateful, to be faithful to all engagements under all circumstances, to be open and generous, promoting in the long run even the interests of both'.[21] But ironically Kissinger states: 'No nation has ever imposed the moral demands on itself that America has . . . No other nation has ever rested its claim to international leadership on its altruism.'[22] Altruism makes foreign policy incalculable, whereas the national interest can be calculated on all sides. Kissinger is fond of quoting Lord Palmerston's saying that there are no permanent friends or permanent enemies, but only permanent interests.

Against this background it is not surprising that President Nixon, the man whom Kissinger advised, is praised as the first and only 'realist' President since Theodore Roosevelt, whereas the peace movement against the Vietnam war is commented on disparagingly even today. But here already it becomes clear what a high price Kissinger had to pay for his amoral foreign policy and how little he was willing to take seriously the pressing problems of domestic policy – here too a successor to Richelieu, Metternich and Bismarck with their authoritarian policies in this sphere – and felt threatened by the power of public opinion which he could only manipulate to a limited extent.

(d) Ethics subordinate to politics?

Even sympathetic observers of Kissinger's foreign policy have described it as a **mixture of diplomacy and force**, which finally made it suspect, for all the world and also in America; indeed it robbed it of **credibility** and not least provoked a growing opposition in Congress and among the student youth. Anyone who would like a precise object lesson in what such power politics looks like, not only in great 'geopolitical' reflections but also in the everyday intrigues and cynicisms at the centre of power and in the secret operations abroad with no moral limits, should take the trouble to read the well-documented 700-page book by Seymour M.Hersh on Kissinger in the White House (1983) or Walter Isaacson's biography of Kissinger (1992).[23]

One remembers all too well the following questionable political operations and ploys by the National Security Adviser and Secretary of State:

– The 'destabilizing' and finally bloody overthrow of the Socialist Allende regime in **Chile** in 1971 and the establishment of the violent military dictatorship of General Pinochet.

– Attacks on the Socialist government of **Portugal** and on the Communist parties of **Italy** and **France**, which were in process of change (1973).

– He excluded the core of the conflict, the **Palestinian problem,** from the agreement between Israel on the one hand and Egypt and Syria on the other, and was then manoeuvred by the predictable coalition of the PLO and Syria into a dead-end from which the USA has still to find a way out.

– It was the oil embargo of the Arab states against the USA and European states in 1973, aimed at a change of policy towards Israel in those countries and the call for a new international economic order, which first showed Kissinger that some of the great **North-South problems** (the squandering or energy, the population explosion, food, poverty and the wretchedness of the masses) could not be solved, like many East-West problems, by balancing power between governments.

– The brutal war in **Indo-China** (secret bombing and then invasion of Cambodia, the Christmas bombardment of Hanoi) showed a lack of all respects for human rights, international law and democracy.

– The **delays over the peace treaty with Vietnam** – according to informed American observers, just as favourable conditions for a solution could have been achieved early in 1969 as in 1973 – led the USA into the deepest crisis in its history.

At the latest since H.R.Haldeman's White House diaries (published despite Kissinger's objections) it has been clear that because of electoral tactics, Nixon's 'real politics', inspired by Kissinger, led to the prolongation of the Vietnam war by three years, from 1969-1972. 20,492 Americans and around 160,000 South Vietnamese had to pay for that with their lives.[24] So would we want the spirit of Teddy Roosevelt, who according to Kissinger lived a century too late or a century too early, still to influence another century, the twenty-first? The consequences of Nixon's and Kissinger's real politics are well known: increasingly vigorous protests among the international and American public, and persecution mania in the White House. At the end came the Watergate affair, which revealed a **hitherto unimaginable abuse of power** and criminal energy in the White House and severely shook the trust of American society in its democratic system of checks and balances. Kissinger was more entangled in the President's intrigues (supported by the perjury of his collaborators) than he was willing to recognize; through the inactivity in the Cyprus crisis – Greek provocation and then Turkish invasion – which was caused by his position, at that time he alienated both Greeks and Turks. And finally on 9 August 1974 came the resignation of the thirty-seventh President of the USA, the allegedly first 'realist' President since Teddy Roosevelt: at any rate the first to resign in the face of the threat of impeachment by Congress. America had to pay a high price in political and moral substance for Watergate, even if Nixon was spared prison by a pardon from his successor Gerald Ford. In 1976 Ford lost the election, and Kissinger his post.

So we must agree with Walter Isaacson, Kissinger's critical bio-grapher (Kissinger's *Apologia pro vita sua* in his own final chapters might particularly have Isaacson's criticisms in mind), when in his review of *Diplomacy* he sees his 'reservations' about the 'lower priority' which Kissinger attached to the values which had made the American democracy such a powerful international force confirmed:[25] 'But Kissinger's power-oriented realism and focus on national interests faltered because it was **too dismissive of the role of morality** ... Kissinger's approach led to a backlash against détente; the national mood swung toward both the moralism of Jimmy Carter and the ideological fervour of Ronald Reagan. As a result, not unlike Metter-nich, Kissinger's legacy turned out to be one of brilliance more than solidity.'[26]

We may also agree with Walter Isaacson when at the end of his book he comes to the conclusion that the American idealism which Kissinger regarded as its weakness in respect of an effective policy in this confused world, also proved a source of strength: 'The greatest triumph of political influence in the modern age was that of democratic capitalism over communism in the early 1990s. This occurred partly because Kissinger and others helped to create a new global balance during the 1970s, one that preserved American influence in the post-Vietnam era.

But the main reason that the United States triumphed in the cold war was not because it won a competition for military power and influence. It was because the values offered by its system – among them a foreign policy that could draw its strength from the ideals of its people – eventually proved more attractive.'[27]

Kissinger dedicated his book 'to the men and women of the Foreign Service of the United States of America'. One would not want it to become their handbook, let alone their 'prayer book'. Instead of that, it would be desirable for them to learn from Kissinger's analyses and ask themselves some fundamental **critical questions** about a 'New World Order' (the title of Kissinger's first chapter):

- Should politics and ethics in principle be separated, and ethics always be subordinate to politics, its effectiveness and efficiency?
- Should ethical criteria hold for the choice of political ends and indeed means, or can the good political goal if need be also justify immoral means?
- Is a realistic policy conceivable but not a realistic ethics, and is therefore the conflict between realist politics and moral claims incapable of resolution?
- In the assessment of the diplomacy of a country or a statesman (Richelieu, Metternich, Bismarck, Stalin), can foreign policy and domestic policy be distinguished in such a way that one gives good marks to the technique of power in foreign relations, but more or less ignores the negative elements of the suppression of freedom and human rights at home?
- Can and should freedom, plurality and human rights simply be sacrificed to international stability and order in a global 'grand design'? Is 'order' the supreme moral principle?

We shall now be investigating these questions. First of all we turn to two of Kissinger's key witnesses. We begin at the beginning of **modern real politics** (Richelieu), progress to its climax (Bismarck) and finally move to the downfall of the modern 'European concert of states' in the First World War. After that we shall examine the **postmodern paradigm of politics** (Wilson) which was already forming at that time but was not at first accepted, and the critical discussion of it after the Second World War (Morgenthau and his successors).

These necessarily brief sections are not concerned with historical research into the sources (this needs to be said to historians who attach importance to detail). Nor are they concerned with the historical influence of individual great personalities or great events, to be played out against a history of structures and processes of long duration. No, this is simply an **analytical diagnosis of the time,** though it is not worked out on abstract principles but (as is usual in realist political science) by historical examples. History is the best teacher of statesmanship – since Thucydides' account of the Peloponnesian war, this is the best European tradition.

2. Sovereign disregard of political morality: Richelieu

At the beginning of the seventeenth century, after eight Wars of Religion, France was torn apart politically and shattered socially by hunger and pestilence. So it was understandable that a policy of reconstruction was implemented and that there was a concern to unite and pacify the country internally and externally by giving state authority a new foundation and reorganizing state finances. This took place first through Henry IV, the Huguenot leader who was converted to Catholicism for the sake of the crown ('Paris is worth a mass'), and then above all by a second, very much more significant, power politician: Armand Jean du Plessis, Comte de Richelieu and Cardinal (1585–1642), by whom, as new publications keep showing – the French are still fascinated.

(a) No *universal values, but reasons of state*

Cardinal de Richelieu, under Louis XIII (Henry's son) for eighteen years (from 1624 until his death) almost an omnipotent prime minister, was the pioneer of the centralistic absolutism which was to become the model for almost all Europe. Though ultimately still dependent on his king, at the same time he was responsible for domestic, foreign and defence policy, for the army and for the first modern secret service, which he himself built up. More attached to the previous structures of state than is often assumed, he was certainly neither an administrator nor a reformer. He was a statesman who practised what could be called 'real politics', indeed the **father of the modern form of the state.**

Specifically, that means that although all his life he was weakened by illnesses, Richelieu pursued two goals with uncanny energy, cold intelligence and reckless courage, as he confirms in his *Testament politique.* **At home,** surrounded by intrigues and revolts and constantly threatened by attempts on his life, he established the absolutist authority and power of the king by every possible means – against anarchy, the autonomy of the feudal lords, parliament, the Protestants and also against any rebellious peasants. **Abroad,** Richelieu established French predominance on several fronts: over against the Spanish army, the English fleet and the German mercenary armies.

Richelieu's **achievements** are beyond dispute: it was primarily thanks to this brilliant strategist who thought in geopolitical terms, the cautiously shrewd tactician in cardinal's purple, that France above all benefited from the downfall of Spain and the Holy Roman Empire of the German Nation. He made France a strong state, indeed the first modern state on the European continent, which became the model for all the others. And it was also basically thanks to Richelieu and his systematic cultural policy that at the same time France developed culturally into a great power and that the 'Spanish age' finally seemed to have been replaced by the 'French Age': all over France splendid new buildings were constructed; art, the theatre and music were encouraged, especially in Paris; and finally the Académie Française was founded to cultivate the French language.

One may gladly concede to recent historians who are more friendly towards Richelieu that in pursuing his far-reaching goals Richelieu was also acting under certain constraints in foreign and domestic policy, and that his hands were tied by the church.[28] Nor is it to be disputed that Richelieu, who fulfilled his priestly duties faithfully, sought to justify his policy to himself and others with universal Christian principles of law. However, at the same time – in this age of baroque façades and Christian rhetoric, in which people were well aware of how to maintain clerical decorum – his real significance must not be exaggerated. This high prelate was certainly not a 'Bismarck *avant la lettre*'.

But only if one does not sufficiently divide up his account of himself, as he gave it in his *Memoirs* and his *Political Testament,* into political rhetoric and reality, intentions and implementation, can one make the French nationalist an internationalist and the secularized cleric a Christian politician.[29] At any rate, Christian principles did not prevent the pious churchman, who was also always discreetly but energetically intent on increasing his own and his family's property, from uninhibitedly grasping further domestic power or foreign territories. Religion was important to him: not, however as an end in itself, but as a means towards the seizure and consolidation of political power, his utterly personal political power. What did this look like in political practice?

The Cardinal, a man of the Counter-Reformation, was not concerned about a reformation of the church, head and members, a programme which still had many supporters in France. His sole concern was the **unity of the nation and therefore also of religion.** Skilfully exploiting the confessional rivalry between the various countries, through his coalitions he helped the Protestants outside France in the Holy Roman Empire to survive, and at the same time suppressed them cruelly within France. Whereas in the Edict of Nantes (1598) Henry IV had assured the 1.2 million Reformed not only freedom of conscience, limited freedom of worship and equal civil rights, but also political and military autonomy in 200 cities with a Huguenot majority as places of safety, Richelieu – unconcerned about any of the king's assurances – withdrew their special political and military rights from the Huguenots, though not their religious rights. Indeed this prelate in purple did not have the slightest moral inhibitions about cruelly shattering the political organization of the Reformed by campaigns in the west and east which he led personally, thus doing away with their 'state within a state' (1628–29). Moreover, he suppressed just as mercilessly the revolts of the peasants, sorely tried by the waves of inflation; he had little time for demonstrations and public expressions of discontent about a particular policy.

How did Richelieu justify all this? In a quite elementary way. A cardinal of the Holy Roman Church and a cold calculating politician, he was the first European politician to put reasons of state (*raison d'état*) – the well-being of the state and its furtherance by every means – in principle above all church and confessional interests.[30] He was convinced that what is done for the state is also done for God, and that was his justification for all the violent expansion abroad and repression at home. He entered into alliances even with Protestant and Muslim powers, certainly not in order to damage the church but in order to break through by force the encirclement of France by the Catholic Habsburgs in Spain, the German Empire and Italy.

Certainly there had always been power politics, acts of violence and wars in the history of humankind. But now for the first time **in principle reasons of state guided solely by political interests took the place of confessional interests and ethical considerations.** Reasons of state and an appeal to the autonomies of politics replaced the mediaeval notion of moral values and obligations binding on all peoples and their rulers. 'Reasons of state', people said at that time; now they say 'national security' or 'national interest' – and by that they think that they can justify (almost) everything in a 'Machiavellian' way.

(b) Machiavellianism realized

The foundations for Richelieu's view of state and politics had in fact already been laid by the brilliant Florentine Renaissance thinker Niccolò **Machiavelli** (1469–1527). This passionate Italian patriot was not un-Christian and admired church reformers like Francis, Dominic and Savonarola. But he regarded the Roman Church as the chief culprit in the decline of Italy. As more recent research demonstrates, Machiavelli did not seek to be the founder of a politics which is in principle free of morals or even amoral. But with his book *Il Principe* (1513), his glorification of Cesare Borgia and his bloody crimes and countless amoral counsels, in fact he provided an excellent textbook in power politics for all politicians without a conscience in the subsequent period.

As an advocate of *'ragione di stato'* (first used as a technical term by Giovanni della Casa around the middle of the sixteenth century), Machiavelli made the good of the state, or more precisely the acquisition, maintenance and extension of power, the criterion and maxim for state action: 'the self-preservation of the state with all means and at any price', which is synonymous with the 'suppression of any morality with a transcendent basis from the field of politics'.[31] And now Richelieu is the classical embodiment of that principle of state political action propagated by Machiavelli's 'Prince' which, when necessary, **ignores existing law or prevailing morality**. The revolution in politics which the Italian thinker, a political failure, had thought out in theory in his wretched exile was realized in a bold and sovereign way a century later by the French cardinal who, after initial failures, had arrived on the scene.

What impresses Henry Kissinger (who knows Machiavelli very well indeed but remarkably never quotes him) so positively about Richelieu (and what he misses in 'idealistic' American policy) has its basis here: such **'reasons of state'** can, may and should deviate from ethical norms which **individual reason,** the individual conscience, has to follow. Of course, on Machiavelli's advice the statesman will sagely always give the impression of being mild, merciful, humane, even Christian; but he may and indeed should also offend against loyalty and faith, mercy and humanity for the sake of his rule and the state: act morally and do good as far as possible, but act immorally and do evil as far as necessary! Moreover, Richelieu's policy, which is allegedly dictated by 'reason', is in fact an unscrupulous policy of interests orientated on power, its preservation and extension – in favour less of European 'balance', as Kissinger thinks, than of the absolutist French state.

One asks oneself: **then is the state allowed to do anything**? Perfidy, breaking treaties, deception, treachery, intrigue and murder – is all this allowed in the same way as the suppression of minorities or the unscrupulous alliance of 'the most Christian of all kings' with 'ideological opponents', Protestants and Islamic Turks? In such real politics, modelled on the criterion of autonomous 'reasons of state', **wars of conquest are pre-programmed;** not, however, as is later anachronistically attributed to Richelieu, because of 'natural frontiers', but for strategic military considerations. Wars, now wholly 'secularized', are more than ever regarded as unavoidable in principle and ineradicable in practice, and are waged with increasing expense, refined methods and growing unscrupulousness.

But wars have to be paid for. Already at that time war was expensive, and easier to begin than to end. Richelieu, too, like many 'real politicians' after him, had to give up his urgent plans for the social and political reform of his country (abolishing the salt tax, reducing the poll tax, putting an end to simony); time and again he had to suppress revolts by the exploited peasants and smash the plots of the disempowered nobility in the various provinces. But the impoverishment of the people hardly bothered the architect of the Palais Royal in Paris, which is still marvelled at today. Expansion abroad was matched by despotism at home with its system of spies and its summary justice, including executions and the Bastille.

So the whole of France literally breathed again when the feared real politician finally died of exhaustion in 1642. Political turmoil, the civil wars of the Fronde, a tremendous burden of taxation and social misery were the legacy of this real politics of which Kissinger does not take account in his analysis. But the Thirty Years' War, which had increasingly developed from a 'war of religion' into a sheer 'war of power', that the cardinal first stoked up financially and then intervened in with the army (on the side of the Protestants), was to be the prelude to very much more cruel European wars in which 'sovereign' European nation states were to wage a fight to the death, of all against all.

How self-destructive these principles of real politics are can thus already be established with Richelieu, and even more with **Louis XIV**, under whose rule the sovereign nation state brought reasons of state and the struggle for hegemony to a climax. A great anti-French coalition came into being, which finally brought about the failure of his whole policy. The glorious reign of the 'Sun King' ended ignominiously: a quarter of a century of almost uninterrupted wars and unprecedented waste led to a decline in the population, impoverishment and state bankruptcy (a state economy overdrawn by around eighteen budgets), to which the people of Versailles responded by throwing stones at Louis' coffin at his funeral in 1713. And neither Louis XV nor Louis XVI had the political and moral strength to change the social power structures which had been established by Richelieu and which had already become untenable under Louis XIV. This was a main cause of the Revolution of 1789. That, too, raises some critical questions for us here.

(c) The alternatives: religious fanaticism or political cynicism?

Let us look back, in order to get a clear view of the politics of the future. A statesman who attempts to counter the geopolitical threat to his country and in so doing dovetails his tactics with his strategy acts legitimately. But does that already mean that he may set himself above law and morality in the interests of national security, the national interest and national prestige?

This question is not prompted, like that of Richelieu's conservative contemporaries, by thoughts of a restoration of the mediaeval order, but by Richelieu's Machiavellianism, which was already criticized at the time. Henry Kissinger takes a quite different view. He cannot put Richelieu's 'novel and coldblooded doctrine', which 'was deeply offensive to the universalist tradition founded on the primacy of moral law', in too favourable a light: 'In an age still dominated by religious zeal and ideological fanaticism, a dispassionate foreign policy free of moral imperatives stood out like a snow-covered Alp in the desert.'[32]

Instead of following Aristotle in putting virtue at the centre between two vices (too little and too much, like boldness between cowardice and foolhardiness), Kissinger, like Machiavelli, is fond of constructing an all too simple opposition in a black-and-white scheme like that between ideological fanaticism and amoral realism, in order to destroy the one position and highlight the other. But perhaps there is no ground between Alpine peaks and desert? As in some modern violent films, in which because of the script the 'realistic' Rambo has no alternative than to murder or be murdered, Kissinger brings the political problems to a head where he can, and then suggests the only alternative. But is there really only an Either–Or here?

- Either mediaeval religious zeal and ideological fanaticism (*à la* Emperor Ferdinand II) – or a foreign policy orientated on interests and completely free of moral imperatives (*à la* Richelieu and Kissinger)?

- Either the state unconditionally subordinated to religion – or religion and morality serving the state and having to bow uncompromisingly to reasons of state? The state as the supreme value which also stands above morality?

Hence the question: at the time of the Reformation and at the beginning of modernity was there not a 'third force'? In fact there were politicians, theologians, lawyers, on the central, reform line of **Erasmus of Rotterdam**, who called for an ethically responsible, realistic peace policy, far removed from the mediaeval fanaticism of the Counter-Reformation or the cynicism of modern real politics.[33] Thus for example in 1629 (already in the eleventh year of the Thirty Years' War), a ruler like Ferdinand II who was not imprisoned in the mediaeval Counter-Reformation paradigm could certainly have accepted the compromise solution put forward by the weakened Protestant rulers and granted them freedom of religion in exchange for recognition of his political supremacy.

At all events, Kissinger should certainly have discussed the formation of **international law**, which is part of the history of diplomacy. International law was prepared for by the Spanish theologians Francisco di Vitoria and Francisco Suárez, and given the most convincing basis by the great Dutch statesman and philosopher of law **Hugo Grotius**, who was living in exile in Paris. Grotius discussed the idea of an international society and the fundamental questions of international relationships, the distinction between the just and the unjust war, and limitations on the monstrous atrocities in war in his book *On the Law of War and Peace*, published in 1625, a year after Richelieu's rise; it was a fundamental work in favour of morality also in foreign policy.[34] But none of these names from the third force appears in Kissinger's work.

On the one hand he quotes a defender of the old system of state and church, the theologian Jansenius (father of Jansenism), and on the other 'Richelieu's defenders', who 'demonstrate how well they had absorbed the **cynical methods of the master himself**'.[35] Indeed, Kissinger uncritically takes sides with the cardinal, who, in the Thirty Years War ('one of the most brutal and destructive wars in the history of mankind'[36]), 'determined to prolong the war until central Europe had been bled white'[37]: 'In order to exhaust the belligerents and to prolong the war Richelieu subsidized the enemies of his enemies, bribed, fomented insurrections, and mobilized an extraordinary array of dynastic and legal arguments. He succeeded so well that the war that had begun in 1618 dragged on decade after decade.'[38]

Kissinger's knowledgeable and exciting historical account of Richelieu confirms the general impression given by his book *Diplomacy*: it is a large-scale, skilful **apologia for real politics,** which in his view should have been self-limiting. Kissinger criticizes only their 'excess': Richelieu's concept of reasons of state contained no principle of self-limitation and therefore proved self-destructive, as in the case of Louis XV, and thus 'supplied no answer to the challenge of world order'.[39] But is 'moderation' sufficient here as a criterion for action when the aims and methods otherwise remain the same? And, one asks, must not the criticism of Louis XIV already begin radically with Richelieu, who was not unjustly the most hated man of his time? His 'reasons of state', which could just as well have justified the prolongation of the Vietnam war and the Watergate manipulations, in fact give no answer to the question of a new world order, either then or now.

But, we may go on to ask, do we find an answer to the 'challenge of the world order' if we now look at Kissinger's second great protagonist of real politics and here move from the seventeenth/eighteenth to the nineteenth century and from France to a Germany striving for unity and a position in the world – having been delayed for 200 years by Richelieu's successful policy?

3. The embodiment of real politics: Bismarck

It was understandable that in Germany, following the failure of Romantic idealism, which had not been able to bring about the political unification of Germany after the wars against Napoleon and particularly after the failure of the 'politics of ideas' of the Frankfurt National Assembly, **'real politics'** had the upper hand in the conservative reaction of the 1850s. The term had only just been coined – by Ludwig von Rochau in his *Principles of Real Politics*,[40] which appeared anonymously. It was Otto von Bismarck who – the match of Richelieu – appeared in Germany to put it into practice. It is not easy to do justice to this complex personality without flights of Bismarck worship or Bismarck condemnation.

(a) Not ideas, but interests

In the second half of the nineteenth century, Otto von **Bismarck** (1815–1898, Prussian Prime Minister and Imperial Chancellor 1862–1890) is the **prototype of the real politician** who does not believe in ideas but merely in interests. He was beyond question a political genius of the highest rank, a charismatic personality with a sharply analytical mind, an intuitive grasp of complex problems and unique tactical gifts. He more than anyone else understood 'the art of the possible' on the European continent after the 1848 revolution, the violent repression of which he had energetically called for as a young man. Indeed, this revolt was a key experience in Bismarck's life, and explains his anti-democratic support of the Prussian monarchy as *the* authority.

No historian today will deny Bismarck's **achievements**, which for all the widespread comparisons clearly distinguish him as Chancellor of the Second Reich from the Chancellor of the Third Reich, the megalo-maniac Adolf Hitler, who saw himself as the successor to the 'Iron Chancellor'. Bismarck united Germany (excluding Austria) without making any attempt to dominate Europe. He had the capacity to recognize fatal challenges and to foresee long-term developments. In preparing for his actions he was cautious and shrewd, but moderate in exploiting his victories. Like almost all statesmen of modern times he had no moral objections to war as the last resort and the 'continuation of politics by other means' (as Clausewitz put it), and in six years he was able to wage it three times, resolutely and victoriously: against Denmark (1864), Austria-Hungary (1866) and France (1870-71). But in princi-ple he gave priority to diplomacy in achieving his political aims. He waged war only when it was necessary for achieving his political plan, and set clearly limited aims to it: against the generality of the Prussians, in 1866 he did not allow the troops to march through to Vienna to destroy the Habsburg monarchy.

Instead of striving for the hegemony of Germany in Europe, even after 1871 Bismarck contented himself with the **balance of power** which was already favoured by England; he held in check a France which was meditating revenge for the annexation of Alsace and Lorraine, but explicitly declared that Germany's foreign policy was now 'saturated'. At the same time he brought about internal consolidation and unifica-tion (one currency, one imperial bank, one civil law, one imperial court), introduced universal secret suffrage, and was the first in Europe to bring in universal social security. At the same time he safeguarded the new German Reich by an artistically woven system of alliances. In this way he made almost four decades of peace possible for Central Europe through a policy aimed at stabilization.

We must not make the *a priori* moral objection to Bismarck that in all his political enterprises he was a virtuoso in provoking, heightening and then again resolving crises at home and abroad; that he played off the

European great powers against one another in a masterly way and knew how to exploit brilliantly for his own ends every diplomatic situation and every error on the part of his numerous opponents at home and abroad. But this raises even more acutely the question of the morality of his policy.

(b) In place of a vision of the future, will to power

For Bismarck, 'power always had priority over law in his politics, right down to the founding of the Reich'.[41] That is the verdict of Anselm Doering-Manteuffel, a representative of the younger generation of German historians. Even historians who are well-disposed towards Bismarck can hardly dispute that in the subsequent period, too, while this real politician did not lack a perception of national interests, he did lack an **openness to trend-setting democratic ideas and tendencies**. Thus in the last resort his main political thought, the strengthening and expansion of the monarchical Prussian state, remained rooted in the past: it was anti-liberal, anti-parliamentarian and anti-democratic.

Bismarck's policy was finally regarded by many people as 'outlived and without a future, as the politics of an aging or an old man; he even repeated the old methods . . .'[42] Surrounded with an aura of infallibility after his victories, he could not see that with the industrial revolution, the population explosion and democratization, all over the world the **future** would belong **to the modern, liberal and democratic forces** which were pressing for power (and not to the imperial house, the nobility, the military and bureaucracy).

– Simply for reasons of tactics and time, this deeply anti-democratic monarchist arrived at an understanding with the nationalistically-inclined liberal middle class and destroyed the political credibility for the **rising working class** of his system of state social security, which was so promising, and a model for the whole of Europe, by simultaneously engaging in oppressive measures against the Social Democrats (the Socialist laws).

– At the same time the intolerant Prussian Protestant alienated himself from the great **Catholic part of the population** which he had gained by an unnecessary 'Kulturkampf' against a Catholicism which, while weakened by the secularization of church property, was for the first time organizing itself as a powerful political party (the 'Centre' Party).

– He soon regarded even those in his **own conservative ranks** who opposed his policies as 'enemies of the Reich'.

Bismarck's quite **personal political morality** also played a major role:

uninhibited by any 'moral feelings' and 'pieties of the age', and no less mistrustful and devious than Richelieu, Otto von Bismarck always knew how to eliminate any possible rival mercilessly at an early stage. He pursued political opponents with irreconcilable hatred and, if his real politics called for it, he equally uninhibitedly dropped old friends. Not only did he lack any of that loyalty the absence of which he lamented in others, but he even unscrupulously changed political course whenever this seemed right to him. If he was under pressure to justify his policies, he did not hesitate to lie in public. Finally, in his own mind he always provided treaties with the secret clause *rebus sic stantibus*, as things are, and in his traumatic recollection of the 1848 Revolution he kept flirting with the idea of a *coup d'état* against his own Reichstag if need be. Crises which he inflated artificially, ugly press campaigns and subtle disinformation (the Ems Dispatch as a provocation to France before the 1870 war) were political means for him. So, too, were secret funds and bribery, for example of the King of Bavaria in 1871 so that he offered the crown of the German Emperor to the Prussian king in the name of the rulers (and not, say, of the people or the parliament as in 1848!), in an act of arrogant 'self-promotion of the ruler state'.[43]

But Bismarck's most serious mistake in foreign policy was to have momentous consequences: the annexation of Alsace-Lorraine, forced by a prolongation of the war. Only when we add the proclamation of the German Empire in the Versailles Hall of Mirrors and the agreement to the peace treaty with its high reparation payments, deliberately postponed for months, does the extent of the **national provocation and humiliation of France** really become evident: 'Through this the hostility of France to Germany became the defining element of the foundations on which the Reich had to stand. The symbols of German-French enmity – Versailles 1871 and 1918 and the railway carriage at Compiègne in which the cease-fire agreements of 1918 and 1940 were signed – run through the history of the German Reich from the day of its foundation to its destruction.'[44]

Furthermore, Bismarck's quite personal **will to power**, hardly restrained by ethical considerations, sought not only the pre-eminence of Prussia over Germany but also that of the King over Prussia and finally that of the Chancellor over the King. This untamed will to power finally led to Bismarck's overthrow, at the age of seventy-five, by the thirty-one-year-old Wilhelm II in 1890. Bismarck spent eight last years as the 'old man in Sachsenwald', terminally ill and irreconcilably grumbling and agitating to the end.

The 'real politician Bismarck' with no faith in a new future, remained a man of the old order and an authoritarian, undemocratic figure to the last. In so far as he placed himself on the side of the old power elites (nobility, army, upper middle class, civil service) in a new industrial society and practised an extremely effective real politics, **abroad he achieved the victory of the military power state and at home the victory of an authoritarian state building on the spirit of subjection** ('Chancellor's dictatorship'). But at the same time in so doing he obstructed the development of Germany into a democracy with a liberal pattern, so that Bismarck's spirit was ultimately also responsible for the disaster of German history in the first half of the twentieth century. Hence there is also a critical question here.

(c) Power – the supreme criterion in politics?

Here, too, let us look back, in order to get a clear view of the politics of the future. We can well understand why Henry Kissinger found Bismarck a kindred spirit, because he too does not see the world in a rigidly ordered system (*à la* Metternich's holy alliance) but as a world in constant flux and constant struggle (*à la* Charles Darwin's survival of the fittest). In international conflicts neither was concerned with applying any preconceived doctrines or ideological positions, but only with the national interests. Therefore foreign policy was to be based neither on feelings nor on historically outdated legitimacies, but solely on an assessment of the real balance of power and prospects of success, which was difficult but still possible.

However, there is an obvious question here: does power legitimate itself, so that might is right? And may might, on any favourable opportunity, also impose itself with violence and war? So in the future, on any favourable opportunity, may a policy of 'blood and iron' be implemented quite separately from any system of values, obligated solely to the power of the state, the needs of national security and prestige? In loyalty to Machiavelli, is any favourable opportunity that offers itself to be exploited unscrupulously in order to extend one's own sphere of power, even if there is no legitimate reason for it? This was the practice, long before Bismarck, of the Prussian king Frederick II, who as crown prince wrote an 'Anti-Machiavelli' with the conquest (which could not be justified in any way) of Austrian Silesia (a seven-year war!). Moreover Bismarck himself practised it again when, driven by the nationalist wave, in 1871 he called for and implemented the annexation of Alsace-Lorraine against the will of the majority of its population, an action which time and again inevitably rekindled the French policy of revenge.

Kissinger's account of Bismarck, like that of Richelieu, forms an essential pillar of the historical apologetics of his real politics. By an **over-sharp contrast** between two political options (religious fanaticism or political cynicism) and a complete disregard of the third force (ecumenical understanding and peaceful agreement) he had made the Cardinal *a priori* seem to be in the right. By contrast, he exonerates Bismarck, who in preparing his political ploy had considered several options of equal merit (partner in an alliance), and then resolutely decided on the one which was most favourable to his interests at that moment, with a second methodological trick: **by blaming his successors,** who unfortunately by no means had the same stature and also did not carry out the necessary institutionalization, so that they and not 'the master' were responsible for the German disaster in the twentieth century. Kissinger's final conclusion is: 'Where Bismarck failed was in having doomed his society to a style of policy which could only have been carried on had a great man emerged in every generation. This is rarely the case.'[45]

To put it bluntly: Bismarck's policy itself was all right, but not that of his successors, because they did not have the stature of the 'master'. But the opposite emerges from Kissinger's own account, and more recent biographies of Bismarck provide abundant confirmation:[46]
– that **Bismarck himself already** systematically changed fronts in both domestic and foreign policy, with endless manoeuvring and manipulations, with threats and counter-threats, in unscrupulous flexibility, and sowed disastrous mistrust among the nations of Europe, above all against Germany;
– that in foreign policy, in an unprecedented way, uninhibited rivalry and constant reassessment of military strength set in and a warlike atmosphere could spread;
– that Bismarck himself showed how the favourable opportunity of the hour can be sufficient justification for an armed attack on one's opponent in the tactical struggle for political advantage;
– that to achieve a peaceful world in these circumstances it is better to rely on large armies and armaments than on diplomacy.

To this degree – for all the essential differences – there is **a fatal continuity in Prussian-German history**: from Frederick II, through Bismarck and Wilhelm II, to Adolf Hitler. The Great German historian Theodor Mommsen, who won the Nobel prize for literature, is right about the internal situation in Germany when he argues that Bismarck 'broke the spine of the German nation': 'The damage of the Bismarck period is infinitely greater than its usefulness, since the gains in power were achievements which were lost again in the next storm in world history. But the enslaving of the German personality, the German spirit, was a disaster which cannot be made good again.'[47] And the German-Jewish historian Hans Rothfels, who remained sympathetic to Bismarck, even though he was forced to emigrate by the Nazis, observed in 1945: 'However long and complicated the way from Bismarck to Hitler was, the founder of the Reich appears as the one responsible for a shift, or at least for the legitimation in our day of a shift, which has all too obviously reached its fatal culmination.'[48] Hans-Ulrich Wehler, an expert in German social history, remarks that along with the authoritarian state and pseudo-parliamentarianism, 'the anti-democratic belief in a Führer and redeemer' is part of the 'evil legacy of the Bismarck period'.[49]

In retrospect it becomes clear that the **political paradigm of modernity** was
– initiated by France under Richelieu in the seventeenth century: morally uninhibited politics in the interest of the nation state;
– moderated in the eighteenth century by England: the struggle for hegemony among nation states given equilibrium by the principle of the balance of power;
– stabilized in the first half of the nineteenth century (after a period of French hegemony under Napoleon) by Austria under Metternich: a 'concert' of the European great powers with an anti-revolutionary orientation;
– shattered in the second half of the nineteenth century by Prussia – Germany under Bismarck and a renewed cold-blooded politics of the 'real' national interest;
– **taken** *ad absurdum* by the First World War, sparked off above all by Germany but also aimed at by the other great powers.

'Traveller, there are no roads. Roads are made by walking.' At the end of his great work Kissinger cryptically quotes a Spanish proverb. Are there really no roads, at least for politicians and diplomats? So are they to continue to act as they have done so far? As an **interim result** of our historical-systematic reflections with a view to the future it is worth noting:

- The **political paradigm of modernity** governed by real politics is caught up in a fundamental **crisis** which reveals the moral doubtfulness of all real politics. For:

- What is **not reprehensible** about real politics is that it distinguishes between dreams and realities, orientates itself on given political possibilities, and goes by the interests of its own state – shrewdly taking other interests into account.
- Such real politics is **reprehensible** only if at the same time it opposes the orientation of state action on political ideas and ethically grounded values and thus runs the risk of succumbing to its own way of thinking, purely in terms of power.

It follows from this that it is impossible simply to respond with an idealist political ethic to Kissinger's plea for a realist power politics in the present multi-polar international system which has replaced the bipolar system of the Cold War. So here, to continue our historical systematic analysis, taking up voices particularly from our century, I shall develop a counterpoint.

II

No Moralizing Ideal Politics

In 1917/18 the United States of America first made an appearance on the European continent (with two million soldiers!) by entering the war against Germany, and prepared the end of the 'European concert' of the great powers. At the same time, with the collapse of the German Reich, the Habsburg empire and the Tsar's empire, along with the Ottoman empire and the Chinese empire, this was an abundantly clear symptom of an **epoch-making global upheaval** that was to replace the Eurocentrism which had held since the beginning of modernity with a polycentrism which, as many people are only now realizing, will hold for postmodernity. Time, too, for a new politics! In fact already at that time the unprecedented catastrophe for humankind represented by 1914–1918 had prompted the call for a **new paradigm of politics**. At least the beginnings of a new orientation had become visible.

1. An attempt at a new politics: Wilson

As early as 1917/18 a new world order was called for, as we saw, by Woodrow Wilson, the President of the United States. But surely Wilson, some 'realists' comment mockingly today, was a hopeful-hopeless 'idealist'! However, it is worth making a critical investigation.

Woodrow Wilson (1856–1924), who from 1885 had taught history, law and political science, from 1890 at Princeton University, whose President he was from 1902 to 1910, won the election for the Democratic Party as in every respect the best hope of the Progressive Movement. He was standing against William H. Taft and Theodore Roosevelt who, self-willed power politician to the end, had split the Republicans. On 8 January 1918 Wilson, as President of a now strong and self-conscious nation, proclaimed the American **peace programme** in the famous **Fourteen Points**. On 6 October there followed the German request for a cease-fire on the basis of the Fourteen Points, and on 11 November a cease-fire was finally concluded.

Thus far at least the peace message of the American President had accomplished its purpose. However, the 'realists' of world politics, and here Kissinger is truly not alone, are anxious to dismiss this novel peace programme as an idealistic programme, in order in this way to provide theoretical justification for power politics in the old European style and to continue it in practice – mindless of the fact that although the United States entered the war so late, it too had to mourn 112,432 dead and 230,074 wounded. This might better also be called a 'reality'. But what did Wilson want?

(a) A new peaceful order

President Wilson wanted a new peaceful order without annexations and demands for reparations. Of course as a politician and political theorist he was also clear how a policy of national interests had been pursued in Europe hitherto – to be truthful, not always simply in favour of a balance of power! The result was a World War and already a total of 20 million dead. Wilson's conviction was that states and their governments simply could not go on like this. To this degree Wilson, as Kissinger critically observed, was concerned not with 'geopolitics' but with a 'conversion', of the kind that is necessary at any epoch-making paradigm shift (Thomas S.Kuhn has demonstrated this in terms of the replacement of the Ptolemaean paradigm with the Copernican paradigm).[1] His new global policy can be understood in the light of three interlocking principles:[2]

(1) **Freedom for all peoples:** 'The day of conquest and aggrandizement is gone by; so is also the day of secret covenants entered into in the interest of particular governments and likely at some unlooked-for moment to upset the peace of the world.' And for the advocates of traditional real politics then and now the President notes: 'This happy fact is now clear to the view of every public man whose thoughts do not linger in an age that is dead and gone.' Is that why Henry Kissinger, who trusts in the methods of the past, speaks so badly of Wilson?

(2) **Justice for friend and foe:** 'What we demand in this war, therefore, is nothing peculiar to ourselves. It is that the world be made fit and safe to live in; and particularly that it be made safe for every peace-loving nation which, like our own, wishes to lead its own life, determine its own institutions, be assured of justice and fair dealing by the other peoples of the world as against force and selfish aggression. All the

peoples of the world are in effect partners in this interest, and for our part we see very clearly that unless justice be done to others it will not be done to us.'

(3) **Securing peace by a league of nations:** 'A general association of nations must be formed under specific covenants for the purpose of affording mutual guarantees of political independence and territorial integrity to great and small states alike.'

The peace message of the American President culminates in this fourteenth point. Wilson had considered the previous concrete points in the programme thoroughly, and he was ready to combine his moral arguments with political pressure. First, fundamental requirements (points 1–5): open peace negotiations and peace treaties, absolute freedom of navigation, the removal of every possible economic barrier and the establishment of equality of trading conditions, the reduction of armament potential to the lowest point consistent with domestic safety, and finally an adjustment of all colonial claims in which the interest of the populations concerned must have equal weight with the equitable claims of the government whose title is to be determined. The last point in particular shows how good it would have been, already after the First World War, to have taken some voluntarily and ordered action to liberate these peoples, a course which after the Second World War was often forced on the colonial powers by armed violence.

Then follow eight demands (points 6–13) relating to the individual countries, the next two of which seem equally indispensable to Wilson: the restoration of Belgium and the evacuation of the occupied territories of Russia. After that came the liberation of the whole of French territory and the restoration of Alsace-Lorraine to France ('a wrong which has unsettled the peace of the world for nearly fifty years'). Furthermore, the peoples of Austria–Hungary were to be given the possibility of autonomous development; Rumania, Serbia and Montenegro were to be restored, an independent Polish state to be created, and the Turkish parts of the Ottoman empire to be guaranteed unconditional independence; the other nationalities which hitherto had been under Turkish rule were to be able to develop autonomously.

This was a truly comprehensive programme for the Europe of the time, even if important problems like the application of Wilson's principle of self-determination in the states bordering on Russia and the states which followed the Austro–Hungarian empire, and the establishment of minority rights remained unresolved – and do so to this day. But now, even more than then, one asks oneself, was it

(b) All an idealistic illusion?

That Wilson was not a deluded idealist from the start is already clear from the fact that he was largely able to implement his **reform programme for domestic policy**, 'New Freedom'. The American economy was freed from paralysing constraints by the lowering of duties and the reorganization of the banks and the credit system; social reform measures followed, like the prohibition of child labour and the introduction of an eight-hour day for railway workers.

Nor had Wilson acted in any way idealistically in his **foreign policy prior to the entry of America** into the war. On the contrary, one can ask whether his reforming impulses were not all too bound up with economic interests, in so far as the demand for the removal of trade barriers was of course in the real political interest of the new economic great power, the USA; and even under him there were also sometimes violent interventions in other states, especially in Central America and the Caribbean.

That Wilson did not maintain the neutrality of the USA proclaimed at the beginning of the First World War was to be attributed not only to the close cultural and economic ties with France and Great Britain, but also to the German way of waging war, which caused offence in many respects (the violation of the neutrality of Belgium, unrestricted U-boat warfare, the sinking of an American ship, and other things). Having first vainly sought a 'peace without victors' through an envoy, Wilson finally resolved to **enter the war** on the side of the Western democracies.

That decided the war – and it was to be the same in the Second World War. However, the peace was by no means yet won. And after the announcement of Wilson's Fourteen Points, the question was now universal: what kind of peace would this be? A peace with justice of the kind that the 'idealist' Wilson had demanded of the world public? Or a dictated peace, of the kind that the 'realists' Clémenceau and Lloyd George strove for, which would exclusively put the blame for the war on Germany and exclude it from the peace negotiations (unlike conquered France at the Congress of Vienna)?

(c) The victory of the 'realists'

We may readily agree with Kissinger that this world-historical controversy was not least a **conflict between two different conceptions of diplomacy.** But looked at closely, this is not a conflict between American and European diplomacy, but a conflict between the **old and the new**

diplomacy. And it is the tragedy of the situation that after the First World War – unlike after the Second – at least among the victors there was not a single European statesman of stature who, like Wilson, had recognized the 'signs of the time' and argued for a new foreign politics and a **peace with justice** with the intelligence, resolution and persuasiveness of a Richelieu or a Bismarck. The peace with justice of the 'idealists' would have been more realistic than the **dictated peace** of the 'realists'; it could have spared the world a second, even more devastating, world war.

For who were being truly realistic? Was it the representatives of the old diplomacy?

– Perhaps Clémenceau, who mocked Wilson's utopian tendencies, prevented the annexation of Austria to the German empire (which was wanted by the majority of the population) and finally had the Rhineland occupied?

– Perhaps Lloyd George, who (against the protest of John Maynard Keynes, the clear-thinking and fair head of the delegation from the British Treasury) along with France attempted to exact tremendous reparations, only reluctantly granted the USA parity in the question of fleets, and opposed Wilson over the question of decolonization?

At the latest after the Second World War, which France and England had again won, it was clear that the **old diplomacy had not realized its aims**:

– **England** had not remained the leading naval power, had had to cede rule of the seas to the USA after 1918, and after 1945 had lost its giant empire.

– **France** did not remain the leading military power of Europe as in the eighteenth century and the beginning of the nineteenth, and after 1945 similarly had to give up its colonies (along with Algeria as a department of France) and recognize the military and political supremacy of the USA also in Europe.

– **Germany** again attained state independence; the reparations imposed on it were paid more rapidly after 1945 than after 1918; the 'economic miracle' did not take place among the victors but among the vanquished; in 1990 West and East Germany were finally united.

Would it not perhaps have been better had the 'realists' listened more to the 'idealist' Wilson and already striven for a reconciliation between France and Germany after the First World War, as the foreign ministers Aristide Briand and Gustav Stresemann did at the end of the 1920s, when it was already too late? Or is thinking like this anachronistic? Only for the eternal men of yesterday; not for those open to the future. For if one can make one criticism of President **Wilson**, it is that, temporarily under pressure and sorely oppressed by the opposition at home, he did not exercise his power, did not venture on the great confrontation, and thus did not call for the final decision in favour of a peace with justice. But at any rate he was able to realize something that lay close to his heart, the foundation of the **League of Nations**, although because of the obligation of unanimity it could be paralysed (like UNO after the Second World War by the veto of the great powers in the Security Council).

The League of Nations was not, as Kissinger thought, 'a quintessentially American institution',[3] but an idea which, put forward by the British philosopher Jeremy Bentham (1748–1832!), a freeman of the French Revolution, was first popular in Great Britain and from there spread to America: an organized common peace instead of organized rivalries. For Wilson this meant the self-determination and collective security of the nations in place of the fluid balance of power of the 'European concert': **power in the service of peace!**

After his retirement, in the USA Wilson devoted himself literally to the point of exhaustion to the League of Nations and the US membership of it, in the face of the isolationist Republican opposition. During a public campaign for the ratification of the treaty, long since worn out physically, on 25 September 1919 he collapsed in Pueblo, Colorado. He was no longer capable of playing an active role in the 1920 presidential election, but in December 1920 was awarded the Nobel Peace Prize and until his death on 3 February 1924 lived a completely withdrawn life in Washington. To this degree Wilson's foreign policy failed: the United States did not join the League of Nations; America was not yet ready to take on a permanent global role.

But did that mean that Wilson's global programme had also already failed? Even died-in-the wool realists must concede that some of the finest acts of twentieth-century diplomacy had their roots 'in the idealism of Woodrow Wilson: the Marshall Plan, the brave commitment to containing communism, the defence of the freedom of Western Europe, and even the ill-fated League of Nations and its later incarnation, the United Nations'.[4] Only Wilson's programme failed to be realized. And for that to happen it urgently needed correction and realistic de-ideologizing.

(d) Crusade for democracy

However much Wilson must be defended against the sweeping charge of a naive idealism, the fact cannot be overlooked that with his missionary thinking and the universal claim that it was a 'crusade for democracy' he finally overplayed the war. This **morally-motivated American idea of a global crusade** which was also widespread later has rightly been criticized by Kissinger and all 'realists'. For here not only do the problems of Wilson's programme and policy become evident, but we also see the weakness of the kind of ideal politics generally which an American theologian and advocate of a 'Christian realism', **Reinhold Niebuhr,** had already shown up at the beginning of the 1930s when, under the title *Moral Man and Immoral Society,* he analysed the pride and the hypocrisy of nations and classes and argued for justice and the preservation of moral values in politics.[5]

- An ideal politics can be **hypocritical:** one criticizes power politics elsewhere, and practises it in one's own sphere of influence.

In often unconscious moral arrogance – and truly not only in America, but also in Switzerland, in Israel and elsewhere – it is presupposed that only one's own politics and one's own institutions are following moral principles as a matter of course: all selfish aims (and often scandalous circumstances) are veiled by moral speeches. National self-righteousness can lead to a political claim to leadership not only on the basis of obligations to democracy, freedom and human rights but also the basis of the alleged superiority of one's own civilization and culture, as a model for the world. Blind zeal, intolerance, oppression and even military intervention can be the consequence of such national self-righteousness. That American democracy in particular has combined the pursuit of national interests with the propagation of values and ideals has indubitably led to ambivalence, indeed to hypocrisy: on the one hand sharp criticism on the part of the USA of the power politics and colonialism of the Europeans, and on the other the expansionist power politics of the USA itself in its own hemisphere, from Puerto Rico and Cuba in the Caribbean to Guam and the Philippines in the West Pacific. Here, though, it is declared to be 'manifest destiny', given by God himself ('God's own country' can be as self-righteously nationalistic as the 'God with us' of the German army in 1914). Reagan's and Bush's interventions – open in Grenada and Panama, 'covert' in Chile and

Nicaragua – confirm that we are still far from President Wilson's visions.[6]

- An ideal politics can be **illusory**: in cases of failure, global interventionism without criteria of selection easily tips over into national isolationism.

In disappointments, the extreme optimism which believes in a special election of one's own country can also easily result in an extreme pessimism which finds everything in the country bad. Excessive expectations like 'the new heaven and the new earth' of the Puritans, Lyndon Johnson's 'great society', or Ronald Reagan's 'America against the dark empire', easily lead to the disillusionment and cynicism against which Niebuhr already warned. Even America as the 'beneficent global policeman', which is in fact what Wilson already had in view, asks too much of even the immense possibilities and forces of the United States and leads to frustrations and 'do-nothing politics' in other cases. In any case, how far the specifically American form of democracy can be transferred to all the states of the world is an open question.

- An ideal politics can be **ineffective**: a politics solely based on moral convictions and ideals, not backed up by any effective political (often military) power, is ultimately doomed to failure.

In other words, even moral politics remains **politics**. It is not to be confused with moralizing, which only encourages the unscrupulousness of politicians on the other side, as became evident after the First and Second World Wars. The War-Prevention Pact of 1928 (the Briand–Kellogg pact) is an example of such ineffective idealistic politics, which thought that it could settle disputes and stop aggression simply through moral convictions, without the backing of political and military strength. Germany, France, Italy, Japan, the USA and other states had solemnly renounced war as a means of establishing national goals, but without at the same time resolving on effective sanctions against possible aggressors.

The criticism of any idealistic policy begins with such frustrating experiences. After the Second World War the political scientist who mainly engaged in it – apart from Reinhold Niebuhr, who in fact always clearly asserted the need for ideals, values and norms – was Hans J. Morgenthau. Unlike Niebuhr he above all emphasized power politics and interests. And anyone who wants to deal with the question of power and morality must move from what happens in history also into the depths of the formation of scientific theories. These – directly or indirectly – in turn influence the perception and shaping of political practice.

2. A dispute over political science: Morgenthau

From early in modern times scholars had also begun to investigate international relations: on the one hand there is the history of **diplomacy**, which attempts to follow the dynamics of the political process with its changing events and developments and above all its wars; and on the other the history of **international law**, which tries more to establish the static elements of behaviour, the continuity and uniformity of relationships. However, already since the nineteenth century something like an **opening up** of foreign politics had come about. On all sides, and of course particularly in the parliaments, which were becoming increasingly strong, people had become mistrustful of the secret foreign, military and arms policies of the rulers and the 'cabinets' (an invention of Louis XIV); President Wilson's demand for open negotiations in 1917 was also directed against this. It is not surprising that Wilson could not implement all his demands for a new world order, built less on power than on justice, at the first attempt, but they did have consequences. In view of the failures of Wilson's 'idealist' peace policy, in political science, too, there was a reaction on the part of the 'realists', led by Hans J. Morgenthau. He subjected to radical criticism the hypothesis of a natural harmony of interests which could be maintained with a little good will and sound common sense.

(a) Politics as management of power

The **catastrophe of the First World War** and the **foundation of the League of Nations**, aimed at a new world order, had prompted a whole wave of new studies in the 1920s and led to the foundation of scientific centres, institutions and schools with countless publications, seminars and conferences. Most of this scholarship was directed, in the spirit of Wilson and the League of Nations, towards giving better form to relations between governments, nations and societies and avoiding a similar catastrophe in the future. In particular the new 'science of international relations' – now an autonomous academic discipline – could make a significant contribution to the preservation of world peace, which was constantly in danger. This was not unimportant. The archives of imperial Germany and Tsarist Russia which were opened to the public now offered a glimpse behind the diplomatic scenes and made it possible to get to the bottom of the causes of the First World War. Thus the question why a war could happen was central.

But it was understandable that the **failure of the League of Nations** and the threatening increase in the power of the dictatorships brought a shift in political-science research: people began to criticize the allegedly idealistic studies which were orientated only on peace, glibly overlooking the fact that this research had subjected a whole series of highly concrete questions to thorough empirical treatment: the effect of racial and ethnic minorities or even the population explosion on foreign policy; the strategic and geopolitical aspects of international relations; the significance of raw materials and the effects of colonialism and imperialism . . . 'Realism' was now the slogan. The **Second World War** encouraged even more that trend in research into international relations which concentrated on the mechanisms of power politics. Here there was great interest in also coming to grips with the problems theoretically.

Hans J. Morgenthau's[7] *Politics among Nations*, published in 1948, rapidly became a **classic of 'political realism'** and within a year had already been officially adopted in around 100 universities and colleges in the United States as a textbook for foreign politics and international relations. It is a 'realist theory of international politics' with an imposing structure and documented with countless historical and contemporary examples, which provides a thorough analysis of permanent factors and variable constellations. It discusses every possible political question and problem, from the definition of political power, through national power and the balance of power, international morality and international law, to questions of securing peace through limitation, transformation and conciliation – and in the three subsequent editions constantly extended these further.

In contrast to 'historical optimism', Morgenthau's 'realist theory' does not presuppose 'that a rational and moral political order, derived from universally valid abstract principles, can be achieved here and now', nor does it assume 'the essential goodness and infinite malleability of human nature'.[8] Rather, its starting point is that human nature is driven by different contradictory forces and that 'this being inherently a world of opposing interests and of conflict among them, moral principles can never be fully realized'.[9]

Here we must limit ourselves to Morgenthau's basic approach and basic principles. The 'realism' of his theory consists in the fact that it puts right **at the centre** the concept of an **interest understood as power.** According to Morgenthau, one must accept human nature as it is: with it there is a constant struggle for existence in all its forms. Now for politics that means:

– Politics, whether domestic or foreign, is essentially a struggle for political power, which means the domination of human beings by human beings.

– The issue everywhere is the maintaining, expansion and demonstration of power; these are the three basic types of political action.

– The criterion for the foreign policy of the nation state as long as it exists must be the national interest; where peace is the main goal of a state, it puts itself in the hands of the most reckless member of the community of states.

– In the struggle for power a competition or alignment of interests is possible.

– Where interests coincide, collaboration between the nations is possible; where interests collide, rivalries and conflicts between them are unavoidable.

– In order to avoid the war of all against all, there is need for competent diplomacy which approaches the struggle for power with a rational assessment of its own and other interests and shrewdly keeps working towards a 'balance of power'.

– Thus where possible, peace should be secured by diplomacy, but where necessary through the threat of force; it is not a gift of heaven, as idealists and utopians suppose, but a by-product of stability and a balance of power between the nations.

In a word, Morgenthau is pleading for **power management** – and here again we recognize Henry Kissinger (who was a student of twenty-five when Professor Morgenthau's basic work was published, but who quotes his master only once in *Diplomacy,* in a subsidiary context).[10] His basic thesis is that in the system of sovereign states, the survival both of the states and of the whole system, depends on the national interest being pursued intelligently, and the power of one's own nation and that of the others being assessed rightly. But the national interest makes it possible for statesmen and professionals to define the goals and tasks of foreign policy realistically. By contrast, religious and ideological crusades threaten the stability of both states and the system. Every effort to lead nations to the ideal of mutual trust, understanding and collaboration can only end in catastrophe.

One can easily see how illluminating this theory of power politics was to many political scientists, and even more to many politicians in Washington (in the State Department and the Pentagon), and how difficult it seemed to the 'idealists', who thought that legality and morality were the important thing in all considerations of power. Subsequently it proved that much, indeed almost anything, could be justified in terms of the 'national interest' (or 'national security'). The illegal and often immoral actions of the CIA (founded in 1947 with a strictly limited responsibility for providing information) could hardly have established itself so strongly in Washington without this new 'realist' thinking, nor could some Latin American dictatorships. However, many political scientists did not make up their minds in the dispute over power politics, and increasingly moved over once again to empirical research under the aegis of political 'behaviourism', that value-free social science which thinks that it can measure and calculate the balance of power almost scientifically, or to individual theories, for example to the political decision-making process, to conflict resolution, to deterrence, to development . . .

After the experiences of the Nixon/Kissinger and then the Reagan/ Bush years, the suspicions of unscrupulous power politics in the 'national interest' (the *coup d'état* in Chile, intervention in Grenada, political murder in Guatemala, the mining of the harbours of Nicaragua, the bombardment of Panama, and so on) have finally once again been taken up by political scientists. As most recent discussion has shown, in particular the central concept of **'national interest'** is only apparently clear: it is easier to know what it is directed against than what makes up its positive content:[11]

- Is the theory of power politics in the national interest descriptive, indicating **how international politics (in fact) functions?** Or is it normative, showing how international politics **should function?**
- Is 'national interest' identical with the interest of the **nation** and thus the whole people, or only with the **state** and those who hold power in it, those who have foreign policy in their hands? The 'national' interest (power politics in foreign policy) often does not coincide at all with 'public' interest (a reform policy in domestic politics).
- Are not all too often the interests of a particular party, class or even **pressure group** (what is good for General Motors or United Fruits is also good for the United States) concealed behind solemn talk of national interest? Many parties join in the decision-making process

which have elevated their own interests to the level of the 'national interest'.

- May a national government, if this is 'necessary', finally override the interests of another nation or even the community of nations? This could hardly be a pioneering slogan for the increasingly global problems of economy and ecology, poverty and overpopulation.

Thus in respect of a future better world order, doubt is in order as to whether the 'realist' theory of politics as power management is enough to explain international relationships and give them a more peaceful form in the future. If we want to know whether the political theory of power management has a **future**, it certainly helps us to know better what its **origin** is.

(b) Where does the power politics theory come from?

Of course Morgenthau's political theory, too, did not fall from heaven: in the preface to the German edition he described his book as 'the fruit of twenty years' intellectual experience'. But when Morgenthau died on 19 July 1980 (a few months after his wife), there was no one who could speak at his funeral about the first forty years of this highly gifted and highly educated German Jew from Coburg, who had left a largely antisemitic Europe in 1937 and after his first six miserable years in New York and Kansas City was able to begin his meteoric academic rise in 1943 at the University of Chicago. And only since 1993 have we had real information about Morgenthau's intellectual background. Christoph Frei (a pupil of A.Riklin in St Gallen) has done us the service of producing a convincing 'intellectual biography' on the basis of previously unpublished material – school essays, diaries, manuscripts and around 30,000 letters.[12] As far as they are necessary for the analysis of our problems, the amazing results of this quest for Morgenthau's fascinating career – so far not noted in the American discussion – will be reported here.

So who was the **decisive stimulus** for the political theory of this completely assimilated, secularized German Jew, who had already lost his childhood belief in God before his university studies but who, now the complete American, constantly quoted Anglo-Saxon authors (in particular the theologian Reinhold Niebuhr, with his pronounced 'Christian interpretation' of the nature and destiny of human beings[13] to confirm and deepen his view), and skilfully kept quiet about his many German kindred spirits? Morgenthau's decisive stimulus was not Max

Weber and his sociology of domination, as has been thought on the basis of a single remark, important though Weber was for him, but – and here one is amazed and yet is not amazed – their common 'teacher', Friedrich Nietzsche! In a diary entry of 4 May 1928 Morgenthau even describes Nietzsche as 'the God of my youth',[14] and is more indebted to him than to anyone else for fundamental insights.

Morgenthau had already thoroughly studied Nietzsche's complete works together with individual works of 'kindred spirits' (above all Machiavelli and Max Weber) in his student days in the 1920s, and continued to make use of him continually (in 1945 he admonished the University of Chicago with the utmost urgency to acquire the volumes of Nietzsche's Complete Works which it lacked). In a 1962 letter (though this is utterly private), he acknowledges: 'As far as the dominant intellectual influences on me are concerned, Nietzsche was by far the strongest and was probably decisive.'[15] And whereas in an autobiographical fragment of 1976 he keeps quiet about Nietzsche's influence in favour of Max Weber (who had meanwhile become fashionable in America), at the same time his answer to the questionnaire in a newspaper (which, is unknown) about the ten books which are most important to him culminates in 'The Collected Works of Friedrich Nietzsche'.[16]

Why was the student, doctoral student and civil service candidate Morgenthau so fascinated by Nietzsche between 1923 and 1930? An evaluation of the diaries which have been discovered only recently allows us to sum this up in three points:[17]
– The Jewish outsider Morgenthau, who had already often been harassed in Coburg, and then in the universities of Munich, Berlin, Frankfurt and even in Geneva, had at an early stage found a **companion in suffering** in Nietzsche, the lonely outsider and spiritual aristocrat. Nietzsche gave him a deep insight into the tragedy of human existence. What Morgenthau admired about him was his unassuming intellectual honesty, which also impressed Max Weber (who similarly was strongly influenced by Nietzsche).
– The acute observer and analyst Nietzsche provided Morgenthau with a **psychology of the drive towards power,** which also investigates the unconscious and recognizes the basic human drive in the 'will to power'. Behind so many ideals of morality, metaphysics and religion Nietzsche's psychological perspicacity detects motives and drives, all of which can be derived from the 'will to power'.
– Nietzsche, the master of exposure, also leads Morgenthau to under-

stand **power** in the broadest sense as a life force and thus also as a **primal fact of history** generally. Life itself is an ongoing struggle to maintain and increase power and prestige: there are interests concealed behind all morality. Morgenthau is deeply stamped by Nietzsche's unadorned realism, which is concerned to establish not what should be, but what is. Morgenthau has taken over from Nietzsche the universal concept of power, which is often not understood in America.

So this is a **first** result of this historical quest: along with numerous other influences, especially those of Machiavelli and Weber, **Nietzsche** is the **spiritual father of the realist Morgenthau**. In the light of this intellectual origin, we can understand, first, how Morgenthau arrived at his political realism and his central notions, concepts and categories; secondly, why **in America he kept quiet** about his deep roots in German cultural life and in the thought of Nietzsche, indeed deliberately obliterated them. Since America's entry into the war in 1941, for many Americans 'German' had become synonymous with 'Nazi', and the 'German' political theory of an unknown would hardly have gained much sympathy. Moreover, particularly since the accession to power of the 'supermen' Mussolini and Hitler, Nietzsche with his ideas – will to power, justification of war, the breeding of the new realistic type of human being and the rejection of democracy and parliamentarianism – was regarded as the spiritual pioneer of Fascism and Nazism. This though, as is well known, Nietzsche had been an anti-nationalist and a European who despised German bourgeoisie, beeriness and nationalistic boasting, and admired Latin form, French *esprit* and the Mediterranean temperament.[18]

In view of this origin in Nietzsche – though that was not acknowledged to the Americans – is it surprising that after the publication of his theory of a realistic politics, Morgenthau himself was criticized by some as an admirer of power politics and a despiser of law and morality? All too often it was not clear whether this polemical spirit only wanted to achieve rationalism, legalism or moralism, or reason, law and morality. 'Hans was very much criticized in those days for his alleged amorality,' Henry Kissinger remarked years later.[19] But at the bottom of his heart Morgenthau was the opposite of an amoralist and a cynic.

(c) The unresolved ethical question

Morgenthau had another side, to which political scientists pay too little attention, and a description of it will take us a step further in our analysis of the substantive problem.[20] As early as 1922, as a senior schoolboy he had experienced Hitler's triumphal appearance in Coburg and then written a 44-page (!) essay on 'morality, civilized behaviour and custom': it was about the flourishing social life of people under a supreme moral law which at that time he still saw as a revelation of the will of God: 'In former times or in another country I might perhaps have become a great scribe and priest; but this age has forbidden us to believe,' Morgenthau later wrote in his diary.[21] For his belief in God had already collapsed in the following months and the ideas of a revealed moral law or a natural law now lacked legitimacy. Morgenthau was now **threatened with radical scepticism and nihilism**: unconditionally valid concepts like 'good' and 'evil' did not seem to exist for him any more than they did for Nietzsche; in his view everything was ultimately dependent on the ultimate value he himself had chosen.

But Morgenthau the student by no means succumbed to Nietzsche completely: in the end he did not even want to devote his doctoral dissertation to him. All his life he remained true to the realistic analyst of psychological and social reality, but he would not follow the prophet of the 'superman' and the 'transvaluation of all values'. Indeed soon he arrived at an at least momentary emancipation from the 'God of his youth'. **National Socialism** under a 'Führer' who embodied the unbounded will to power, who had come threateningly near to power with the world economic crisis and mass unemployment of 1929, opened Morgenthau's eyes: in the face of a totalitarian movement which had written dictatorship and war on its banners, was there not a need for a firm standpoint, transcendent, supreme values, clear and binding criteria? This is a **second** result of our historical quest: in **distancing himself from Nietzsche** at a very early stage, Morgenthau advocates the need for a table of values, the courage of the scientist in particular to make value judgments and to engage in values – even in the face of a naive, value-free positivistic doctrine of the constitution (and the young Marxists of the Frankfurt Institute for Social Research engaged in the exegesis of Marx).

That landed Morgenthau with a tormenting **problem**: he certainly wanted to **overcome ideological relativism,** but since like Nietzsche he had bidden farewell to belief in God and metaphysics, he had no firm **standpoint and table of values.** In these years he struggled indefatigably for an ethic. In Geneva he wrote his Habilitation thesis *La réalité des normes*[22] – in the face of Hitler's seizure of power in 1933: Hitler put all previous values and criteria in question and immediately issued a ban on Jews in the professions. Like other treatises on the precarious reality of law, custom and morality, these led him basically simply to note the downfall of these normative systems.

And indeed, in the face of violent Nazi rule, the failure of the League of Nations and international law, and Italy's war against Abyssinia in 1935 which no attempt was made to stop (and the Japanese occupation of Manchuria which had already happened in 1931), who could still maintain that law, custom and morality really fulfil the function attributed to them, namely of restraining and limiting the struggle for power? Morgenthau argues that only the expectation of an effective sanction (through conscience, public opinion or law) gives the norms validity, and precisely this is difficult in international law. Indeed, he contends, formerly religion and metaphysics had given normative force to ultimate values and criteria. But – and here his reading of Nietzsche shows its influence again – where are these to be got at a time when religion is dying and metaphysics is declining? Instead of an objective order of values, only the political is left as the criterion of all things, and rational regulation of power as the sole form of political behaviour.

Yet the **unresolved ethical question** would not let Morgenthau go. Still in 1937, immediately before he emigrated to America, in a systematic discussion of Kant, Hegel, Comte and Nietzsche he once again dealt with the question whether an objective moral order can be established in our time. But Morgenthau cannot ultimately express more than an uncertain hope that it will come like the Messiah: today, tomorrow or never. Two souls are clearly struggling in his breast: the passion of the moralist and the cool understanding of the realist.

Now, however, in **America** the German emigrant who had grown up in a world which valued theory and history, art and culture highly, experienced the culture shock of a **world of optimistic belief in scientific progress and political moralism**. Morgenthau addresses himself to the new situation: by temperament tending towards one-sided polemic, he conceals his moral idealism; indeed, in 1948 in his *Politics among Nations* with its well-formulated synthesis enriched with abundant historical and contemporary material, he demonstrates his power-political realism and his ideological criticism in a highly one-sided way. Instead of moral principles like freedom, democracy, human rights there is a sober calculation of power and interests. Instead of all the American utopianism, idealism, legalism and sentimentalism we have **foreign policy as rational power politics**, which presupposes that as the main actors in world politics, the states are striving for power and here on the whole must behave rationally and in a way that is clear to outsiders![23]

(d) In search of universal values

The vigorous criticism made at times that his theory of power politics, which he sometimes presented in a very dogmatic way, was amoral led in the third edition of 1960 to an apologetic preface with 'six principles of political realism'. Here, too, Morgenthau sees statesmen thinking and acting in terms of an interest understood as power. However, it is now stated, this approach should **not** sanction or even require **indifference towards political ideas and moral principles**, as long as a foreign policy is rational in its moral and practical aims.

Nevertheless, the question of universal ethical norms, hitherto unanswered, recurs as the assertion 'that universal moral principles cannot be applied to the actions of states in their abstract universal formulation'.[24] But that such an application has to take place 'filtered through the concrete circumstances of time and place' (and to this degree not in an 'abstract' way) does not make the question of universal moral principles for state action superfluous, but on the contrary urgent.

What is suspicious about Morgenthau's *Politics among Nations* is not the emphasis on power and interest but the constant **devaluation, relativization and political subordination of morality** which likes to dismiss universally binding ethical criteria as 'abstract' and political morality as 'unrealistic', and hardly seems to acknowledge supreme values and universal moral principles. Does that not mean, one asks oneself, an almost positivistic exclusion of morality from politics, from all that goes with power? Perhaps at this point Morgenthau has learned all too much from Hans Kelsen's 'pure' theory of law, for which only legal questions are the jurist's concern. National Socialism took this moral-free 'pure' theory of law *ad absurdum*, and along with it a moral-free 'pure' theory of power and interests.

Thus the **'autonomy' of politics**, understood in absolute terms by Morgenthau, gives no answer to the serious **questions** which have to be addressed to this political theory:[25]
– Is the autonomy of politics which is to be affirmed in principle to be understood relatively rather than absolutely, in so far as *a priori* it involves a reference to ethics?
– Or may the political 'realist' simply think 'in terms of an interest defined in terms of power' and here simply leave any thinking 'in terms of an accord between action and moral principles' to the 'moralist'?
– Should only the 'moralist' ask whether this politics is in accord with moral principles, whereas the political 'realist' needs to ask 'what effects this politics has on the power of the state'?

– May the political 'realist', in the face of a 'legalistic-moralistic' approach to international politics, simply 'subordinate the standards of morality' (like those of law) 'to those of politics'?

– Cannot such a subordination of moral principles to politics if need be also justify war, tyranny and terror, indeed any kind of politically motivated lies and deception, hypocrisy and treachery: to be specific, like the prolongation of the Vietnam war and Watergate?

– Is not that social insensitivity to the domestic political consequences of their foreign policy which can be found from Richelieu and Metternich to Kissinger (in America the widespread poverty, the misery of the blacks, the unrest in the universities, the decadence of the inner cities, the destruction of the environment . . .) connected with this?

But no, Morgenthau in no way wanted to justify any of this; indeed, he expressly criticized it. The moralist in him which had formed in confrontation with Nazism had not died. So as soon as he had to recognize that his theory of power politics had become established all too easily among Washington's dominant elites (especially in the planning staff of the State Department newly created by George Kennan), and that in the Cold War foreign policy was concentrated completely on military strength and deterrence, he began to steer an **opposite moral course**. As early as 1952, he stated in an article: 'To say that a political action has no moral purpose is absurd; for political action can be defined as an attempt to realize moral values through the medium of politics, that is, power . . . In order to be worthy of our lasting sympathy, a nation must pursue its interests for the sake of a transcendent purpose.'[26] And what is this 'transcendent purpose'?

Morgenthau feels compelled to note a crisis and decadence in American society in the Eisenhower years, characterized by self-satisfied ease and the hedonism of the *status quo*. In 1960 he wrote a book on the ideal goals of American politics, *The Purpose of American Politics*, which amazed friends and foes equally. Over several hundred pages he expatiated on the significance and necessity of ultimate values: 'Society has not created these standards and, hence, could not abolish them . . . The validity of these standards owed nothing to society; like the law of gravity, they were valid even if nobody recognized and abided by them.'[27] Even power and interest are subordinate to these moral values – above all the preservation of life and freedom in the sense of the Jewish-Christian tradition and Kantian philosophy. No wonder, then, that Morgenthau followed the global American policy increasingly critically, and objected to the Vietnam war at a very early stage, arguing that it was not worth the cost and could not be won. As a result, he was engaged in a public controversy with Henry Kissinger in 1966.

Moreover Morgenthau's personal life and scholarly development show how little politics and morality can be separated from each other. In principle, it is now clear to him that 'while military strength and political power are the preconditions for lasting national greatness, the substance of that greatness springs from the hidden sources of intellect and morale, from ideas and values'.[28] But has Morgenthau reconciled the dimension of politics related to power with that related to values? Here he is fond of referring to the virtue of intelligence, understood as the power of judgment. However, some fundamental questions remain open, above all:

- If the 'substance of national greatness' is ultimately determined by ideas and values, can the thesis be maintained that all politics is power politics and that all states are always **driven only by power-political interests**?
- Are Morgenthau's polemics against idealism, legalism and sentimentalism, and also his counsels for a realistic foreign policy, not at least an indirect argument against the view that *de facto* the politics of states are not exclusively determined by interests of power but often **also by ideal goals and moral claims**?
- Is it therefore correct to propagate **the pursuit of the national interest as an overall strategy for successful foreign policy**, indeed to super-elevate it as a moral obligation and attribute 'moral dignity' to the national interest in respect of a stable world order?
- Cannot such national power politics, as was demonstrated earlier by Richelieu and Bismarck, justified philosophically by Machiavelli and Nietzsche, and 'imitated' by Nixon and Kissinger, have at least as **disastrous consequences** as the crusades of the eleventh/twelfth centuries (which are rightly criticized) and the wars of religion of the sixteenth/seventeenth centuries?
- Must not power politics in the twenty-first century then again be subjected to humane **ethical criteria**, as Morgenthau sees these already formulated in Plato's ideas, in the biblical moral law and in the natural law tradition?
- But in that case what is their concrete **content**? Is a general reference to the preservation of life and human freedom, and a reference to the virtue of intelligence enough? Does this not need at least a counter-

balance in the virtue of **justice,** which for Plato, Aristotle and Cicero is the supreme virtue, in Machiavelli is by no means the least, and in Morgenthau plays only a subordinate role?

Hardly any political theorist in the Anglo–Saxon world had argued so impressively, before Morgenthau, on the eve of the outbreak of the Second World War, that the power factor – and alongside military power, also economic power and the power of public opinion! – should no longer be ignored, than the Englishman **Edward Hallett Carr** in his study *The Twenty Years' Crisis 1919–1939.*[29] But this very advocate of a realistic power politics, who in the inter-war period had analysed 'the abrupt descent from the visionary hopes of the first decade to the grim despair of the second',[30] concludes his book with a section on '**Morality in the New International Order**': 'If, however, it is utopian to ignore the element of power, it is an unreal kind of realism which ignores the element of morality in any world order. Just as within the state every government, though it needs power as a basis of its authority, also needs the moral basis of the consent of the governed, so an international order cannot be based on power alone, for the simple reason that mankind will in the long run always revolt against naked power. Any international order presupposes a substantial measure of general consent.'[31] At the same time, Carr warns against the 'disappointment if we exaggerate the role which morality is likely to play'.[32]

Remarkably, later Hans Morgenthau himself criticizes the new synthesis of realism and utopianism, theory and practice, politics and ethics for which Carr strives: in his view the British diplomatic and historian has sought a new morality in the world of politics 'without a clear notion of what morality is'; in so far as he simply identifies utopia, theory and morality, this 'leads of necessity to a relativistic, in-strumentalist conception of morality'. Carr has 'no transcendent standard of ethics'.[33] But Morgenthau, too, leaves us without a clear answer here. Has perhaps the more recent discussion with and after the classic figure of political realism allowed us to see more clearly? At all events we must now consider in principle the conflict between power and morality.

3. The conflict between power and morality

Many people today are asking: isn't ethics *a priori* a lost cause in the great world-historical dispute between power and morality, as the

Machiavellians among politicians and columnists keep wanting to make us believe? Is someone who wants particular humane 'values' to be observed even in foreign policies a naive 'preacher' or 'prophet'? And is someone who constructs politics purely on the basis of interests a cool and intelligent 'strategist'? Are politics and morality as a rule compatible only so long as no important interests are touched on? At all events, do not trade interests in particular prove stronger than political and moral postulates?

(a) Man, the ambivalent being, and power

The relationship between power and morality is an extremely difficult problem. There are famous political theorists who have never discussed it as a topic, and very recent works on international politics taking the line of Morgenthau the realist (but not the moralist) which hardly devote a word to it. However, we cannot evade the question here and must begin at a deeper level. A short anthropological reflection is unavoidable.

Ever since Aristotle, philosophers have reflected that man is a 'political being', a 'community being'. But Nietzsche and with him Max Weber and Hans Morgenthau were the first to understand this 'political being' essentially as one 'striving for power'. Particularly if we adopt this broad concept of power (against which some have important objections), we will have to remember that the evaluation of power in politics always depends fundamentally on a particular **view of human beings:**
– Anyone who, like the optimists of the Enlightenment and naive liberals, regards human beings as by nature good, rational, capable of learning and being trained, and the world as an ordered cosmos, will see politics as a means of human progress and of improving of the world, and **power as something good and beneficent.** But that raises the question: cannot evil also arise from what is good and well-meant?
– Anyone who, like the pessimistic analysts and ideological critics with a philosophical or theological background, regards human beings as by nature corrupt, irrational and dangerous and the world as chaotic will always see politics as a dirty business, an unavoidably immoral activity and **power as something evil and demonic.** But that raises the question: is any political use of power bad and any action unavoidably evil?

Considered from a truly **realist** perspective, the world is a split reality, and both good and evil are also mixed in human beings. Human beings are neither angels nor devils. If they were devils, it is said, no government would be possible; if they were angels, no government would be necessary. But **human beings** are **complex and ambivalent,** midway between reason and unreason, good and evil, a mixture of egotism and virtue, who can use power rightly or badly – in small things as in great, in private life as in politics.

But what is **power?** Power, generally speaking, is the competence, possibility or freedom to determine something else, people or circumstances. Or more precisely, according to Max Weber's classic sociological definition: power is 'any opportunity to impose one's own will within a social relationship even against opposition, no matter what the basis for this opportunity'. Thus 'every conceivable quality of a person and every conceivable constellation could put someone in the position of imposing his will in a given situation'.[34] And in so far as every individual has his qualities, he also has power – though this is often unutilized or minimal. Even extreme powerlessness does not yet mean the loss of inner force and power, feared so much by omnipotent dictators in particular that they think that they can master their opponents only by physical liquidation.

Power and power politics, understood in this broad sense, are in fact given with human nature, but they also share in the ambivalent character of that nature:

* Human power can be used **well,** in a truly **humane** way, for the well-being of those concerned, those around them and their environment. A humane peace policy is at least possible.
* Human power can also used **badly,** in an inhuman, **inhumane** way, to the detriment of those concerned, those around them and their environment. An inhumane power politics is often usual.

In politics least of all can one overlook the fact that since human beings are ambivalent by nature, power is always and everywhere not only used well but also abused. Therefore from antiquity human beings have made tremendous efforts to oppose the abuse of power, above all by those with political power.

(b) Inventions to counter the abuse of power

In the course of the twentieth century a start had increasingly been made on investigating international relations, too, from new perspectives: geography, economics, psychology, sociology, philosophy and political science, which was increasingly growing in strength. An analysis by the

Swiss political scientist **Alois Riklin** of St Gallen on a historical and philosophical basis is an example of how fruitful a political science which takes the broadest possible approach can be in investigating **power and the abuse of power.** Such an approach demonstrates with welcome systematic clarity by what means attempts have been made since the advent of Western civilization in ancient Greece to regulate the use of power in some way. In a process of trial and error lasting for almost three thousand years, six great **inventions to counter the abuse of power** can be said to have been made, which 'today form the provisional nucleus of legal and constitutional democracy': 'political innovations devised by human beings, tested experimentally and developed further', which 'are at least as significant in the history of civilization as the invention of the printing press, the steam engine or the computer'.[35] Briefly, according to Riklin, the following are the six inventions which remain significant to the present day as **institution-orientated political ethics.**

First invention: **the restraining of power by constitution and laws.** Power is controlled by binding even rulers to the laws. Plato already laid the philosophical foundation for a rule of law (nomocracy) instead of an arbitrary rule, and it was developed further by Aristotle, who distinguished between law and constitution (initially unwritten). Not human beings, but laws should rule, and these should be constitutional. However, a first written constitution appears only at the beginning of modern times (in 1654 under Oliver Cromwell); in the nineteenth and twentieth centuries written constitutions have become generally established.

Second invention: **the division of power by a mixed constitution, or the division of authorities.** The mixed constitution, made up of monocratic, oligocratic and/or democratic elements in the basic order of the state, was also founded already by Plato and developed by Aristotle, Polybius, Cicero, Thomas Aquinas and Italian Renaissance thinkers. This division of power between several holders of power controlling one another was described realistically in the sixteenth century by Donato Giannotti (who distinguished four functions of the state and three phases of decision-making). and proclaimed in its modern form in a historically effective way by Montesquieu against princely absolutism, though he himself did not yet use the term '*séparation des pouvoirs*', and made a strict division between legislative, executive and judicial authority. But since then it has been clear that any uncontrollable power, any concentration of power and above all any monopoly of power endangers the freedom of the individual, and that therefore limits must be set by power to power ('*Que le pouvoir arrête le pouvoir*').

Third invention: **limitation of power by unassailable basic rights.** That there are basic rights which are unassailable and inalienable in their substance, which are grounded in human nature before and above the state but which must be guaranteed by the state, was only formulated in the Enlightenment, though on the basis of antiquity and Christianity. They appear above all in John Locke and in the 1776 American Declaration of Independence which he influenced (from which Thomas Jefferson deliberately omitted the right to property). This was the model for the French Revolution's Declaration on the Rights of Man in 1789. The Universal Declaration of Human Rights was proclaimed by the United Nations in 1948. Thus human rights are to be found in almost all modern constitutions: they were finally also given a home in the Catholic Church, in which they had so long been condemned by Rome as contrary to God, by John XXIII and the Second Vatican Council.

Fourth invention: **moderation of power by the principle of proportionality.** The state and any holder of power may use only the means appropriate to the legitimate end. This is to be safeguarded by the principle of the proportionality of means (the prohibition of excess), which has developed out of modern criminal law, and in international law above all, in respect of the state's recourse to retributive measures (retaliation), reprisals and the right of self-defence. In our time moderation of power is the principle behind all legislation and administration of the law.

Fifth invention: **participation in power of those subjected to it.** What is meant here is democracy as already invented by the Athenians: at least a partial identity between those who hold power and those over whom it is exercised. This, too, became established only in modern times, above all through the English Parliament and the American and French Revolutions. In the twentieth century it attained its full form through universal suffrage, first for all adult male citizens and finally also for all female citizens.

Sixth invention: **balance of power through reduction of differences in power.** A reduction in the difference in power which exists between strong and weak individuals and groups, between the privileged and the underprivileged, and between employers and employees, producers and consumers, professionals and those excluded from the process of work, is a just demand. This difference in power, which can never simply be removed, always needs to be balanced to some degree by the state and other institutions. Here a way must be found between a formalistic egalitarianism and a social Darwinian utilitarianism, as the most significant theoretician of justice in our century, John Rawls, has attempted to demonstrate.

All these inventions for regulating power also have indirect significance for foreign and world politics, but they have all primarily been developed within the framework of a particular people or state. But what about **regulating power between the nations**? That has already been the concern of 'neorealist' political scientists – following Hans Morgenthau but distancing themselves from him.

(c) 'Scientific' disregard for ethics

Already at an early stage there was criticism of Morgenthau's theory, even among the 'political realists', though as Stanley Hoffman comments, he was recognized among the political scientists of America as a 'founding father'. Above all his central concepts, which were meant to explain international relations, were criticized as being too woolly and imprecise.

– The **concept of power** was thought to be too broad (at that time no one hit upon Nietzsche's influence!); striving for power as a universal human quality and an end in itself was thought to ignore other more philanthropic human characteristics, which were ultimately responsible for the fact that there was not constant war between the nations.

– **Rationality** in relations between states was also said to be presupposed too generally: the irrational factors which were always possible, along with information and negotiating tricks, were not factored in.

– Finally, the **balance of power**, too, was said to be understood too much as a universal concept: it covered only situations of real equilibrium and not all situations in the power struggle.

Contradictions would follow from such improper generalizations, which could be overcome only with a new 'more scientific' theory: thus the 'new realists' or **'neorealists'**, who were often distinguished from the classical realists (Morgenthau, Kissinger). They no longer wanted to start from human nature to explain the constantly new dissent and collaboration in world politics, but from the anarchical nature of world politics as such, with its proneness to rivalry. The fluctuations in world politics between stability and instability, war and peace, were to be explained with the aid of a **theory of the international system** which concentrated above all on **structures** and the distribution of power within the system. This structuralist system theory was meant to provide an unassailable theory of power and the balance of power. After significant predecessors, who criticized Morgenthau at a very early stage,[36] finally in 1979 the neorealist synthesis which is still normative today was presented by **Kenneth N.Waltz,**[37] who in the view of many people had succeeded in presenting a strictly coherent deductive theory of international politics: instead of the 'subjectivism' and 'common sense' which was still all too dominant with Morgenthau, there was now an even stronger rationalization of world politics.

But some critics found inadequacies even in this neorealist synthesis. The discussion documented by the Harvard political theorist **Robert O.Keohane**[38] reveals the following problematical points: the ambiguity of the terms power and balance of power which has still not been overcome; the neglect of the significance of domestic policy for foreign policy; the difficulties inherent in the structuralist system theory with the change in international relations; and finally the tendency simply to ignore history, in which any international system is ultimately grounded, because of a positivistic methodology.

I need not pass judgment here on neorealism as an overall political theory. However, the last point of criticism must be of interest to us: the ignoring of history or at least some of its primary aspects. Keohane notes that 'the widespread, if varied, sense of dissatisfaction with Waltz's version of neorealism' has its roots not only in the danger of nuclear war, which puts any realistic theory in question, but above all 'in the critical, idealistic tradition of commentary on world politics'.[39] But what do 'critical' and 'idealistic' mean here? Keohane himself, a wise Harvard brain, demonstrates the system-conditioned weakness of all neorealist positions, and also his own, when he concedes willy-nilly to the all too justified question of Richard K.Ashley, 'How can anyone integrate history into the type of theory that I have constructed?'[40]

Indeed, all these neorealist (or whatever name they go by) theoreticians of international relations are today (unlike Morgenthau and Kissinger) concerned intensively with economic interlocking, the role of the formal and informal international organizations, and thus with the problem of interdependence.[41] However, because of their methodology, which is positivistic and structuralist and constantly prone to reductionism, they ignore primary aspects of history, above all the **ethnic, ethical and religious dimension of world-political conflicts.** The outsider is sometimes almost reminded of neoscholasticism when following the basic neorealist discussion: so many conceptualities, nuances and distinctions, and at the same time so much abstractness, remoteness from life, so many acrobatics with concepts and ideas which one does not find in Morgenthau, the man who is claimed to be less 'scientific' but who offers rather more for practical politics.

And anyway, one asks oneself, how will such a structuralist theory explain the wave of European revolution in 1989? How will it give a convincing explanation of the war in Yugoslavia and the conflict over Jerusalem, if for 'systemic' reasons it abstracts, and has to abstract, from ethnic, ethical and religious dimensions? Despite all this expenditure of science, can it carry conviction as a truly **realist** theory, indeed as a problem-solving theory?

One of the most prominent advocates of the neorealist trend, the Princeton political theorist **Robert Gilpin**, is convinced that 'many, especially among the younger generation of international scholars, abhor realism'. Why? 'Because it is believed to be an immoral doctrine at best and a licence to kill, make war, and commit wanton acts of rapine at worst.'[42] This last is of course false: the realists are not 'immoral monsters'. But 'this rap of moral neutrality bordering on immorality is obviously a difficult one to beat'.[43]

In fact Gilpin himself, who has written outstanding books on war and change in world politics, political economy and, within that, even on monetary policy in historical perspective,[44] is amazingly unsatisfying on the **question of morality in neorealist theory**. A reference to Machiavelli's *Morality* is not really enough here, even if one appreciates his clear distancing: 'This amoral version of realism, which holds that the state is supreme and not bound by any ethical principles, is not my own view of realism.'[45]

Then what is? Already to offer the political 'counsels' of the realist theory as morality does not help here, any more than Gilpin's eventual flight into a 'confession'. He says that he is 'a closet liberal' who believes in the 'liberal values' – note the sequence – 'of individualism, liberty and human rights'.[46] As if all the immorality in politics has not been justified and cannot continue to be justified by an appeal to individualism and freedom! Should not liberals in particular realize that political morality comprises not only quite specific freedoms and rights but also quite specific obligations and criteria?

Questions arise here – not only to persons, but also to nations and their politics – which await an answer. So I shall end this chapter with some basic reflections on politics and ethics which will lead on to a systematic answer to the questions which have arisen in modern and contemporary history.

(d) The irresolvable tension between politics and ethics

The realist position has its truth, which must not be given up: it would be illusory to practise politics with abstract ideals, deceptive hopes and utopian wishes. Ideologies which veil and conceal the balance of power need to be exposed by ideological criticism. The reality of the political dimension, which may in no way be identified with rationality, must be taken seriously as such.

Even those political theorists indebted to the structuralist systemic theory will concede that political strategy and decisions cannot simply be replaced by more 'science', a 'scientific' system and 'scientific' solutions, **nor may politicians simply be replaced by 'experts'**. As Bismarck remarked on occasion, politics itself is no science, as the professors imagine, but the art of intuitively recognizing the right course at the right time in each new situation. Even when all the facts have been weighed up scientifically, a certain degree of subjectivity and a residual risk remain. On the other hand, political strategy and decisions cannot simply be replaced by more 'morality' and moral commands, **nor can the politician be replaced by the ethicist or theologian**.

Rather, a certain **autonomy of the political** must be recognized, which cannot be totally subjected either to scientific logic and the laws of economics or to legal norms and moral ideals, as scientists and economists on the one hand and legalists and moralists on the other would like. At any rate, one thing has become clear: there is a relationship of irresolvable tension between politics and ethics which must be maintained. And this means:

- The 'idealists' should note that a complete **subordination of politics to ethics** does not do justice to the autonomy of politics and leads to irrationalism. The calculation of power and interests must not be neglected: in the face of crusading politics inspired by 'morality' and its excesses, **sober matter-of-factness** is called for.
- But the 'realists' should not overlook the fact that a complete **detachment of politics from ethics** violates the universality of ethics and leads to amoralism. Values, ideals and criteria must not be neglected by politics. In the face of a largely individualistic and hedonistic society and a militarized foreign policy, there is a need for **ethical responsibility**.
- Even political science must note realistically what **is**: the highly ambivalent **reality** of human beings and their world. But at the same time it may not neglect what **should be**: the **humanity** of human

beings and the great unexhausted possibilities of being human, specifically in its relationship to power. The supreme criterion, even for political action, must not be reality, which can also mean bestiality in politics, but humanity.[47]

Since politics is concerned not only with power and systems but with human beings, it can never simply be left to politicians and political scientists. After all the experiences of modernity a new ethically determined, humane paradigm of politics is called for. It may be worth attempting to sketch it out in the next section.

III

Responsible Politics

Our whole account has shown that neither real politics along the lines of Richelieu, Bismarck and Kissinger nor ideal politics along Wilson's line is adequate for the postmodern polycentric world era which has definitively arrived after the Second World War. We need a new paradigm of politics, which **combines a sober perception of interests with a basic ethical orientation**.

1. Outlines of a new paradigm of politics

In venturing to speak here, perhaps all too boldly for some, of a 'new paradigm of politics', as a theologian of course I do not want to present the outline of a theory of international relations, their changes and their continuity, thought out in detail. Such a theory was presented, for example, by the American political scientist James N.Rosenau immediately before the great European revolution of 1989.[1] Against the background of a world situation in which there are no longer great conflicts which overshadow everything, and a number of power centres have formed, sometimes with very different interests, I want to concentrate on the **basic ethical structure** of the new paradigm of politics, though this has a variety of consequences for political practice. For in my view 'a new global politics' cannot be realized without '**a new global ethic**'. And this primarily concerns the question how the 'interests' which are constantly expressed in politics can be implemented. In what follows dramatic narrative must necessarily give place to analytical argument; the substantive problem has its own tension.

(a) Identification of interests – but how?

In international relations, too, there is a struggle for power – though that is not all! However, as the school of political realism has understood in our day, this struggle need **not primarily** be fought out **with military and political means**, as was supposed in the modern paradigm from the Peace of Westphalia in 1648 and the establishment of the European system of nation states down to the Cold War. Certainly military strength remains an important factor in international relations, particularly in the extreme case of collective defence – even if only as a threat. However, in the postmodern era of history, which is no longer Eurocentric and colonial but global, **economic achievements and resources** are often more important power factors. Here of course the geopolitical situation and size of a country play a role, as ultimately does also the diplomatic skill of its political leaders.

In the paradigm of modernity, since Richelieu, who exploited every opportunity in this direction, the concern was with a systematic **increase of power**: an **imperialistic policy**, which made use of all military, economic and often also cultural methods to achieve as extensive a hegemony as possible. Of course such an expansionist policy was often at the expense of others and necessarily endangered peace and stability, as is attested by the countless wars in modern Europe, culminating in two world wars. Such an imperialist increase in power, at least in military power, has been clearly rejected in contemporary international law, in the statutes of the United Nations, and in the European treaties. Although there are and will continue to be constant attempts in this direction in certain parts of the world, such an imperialistic policy can no longer be tolerated in any way in the postmodern paradigm, as I shall go on to demonstrate in more detail.

Maintaining power is another matter: a **policy of the** *status quo*, usually prescribed by legal agreements after military clashes (a peace treaty), makes sense in principle and should also be allowed in the future, albeit in the correct form. Such a policy should **not** be based on mutual **deterrence**, as in the earlier East–West conflict, for which all those involved must pay with expensive armaments and a squandering of resources; this at best makes it possible to achieve a precarious equilibrium. **Rather,** it is important to achieve a **balance of interests**, as for example in the European Community, where such a close network of interests has come into being in the political, military, economic and cultural sphere that even for the British it would bring more disadvantages than advantages if they were to detach themselves from this fabric of relationships.

Precisely because the issue is always a balance of interests, and today political and economic interdependence plays an incomparable greater role, there must be a **differentiation between all interests**. The annexing of Alsace and Lorraine in 1871 seemed to be in the interest of the German Reich, but in the longer term it was not. Conversely, the incorporation of the Saarland into the Federal Republic of Germany in 1957 seemed to be against the interest of France, but in the longer term it was. In the longer term it was not in the interest of the state of Israel to regard good relations with the USA as the only thing of importance and to disregard relations with the Palestinians, with the Arab world and with the government and Jewish communities of Egypt, because the Israeli governments did not take into account the threat from within (the Palestinians, and the extreme Right in their own country).

However, in these and similar cases it would have been little use investigating 'scientifically' the chances of gaining, maintaining and increasing power in a kind of cost-benefit calculation and, as some political scientists have attempted, to make a 'marginal-utility calcula-tion' about the use of power. In fact the scholarly discussion has indicated that the substance of interests is far more difficult to define than Morgenthau himself assumed.[2] At any rate, those who think that they need only consult the history of a nation to be able to determine the **content of the national interest** empirically and objectively will have been able to note in recent years that national interests also change over time and in no way remain constant: friends can become enemies and enemies friends. Great Britain, which for a long time had a vital interest in an empire and a Royal Navy operating all over the world, now needs Europe and a tunnel to the continent more than ever. And was the most recent 'protection' of Croatia in the interest of Germany, and that of Serbia in the interest of France and England?

Discussion of the 'national interest' seems very confused even to political scientists. Many periphrases of what one might almost call the empty formula of 'national interest' are only apparently clear. Self-interest should be 'enlightened' – but by what criteria? Many distinc-tions are not very practicable: 'vital' and 'non-vital' interests – but how are these to be distinguished in practice? Anyone who seeks to define the content of the national interest clearly in political theory fluctuates between a maximum and a minimum:

– Should one perhaps declare **everything possible** (from the importation of raw materials through foreign bases and the balance of power to the introduction of democracy all over the world) to be the national interest?

– Or should one limit oneself to what is **necessary**, namely the preservation of the nation, here at most including territorial integrity, political independence, maintaining the fundamental state institutions, and economic prosperity?

– And should the national interest be defined **from above,** by the government (in some circumstances even against the vast majority of the people) as the 'state interest'? Or should it be defined **from below,** from the people, so that the interests of the various population groups are reflected in the 'national interest'?

– Is it possible that only the preservation of the nation (and its culture) is the **end,** and everything else, even territorial integrity and political independence, merely the **means**?

If one regards particular interests as the means rather than the end, in cases where they conflict one is more flexible and thus, if necessary, also capable of negotiation and compromise. In fact Austria can exist quite well even without the South Tyrol (and territorial integrity), and the South Tyrol can equally well exist in the Italian state federation (without political independence). It remains to be seen whether Slovenia and Croatia will flourish better as sovereign states than in a truly federalist Yugoslavia; that will certainly not be the case with Bosnia and Montenegro. And as far as economic, political and military interests are concerned, perhaps one day the Czech Republic and Slovakia, indeed the Israelis and Palestinians, will understand each other better as partners than as rivals, after the example of France and Germany. At all events an economic union would be in the interest of both sides, and a new military conflict would be in the interest of neither. In the European Community, which is a example in this respect, people have already got used to subordinating state sovereignty to the common interests of the union of states in an increasing number of areas. The conclusion to be drawn is that we need to be careful in talking about national interests as the unchangeable constants in foreign politics.

(b) Identification of interests – being ethically responsible

One can already ask: what is and what will be the 'national interest' for this or that nation here and now and tomorrow and the day after? In such a serious conflict as the Vietnam war, even the American 'realists' held very different opinions here. No wonder that some political scientists describe interests as **purely subjective** (for example, the very different foreign policies of Israeli governments) while others, in vigorous contradiction, describe them as **completely objective** (for example, the foreign policy of different American governments, which has remained the same). Some political scientists, at a loss, have abandoned the concept as undefinable and impracticable. But here they have come up against political reality, in which national interests still play a major role for national governments. It seems to me better to differentiate the term than to eliminate it.

- Interests are not purely subjective ideas: they have a substantive basis, a **foundation in political reality,** when one thinks for example of the geopolitical situation of a country or the availability of certain raw material. Only if interests are not merely the daydreams of individual statesmen; only if there is at least a rational nucleus to the national interest, is it possible to judge whether a particular government is acting in the national interest or not; at all events, not every policy can *a priori* be in the national interest of every government.

- But interests are not purely objective facts either: they are open to **subjective assessment.** They cannot simply be calculated rationally, or quantified: whether there is a real interest of the country concerned in this case or that can only be determined by taking into account numerous factors, constants and variables. One would have to be omniscient to identify them all. Therefore at best there can only be 'core elements' or 'crude generalizations' of the national interest.

- In a new era of multilateralism, economic integration, governmental and non-governmental, international and supranational organizations, and thus of growing **interdependence,** national interests are at best capable of being defined to some degree objectively only by a highly complex process. Even 'realists' nowadays speak more modestly of 'core elements' of the national interest.

- So national interests are not to be brought into play naively or even demagogically. They have to be **accounted for ethically,** not only in the 'cabinet' which is directly responsible for policies, but, in view of the new significance of public opinion (the media as the 'fourth force' in the state) before the forum of the nation (and often even of the nations), whose verdict on the viability of government policy was in the last resort decisive in the case of the Watergate scandal and the Vietnam war.

In 'realist' political science, too, attention is increasingly being drawn to the problem of **global ethical responsibility.** It is worth listening when a political scientist like **John C.Garnett** (of the University of Wales) in his discussion report entitled 'The National Interest Revisited', ends by concluding that a 'major disadvantage' of an attitude to foreign policy orientated on the national interest is 'that it emphasizes "taking" rather than "giving", and pays scant attention to the notion that states may have **responsibilities and obligations** as well as interests'.[3] The recommendation of his colleague Andrew Scott that states should be encouraged to develop interests centred on the international system of states is said to be a 'useful way of smuggling the idea of responsibility into the national interest, thereby adding a genuinely positive dimension to a concept that is normally associated with purely selfish state behaviour'.[4] But why 'smuggle'? Garnett's final conclusion is: 'There is nothing to prevent the concept of **national interest** from being expanded to include wider milieu or system-centred interests, and given the wider problems that confront us, there are very good reasons why we should do this.'[5]

Every observer of international politics knows how difficult national governments find it to subordinate very tangible, short-term national interests to **less tangible, long-term global interests**. The great cycle of UN conferences in the last six years on education, protection of children and of the environment, human rights, precautions against catastrophes, population development and social reforms, and going on to the topics of women, children, settlement policy and nutrition bears abundant witness to this.

Among present American political scientists no one has been more concerned to awaken an awareness of global values and norms than **Richard Falk** (of Princeton), who with a large international team and conferences in Moscow, Yokohama, Notre Dame, Indiana and Harare between 1988 and 1993 has impressively worked out a 'World Order Models Project' which in 1995 he summed it up in a synthesis.[6] Falk develops ten concrete global dimensions in his 'essential vision' for a 'humane governance': restraining war, abolishing war, making individuals responsible, collective security, the rule of law, non-violent revolutionary politics, human rights, the stewardship of nature, positive citizenship, cosmopolitan democracy – all very important fields of action which cannot be discussed here. However, after discussing the basic problem I do want to go into the problem of human rights, where the clash between ideals and realities is especially harsh.

(c) The middle way between real politics and ideal politics

At least since the new US policy on Latin America, more orientated on collaboration than on hegemony, even Henry Kissinger sees a 'confluence' of the geopolitical and moral aims of Wilsonianism and real politics.[7] At the end of his book, even Kissinger has to concede: 'In travelling along the road to world order for the third time in the modern era, American idealism remains as essential as ever, perhaps even more so, which must combine with a thoughtful asssessment of contemporary realities to bring about a usable definition of American interests.'[8]

However, Kissinger should have introduced such correct insights positively right from the start and kept reflecting on them, instead of discrediting them: his chapters on Bismarck, Theodore Roosevelt and Woodrow Wilson (presumably written very much earlier) would then have turned out differently, as also, in some respects, would his own foreign policy. At the latest since the Second World War, despite all too manifest resistance, **a new postmodern paradigm of politics** is now **slowly and laboriously** becoming established, which is no longer Eurocentric but polycentric, and which in a post-colonial and post-imperialistic way aims at truly united nations. And it is certain that in this new epoch the united Europe, and also America, indeed the whole world, no longer needs old-style geopolitical power strategists, but rather authentic statesmen, who, while showing as much of Kissinger's intelligence, power of decision and understanding as possible, at the same time have an ethically determined vision and concrete plans which they can realize with a high awareness of their responsibility.

From the historical and systematic account given so far, it should already have become clear that there is a **middle way between real politics and ideal politics.** This is the way of a **politics in the spirit of an ethic of responsibility,** of the kind that I have already sketched out in my *Global Responsibility*, along the lines of Max Weber and Hans Jonas. Where foreign policy is concerned, it first of all means two negative demarcations.

- The **mere ethics of success of the real politician,** for whom the political goal 'hallows' all means, even immoral ones like lying, deceit, betrayal, political murder and war, is of no use for a new world order. Neither diplomacy nor the secret services nor the police are above morality.

Such Machiavellianism, which adopts only Machiavelli's immoral counsels, has brought an infinite amount of suffering, blood and tears upon the nations. Here one is thinking not only of horrific figures like Hitler and Stalin, Pol Pot of Cambodia and Idi Amin of Uganda. Nor is one thinking only of the secret police and secret services of various states which (like the Soviet Union's KGB and the United States' CIA) forged murder plots and broke the law, and indeed (according to a US army handbook for Latin American soldiers) even successfully taught others extortion, torture and murder. Ultimately one is also thinking of the many politicians who were less statesmen than characterless opportunists, for whom the only political constant at home and abroad was the furtherment of their own re-election (and thus the preservation of their influence, prestige and income) and who precisely because of this did not deserve re-election. Nevertheless:

- The **mere conviction ethics of the idealistic politician**, for whom a purely moral motivation and good aim ('national unity', 'peace', 'human rights') is sufficient, but who thinks all too little about the real balance of power, the possibilities of concrete implementation or possible negative consequences, is no use for a new world order either. In world politics too, 'well meant' is 'the opposite of good'.

Good motives do not in themselves guarantee good politics. Anyone with good intentions can certainly seem good to himself and to others, but that does not mean that his policy has good results. The art of politics includes the assessment not only of the consequences aimed at (say, of reform measures in domestic politics or moves abroad), but also the side-effects which, while in no way intended, are often extremely serious. Anyone who merely wants to act well, with no concern for possible bad consequences and side-effects, is acting irresponsibly, indeed culpably, even if in cases of failure he is fond of blaming others or the circumstances. False idealism, too, has sometimes led whole peoples astray towards an unrealizable 'no-where' ('u-topia'). Moreover this has happened not only in the crusades and so-called wars of religion but also in the modern wars of nations and ideologies. Not only the motives but also the results are important, and so a political ethic orientated on institutions needs to be supplemented by an **ethic orientated on results**. The positive conclusion to be drawn from this is:

- Only an **ethic of responsibility** is of any use for a new world order. It presupposes a conviction, but realistically seeks the predictable consequences of a particular policy, especially those that can be negative, and also takes responsibility for them. The art of politics in the postmodern paradigm consists in combining political calculation (of modern real politics) convincingly with ethical judgment (ideal politics).

Anyone who thinks that this demand would ask too much of the politician should reflect that already according to **Max Weber** the ethic of responsibility presupposes a conviction; indeed, just as an ethic of conviction is not to be identified with irresponsibility, so an ethic of responsibility is not to be identified with a lack of conviction.[9] Max Weber was unable to give closer thought to this ethic of responsibility which he had sketched out in the last dozen pages of his Munich lectures given to students in the revolutionary winter of 1918/19, and which appeared in print in 1919. At the end of the lecture he remarked that in ten years' time he would like to say more about it, but the following year he was dead. In conclusion he also declared that an ethic of conviction and an ethic of responsibility were 'complementary' and 'together first make the authentic human being who **can** have the "call to politics"'.[10] How that can be, however, Weber left open.

(d) From national to international responsibility

Max Weber had sketched out his ideas on an ethic of responsibility in the middle of the epoch-making upheaval of the First World War, which ushered in the end of a Eurocentric modernity that believed in reason and progress, still within a narrow nationalistic framework. In a postmodernity that has become critical and no longer Eurocentric (since the Second World War increasingly conscious of being a new era), such an ethic has to be reflected on in a **global context**. The scientific and technological power of humankind, which has grown to immense proportions, brings with it a moral responsibility which has become equally immense. The many manifest negative consequences of modern progress, which is intrinsically so grandiose, make it abundantly clear that here too much is being asked not only of individual human beings and human communities, but also of nation states. Indeed another characteristic of postmodernity is that a humanity which has grown together can for the first time in its history produce its own downfall.

If humankind is to survive, global solutions must be striven for. Of course these can only be realized step by step, but in some areas they have already been introduced. In his major book on *The Imperative of Responsibility* (1985), **Hans Jonas** has demonstrated with reference to the danger to the ongoing existence of the human species[11] that in this world situation which has been changed in such an epoch-making way the issue is one of a **truly global responsibility**. This extends to the whole bio-, litho-, hydro- and atmosphere: it is a responsibility for the world around us, the environment and posterity in the face of the danger to the future of the human race. It is evident that in these circumstances foreign and domestic policy can no longer simply be separated. **Carl Friedrich von Weizsäcker**, who as both a physicist and a philosopher is constantly preoccupied intensively with these problems, has coined a term for this situation which is as precise as it is challenging, namely 'world domestic policy',[12] and **Ernst Ulrich von Weizsäcker** has proposed an 'earth politics', an 'ecological real politics' for the next century.[13] The most significant American contribution to the ecological problem has come from the American Vice-President **Al Gore**, who in the face of the real dangers to the environment calls for a radical rethinking of our relations to nature, in order to preserve the world for coming generations: a Marshall Plan for the earth.[14]

A politics which in the perspective of this world domestic policy does not ask under what basic conditions human beings can survive on a habitable earth and give their social life a human form will not achieve its goal. It is no help in saving human civilization for the third millennium. More than ever, in the face of a responsibility which has become immeasurable in areas from gene technology to nuclear energy, the **human being** must be the **goal and criterion of politics**: the human being, who should also become more humane in relations between peoples and states and also in relations with nature. Politics is an essential means of drawing on the **human potential** which does exist in order to further **the most humane and intact environment possible**. The postmodern movements which already broke through after the First World War, but only developed their full force after the Second World War, have long since become political factors of the first order: the disarmament movement, the peace movement, the women's movement and the ecological movement have assumed global dimensions.

Thus here already the question arises whether a new world order is possible at all without an ethic for the whole of humankind which is binding and compulsory – even though it may be historically-conditioned: a global ethic which in its most basic features can be supported by different religions, indeed by both non-religious and religious people. But before we turn to this fundamental problem of global religions, global peace and a global ethic, which is not being reflected on even in the most recent American political discussion, we must first ask ourselves rather more concretely that serious question of serious politicians, namely how an ethically motivated politics can be achieved in the face of all the real difficulties. The test case for this since Machiavelli has been: is not one sometimes simply compelled to act immorally, particularly in politics?

2. Ethics – a challenge for politicians

Max Weber depicted an ethic of conviction, particularly in so far as it involves the New Testament and the Sermon on the Mount, in a polemically one-sided way. At the same time he had brought what in his last years he had called an ethic of responsibility far too close to an ethic of success (earlier he had spoken of 'power politics' instead of 'politics of responsibility'[15]), as is clear in his superficial remarks on truthfulness, which is not among the decisive **qualities** which he requires **of the politician.** There are three of these: 'passion', in the sense of commitment to the cause; 'responsibility' towards this cause; and 'proportion', in detachment from things and people. All three are doubtless of great significance for any politician; they comprise 'the strength' of a 'political 'personality'.[16] But precisely what does 'responsibility' mean? At all events the ethical test-question remains unanswered, namely whether even immoral means may not be employed for the 'cause' and its success, and conversely whether moral means may be employed as a pretence. First, we look at the second strategy.

(a) More semblance than reality?

One thing has become clear: what has been said so far in political ethics about political institutions (against the abuse of power) and the results of policies (assessment of consequences) is not enough. Certainly the 'restraining of political power' and the 'abuse of power by **institutions**' is emphasized from Donato Giannotti, the last great Florentine statesman, through Immanuel Kant to Karl Popper as 'a fundamental problem of state theory'.[17] But conversely, it must be asked: what are laws without morals, what are institutions without **persons** who use them morally? From where else do the giant scandals in our democratic constitutional states and institutions come? And if politics is already said to corrupt the character, conversely corrupt characters certainly affect politics. Particularly against the global horizon of the problem, there is need for what A.Riklin calls – and here I see my concern well taken up – 'unconditionally' a '**synthesis of result-orientated, institution-orientated and person-orientated political ethics**'.[18]

Power politicians could always refer to **Machiavelli** – even if they did not quote him ('realist' political scientists have fewer inhibitions here). It was Machiavelli's conviction that the politician who aimed to be successful sometimes had to act immorally and that conversely the politician who always acted morally must necessarily fail. Hence his counsel not only for the extreme situation of the politician but also the normal situation: act morally as far as possible and immorally as far as necessary. Moreover, **appear more than be,** as he bluntly demands in the notorious Chapter 18 of *Il Principe*: people are to have the impression 'that he (the ruler), when one sees and hears him, is all gentleness *(pietà)*, all faith *('fede')*, all trustworthiness *('integrità')*, all humanity (*'umanità'*) and all piety (*'religione')*'.[19] And he adds: people are simple, judge by appearances and like to be deceived. He wants to give just one example of this, the Pope and father of Cesare Borgia whom Nietzsche also admired: 'Alexander VI did nothing else, he thought about nothing else, except to deceive men, and he always found the occasion to do this. And there never was a man who had more forcefulness in his oaths, who affirmed a thing with more promises, and who honoured his word less; nevertheless, his tricks always succeeded perfectly, since he was well acquainted with this aspect of the world.'[20]

So here already we have him: Nietzsche's modern **man beyond good and evil,** who does good when possible and evil as far as necessary. So are we not to grant politicians in particular not only guile and cleverness, but if need be also any lies and perfidy, any treachery and corruption? But the most recent political scandals, which have also affected Europe, have shown that the long-sufferingness of the electorate does have its limits, and that such scandals can lead to the downfall of politicians, indeed of a whole political class (in Italy, Japan and Korea), including the judiciary (in Belgium and elsewhere).

Nevertheless it would not make much sense to hark back, in the spirit of a purely person-orientated ethic, to one of the many **codes of conduct for rulers** which go back to the ancient Egyptians, Babylonians and Israelites, but which were difficult to translate from the feudal period into a democratic society (that applies even to the famous version by Erasmus of Rotterdam), and to make a universal **code of conduct for politicians.** However, the fact that in literature and also in art (they are often displayed in town halls and public places), these codes of conduct for rulers almost unanimously require more of the statesman than Max Weber – not only to be bold, prudent and wise but also to be just, generous and peaceful – could give present-day politicians and political scientists, too, something to think about. Still, I do not want to point a moral finger here, but to say something which may perhaps be helpful for political practice: perhaps a contribution to a 'code of conduct for politicians in a media age'.

(b) Immoral if need be?

I shall not engage here in any dreary casuistry, which has its own way of dealing with all cases. Nor in any moralism, which self-righteously dictates its own terms and sees only its own virtue and the vices of others. But in the face of the conflict between moral standards and political success and in the face of the public discussion over politicians and morals, there is a pressing need to offer some, so to speak, **anti-Machiavellian counsels** for politicians, and not only for them:

(1) **No professional pessimism.** One perhaps has to be a politician who has been thrown out and banished from his ancestral city, like Machiavelli, in despair about the situation of his own country and embittered at the shameful failure of his personal career, to share in the deeply pessimistic view that all human beings are deceitful, hypocritical, cowardly, ungracious, greedy and bad. Is virtue, as Bernard Shaw thought, only a 'lack of opportunities'? Were that the case in politics, one's starting point would have to be that all human beings are evil and follow their evil inclinations as soon as they have the opportunity. But is that true for everyone, always, everywhere? Do not other people have a wealth of other experiences? Do not many people refrain from lying, stealing and murdering, even when they have a favourable opportunity? So in politics, too, one should not act as though the abnormal were normal and there were no respectable politicians at any level – for all their weaknesses. Moreover, in humankind, in addition to an infinite amount of immorality, an amazing amount of moral inhibitions and motivations are also at work, so that even when treaties are broken opportunistically, and there are shameful judicial verdicts (masses of them in totalitarian states and not a few in democratic states), there is always a concern for the semblance of legality and morality. Therefore for politicians, too, there should be

(2) **No special morality.** Certainly in many political decisions the moral decision must be balanced with political necessity, and this is sometimes difficult. But it would be greatly to overestimate the position of the politician (or the businessman) to want to grant him a special morality in society which would allow him if 'necessary' to lie in the face of fellow citizens or the representatives of other states, to attack them, or even to destroy them morally, if not physically. Is it right for not only the fit but also the addicts, those addicted to power, influence, prestige and sex, to have their own way? No, even the utmost tolerance and liberality cannot go so far that one allows a politician, as in Cesare Borgia's time, poison (now disseminated through the media) and the dagger (for

treacherous democratic murder). As is well known, elementary ethical imperatives for individuals as such ('You shall not . . .!) seldom tend to be applied directly to state decisions, but they are applied to the personal decisions of statesmen. As the sexual infidelities of politicians do not affect the general public, unless they have political implications (betrayal of secrets, intrigue, Mafia), the public tends to forgive politicians for them more than for open lies, corruption in office or even political murder. But two or three divorces along with new affairs presumably does not strengthen the confidence of the electorate in the reliability of such a politician; indeed it creates some doubt as to whether such a person is suitable for the highest state office. But on the other hand a warning is needed:

(3) **No rigorism.** All too often, following Machiavelli, exclusive alternatives have been constructed between political and moral imperatives, as if in practice there were no third middle way, as if one had to act either rationally and immorally or morally and irrationally. 'Realist' political scientists have taken great trouble to find concrete examples in which particular moral principles either were not allegedly applicable or had pernicious consequences in the reality of world politics. Here further ethical reflections would have been appropriate. After all, traditional moral theology since the Middle Ages has already reflected in a quite rational way on the question of the **double effect** (both good and evil) of particular actions (*actus duplicis effectus*), in which the foreseeable evil effect may never be striven for directly and positively (the good end does not hallow evil means), but can be taken into account indirectly for the sake of an appropriate or higher good (abortion where the mother's life is endangered, the killing of a person in self-defence). Attempts have been made to answer the associated question of the **clash of obligations** in cases where it is impossible to fulfil both obligations at the same time, and therefore there must be an **assessment of goods** in order to choose the lesser evil. In practical life moral decisions often involve the weighing up of substantive arguments in order to arrive at a verdict as to whether this or that particular good (truth or life?) has priority. Must one, for example, speak the truth in all circumstances, even if in so doing one deprives an innocent person of his or her life (not to mention contraception for the well-being of a marriage and family). In real life the choice is usually not so much between absolute good or evil as between two competing goods and sometimes even between two evils.

So an ethic of responsibility as I understand it does not mean a modern 'life without norms', but it does not mean a quasi-mediaeval 'life in accordance with norms' either. Rather, here, too, I would plead for **a middle way of responsible reason between**

– an irresponsible **Machiavellianism and libertinism,** which in politics as in personal life means being able to dispense with all ethical principles, criteria and maxims, which seeks simply to orientate itself on the given situation, that is constantly changing: a decision focussed only on the case in question, purely in the light of the present moment. In this view even treaties are valid only 'as things are' (*rebus sic stantibus*); if the situation changes, breaking the treaty is a matter of course; loyalties and alliances in any case change; and

– an irrational **legalism and dogmatism,** which in politics as in personal life wants to act inflexibly, simply by the letter of the law. Principles, criteria and maxims here have become infallible paragraphs which apply unconditionally in any situation, without exception and in all circumstances – on questions from contraception and population policy to abortion and euthanasia.

Are there not for politicians, too, situations in which Luther's 'Here I stand, I can do no other!', a completely personal **decision of the conscience,** is needed? Yes, since after all the ethical imperative always relates to a situation. In a particular situation the ethical imperative can be quite categorical, an obligation of conscience without any ifs or buts, not hypothetical but unconditional. For political ethics all this means:

- Political ethics does not imply an inflexible **doctrinaire standpoint** which allows no compromise. Ethical norms which take no account of the political situation are counter-productive; ethical decisions are always concrete.
- Nor does political ethics imply any **crafty, sharp tactics,** which have an excuse for everything. Unless the political situation is assessed by ethical norms, the result is a total lack of conscience.
- Instead of this, political ethics implies an **obligation of conscience** which is not focussed on what is good or right in the abstract, but on what is good or right in the concrete situation. Here a universal norm as a constant is combined with specific variables determined by the situation.

Only in a particular political situation does a moral obligation become concrete (here the realists are right). But in a particular political situation, which only those involved can judge, the obligation can be unconditional (and here the idealists are right). Does that also apply in politics to such a tricky question as 'speaking the truth'? To be specific:

(c) May politicians lie?

There should be no doubt about it: in particular the requirement of **truthfulness**, which since the Enlightenment has been recognized as a basic condition for human society, applies not only to normal citizens but also and in particular to politicians. Why? Because by nature they bear a special responsibility for the common good and therefore also have some privileges. These do not include *carte blanche* where truthfulness is concerned. With justification, a lack of truthfulness is particularly frowned on in their case. However, here there are so to speak **degrees in the lack of truthfulness** which need to be reflected on.

(1) The **lie** is a bad thing. A lie is a statement which does not correspond with the opinion of the speaker and, unless it is merely a jest or a polite formula, is meant to deceive others for the sake of an advantage or disadvantage. Lies are sometimes difficult to avoid in an emergency, and even someone who is basically truthful can lie when really pressed. But calculated lies are rather different, and efficient diplomacy, at least today, certainly does not consist in two people lying in each other's face, each knowing full well that the other is lying (Metternich and Talleyrand are no longer quoted as examples nowadays). Rather, particularly in secret diplomacy, openness is needed despite all shrewd negotiating tactics. Tricks and deceptions ultimately do not pay; they undermine trust, and without trust no politics which can shape the future is possible.

(2) Worse than the lie is **untruthfulness** which does not relate to an individual statement and primarily to others, but affects the core of the person and his or her basic attitude: even someone who does not actually lie can be untruthful in his or her whole person and behaviour. But such individuals can still have an awareness of conforming to or transgressing norms, for all their hypocrisy.

(3) Worst of all is **mendacity**, which can permeate the whole of a person's life, so that he no longer even notices the way in which he is constantly coming up with untruths and half-truths. According to Martin Luther, in any case a lie must bring seven others with it, if it is to become like the truth or to emanate a semblance of truth. A mendacious person has possibly identified himself slavishly with an authoritarian political system (a state, a party, a church) and denies even the lie of his life to himself; indeed it constantly lies itself away. After all, he has done

everything well, so that he can even seem honest to himself, as he believes his own lies and has an answer to all objections. He did not allow himself to be driven to untruth for his own advantage (he is not in himself a malicious person), but for the sake of the state, the party or the church, which calmly allows him to lie without worrying his conscience about it. After all, he is not lying for himself but for the greater whole which he represents. He need not take responsibility; the institution does that. Here it becomes quite evident that the view propagated by the advocates of real politics and reasons of state, namely that the state may claim a special morality for itself, presupposes a certain mendacity in the statesman, whose politics reflects quite different moral criteria from his personal ethic – if he has one at all.

There is another variant of mendacity, **opportunism**. It need not necessarily be the adaptation of politicians to an authoritarian or totalitarian state that leads them to mendacity. An uncritical, irrespons- ible adaptation to a milieu, a trend, a social, political or cultural tendency of the time, the spirit of the time or even a particular constellation of power can be enough for a politician to lapse into untruthfulness, so that he no longer comes clean with himself, and is no longer completely transparent to himself. Thus opportunism and authoritarianism are related. The opportunism of the many in a party, a grouping or community, makes possible the authoritarianism of the few, and the authoritarianism of the few encourages the opportunism of the many. Authoritarianism and opportunism can even appear in the same person and admirably supplement each other, particularly in those who hold office. In that case one is authoritarian to interiors and opportunistic to superiors. This is what is usually described as the official bicycling position: bend one's back at the top and push down at the bottom.

However, a rejection of opportunism does not mean its precise opposite; it need not mean a **fanaticism for the truth**. Much as there is an ethical obligation not to utter untruths, there is no ethical obligation to disclose the truth at any time in any place to anyone, as if any individual had the right to learn the truth and the whole truth from another person at will. Should, for example, someone who had hidden a Jew have betrayed the hiding place to a Gestapo man? In a democratic constitu- tional state cannot any accused refuse to testify in a criminal trial? And do I have to give information if I am asked about the weaknesses of my friend? Conversely, cannot it be cynical to spring a truth on someone who is totally unprepared for it? Silence can certainly be an expression of untruthfulness, but it can also serve truthfulness. Discretion about others can be an obligation, and discretion about oneself can be a right. Silence can be a virtue if it is not rooted in cowardice. Nor are circumlocutions or exaggerations already lies.

No *a priori* legal definition can be given of the point at which secret reservations and diplomatic ambivalence become lies, nor can any casuistic moral theology replace the virtue of cleverness in the concrete instance. That is also true of politics. For example, for a statesman like Charles de Gaulle to give only limited information to the supporters of 'Algérie française' about his strategy for Algerian independence was a justified political tactic in such an impossible situation, and one which did not offend against the truthfulness of the politician. Nor did de Gaulle's strategy and tactics serve only his instinctive will to power; they also served the peace and prosperity of France and its former colony, which were under threat.

Now like anyone else, in an emergency a politician can get into a conflict situation which is so extraordinary that it cannot be resolved by any existing law, and he or she is compelled to decide and act for the best possible outcome. If, for example, a Swiss Minister of Justice hears as an official secret about an impending investigation of her husband on a serious charge and warns him about it, she is clearly offending against the law; but she would perhaps find public opinion understanding if, on being discovered, she openly confessed her wrong behaviour and apologized. But if she lies, attempts to put the blame on others and still cannot clear herself, she is rightly forced to resign. However, has the Minister of Justice not perhaps acted in the interest of the state, which would have been severely shaken by such a scandal?

Here it becomes clear how **dangerous** it would be for our democracy if – as some 'realists' want – one sought to **detach the morality of the state from the morality of the individual.** Thomas Jefferson seems to be right (against Morgenthau, Nixon and Kissinger): there is only one, undivided ethic. The same ethical criteria must apply to states as apply to individuals. And the argument (here anti-idealistic 'realists' in particular treacherously appeal to moral heroes) that only the individual has a right to sacrifice himself in defence of a moral principle, and that the statesman does not have the right to sacrifice the state, say in defence of freedom if the survival of the nation is in danger, does not tell against this.

But neither the one case nor the other is as clear as it seems; questions need to be answered in both.

– Where **individuals** are concerned: do individuals perhaps have the right to sacrifice themselves in defence of a moral principle if they so wish? At most by way of exception. Not only are there completely meaningless sacrifices, but even an intrinsically meaningful sacrifice can be morally unjustified; the old Catholic Church of the Roman Empire rightly banned believers from voluntarily exposing themselves to martyrdom for the Christian faith.

– Where the **state** is concerned. Could not a statesman in extreme emergency, contrary to widespread opinion, perhaps regard it as his duty to require a 'sacrifice', indeed a fatal confrontation, of his state in order to preserve the freedom of the people? Winston Churchill (like de Gaulle) could have capitulated to German supremacy, as Marshal Pétain did. But he called on his people to engage in a military confrontation with Germany, the outcome of which at that time was completely open, in order to fight for the freedom, first of England and then also of the continent. A good deal could certainly be said about these examples; they are cited here simply to show that the separation between individual and state morality proposed by 'realists' is unconvincing because it is abstract, simplistic and alien to reality.

However, even for those holding political power, a gap will often remain between what is desirable and what is possible. More important, though, is another question, which once again brings us back to the question of power. To what end is power used?

(d) What is power for?

Charles de Gaulle, Konrad Adenauer, Robert Schuman, Jean Monnet, Alcide de Gasperi, all the great European politicians who came to power after the Second World War, had not given way in the time of Fascism and Nazism and had learned what powerlessness means. They were certainly no saints; all had their weaknesses. But one can hardly claim that they strove **for power for its own sake.** Max Weber had already made a precise distinction: 'Anyone who engages in politics, strives for power: power either as a means in the service of other ends (ideal or selfish) – or power "for its own sake": to enjoy the feeling of prestige that it gives.'[21]

In fact there is also the other genre of the **pure power politician,** and here one does not think just of Hitler and Stalin. Looking back on the defamatory statements, intrigues and treachery of the German Social Democrat politician Herbert Wehner (though he has his merits), his friend in the party Egon Bahr concluded: 'But what was all this for?

German unity? Democracy? The unity of the working class? He did not have a vision or a strategy for any of all this. He was a power centre that was sufficient in itself.'[22] Some German Christian Democrats would use at least the last sentence (mindful of so many manipulations, intrigues and defamatory statements) of their party friend Franz Josef Strauss, who also has his merits. But whether or not one shares these sharp judgments, one has to have a healthy mistrust of any politician of any party who is said above all to have a 'will to power' ('instinct for power', 'drive for power'). For such men of power are usually capable of almost anything, even if quite often (like Wehner and Strauss) in the end they fail in their ambitions.

So if one should limit such men of power ('power centres') in a country, one cannot simply abolish power, as the anarchists ('anarchy' = 'without rule') wanted; that was an illusion. But one should make demands on and encourage politicians, elect and re-elect them, to strive not only for power for its own sake but for **power as a means in the service of humane ends**. Power in politics can and should be relativized, in favour of the people. In politics at whatever level, power must be used for service rather than domination – whatever the personal commitment.

Power and domination are by no means identical, even if many politicians and political scientists do not see this. In politics at whatever level one can constantly see that wherever a politician, a political grouping or a government **uses power as an instrument for domination instead of service**, power dominates political thought and action and foments hatred and enmity; indeed it leads to the waging of wars, hot or cold. But wherever a politician, a particular group or a government at least attempts to see that **power is there for service instead of domination**, in the struggle for power they help to humanize the cut-throat rivalry on all sides, and to promote respect and esteem for others; mediation, understanding and peace among the nations.

Power in the **service of peace**: this applies especially to **foreign policy**. Power blocks and political camps were and are fixated on hostile stereotypes in foreign policy which are meant to justify the position adopted. Such hostile stereotypes and prejudices about other countries, peoples and races are convenient because they are popular. And precisely because they are rooted in the psychological depths of human beings, they prove extraordinarily difficult to correct. Thus the political situation of the power blocks, great and small, was and is mostly characterized by an atmosphere of anxiety, distrust and collective suspicion: a vicious circle of mistrust which makes any peaceful intentions and readiness for reconciliation questionable from the start, by regarding them as a weakness or a tactic of the opponent.

Here the mechanism which political scientists call the 'security-power dilemma' comes in: out of anxiety about their security, weaker individuals or nations attempt to achieve more power (territory, power bases, allies, weapons . . .) so that they in turn seem a threat to the others. Thus in international crises there is all too easily that spiral of violence and counter-violence in which each side attempts to out-manoeuvre the other by power politics. Consequently in particular regions of the world, as in the Middle East, there is no real peace, because no one can see why he and not his opponent should renounce a position of power and right, why as long as he has the power to do so he should not establish his standpoint, even with brute force: an eye for an eye, a tooth for a tooth, or sometimes even more than a tooth and an eye.

Yes, **right** too can be **abused by power politicians.** Wherever nations or ethnic groups do not realize that right is there for human beings and not vice versa, as is shown by the post-war history of German ethnic groups and their eastern neighbours (in most recent times the Sudeten Germans and the Czechs), they play their part in establishing the merciless standpoint of being in the right, with the result that the supreme right (*summum ius*) all too often becomes the supreme injustice (*summa injuria*), thus constantly disseminating new hatred, war and inhumanity between nations or ethnic groups.

Conversely, wherever nations or ethnic groups remain aware that right, too, is there for human beings, they relativize positions which are theirs by right; they facilitate giving and taking, those concessions and compromises without which politics is quite impossible. They practise the humanizing of the legal order and, as is shown by the post-war history of Germany and France, and finally also that between Germany and Poland, they make peace and reconciliation possible.

But while we may recognize these positive examples, do not ideals and realities keep clashing, particularly in politics?

3. Ideals and realities

There is an apparently convincing argument against any concern for ethics in private or public life which is in reality trivial and in any case is not new, but which keeps being put forward time and again as if it were. What is the use of all this, since none of the ethical rules are observed? Therefore here are some elementary but by no means trivial observa-

tions on the question – less for the naive and those of good will than for
the cynics in politics and journalism.

(a) Is ethics inefficient?

The six successful 'human inventions to counter the abuse of power'
listed by A.Riklin, behind which there was always an ethical impulse,
prove convincingly that in its struggle with power, ethics is by no means
fighting a lost cause. But the efforts of humankind do not just embrace
these **basic political innovations**, which already began with the ancient
Greeks and today form the provisional nucleus of legal and constitutional democracy. The efforts of humankind also, and even primarily,
embrace those **elementary ethical norms** which go back far beyond the
Greeks, are connected with the humanization of human beings in a
prehistory which is by no means only grey, and to the present day form
the basic substance of universally binding rules for human behaviour
and social life, and thus of authentic humanity, the *humanum*, even if
this basic substance is in danger.[23]

Human beings could not simply get these ethical norms as fixed
solutions from heaven, nor even derive them from an immutable essence
of human nature. Rather, they had to discover, practise and prove
particular rules of behaviour and social life, on the basis of numerous
and sometimes cruel experiences, 'on earth', where human life all down
the millennia has been governed by religion. No, human beings had to
take into account not theoretical considerations, but quite **practical
needs of life,** as individuals, as a tribe or a people, if they were to survive
and live together. In other words, where particularly urgent human
needs and necessities emerged – say to protect life, marriage or property
– in time regulations for action, priorities, conventions, laws, customs,
in short norms for human conduct, imposed themselves. After periods of
testing and acclimatization, such embodied norms finally gained general
recognition.

Even the **Ten Commandments of God** – 'the Ten Words',[24] which
occur in two versions in the Hebrew Bible[25] – have undergone a history.
The instructions on the 'second table' which relate to relations between
individuals (respect for parents, protection of life, marriage, property
and the honour of the neighbour) go back to the moral and legal
traditions of the pre-Israelite semi-nomadic tribes and have numerous
analogies in the Near East. It took long centuries of practice, refining
and testing, for the Decalogue to assume such a universalistic and
succinct form and content that it could be regarded as an adequate

expression of the will of Yahweh, the covenant of God with his people. So these age-old minimal ethical requirements are not specifically Israelite; however, the way in which they are put under the legitimizing and protective authority of Yahweh and his covenant, the 'subject' of the 'first table' (obligations towards God), is. And in so far as Christianity, too, has appropriated the 'Ten Words', and in so far as the Qur'an, too, offers a corresponding summary of the most important ethical obligations, here already one can speak of a **common basic ethic** at least of the three prophetic religions, which seeks to guarantee the elementary humanity of human beings with reference to divine authority.[26]

Some norms which were lived out at a very early stage have been undermined and abandoned in a completely different age. However, it was only when **at the end of modernity** the 'man beyond good and evil' was proclaimed, with his attempt at a 'transvaluation of all values', that they were **fundamentally put in question**, in particular the basic demands of the Decalogue. At a very early stage Friedrich Nietzsche, who proclaimed the man who was governed only by the 'will to power' ('superman'), recognized that with the 'death of God', even the morality for human beings which had hitherto been guaranteed by God was on the way out. So today we must already be aware what an age-old tradition of humanity is being put at risk with a nihilistic acceptance of all and everything, if there is a concern not only to demonstrate the inefficiency of ethical norms but if possible even to promote it. However, more and more people, whether or not they are religious, can now see that since the substitute religions of the nineteenth and twentieth centuries with all their terrors have proved to be false belief, humankind is exposed to a complete vacuum in orientation.

Against this historical background, some basic observations on the efficiency or inefficiency of ethical norms under discussion here may suffice:

(1) If humankind lived like saints, there would be no need for ethical rules of behaviour. But it is a fact that since its ascent from the animal world, governed only by drives, humankind has needed regulatory, ethical norms. To this extent, from the start **ethics goes against the facts**: it does not state what is, but what should be.

(2) From the beginning, ethical rules of conduct have **constantly been violated**: it is not normally given to human beings to go blamelessly through life. And even those who have been 'beatified' by

the church authorities in accordance with mediaeval custom have regarded themselves more as sinners than as saints.

(3) Nevertheless, despite everything, the ethical rules of conduct have **constantly been observed** to an amazing degree – out of conviction, adaptation, compulsion or for whatever reason. And even those who did not want to observe them were, on Machiavelli's advice, at least to seem to keep them. Without some elementary ethical norms in fact neither family nor social life, business nor politics nor culture, can function.

(4) If nowadays often even the Ten Commandments are ignored in principle or simply *de facto*, this is **no argument against the Ten Commandments,** but against the people who are not humane enough to observe these imperatives of elementary humanity. The argument 'The world looks so bad despite the Ten Commandments' can easily be reversed: 'How bad would this world look without the Ten Commandments?'

A further insight has emerged from this retrospective consideration of the history of humankind: **the formulation of universal human responsibilities** is millennia **older than the formulation of universal human rights** (the great achievement of the modern Enlightenment). And we shall have to raise the question whether a better respect for human rights can be established without a better respect for human responsibilities.

It is a welcome development that among social scientists the insight is slowly being established 'that human history is at the transition to a new and uncertain age'. This insight has 'almost unimaginable philosophical implications' and is connected with the question what human nature is. Arguing against this contemporary background, the American political theorist **Zbigniew Brzezinski,** the former Security Adviser to President Carter, remarks: 'The needed correction will not come from a catalogue of policy recommendations. It can only emerge as a consequence of a new historical tide that induces a change both in values and in conduct; in effect, out of a prolonged process of cultural self-reexamination and philosophical reevaluation, which over time influences the political outlook both of the West and of the non-Western world.'[27]

But some politicians may be less interested in this world-historical perspective than in their own immediate situation. They may object, 'I need first to be elected or re-elected.' That raises the question:

(b) Can one win elections with ethics?

There is no mistaking the fact that **elections, too, have an ethical**

dimension. No topic has been so much discussed in and even after the 1996 American presidential election campaign as the topic of ethics, though in the context of election politics it has proved very complex. It would take me out of my way to evaluate reflections of this kind on the elections of Jimmy Carter, Ronald Reagan, George Bush and Bill Clinton; I must limit myself to the following conclusions:

– A lofty ethic is no obstacle to an election victory (see Carter's election in 1976).

– A lofty ethic is no guarantee of an election victory (see Carter's defeat in 1980).

– A lack of ethics is not necessarily an obstacle to an election victory (see Clinton's re-election in 1996).

– A lofty ethic can, if credible, be decisive for an election victory.

In fact, in the end even the *New York Times*, after much heart-searching, made a formal commendation of Clinton in the 1996 election, although it was aware of the worries of many Americans about the candidate's decisiveness and sensitivity to ethical standards in the government, his personality and character. However, all in all he was regarded as the better candidate, and he was given a whole series of urgent recommendations on how to solve his 'most significant leadership problem': 'Many Americans do not trust him or do not believe him to be a person of character.'[28] Be this as it may: in retrospect it is clear that a younger, more optimistic and charismatic opponent with a convincing character and more social sensitivity could have won against Clinton. Such a candidate could also win in the future.

After the 1996 election at any rate, serious consequences arise; for what are realities in the USA **threaten also to be a 'model' for other countries.**
– An excessive **lobbying** which undermines the democratic decision-making process. In the opinion polls, in answer to the question 'Who really controls what goes on in Washington?', the President is seen to have diminishing significance (from 8% to 6% in 1991 and 1993); the Democrats have as limited significance (from 19% to 16%) as the Republicans (from 10% to 5%). But the influence of the lobbyists and special interest groups was already estimated at 38% in 1991 and at 57% in 1993; so far one can only guess what percentage will apply in 1996. As a background: the number of lawyers in Washington today amounts to 50,000 and the number of registered lobbyists to 90,000 (40,000 themselves lawyers). In addition to countless government officials, more than 50% of Congress members become lobbyists when they leave Congress, and of course this already influences their activity

in Congress.²⁹ So what is already regarded as 'part of the game' in Washington is also coming to be so in other capitals (especially in Brussels).

– Large-scale **media manipulation.** Since the trained film actor Ronald Reagan showed the way, all public appearances of the President and his opponent have been planned above all to make a visual and emotional impact: this is often not so much effective leadership as seduction by the media for illusory goals. The national election of the candidates is always governed less by serious information than by skilfully chosen moving testimonies by members of the family and 'those involved', which transform the electoral process into a sentimental melodrama. In addition, the demagogic election TV spots are terrifyingly devoid of content and morality, attempting with every means possible to do down the opponent. 'All means are allowed, but not all are successful . . . Playing it rough is the nature of this election campaign . . . Apart from that there is only one law for any candidate in the election. How can I benefit myself and how can I harm my opponent?', remarks Phil Noble, the not very noble electoral adviser for George Bush in 1988 and Bob Dole in 1996.³⁰

– A **globalization** even of election campaigns. Both American parties stand accused of having received gigantic sums of money which in fact came from abroad: President Clinton from Indonesia, Thailand and China, and the Republicans previously from the Philippines (the Marcos clan). In both cases the money was given to foster trade relationships, to place friends in important trade commissions and to counter demands for human rights. Through US branches the Canadian alcohol producer Seagram alone paid $1,055,000, a British tobacco firm $400,000, the Australian media mogul Murdoch $351,000 and Indian backers $325,000 for the last election. That these tremendous sums of money go to the party committees ('soft money', which is still allowed) instead of to the candidates (which is forbidden) does not improve matters; in just one case $253,000 was paid back because it was shown up as being illegal. What these global players did in the USA, they and others could also do in other countries.

– A **de-democratization** which makes active political participation seem meaningless to more and more citizens. They mistrust the media, with their focus on entertainment and greed for scandal, along with the squads of opinion makers. Many Americans regard their electoral system as corrupt, what the *Washington Post* has called 'a greasy system', which for an appropriate gift allows invitations to the dozens of Clinton coffee meetings, dinners or even (for a gift of $100,000) a night in Lincoln's bedroom in the White House. Furthermore, Clinton's officials and friends have established a dozen private funds with mostly unknown donors which pay for all kinds of things: from Clinton's legal costs in the Whitewater and Paula Jones affairs ($640,000 for the Legal Defense Trust alone), through the building of a jogging track in the garden of the White House, to the restoration of the house in which Clinton was born. Since 1992 the expenses for the presidential election campaign have tripled and now stand at a proud $800 million, with a further $800 million for the congressional elections; according to most recent estimates around $2 billion dollars were spent in 1996. Even apart from what social organizations have been deprived of, this is an exorbitant sum, but it has been given not so much by the ordinary American as for the most part by firms with particular interests and a small handful of the super-rich (Wall Street alone – not Main Street! – donated around 50 million dollars in 1996).[31] Is it all that amazing that despite the tremendous financial expenditure and an unprecedented media spectacle, only 49% of those eligible to vote took part in the presidential election (and only 36% in the election to the US Congress!)?[32]

Sometimes, of course, this process of de-democratization can also turn into a spontaneous mass **popular movement** which, as has already been observed, can sweep a whole political class from the national stage for **ethical motives**. Well known examples are Italy, Japan, the Philippines and South Korea; there are real signs of this also in Belgium, Indonesia and elsewhere, where people have taken to the streets in mass demonstrations against preferential treatment, scandals and favouritism, and have called not only for new laws but for a new political culture. No, in the longer term, ethics is by no means a lost cause in the face of power! But is this not true, at least in the short term, in the question of human rights?

(c) A realistic human rights policy?

To pursue an honourable policy on human rights and an efficient trade policy at the same time seems to come close to squaring the circle. President Carter already had to discover how easily, even with the best intentions, a principled policy of human rights can collide with a policy of détente. Basically it should be clear that a **policy of human rights** in the spirit of an **ethic of responsibility** cannot be content with lip service and 'silent diplomacy', but must on the other hand **calculate coolly the real conditions in which it can be successful at all.**

That means that pragmatically a government must decide what ways and means are most effective in a particular situation. Human rights are promoted effectively only by someone who uses them in a difficult situation and does not infringe them. Spectacular actions which are doubtless allowed by and perhaps asked of the human rights organizations can be counter-productive for governments: at all events it is right to press openly for more constitutionality. A differentiated assessment and control of the constellations of power in politics at home and abroad is an indispensable presupposition for a politics orientated on ethical criteria. And this cannot happen once and for all. Rather, the potential dangers and opportunities of a particular policy must constantly be re-assessed in the light of the situation. However, hardly anything can be achieved without public opinion. And here the human rights associations (Amnesty International and other non-governmental organizations), which need not take politics into account, are of course much freer. Their informative and bold actions need more support from politicians.

This is also true of the last great country which on the basis of its Party ideology is as opposed in principle to a policy of human rights as was the Soviet Union earlier: **the People's Republic of China.** A land with more than a billion people and frontiers of umpteen thousand kilometres cannot simply isolate itself internationally. Nevertheless, the pressure of international public opinion on the Communist leadership must insist on not only economic but also political liberalization. For the introduction of the market economy by no means automatically leads to a free democratic system. Simply because of other developments, say in the oil states, one must have reservations about the statement of a sociologist, S.M.Lipset, that 'the richer a country, the freer it is'. However, we cannot overlook the fact that not only Spain and Portugal, Chile and Argentina, but also South Korea and Taiwan have achieved a transition from *de facto* dictatorship to democracy with increasing prosperity, better education and greater political awareness. And is not China already today – despite all the party dictatorship, giant prison camps and numerous executions – on the other hand a land in transition, with increasing liberality and freedom for the individual, more freedom in the media, and a stirring of 'grass-roots' democracy in villages and large coastal cities? However, the slogan 'change through trade' and the furthering of economic relations are not enough for an ethically responsible policy on China.

The democratic states (and churches!) of the West have taken two centuries to implement human rights fully. It might therefore be meaningful to note a certain hierarchy of human rights (not a chronological sequence) in countries which are on the way to democracy.[33] There is no justification whatsoever for the violation of the **fundamental rights** of the human person: to life, freedom (not slavery), protection from torture and arbitrary deprivation of freedom; and there is a need for a ban on discrimination on racial, religious and similar grounds. These fundamental human rights are in fact by no means only of Western origin, but simply form the other side of responsibilities which are expressed in most religious and moral traditions, as we shall see later. In particular, freedom of opinion and religion, which are part of cultural freedom, are intrinsically connected with the ban on any discrimination. Economic and cultural freedoms seem subordinate to these fundamental rights, but that does not mean that therefore they can simply be neglected.

Specifically, for the **success** of a policy of human rights it may be noted:

– Those who **a priori** abandon their ethical criteria for the sake of market advantages (which in China are often very dubious) will **lack** that **dignity and self-respect** which are a presupposition for any successful policy. Neither democracies nor democrats must subserviently flatter any dictatorship – whether brown, red or black – but must be resist it unyieldingly. They must point out shortcomings without arrogance and call for them to be removed.

– Right from the run-up to taking office a government (or a presidential candidate) advised by experts must use common sense and political judgment in considering what **instruments** it has at its disposal for implementing demands for human rights generally.

– To have to **withdraw general idealistic demands under pressure encourages the political cynicism** at home and abroad which was meant to be overcome. Examples are: the announcement of Clinton as presidential candidate that he would offer asylum to all refugees from Haiti; the attempt of President Clinton, against powerful forces in the USA itself, to withdraw from China most-favoured nation treatment accorded by GATT/WTO (two promises not kept).

– Therefore political instruments must be well planned and **used in a** highly **purposeful way**. One example is the detailed embargo threatened by President Clinton on the import of a series of Chinese products to combat effectively the Chinese piracy of software, videos and compact discs.

– The **government** must **speak** with conviction and therefore **with one voice**: finance and trade ministries must not speak differently from the foreign ministry, and local ambassadors differently yet again.

– In business negotiations, the most influential **business communities** should not just fawn on those who scorn human rights, but should similarly (in their own discreet way) insist on the need to observe moral criteria.

– In the case of all unavoidable **trade agreements,** the government should constantly emphasize in public and in private that ethical perspectives are and remain of prime importance to it, and that without them real friendship between nations cannot be realized in the long term.

– A government should draw the attention of others to their **own laws** (which are often not observed: torture violates even Chinese law), and the UNO should implement human rights as universal (and not just Western) values and norms.

– A policy of human rights is credible only if it is also **measured by the same criterion** where there is the necessary influence to implement it (unlike the USA with the massive violations of human rights in Cuba, Libya, Iran and Iraq on the one hand and in Pinochet's Chile, in Indonesia, Saudi Arabia and Israel on the other).

– A human rights policy is questionable if it is combined with massive **arms exports** to countries in which human rights are trampled under foot (according to the US State Department, in the last four years 78% of arms purchases went to such countries, including the poorhouses of this world like Somalia, Liberia, Zaire, Guatemala and Haiti . . .).

The West must beware of any arrogance in the question of human rights, above all towards the Third World. For there one often has the impression that in past decades the West has subjugated the whole of the rest of the world, and in so doing has violated almost all human rights. But now, in a changed situation, it is calling on the rest of the world finally to observe human rights, as these are often in the interests of the West . . . Here the policy of human rights is nevertheless having considerable success even in the Third World.

(d) Successes in human rights policy

Allegedly 'realist' postulates against a policy of human rights should no longer be presented without reflection, now that even the Eastern European Communist dictatorships which operated so cynically with the means of real politics have finally had to capitulate to the moral postulates of their own population. The same has been true in South Africa, the Philippines, South Korea and Chile. And just as in Rumania a single Protestant pastor (László Tökés) began the revolution for human rights against the dictatorship of Ceaucescu, which was armed to the teeth, so in Haiti a single Catholic priest, Jean-Bertrand Aristide, has carried on the revolution against Duvalier's inhuman police regime.

How many clever real politicians of the West thought for long years that **fighters for human rights** like Albert Lutuli (the ANC leader), Alexander Solzhenytsin, Andrei Sacharov, Lech Walesa, Nelson Mandela, Bishop Desmond Tutu, Rigoberta Menchu and Václav Havel did not have the slightest chance against the omnipotence of a regime which scorned humanity! Today, however, the wise 'realists' of the time are paying their respects to those 'idealists' who in the end, despite all the setbacks, have proved more realistic than the 'realists'. Today they are all victorious, and most of them have been opportunely honoured with the Nobel Peace Prize. No, once again, in the longer term, the cause of ethics is by no means lost in the face of power.

This is also a sign of hope for the Nobel Peace Prize winner **Aung San Suu Kyi**, the head of government in Burma (Myanmar), elected with a phenomenal 82% of the vote but so far prevented by the military regime from taking office, who has now herself called for international **sanctions** against her own regime. And indeed, if their political and social implications are carefully worked out, while sanctions like a ban on credit and investment may not have had much success against China, they were right and successful against the apartheid state in South Africa, and may not *a priori* be false and hopeless against the socialist military dictatorship in Burma where (according to Human Rights Watch/Asia) there are two million slave workers, and which is the source of 60% of the heroin smuggled into the USA. It is better to cut off the money supply than to restrict trade, an action which usually affects the populace more than the political leadership. The clearer the aims and the more finely tuned the sanctions, the more effective they are.[34]

Of course the **energy concerns** with all their lobbyists (the energy giant Unocal has a $1.2 billion natural gas contract with Burma) object to the stop on development aid and World Bank credits resolved on by the US Senate but not yet implemented by the President. In view of all the oppressive measures, e.g. in Nigeria, often combined with pseudo-trials and executions (Ken Saro-Wiwa!), particularly oil multinationals like Shell, which for example has constantly influenced tax policy, environment legislation, employment laws and trade politics there, should not shirk their responsibility but also exercise their real political influence for humane ends. Moral pressure on the mother society and threats of boycotts in connection with the planned sinking of the Brent Spar platform in fact led to a rethink by Shell. But in the long term would not both the peoples involved and the energy concerns be helped better by democratic governments which take action against slave labour, child labour, corruption and oppression? So it is to be hoped that not only Aung San Suu Kyi but also other Nobel Peace Prize winners like the Dalai Lama and Carlos Belo and José Ramos-Horta of East Timor will one day be justified in their dedication to human rights and democracy.

But, it may rightly be asked: do not all these ethical demands on politicians, governments and nations simply ask too much of them? What is to be the motivation for a more humane use of power and justice in the service of humankind, of peace, of freedom and of justice generally? It is by no means a matter of course that human beings are humane, and behave humanely rather than inhumanely. Even more laws are of no help here. It already struck Hans Morgenthau that while law and morality have features in common, the law receives its normative substance from morality (e.g. 'You shall not steal'). However, what if the moral values and norms have simply lost their normative force? That was already his question, and it is a question of many people today. If morality is shaken, the inevitable consequence must also be a shaking of the law on all sides. But how can the rising world society find **a moral basis which is viable for all**? If one is to convince human beings on questions of might and right, is it not necessary to strike up religious tones? But on the other hand, is it not the religions which often represent a hindrance rather than a help towards peace and understanding between the nations? How can the new world society arrive at a consensus of values and norms, an ethical consensus?

IV

A Global Ethic as a Foundation for Global Society

An **ethical consensus** – an agreement on particular values, criteria, attitudes – as a basis for the world society that is coming into being: is that not a great, beautiful illusion? In view of the differences which have always existed between nations, cultures and religions; in view of the current tendencies and trends towards cultural, linguistic and religious self-assertion; in view even of the widespread cultural nationalism, linguistic chauvinism and religious fundamentalism, is it possible to envisage any ethical consensus at all, let alone in global dimensions? However, one can also argue in the opposite direction: precisely in view of this oppressive situation, a basic ethical consensus is necessary.

1. Challenges and responses

Here in practice I shall be taking up terms used by the British historian Arnold Toynbee: the 'challenges' which arise from the present situation in world history, and the 'responses' which are to be given to these challenges. I can begin by presenting in the form of theses what I have described at length in my book *Global Responsibility* and the publications that have followed. I shall then go on to illuminate the problems from yet another perspective.

(a) Key questions and principles

(1) We live in a world and time in which we can observe new dangerous tensions and **polarizations between believers and non-believers**, church members and those who have been secularized, the clerical and the anti-clerical – not only in Russia, Poland and East Germany but also in

France, in Algeria and Israel, in North and South America, Asia and Africa.

My response to this challenge is: **there will be no survival of democracy without a coalition of believers and non-believers in mutual respect!**

However, many people will say: do we not also live in a period of new cultural confrontations? That is true.

(2) We live in a world and a time in which humankind is threatened by what S.Huntington has called a '**clash of civilizations**', for example between Muslim or Confucian civilization and Western civilization. However, we are threatened not so much by a new world war as by every possible conflict between two countries or within one country, in a city, even a street or school.

My response to this challenge is: **There will be no peace between the civilizations without a peace between the religions!**

And there will be no peace between the religions without a dialogue between the religions.

However, many people will object: are there not so many dogmatic differences and obstacles between the different religions which make a real dialogue a naive illusion? That is true.

(3) We live in a world and a time when better relations between the religions are often blocked by every possible **dogmatism**, which can be found not only in the Roman Catholic Church but in all churches and religions and also in modern ideologies.

My response to this challenge is: **There will be no new world order without a new world ethic**, a global or planetary ethic **despite** all dogmatic differences.

What should the precise **function** of such a global ethic be? I can only repeat that a global ethic is not a new ideology or superstructure; it does not seek to make the specific ethics of the different religions and philosophies superfluous. Thus it is no substitute for the Torah, the Sermon on the Mount, the Qur'an, the Bhagavadgita, the discourses of the Buddha or the sayings of Confucius. The one global ethic does not mean a single global culture, far less a single global religion. To put it positively, a global ethic, a world ethic is none other than **the necessary minimum of common human values, criteria and basic attitudes**. Or, to be more precise: the global ethic is a **basic consensus** on binding values, irrevocable criteria and basic attitudes which are affirmed **by all**

religions despite their dogmatic differences, and which can indeed also be contributed by **non-believers**.

(b) Universal ethical standards

It is certain that even science and technology cannot create this consensus; rather, they need it, if their own intrinsic dynamic is not to overflow. For the great economic and technological problems of our time have increasingly become political and moral problems which seem to ask too much of any psychology, sociology, political theory and sometimes even **philosophy**.

Some philosophers think that a basic global consensus on ethical questions is impossible, since there are only regional ethics,[1] and thus, themselves well protected in their academic ghetto and its regional environs, leave aside the globe with all the challenges of our time. Yet other philosophers defend a radical pluralism which in a 'postmodern' fashion claims to be content with 'truth, justice, humanity in the plural'.[2] However, a third group, also philosophers, say that perhaps there is something that is held in common and deserves to be brought to light, something like universal **ethical standards,** even among human beings of different nations, cultures and religions.

'**Standard**' (originally meaning 'banner') nowadays means something that is accepted as a model, and by which other things are also orientated, i.e. a measure, criterion or norm. Here we are speaking of **ethical** standards, namely of moral **values, norms, attitudes**.

I use '**ethic**' to denote the basic moral attitude of an individual or a group, whereas '**ethics**' means the (philosophical or theological) theory of moral values, norms and attitudes (often, though, the distinction is not drawn so clearly). In English the distinction between 'ethic' and 'ethics' is harder to make than in German, where it would be between '*Ethos*' and '*Ethik*' (but to translate the German '*Ethos*' as 'ethos' does not really work).

But what has this to do with the ethical **consensus**? Here I must obviate one misunderstanding from the start:
– The **differences** are so great, not only between the nations, cultures and religions but also between the forms of life, scientific views, economic systems, social models and communities of faith, that a complete agreement on an ethic is inconceivable: so there can be **no total ethical consensus**.

– However, varied and complex as the national, cultural and religious differences may be, they all concern **human beings,** and nowadays in particular through modern systems of communication, above all radio and television, these human beings experience themselves increasingly as a community of destiny on our spaceship earth, in which even a leak from a nuclear power station or a mistake in manipulating biology or genes could threaten whole continents. And here the question arises whether there cannot, should not, be a minimum of values, criteria and attitudes that are common to all human beings, in other words a **minimal ethical consensus.**

(c) The quest for the universal: truth and justice

We do not start from a theory but from a **fact:** nowadays the whole world is indignant about particular local events. When masses of people are driven on to the streets and their protest march – whether in Beijing, Buenos Aires, Rangoon, Brussels or Belgrade – is broadcast on television all over the world, countless men and women everywhere share in the event, identify themselves with the local people and are with them in spirit. They are often the first to compel the frequently so opportunist and pussyfooting politicians of the West to act. In this phenomenon we see a sharing of basic values, of which we need to be made aware.

We are indebted to **Michael Walzer,** Professor of Social Sciences in Princeton, for having published at the beginning of the 1980s an important book in defence of pluralism and equality under the title *Spheres of Justice,*[3] for investigating this phenomenon in connection with what is held in common ethically. For in his new book *Thick and Thin,* this 'pluralist' points out that in particular a universal element can be detected in the perception of political conflicts.[4] When in 1989, the revolutionary year for Europe, the people marched through the streets of Prague, carrying signs some of which said 'Truth' and others 'Justice', television viewers all over the world, beyond any barriers of nation, culture and religion, understood quite spontaneously what (global) values and criteria were being required here (locally) of the Communist dictatorship.

Walzer notes that it was evident to him and to others on such occasions that there was an **'easy friendliness and agreement with'** the values of 'truth' and 'justice'.[5]
– **Truth?** The citizens of Prague 'were not marching in defence of the coherence theory, or the consensus theory, or the correspondence theory of truth. Perhaps they disagreed about such theories among themselves;

more likely, they did not care about them.' But the demonstrators wanted 'to hear true statements from their political leaders; they wanted to be able to believe what they read in the newspapers; they didn't wanted to be lied to anymore'.

– Justice? The citizens of Prague 'were not marching in defence of utilitarian equality for John Rawls's difference principle or any philosophical theory of desert or merit or entitlement'. But with this one word they did demand quite simply 'an end to arbitrary arrests, equal and impartial law enforcement, the abolition of the privileges and prerogatives of the party elite – common, garden variety justice'.

What does this mean for the question of universal norms? In that we are identifying in spirit with the protesters, if truth and justice are openly trampled under foot, an international solidarity can come into being beyond all national, cultural and religious limits. Contrary to all those who dispute ideas of universal values and moral claims and argue for regionalism or relativism, Michael Walzer demonstrates in a differentiated way that there is something like a '**core morality**': a whole set of **elementary ethical standards**, which include the fundamental right to life, to just treatment (also from the state), to physical and mental integrity. Walzer calls this a 'minimal morality' or a 'moral minimalism'. What is meant here are moral concepts which have a minimal significance and are indicated by a 'thin' description: in other words, this is a 'thin' morality, the content of which, of course enriched in the various cultures, appears as a 'thick' morality in which every possible historical, cultural, religious and political view comes to be involved, depending on place and time.

This concrete approach distinguishes Walzer from two significant social philosophies of our day, which like him regard the utilitarian arguments as an inadequate basis for normative obligations but which proceed in a rational abstract way:

– on the one hand from **John Rawls**, who deduces and applies ethical rules from general principles of justice understood as fairness, but deliberately abstracts them from concrete contexts and situations:[6] only an expanded idea of justice makes it possible for Rawls in retrospect to develop a conception of right and justice which can also be applied to the principles and norms of international law and international relations.[7]

– on the other hand from the constructivist discursive ethics of **Karl-Otto Apel** and **Jürgen Habermas**, who rightly emphasize the significance of rational consensus and discourse, but think that they can develop from the human community of communication and argumentation,

supposedly independent of context, norms which should apply unconditionally.[8] The religious grounds and interpretations of morality which
have allegedly been devalued for the public are to be replaced by rational
discourse, by moral language games, by the 'compulsion of arguments
which are not compulsory'.[9]

In view of the concrete relevance of the religions and cultures, it seems
very questionable whether a really binding and obligating ethic can be
established globally (as it were down to the last Indian or African
village) with the help of an abstract rational discourse. Walzer, thinking
concretely in quite a different way, shares the scepticism of those who do
not believe that the moral language game and the argument which is not
compulsory have the same binding and obligating force as the traditional ethical standards in which a certain degree of accord can be noted,
even world-wide; and these are evidently still quite effective even in the
public political sphere, though they are unjustly neglected by those
sceptical philosophers. However, I would differ from Walzer in
preferring to speak of elementary and differentiated morality rather
than of 'thin' and 'thick' morality.

But a more important matter is: what is the significance of Walzer's
distinction for an ethical **consensus?** It is important in two ways:

- A global **consensus is possible** in respect of **elementary** ('thin')
  morality which limits itself to some fundamental demands. Only such
  a 'thin' morality can also be expected of other nations, cultures and
  religions and promoted world-wide. Here we have the claim of a
  'pure morality' which may never be given up.
- A **consensus is not necessary** in respect of culturally **differentiated**
  ('thick') **morality**, which necessarily contains numerous specific
  cultural elements (particular forms of democracy or pedagogy). In
  disputed concrete questions like abortion or euthanasia, no unifying
  demands should be made on other nations, cultures and religions to
  have the same moral praxis.

As I have remarked, in the specific local or regional instance, 'thin' and
'thick' morality are mixed. Nevertheless, the distinction is important.
For example, that one may not torture children is elementary morality
('thin' morality) in the various cultures and is as true in San Francisco as
it is in Singapore. But the point at which corporal punishment becomes
torture for a child is obviously not the same in San Francisco as it is in
Singapore, and here very many historical, cultural, political and
religious elements come into play. And it would be nothing but cultural

imperialism to want to introduce the specific customs of San Francisco in Singapore or those of Singapore in San Francisco.

Whether or not one can accept Walzer's terminology, what is meant by his distinction between 'thin' and 'thick' morality is understandable and immediately clear. And as far as the **'certain kind of universalism'**[10] here is concerned, I can feel welcome confirmation in Walzer's remarks of my efforts towards a common ethic for humankind. In this connection I myself would prefer not to talk of 'mini-morality' or 'minimal morality', far less of 'moral minimalism'. In any case, in German more than in English '-ism' has the derogatory sense of a new ideology; even Walzer emphasizes that 'minimalism' does not denote 'a morality which is subordinate in content or emotionally' shallow, but on the contrary a 'pure morality'.[11] At all events we may not be concerned with a 'minimized' ethical standard, reduced to a minimum and diminished, far less with a 'minimalized' standard, reduced and hardly observed. Looked at closely, our question is less about minimal standards than about a **minimal consensus**, about the necessary elementary social consensus. For today's pluralistic society, ethical consensus means the necessary agreement in fundamental, ethical standards which despite all differences of political, social or religious direction can serve as **the smallest possible basis for human living and acting together.**

(d) Humanity: the Golden Rule

However, morality is always basically concrete; it does not exist in an abstract universality but in a local or particular situation. Here Michael Walzer feels that he has to note even a 'dualism': between 'minimalism' and 'maximalism', between 'thin and thick', between universal and relativistic morality. But does such a distinction do full justice to reality?

A moral equivalent of Esperanto (a complete objective code or any specific cultural expression) is probably impossible.[12] But though that is impossible and unnecessary, according to Walzer it is 'possible, nonetheless, to give some substantial account of the moral minimum': 'we can pick out from among our values and commitments those that make it possible for us to march vicariously with the people in Prague. We can make a list of similar occasions (at home, too) and catalogue our responses and try to figure out what the occasions and the responses have in common.'[13] 'Perhaps the end product of this effort' could be 'a set of standards to which all societies can be held – negative injunctions, most likely, rules against murder, deceit, torture, oppression and tyranny'.[14]

Now I can imagine that there is another, more convincing way of describing the content of what Walzer calls the moral minimum. Here, following the beginning made by Michael Walzer, are **three questions to reflect on:**
– With good reason, Walzer thinks a consensus on elementary morality, above all in some negative formulations, possible, but believes that a consensus on differentiated morality is so far impossible. Yet is it not evident here that there is really no dualism between a 'minimal' and a 'maximal' morality, but a continuity allowing **different degrees of concreteness** which would need to be researched in respect of a consensus between people of different nations, cultures and religions?
– Walzer has rightly singled out truth and justice as elementary ethical values. But must we not also at least add the equally elementary value of **humanity**, particularly if we keep wanting to talk not only of local and particular situations, but also of 'humankind'? After all, there is hardly ever a more furious outcry than that when someone is being treated really 'inhumanely'; there is hardly a stronger accusation than that this or that system is 'inhuman'; hardly a more important criminal trial than one (whether in Nuremberg, Tokyo or the Hague) concerned with 'crimes against humanity'.
– Walzer, an author with a Jewish background, has convincingly referred to the Hebrew Bible to illustrate his remarks. But what would prevent him and us from referring not only to the Jewish and Christian tradition, but also to the **other great religious or ethical-philosophical traditions of humankind?** And not only as an illustration but to provide concrete content? It could be that one will find some common ethical 'sayings' or instructions for human behaviour in quite different traditions.

What I mean by this can be demonstrated relatively simply by means of that **Golden Rule of humanity** which we find in all the great religious and ethical tradition. Here are some of its formulations:
– Confucius (c.551–489 BCE): 'What you yourself do not want, do not do to another person' (Analects 15.23).
– Rabbi Hillel (60 BCE–10 CE): 'Do not do to others what you would not want them to do to you' (Shabbat 31a).
– Jesus of Nazareth: 'Whatever you want people to do to you, do also to them' (Matt.7.12; Luke 6.31).
– Islam: 'None of you is a believer as long as he does not wish his brother what he wishes himself' (Forty Hadith of an-Nawawi, 13).

– Jainism: 'Human beings should be indifferent to worldly things and treat all creatures in the world as they would want to be treated themselves' (Sutrakritanga I, 11,33).

– Buddhism: 'A state which is not pleasant or enjoyable for me will also not be so for him; and how can I impose on another a state which is not pleasant or enjoyable for me?' (Samyutta Nikaya V, 353,35–342,2).

– Hinduism: 'One should not behave towards others in a way which is unpleasant for oneself: that is the essence of morality' (Mahabharata XIII, 114,8).

The great traditions of humankind know very many much more concrete maxims, as will be demonstrated. And here the structural and institutional problems of modern society are by no means to be left out of account. But some people nowadays would largely like to dispense with ethical norms. They say, 'Why talk so much about morality? Don't we already have laws for all this? Don't we live in a constitutional state? And hasn't the international community of states already created numerous trans-national, trans-cultural and trans-religious structures of law?'

2. Not only rights but also responsibilities

Already in the debate on human rights in the French Revolutionary Parliament of 1789 the demand was made: if a declaration of the **rights** of man is proclaimed, it must be combined with a declaration of the **responsibilities** of man. Otherwise, in the end all human beings would have only rights which they would play off against others, and no one would any longer recognize the responsibilities without which the rights cannot function.

(a) Human beings have responsibilities from the beginning

In our historical retrospect we saw that the responsibilities were formulated millennia before the rights. But 200 years after the 1789 Revolution we are living in a society in which individuals and groups constantly appeal to **rights against others** without recognizing any **responsibilities** of their own. Hardly anyone can build a house or a street, hardly an authority can enact a law or a regulation, without an appeal being made to rights in connection with it. Today countless claims can be advanced as rights, in particular against the state. After all we live in a society of claims which often appears to be a 'litigious society',[15] and thus makes the state a 'judiciary state' – as it has been called in the Federal Republic of Germany. That is above all the case in the USA, where a third of all the lawyers in the world practise; there the costs of damages use up around 3% of the Gross Domestic Product.[16] Don't we perhaps need a new concentration on responsibilities, particularly in our over-developed legalistic states, to balance all the justified insistence on rights?

Responsibility, obligation, duty; in German all are expressed by the same word. And of course as **duty**[17] it has been **badly misused**. 'Duty' (towards those in authority, the Führer, the people, the Party, the Pope), has been hammered home by totalitarian, authoritarian hierarchical ideologies of every kind; fearful crimes are committed out of 'duty' or on the basis of some 'oath' which backs up obedience with divine authority. 'Duty is duty' and 'an order is an order'. Neither of these must again become slogans: blind obedience, whether in state or church, is immoral. But all the abuses should not prevent us from taking up the concept of duty in a discriminating way. It is a term which has had a long history since Cicero (*De officiis*) and Ambrose, Bishop of Milan (*De officiis ministrorum*), and became a **key concept of modernity** through Immanuel Kant.

The fact cannot be overlooked that duty in particular – this was Kant's key thought – distinguishes man as a rational being from animals, who only follow inclinations, instincts, drives or external pressures and training. But human beings are not just rational, quite naturally following their reason and therefore needing no obligation. Human beings, who are both **rational and subject to drives**, have the possibility – which is both an opportunity and a risk – to **make decisions in freedom** and to act in accordance with their reason. In this sense, understood in modern immanent terms, an obligation is a claim of reason which is binding and yet aims at freedom. However, in principle it does not exclude other 'external' authorities (God, positive law), since a human autonomy grounded in theonomy need not mean heteronomy, i.e. being governed from outside.

Moreover, it is important to see that while duty exerts a moral compulsion, this compulsion is not physical. Leaving aside external authorities, it follows from **reason**, which is not purely technical nor economic but **ethical, prompting** and compelling **human beings to moral action**. But in modern discussion of human rights one thing is overlooked. All rights imply responsibilities, but:

(b) Not all responsibilities follow from rights

I shall demonstrate this first by three examples, one more special, one more general and one quite universal, and then make a more precise definition of the relationship between rights and responsibilities.

(1) A special example: the **freedom of the press** enjoyed by a newspaper or a journalist is guaranteed and protected by the modern constitutional state: the journalist, the newspaper, has a **right** to report freely. The law may not only not attack this right, but on the contrary must protect it actively, and if need be even establish it with its authority. Therefore the state and the citizen have the **responsibility** to respect the right of this newspaper or this journalist to report freely.

However, this right does not in any way affect **the responsibility of the journalist or the newspaper itself,** namely to report objectively and fairly, not to caricature reality and not to manipulate the public, but to inform it truthfully.

(2) A more general example: the **right of each individual to property** is guaranteed by the modern constitutional state. It contains the legal **obligation** for others (the state or the individual citizen) to respect this property and not to misappropriate it.

However, this right does not in any way affect the **responsibility of the property-owner** himself not to use the property in an anti-social way but to use it socially, to restrain the unquenchable human greed for money, prestige and consumption, and to develop some sense of proportion and moderation.

(3) A quite general example: the **freedom** of any individual to decide in accordance with his or her own **conscience** entails the legal **obligation** that others (individuals or the state) should respect a free decision of conscience; the individual conscience is guaranteed protection by the constitution of the state.

However, this right by no means entails the ethical **responsibilities of individuals themselves** in every instance to follow their own consciences even, indeed especially, when this is unpleasant or abhorrent to them.

It follows from all this that rights imply certain responsibilities, and these are **legal obligations.** But by no means all responsibilities follow from legal rights. There are also original **ethical obligations.** The Protestant natural-law ethicist Samuel von Pufendorf (1632–1694) and the Jewish philosopher Moses Mendelsson (1728–86) distinguished between:

– 'perfect' obligations, obligations in the narrower sense: these are **legal obligations,** for example, to respect freedom of conscience and religion, obligations which the state may enforce, punishing violations of them; and

– 'imperfect' obligations, obligations in the wider sense: these are **ethical obligations**, for example the obligations of conscience, love and humanity which rest on one's own insight and cannot be compelled by the state, unless it wants to be a totalitarian state. That constitutes their greatness but also their practical limits. Here, though, we should reflect:

(c) What would rights be without morals?

This distinction between legal and ethical obligations is important for a more precise distinction between the levels of law and ethics, which has many implications, in particular for the implementation of human rights. First of all we need to clarify the question: can one develop an ethic valid for the whole of humankind simply on the basis of human rights? The levels of law and ethics are related in many ways: the origin as well as the presence and application of the law already presupposes an ethic. On the other hand, however, ethics is not exhausted in the law. The levels of law and ethic are thus to be distinguished in principle, and this is of particular significance for human rights.

- Human beings have fundamental rights which are formulated in declarations of human rights. To these correspond the responsibilities both of the state and of individual citizens to respect and to protect these rights. These are legal obligations. Here we are at **the level of law**, the laws, the regulations, the judiciary, the police.

In practice that means that outward conduct in conformity with the law can be examined; the law can be appealed to in principle and if need be enforced ('in the name of the law').

- But at the same time human beings have elementary responsibilities which are already given with their personhood and are not based on any laws: there are ethical obligations which are not fixed in law. Here we are at the **level of ethics**, customs, the conscience, the 'heart' . . .

In practice this means that the inner, morally good disposition cannot be examined; so it cannot be brought under the law, let alone be compelled ('thoughts are free').

- The conclusion to be drawn from this is that **no comprehensive ethic of humanity** can be derived **from human rights alone**, fundamental though these are for human beings; it must also cover the human responsibilities which were there before the law. Before any codification in law and any state legislation there is the moral independence and conscious self-responsibility of the individual, with which not only elementary rights but also elementary responsibilities are connected.

The distinction between **law and ethic** has momentous consequences: because law and ethic are not *a priori* identical but can **fall apart**. The law very often does not function. That is particularly true of politics: if, as happened in the recent war in Yugoslavia, one or both partners in a treaty *a priori* do not have the ethical will (which cannot be directly examined, far less be compelled) to observe the cease-fire that has been negotiated, then the cease-fire treaties co-signed by the great powers and all their legal provisions are of no use; the parties will continue the war as soon as there is a favourable opportunity, with whatever political or legal justification. The realization of the fundamental principle of international law, 'treaties are to be observed' (*pacta sunt servanda*), quite decisively depends on the ethical will of the partner in the treaty. It only needs Bismarck's secret addition 'as things are' (*rebus sic stantibus,* which also cannot be guaranteed) for even the most solemn legal treaty to be built on sand, and one-sidely to be declared no longer valid in a changed situation.

On the level of international law, in 1955 **Max Huber** (1874–1960) pointed out the relevance of the distinction between law and ethic. In his reflections, Huber, who was not only a renowned Swiss international lawyer, but also the President of the International Court of Justice at The Hague from 1925 to 1928 and President of the International Committee of the Red Cross (1928–1945), develops the concept of an 'international ethic' transcending the law, standing behind and above it, and therefore not grounded in law.[18] For the international lawyer it is a matter of principle that: 'Neither the law nor morality can assert themselves in the long run without the authority of an ethic which stands behind them and comes from another, higher, realm that elevates mere custom to morality.' In respect of international law, which accords the sovereign states very great freedom of movement for politics, the ethic has 'the task of giving criteria for this broad area of political action, and setting limits'.

So, '*Quid leges sine moribus?*' runs a Roman saying: what is the use of any laws if no morals, no moral inclination, no obligation of conscience stands behind them? What is the use of a peace treaty which only exists on paper, which has not found its way into human heads and, since it is not just a rational event, into human hearts? There is no overlooking the fact that the realization of peace, justice and humanity depends on the insight and readiness of human beings to give the law validity. In other words, **the law needs a moral foundation!** For a **new world order** that means:

- A better world order cannot be created or even enforced with laws, conventions and ordinances alone.
- Commitment to human rights presupposes an awareness of responsibility and obligations for which both the human head and the human heart must be addressed at the same time.
- Law has no permanent existence without ethics, so there will be **no new world order without a world ethic.**

So a **world ethic**, or, as it has come to be called, a **global ethic**, does not mean 'ethics for the world' in the sense of a quite definite philosophical or theological theory of moral attitudes, values and norms; it means the basic moral human attitude, understood individually or collectively. However, the Greek word *'ethos'* is not used much in most non-Germanic languages, and even the term 'world' cannot be combined with *'ethos'* as it can be in German, where we talk quite naturally of world history, world politics, world economy, world society, using a single word. By preference, the terms used for the German *Weltethos* are:
– in English 'world ethic' or 'global ethic',
– in French *'éthique planétaire'*,
– in Spanish *'ética mundial'*,
– in Italian *'etica mondiale'*,
– in Czech *'svetový etos'*, and so on.

However, whether the term is 'world ethic' or 'global ethic', *'éthique planétaire'* or *'etica mondiale'*, the vocabulary is not ultimately decisive; it is the subject that is important. In German one can speak of a 'world ethic' or a universal 'ethic of humankind' or of a 'global', 'universal' or 'planetary' ethic. But much more important than the terminological question is the substantive question: how are the obligations of such a global ethic to be formulated in concrete terms? On what basis are the concrete normative judgments to be made which are constantly required of men and women? Should one perhaps keep beginning at zero – with an appeal to the critical autonomous reason? Or can the great religious and ethical traditions of humanity perhaps offer points of contact for a formulation of a global ethic?

3. A first formulation of a global ethic

To avoid misunderstandings I should repeat here: a global ethic does not mean a new global ideology, far less a uniform world religion beyond all existing religions; least of all does it mean the domination of one religion over all others. As I have indicated, a global ethic means a basic consensus on binding values, irrevocable criteria and personal basic attitudes, without which any community is sooner or later threatened with anarchy or a new dictatorship. But if the question is one of a basic ethical consensus, I will certainly be expected not to keep to universal programmatic words (truth, justice, humanity) and the Golden Rule, but to define the content of this consensus more closely. However, if one is to make the global ethic more concrete, first of all the formal question must be clarified:

(a) How should a global ethic be made specific? Criteria

If we take seriously the discussion so far, in terms of philosophy and political science, we must avoid two things – and here Walzer's terminology is useful:

(1) A concrete form of the global ethic may **not just** offer **a 'thin' minimum** ethic. All the helpful suggestions from philosophy should of course be taken up, whether they are inspired more by linguistic analysis, Frankfurt Critical Theory or a theory of history. The concrete form of the global ethic should be formulated in such a way that philosophers too, like agnostics and atheists, can make it their own, even if they do not share a possible transcendent ground for such a concrete form.

But if one were to keep to more recent philosophical ethics in making a global ethic concrete, possibly one would not get beyond problematic generalizations and pragmatic models (with a transcendental, utilitarian or even merely regional basis). Yet more than intellectuals and the educated should be addressed.

(2) A concrete form of the global ethic may **not** offer **a 'thick' maximum** ethic either. Of course such a concrete form should also be

relevant at the economic and political levels and support the forces working towards a just economic, social and environmental order.

But if such a concrete form wanted to make direct statements on questions of world politics or economic policy like the Middle East conflict or a solution to the debt crisis, too 'thick' a concrete form of a global ethic would immediately be drawn into the maelstrom of world-political discussions and confrontations; it would deepen political dissent rather than bridge it. So no particular modern Western theory of the state or society can be the presupposition for such a concrete form.

To arrive at a more concrete form, **three dead ends** would have to be avoided from the start:.

– A reduplication of the Declaration of Human Rights. A concrete form of the global ethic should provide ethical support for the UN Declaration of Human Rights, which is often ignored, violated and by-passed. But if it only repeated statements of the Declaration of Human Rights, one could do without such a concrete form. As we saw, ethics is more than law, and ethical obligations are more than just legal obligations. Moreover, such a concrete form of the ethic would not escape the charge, made particularly by the Eastern nations and cultures, that this is a typically 'Western' enterprise. That must not happen.

– A casuistic moral sermon. A concrete form of the global ethic should certainly not be afraid of stating inconvenient truths and demands clearly – for example, respect for all life – not omitting the sphere of sex. But if it simply admonished with a raised finger or a threatening fist; if it got lost once again in a jungle of commandments and precepts, canons and paragraphs; indeed if it wanted to make binding statements on every possible difficult case, such a concrete form would justifiably meet today with opposition from many women and men, and not produce anything capable of achieving a consensus. To enter into questions like divorce or euthanasia which are disputed in all nations, cultures and religions would be to torpedo such a concrete form from the start.

– An enthusiastic religious proclamation: certainly a concrete form of the global ethic can be attempted by religiously motivated people (though not only by them) who are convinced that the existing empirical world is not the ultimate, supreme, 'absolute' spiritual reality and truth. But if such a concrete form simply conjured up a cosmic consciousness, global harmony, spiritual creativity, universal unity, all-embracing love and a spiritual vision of a better world, or merely hymned 'mother earth' and in so doing did not take sufficiently seriously the economic, political and social reality of today's highly complex industrial society, such a concrete form would prove alien to reality.

If one wanted to progress in making a global ethic concrete and even to formulate it, the following formal criteria would have to be fulfilled. A formal **declaration on a global ethic** would have to
– **be related to reality**. The world must be seen realistically, as it really is, and not just as it should be. So the starting point must always be what is, with a progression from there to what should be. To recognize the real significance of norms which initially seem universal, it is necessary to begin with certain negative experiences. What is truly human is not always easy to define, but anyone can give many examples of what is really inhuman;
– penetrate to the deeper **ethical levels**, the levels of binding values, irrevocable criteria and inner basic attitudes. It must not remain stuck at the level of laws, codified rights and legal sections with which issue can be taken, nor at the political level of proposing concrete political solutions;
– be **generally comprehensible:** technical arguments and academic jargon, of whatever origin, are to be avoided. Everything must be expressed in a language which at least the ordinary newspaper reader can understand, and which can also be translated into other languages;
– be **capable of securing a consensus**: moral unanimity and not just numerical unanimity is to be striven for. So statements should be avoided which are *a priori* repudiated by particular ethical or religious traditions. Condemnations which are understood as violations of religious feelings are counter-productive.

Anyone who considers the degree of difficulty and the qualities required of a formulation of a global ethic will not be surprised if sceptics and pessimists regard such a project as almost or completely impossible. However, these sceptics and pessimists should be told that while for the sake of a systematic argument I have had to present these formal conditions as it were *a priori,* in practice they are *a posteriori* and had to be worked out laboriously in the process of arriving at a closer definition of the specific content of a global ethic. In other words, a discussion of the possibility of formulating a global ethic is pointless. For a first declaration on a global ethic does not have to be worked out; it has already been promulgated and published, after being worked out precisely in accordance with the formal criteria stated here.

(b) How should a global ethic be made specific? Content

For the first time in the history of the religions, the **Council of the Parliament of the World's Religions**, which met for the first time in Chicago between 28 August and 4 September 1993 with the participation of 6,500 people from every possible religion, ventured to commission and present a declaration on a global ethic: the author of this book had the honour and the burden of drafting this declaration and has given an account of the whole history of its origin and the broad international and inter-religious process of consultation in a publication of his own.[19] As was only to be expected, this declaration provoked vigorous discussions during the Parliament. But the welcome thing was that at a time when so many religions are entangled in political conflicts, indeed in bloody wars, adherents of very different religions, great and small, made this declaration their own by signing it, as representatives of countless believers on this earth. This declaration is now the basis for an extensive process of discussion and acceptance which will certainly last a long time. It is to be hoped that despite all the obstacles the discussion will take place in all religions. For of course this first declaration on human obligations – like the first Declaration on the Rights of Man in 1776 in connection with the American Revolution – is not an end but a beginning.

One of the many hopeful signs for this acceptance is the firm confirmation of the Chicago Declaration by a report of the **InterAction Council** of former Presidents of State and Prime Ministers under the chairmanship of the former German Federal Chancellor Helmut Schmidt.[20] This report was discussed under the title *In Search of Global Ethical Standards* in Vienna from 22–24 March 1996 with experts from the various religions, and approved in a plenary assembly of the InterAction Council in Vancouver on 22 May 1996.[21]

Of course these statesmen are also aware of the **negative role** which the **religions** have often played and still play in the world: 'The world is also afflicted by religious extremism and violence preached and practised in the name of religion.'[22] But that does not prevent them from also taking note of the **positive role** of the religions, particularly in respect of a common human ethic: 'Religious institutions still command the loyalty of hundreds of millions of people,'[23] and do so despite all secularization and all consumerism: 'The world's religions constitute one of the great traditions of wisdom for humankind. This repository of wisdom, ancient in its origins, has never been needed more.'[24] The minimal standards which make a collective life possible at all are important. Without an ethic and self-restraint humankind would revert to the jungle. 'In a world of unprecedented change humankind has a desperate need of an ethical base on which to stand.'[25]

The statements on the priority of ethics over politics are encouragingly clear: 'Ethics should precede politics and the law, because political action is concerned with values and choice. Ethics, therefore, must inform and inspire our political leadership.'[26] In response to the epoch-making change that is taking place, our institutions need a rededication to ethical norms: 'We can find the sources of such a rededication in the world's religions and ethical traditions. They have the spiritual resources to give an ethical lead to the solution of our ethnic, national, social, economic and religious tensions. The world's religions have different doctrines but they all advocate a common ethic of basic standards. What unites the world's faiths is far greater than what divides them.'[27]

The InterAction Council positively adopted the Chicago Declaration on a Global Ethic: 'We are therefore grateful that the Parliament of the World's Religions, which assembled in Chicago in 1993, proclaimed a Declaration towards a Global Ethic which we support in principle.'[28] The legal and ethical levels are clearly distinguished, and it is emphasized that what the United Nations proclaimed in its Declaration on Human Rights and the two supplementary conventions is confirmed and deepened by the Declaration of the World's Religions from the perspective of human **responsibility**: the full realization of the intrinsic dignity of the human person, the inalienable freedom and equality in principle of all humans, and the necessary solidarity and interdependence of all humans with each other, both as individuals and as communities. The statesmen are also convinced 'that there will be no better global order without a global ethic'.[29]

Of course the politicians are also very well aware that a global ethic is no substitute for the Torah, the Gospels, the Qur'an, the Bhagavadgita, the Discourses of the Buddha or the Teachings of Confucius and others. It is concerned simply with 'a minimal basic consensus relating to binding values, irrevocable standards and moral attitudes which can be affirmed by all religions despite their dogmatic differences, and can also be supported by non-believers'.[30] The alliance of believers and non-believers (also including that of theologians, philosophers, religious and social scientists) in the matter of an ethic is important. What is it aimed at?

(c) The core of a global ethic

The basic ethical demand of the Chicago Declaration is the most elementary that one can put to human beings, though it is by no means a matter of course: true **humanity**: 'Now as before, women and men are treated inhumanely all over the world. They are robbed of their opportunities and their freedom; their human rights are trampled underfoot; their dignity is disregarded. But might does not make right! In the face of all humanity our religions and ethical convictions demand that **every human being must be treated humanely!** That means that every human being without distinction of age, sex, race, skin colour, physical or mental ability, language, religion, political view, or national or social origin possesses an inalienable and untouchable dignity.'[31]

In this way, modern men and women with their 'will to power' are shown quite clearly that even in our time they in no way stand 'above good and evil', that rather the criterion of humanity has to be respected by all: 'Everyone, the individual as well as the state, is therefore obliged to honour this dignity and protect it. Humans must always be the subjects of rights, must be ends, never mere means, never objects of commercialization and industrialization in economics, politics and media, in research institutes, and industrial corporations. No one stands "above good and evil" – no human being, no social class, no influential interest group, no cartel, no police apparatus, no army, and no state. On the contrary; possessed of reason and conscience, every human is obliged to behave in a genuinely human fashion, to **do good and avoid evil!**'[32]

Would not only Woodrow Wilson, but also Hans Morgenthau, who had endured so much inhumanity in his life and at the same time was always in search of universal criteria, have been in agreement with such basic demands? At all events it is a sign of the times that today a body of proven and completely realistic statesmen have expressly adopted as the basis of a global ethic the two basic principles:

- **Every human being must be treated humanely!**
- **What you wish done to yourself, do to others.**

These two principles should be the irrevocable, unconditional norm for all spheres of life, for family and communities, for races, nations and religions. Moreover on the basis of them the InterAction Council also affirms **four irrevocable directives** on which all religions agree. (Here they can be given only by title, without further elaboration; one could also render them, recalling the demonstrators in Prague or Rangoon, with ethical imperatives like 'justice', 'truth', humanity or whatever):

- Commitment to a **culture of non-violence and respect for all life**: the age-old directive: You shall not kill! Or in positive terms: Have respect for life!
- Commitment to a **culture of solidarity and a just economic order**: the age-old directive: You shall not steal! Or in positive terms: Deal honestly and fairly!
- Commitment to a **culture of tolerance and a life of truthfulness**: the age-old directive: You shall not lie! Or in positive terms: Speak and act truthfully!
- Commitment to a **culture of equal rights and partnership between men and women**: the age-old directive: You shall not commit sexual immorality! Or in positive terms: Respect and love one another!

Since the question of **truthfulness** has played such a great role in connection with the **ethic of politicians** and we have already drawn some distinctions here, it may be of interest to see how this particular obligation to an ethic of truthfulness was formulated in an elementary way in the Parliament of the World's Religions, and of course not only for politicians. Here it is, word for word:

(d) The obligation to truthfulness

Numberless women and men of all regions and religions strive to lead lives of honesty and truthfulness. Nevertheless, all over the world we find endless lies and deceit, swindling and hypocrisy, ideology and demagoguery:
– Politicians and business people who use lies as a means to success;
– Mass media which spread ideological propaganda instead of accurate reporting, misinformation instead of information, cynical commercial interest instead of loyalty to the truth;
– Scientists and researchers who give themselves over to morally questionable ideological or political programmes or to economic interest groups, or who justify research which violates fundamental ethical values;
– Representatives of religions who dismiss other religions as of little value and who preach fanaticism and intolerance instead of respect and understanding.

A. In the great ancient religious and ethical traditions of humankind we find the directive: **You shall not lie!** Or in positive terms: **Speak and act truthfully!** Let us reflect anew on the consequences of this ancient directive: No woman or man, no institution, no state or church or religious community has the right to speak lies to other humans.

B. This is especially true:

- For those who work in the **mass media,** to whom we entrust the freedom to report for the sake of truth and to whom we thus grant the office of guardian. They do not stand above morality but have the obligation to respect human dignity, human rights, and fundamental values. They are duty-bound to objectivity, fairness, and the preservation of human dignity. They have no right to intrude into individuals' private spheres, to manipulate public opinion, or to distort reality.
- For **artists, writers, and scientists,** to whom we entrust artistic and academic freedom. They are not exempt from general ethical standards and must serve the truth.
- For the **leaders of countries, politicians, and political parties,** to whom we entrust our own freedoms. When they lie in the faces of their people, when they manipulate the truth, or when they are guilty of venality or ruthlessness in domestic or foreign affairs, they forsake their credibility and deserve to lose their offices and their voters. Conversely, public opinion should support those politicians who dare to speak the truth to the people at all times.
- Finally, for **representatives of religion.** When they stir up prejudice, hatred, and enmity towards those of different belief, or even incite or legitimate religious wars, they deserve the condemnation of humankind and the loss of their adherents.

Let no one be deceived: There is no global justice without truthfulness and humaneness!

C. Young people must learn at home and in school to think, speak, and act **truthfully.** They have a right to information and education to be able to make the decisions that will form their lives. Without an ethical formation they will hardly be able to distinguish the important from the unimportant. In the daily flood of information, ethical standards will help them discern when opinions are portrayed as facts, interests veiled, tendencies exaggerated, and facts twisted.

D. To be authentically human in the spirit of our great religious and ethical traditions means the following:

- We must not confuse freedom with arbitrariness or pluralism with indifference to **truth.**
- We must **cultivate truthfulness** in all our relationships instead of dishonesty, dissembling, and opportunism.
- We must **constantly seek truth** and incorruptible sincerity instead of spreading ideological or partisan half-truths.
- We must courageously **serve the truth** and we must remain **constant** and **trustworthy,** instead of yielding to opportunistic accommodation to life.

Thus the Declaration of the Parliament of the World's Religions which, in a thoroughly self-critical way, shows the best side of the religions. However, unfortunately they have another less pleasant side, which we must now also discuss.

V

World Peace – A Challenge
for the World Religions

Since the French Revolution, the wars of kings and cabinets have been replaced by the wars of nations, and since the First World War these have been succeeded by the wars of ideologies. Now, however, we are told – and this is also the sign of an epoch-making change – that we are in the age of wars between the civilizations, which for their part are stamped by the religions. And indeed there is no avoiding the sad recognition that in the transition to the third millennium, **religions** appear not only as the great midwives of the global ethic but also as the great **disturbers of world peace**.

That is true of the civil war between Catholics and Protestants which has already been going on for centuries in Northern Ireland, of the civil war in former Yugoslavia, and the struggle in the Philippines between Christians and Muslims, and finally of the Middle East conflict with so far five wars between Israelis and Arabs, Jews and Muslims. In addition there has been the establishment of often violent and authoritarian Islamic regimes, in Iran, in the Sudan and most recently in Afghanistan, along with the countless terrorist acts of fundamentalist Muslims in Europe, the Middle East and in America. And beyond the sphere of the three prophetic religions, which seem to be particularly aggressive, there are wars between Hindus and Muslims in Kashmir and India, between Hindus and Sikhs in the Punjab, and finally the civil war between Buddhists and Hindus in Sri Lanka. Truly, there is no lack of cruel examples of the way in which religions inspire people to hatred and enmity, just as they can inspire and legitimate wars. Is all that perhaps just the varied prelude to a great new tragedy of humankind, the clash of civilizations?

1. A clash between the civilizations – or peace?

That once again brings us definitively back to the immediate present. I am well aware that I have asked of my readers so far an extremely energetic 'forced march', in two respects:
– It has been a march through the **world politics of modernity**. Starting from the present (Kissinger), as I indicated, we went back to the beginning of modern real politics (Richelieu), progressed to its climax (Bismarck), and finally arrived at the downfall of the modern 'concert of European states' in the First World War. We then moved on to examine the new postmodern paradigm of politics (Wilson) and the critical discussion of it after the Second World War (Morgenthau and his successors);
– It has been a march through the **problems of world politics**: from the strengths and weaknesses of a real politics orientated on power and interests we arrived at the strengths and weaknesses of an ideal politics orientated on moral principles and finally developed the perspective of a politics of responsibility, which tries to take seriously ideals and realities, principles and interests, rights and obligations at the same time – all in the framework of a world society which needs a global ethic as a basis.

(a) The depth dimension of global political conflicts

'Global Responsibility: A New World Ethic in the New World Order.' On 15 April 1992 I spoke on this topic in the Dag Hammarskjøld Library Auditorium in the UN headquarters in New York. In fact, I had announced the slogan 'No world peace without peace between the religions' as early as 1984,[1] presented it for discussion within the framework of a UNESCO colloquium in Paris in 1989,[2] and developed the programme for it within the broad framework of my book *Projekt Welthos* (English *Global Responsibility: In Search of a New World Ethic*, 1991). When I spoke again on the global ethic at the same place in New York on 26 May 1994, I specifically discussed a striking essay that had appeared in the meantime, by **Samuel P. Huntington**, Director of the Institute for Strategic Studies at Harvard University, 'The Clash of Civilizations?',[3] and his hypothesis that in the new world era, wars would be waged above all by civilizations, which are stamped not least by religions. Consequently, in the future, political, economic and military conflicts were to be expected, for example, between Islamic civilization or Confucian–Asian civilization and the West: 'The next world war, if there is one, will be a war between civilizations.'[4]

I cannot judge whether there is any substance to the suspicion, expressed on the American side after my lecture, that Huntington, the long-time Pentagon adviser who has hardly had any positive concern with the religions, but already had a share of responsibility for the strategy of the Vietnam war, was looking for a new theory to justify additional arms expenditure. But when one sees him now on television presenting with a simple multi-coloured map of the world a model which is to replace the Cold War, one has strong reservations. Huntington's suggestion, originally presented with a question-mark, now appears in a big book without a question-mark[5] and is being propagated as though it were a proven theory. The problems it raises are easily overlooked:

– It **encourages thinking in terms of blocks.** The seven or eight 'civilizations' (following Arnold Toynbee's theory of civilizations) are demarcated as cultural entities, as if they did not in reality overlap or often interpenetrate – as they do in the big cities of Europe and America. Is this an attempt to explain to us who are the new 'natural' enemies of the West after the collapse of Communism, namely Islam and China?

– **It presents a simple system of co-ordinates.** Particular civilizations are defined without further examination by their religions (Islamic, Hindu, Confucian, Slavonic Orthodox), whereas this does not happen with others (Western, Japanese). But are not the contrasts, say, within Islam often greater than between Islam and the West, and have not the most recent wars often taken place between rivals of the same civilization (Iraq-Iran, Iraq-Kuwait, Somalia, Rwanda)?

– **It ignores common features.** Within the one Christianity a dividing line is drawn between Eastern Orthodox and Western civilization or even between Western North American and Latin American civilization, and everywhere the opposition of cultures is worked out without even considering the basic elements that they have in common with one another,[6] not to mention what they have in common with Islam. And why do Australia and Israel belong to the West and not Latin America and Eastern Europe?

But despite all the suspicions, if as a theologian one has so long been arguing that the reality of the religions should be taken seriously for world politics and world peace, then it is with great satisfaction that one notes that with Huntington we finally have a prominent political scientist, moreover one from the 'realist' school, who, unlike all the superficial politicians and political scientists, has noted the conscious-unconscious depth dimension of world-political conflicts and thus draws attention to the **fundamental role of the religions in world** politics: 'In the modern world, religion is a central, perhaps the central, force that motivates and mobilizes people . . . What ultimately counts for people is not political ideology or economic interest. Faith and family, blood and belief are what people identify with and what they will fight and die for.'[7] Political scientists, too, are now noting that a multiplicity of cultures and religions goes with the multi-polarity of global politics.

No wonder that Henry Kissinger does not find his Harvard colleague Huntington worth the slightest mention in his *Diplomacy*. After all, Huntington's totally different starting point does not fit well into the scheme of the traditional politics of interest; it has never occurred to the politician concerned with interests. Here in particular, in connection with the assessment of potential future conflicts, for all one's criticisms it is worth assessing with Huntington as a possibility that 'nation states will remain the most powerful actors in world affairs, but the principal conflicts of global politics will occur between nations and groups of different civilizations'.[8]

But in the meantime must it not have struck even so attentive an observer of current events as Henry Kissinger that the state frontiers drawn by real politicians in Eastern Europe and also in Africa are fading before the **age-old frontiers** which were once drawn by the peoples, religions and confessions? Lines of conflict have become visible between Armenia and Azerbaijan, between Georgia and Russia, the Ukraine and Russia, and even between different peoples in Yugoslavia, and finally between the Hutu and the Tutsi in Central Africa.

Huntington is certainly not wrong in his prognosis that **in the future too**, realistically we have **to expect culturally conditioned conflicts**: 'The most important conflicts of the future will occur along the cultural fault lines separating these civilizations from one another.'[9] Why? Not only for 'geopolitical' reasons: because the world is getting smaller and smaller, the interactions between people of different civilizations are becoming ever more numerous, and the significance of the regional economic blocks is becoming increasingly important. But according to Huntington, above all for cultural and **religious political reasons**:
– The differences between the civilizations are not only real but fundamental, often age-old and all-embracing; they extend from bringing up children, through the constitutions of states, to understandings of nature and God.
– Because of the cultural alienation and disappointment about the West caused by the process of modernization and globalization, many people are increasingly reflecting once again on their own religious roots.

– It is less possible to change and abandon human cultural characteristics than political and social characteristics, and religion divides people
sharply and very often exclusively far more than membership of a
people.

But: does that mean that **a conflict of cultures and religions is
unavoidable?** I cannot share Huntington's fatalism or accept his theory
of civilizations as the 'best compass for the future', the slogan used to
promote it in the media. His map seems all too simplified and his interest
in a further dominance of the Euro-American 'West' which in no way
may become multicultural ('A multicultural America is impossible
because a non-Western America is not American'[10]) seems all too
simplified. It is a question of 'maintaining Western technological and
military superiority over other civilizations'.[11] 'In the clash of civilizations, Europe and America will hang together or hang separately.'[12]

Huntington overdraws his thesis: not only when in the last chapter in
great detail he develops the horror scenario of a global war between the
USA, Europe, Russia and India on the one side and China, Japan and
the greater part of Islam on the other,[13] which provides any member of
the military or the armaments industry with brilliant arguments, but
also and above all when he now stylizes his reflection, which in his article
is still a brilliantly worked-out question (with a question-mark), into a
new paradigm of foreign politics, which is to replace the paradigm of
First, Second and Third Worlds. But it is questionable whether after the
Cold War and the bipolar consolidation of fronts in the multipolar
world of today there is still a unitary global explanatory model. By
contrast, my own judgment of the world situation leads to the following
assessment, which takes seriously the cultural and religious dimensions
of world politics, but at the same time does not blot out all the other
dimensions:

- Even in the foreign-political conflicts of the postmodern period, the
  issues are usually territories, raw material, trade and money, i.e.
  economic, political and military power interests.
- But while the **ethnic-religious differences and rivalries** are not a
  paradigm or system of co-ordinates which can explain all territorial
  controversies, economic rivalries and power interests of every kind,
  they are the constant **underlying structures** by which the political,
  economic and military conflicts can always be justified, inspired and
  dramatized, but also blunted and pacified.
- The civilizations or – more clearly – the **religions** thus do not form the
  surface dimension of all conflicts, which can easily be mapped, but

the **depth dimension** of many antagonisms and conflicts between the peoples and nations, and often even more within the nations, in cities, schools and families, conflicts which must not in any way be neglected.

* The allegedly unavoidable **global clash** of civilizations is perhaps the new anxiety-provoking model which is needed by some military strategists. But the vision for humankind which points towards the future is **global peace between the religions** as a presupposition and motive force for a global peace between the nations, and this must be striven for with all our might.

Only on the last five pages does Huntington mention what he has criminally neglected on the previous 300 pages and what now in retrospect relativizes the whole book: that 'the world's major religions . . . share key values in common', so that for peace in a multicultural world a 'commonalities rule' needs to be formulated: 'Peoples in all civilizations should search for and attempt to expand the values, institutions, and practices they have in common with peoples of other civilizations.'[14] Here one can see something like a periphrasis of the 'global ethic project': 'The futures of both peace and Civilization depend on understanding and cooperation among the political, spiritual, and intellectual leaders of the world's major civilizations.'[15] That means that it is not a clash between the cultures, but co-operation between the cultures, which is the model for the future.

(b) Religion – the missing dimension in statesmanship

I found further confirmation of my long-expressed view that the religious dimension in foreign politics has been neglected in the book by **Douglas Johnston** and **Cynthia Sampson** of the Center for Strategic and International Studies, Washington, published under the title *Religion. The Missing Dimension of Statecraft.*[16] The initiators of this volume, with a foreword by Jimmy Carter, start from the following hypothesis: 'The rigorous separation of church and state in the United States had so relegated religion to the realm of the personal that it left many of us insensitive to the extent to which religion and politics intertwine in much of the rest of the world. Such an insensitivity . . . could lead . . . to uninformed and potentially costly foreign policy choices.'[17]

Many concrete instances in fact confirm this working hypothesis: Vietnam, Lebanon, Iran, the Palestinian Intifada, Sudan and West Irian and also Nicaragua, Nigeria, the Philippines, Zimbabwe and South Africa. And they show two things:

– A whole series of fundamental **wrong foreign policy decisions** because the religious dimension of the conflicts was not taken seriously. Examples are Lebanon, Iran, Palestine (Intifada).

– In a whole series of instances the religions have made a specific contribution to **furthering peace** or restoring it. Examples are the reconciliation between France and Germany, peace in Nicaragua and Mozambique, the change of power in the Philippines, and the end of apartheid in South Africa.

Of course we are interested in the reason **why religion**, which so often proves 'an intractable force which hardly addresses any of the normal instruments of state power, even foreign policy',[18] is so often **ignored** in politics and diplomacy. According to **Edward Luttwak,** for many years Professor at Johns Hopkins University and now Director of the Geo-economy Project at the Center for Strategic and International Studies in Washington, the reason is to be seen in a **'secularizing reductivism'** and a 'crude materialistic determinism which slights nonmaterial motivations, always important and not infrequently decisive': 'Such motivations are often ethnic, but as often they are spiritual; the latter in turn are often personalistic and socially inchoate (as in the May 1968 Parisian uprising), but as often they are constituents of structured religious beliefs.'[19] For Luttwak, a long-serving specialist in military strategy, it seems 'quite certain that materialistic determinism, always a poor predictor, is even less likely to be predictive in the future'.[20]

One need not be religious to take religion – a real universal phenomenon, both diachronically and synchronically – seriously. For my part I can only state in a matter-of-fact way that **an analysis of a time which brackets off the religious dimension is defective,** however 'scientific' it claims to be. And a very specific Enlightenment, whether it comes from French lay or German Marxist dogmatics, itself needs enlightenment here.

But as far as the **practice of diplomacy** is concerned, the final conclusion for American diplomats drawn by the Washington political theorist **Stanton Burnett** can safely be generalized: 'American diplomats, raised in the Enlightenment secularism of the Realist school, are unprepared to see spiritual aspects of problems and possible solutions or, for that matter, to cope (as more than a colourful aside) with the whole cultural richness, including the intellectual life and structure of belief of the people (not just the institutions) with whom they deal abroad.'[21] Even if here I must be extremely brief, that can again be demonstrated in narrative and argument by the most recent political test case, with which the diplomacy of the old paradigm is far from having finished:

(c) The warning example: Yugoslavia

Only when it was too late did it also become clear to politicians and diplomats that the complexity of the problems in Yugoslavia can only be understood when one takes seriously the fact that for a thousand years – grounded in the separation of West Rome and East Rome – not only two completely different civilizations but **two different paradigms of Christianity** meet in the middle of Yugoslavia: the Eastern Byzantine with Serbia and the Roman Catholic with Croatia and Slovenia.[22] For more than a millennium, in matters of religion the Serbs have looked towards East Rome, Byzantium or Moscow, while the Croats and Slovenes have looked to Latin West Rome. Different liturgies, theologies, hierarchies, church constitutions, mentalities have developed; so too have different festivals, songs, poems . . . In addition there are the problems of the 600-year occupation of Serb territory by the Turks (since their defeat at the battle of Kossovo, 'The Field of the Blackbirds', in 1389), which particularly among the Serbs has produced the ideology of a lasting suffering and endurance which very often does not correspond (or no longer corresponds) to reality. Thus every ethnic group in ex-Yugoslavia has its own myths, legends, justifications, excuses and prejudices handed down for centuries, in short its history of suffering and guilt. Nationalism, overcome in Central Europe since the Second World War, lives on in South-East Europe in a dangerous way and is now displaying devastating consequences: your own nation or nationality comes first. But it is truly not just in Yugoslavia that fatal mistakes have been made in recent times.

(1) **The failure of politics.** Serbs, Croats and Bosnians (including the only indigenous and originally very tolerant Muslims in Europe) are all 'southern Slavs' ('Yugo–Slavs'). They speak the same language, and despite different religions – a living argument against the allegedly unavoidable 'clash of civilizations' – lived together peacefully for a very long time and often intermarried. Yugoslavia in particular was an example of overlapping and interpenetrating civilizations. For centuries Serbs have lived among Croats, originally recruited against the Turks, as ethnic cousins. So the three groups were very mixed on the territory of

former Yugoslavia, most of all in Bosnia. But what political conclusions should have been drawn from this many-sided and tricky situation?

Instead of striving for some uniform centralistic or antagonistic and separatist solution, it should have been possible to find a 'federal solution' and impose it unconditionally, with support from the great powers, who initially had the power to do this. But what happened? When I studied in Rome with Slovenes and Croats and as early as 1984 lectured in Belgrade, Zagreb and Dubrovnik, which were then peaceful, I followed events with passionate concern. I know from direct information that neither in the Foreign Office in Bonn nor on the Quai d'Orsay in Paris was a serious analysis made of ethnic and religious perspectives at the beginning of the conflict; and it was no different in Washington and London. Had such analyses been made in the foreign ministries of the Western great powers, and had the ethnic-religious antagonisms not been dismissed as the long-outdated quirks of a few surviving fanatics and lunatics, the governments could easily have avoided many of the disastrous mistakes in the various phases of the Balkans conflict after 1989. A short survey of the three phases of this conflict is not meant to pass reproachful verdicts on the past but to draw lessons from it for the future.

In phase 1: **the first fatal mistake** was, despite all the ethnic and religious differences, **to want to establish a single uniform Yugoslavian state.** Thus at that time the EC, the UN and especially the USA, badly advised (as was honestly conceded by their ambassador in Belgrade, Warren Zimmermann) and led by a President George Bush who was uninterested in the Serbian invasion of Croatia in 1991, tied the US super power to a 'do nothing policy' which President Clinton continued until 1995 instead of forging an alliance against the aggressor as in the Gulf War (Huntington totally overlooks phase 1, in which Islam plays no role).

The consequence was **a lack of any ethical will** to resist the blatant Serbian aggression (the bombardment of the civil population of Vukovar, Dubrovnik, Sarajevo and other Bosnian cities) among the European great powers and with them on the part of the American President, without whose leadership nothing in a disunited Europe went or goes. A timely and well-considered threat of economic sanctions and military force (no ground troops but massive NATO air attacks on air bases, military camps, munitions factories and strategically important bridges) could have stopped the aggression at that time: 'Not only would damage to the city (Dubrovnik) have been averted, but the Serbs would have been given a lesson in Western resolve which would at least have prevented something of their aggression against Bosnia,' said US Ambassador Zimmermann later. 'As it was, the Serbs learned another lesson – that there was no Western resolve and that they could advance as far as their power would take them.'[23] So the lack of an ethical will to resist made possible and encouraged the aggression of the 'Yugoslavian', but in fact Serbian, army against Croatia, Slovenia and then also Bosnia. It is already significant that the American Foreign Minister Warren Christopher hardly travelled in the Balkans, but instead went to Syria twenty-four times and to Israel thirty-five (though even there without exerting the necessary political and financial pressure at the right time, so that at the end of his period in office he had to watch the Israeli–Palestinian peace process collapse because of the obstruction of the new Likud government).

In phase 2, **the second fatal mistake** was, conversely, in the face of massive Serbian aggression **immediately to give diplomatic recognition to Croatia and Slovenia as sovereign states** (here Huntington is right). It came first of all from the Vatican, which regards Croatia as a 'bulwark of (Western) Christianity' and had an interest in seeing two more 'Catholic states' in the alliance of European powers. Then one day later, under massive pressure from the Vatican, recognition came from the government of the Federal Republic of Germany – so far its most serious diplomatic mistake. And some weeks later, for the first time under strong German pressure, the whole EC, without any concern to give serious protection to the minorities in Croatia (the Krajina Serbs) – which was urgently necessary in view of the policy of the Croatian president Franjo Tudjman (like the Serb Slobodan Milošević an ex-Communist, now an authoritarian nationalist), who suppressed all opposition within Croatia and engaged in aggression.

The diplomatic recognition of Slovenia and Croatia had **highly negative consequences in two ways**. First for the unity of the multi-ethnic and multi-religious Bosnia and Herzegovina: this land was now in fact delivered over to the criminal games of Messrs Milošević, Karadzić and Mladić. On the other hand, for the common foreign policy of the European Union. In order to restore the balance of power in the Balkans in the face of the unfortunate massive German and Vatican support of Croatia and Slovenia, England and France (supported by the Netherlands) with skilful diplomacy for the moment played the card of their ally since Bismarck's time, Serbia. Officially 'neutral', they sent UN troops as 'observers' to Bosnia and precisely in so doing constantly prevented any serious military intervention against Serbian aggression. That led to the absurd situation that now it was the protectors, unable to protect those who really needed to be protected, who had to be protected, or, as I heard it put ironically by a witty English observer, 'Protect protectors who don't protect!' So after Versailles in 1919, yet again there was a bankruptcy of the old European policy of interests which even now makes a common European foreign policy impossible. Attempts are being made with the Euro to build the house of Europe from a golden roof downwards, while at the foundations a common foreign and economic policy is evidently impossible!

In phase 3, the **third fatal mistake** was **to draw arbitrary frontiers** in the style of colonial powers, in the face of a civil war in Bosnia which had not been prevented, to recognize *de facto* 'ethnic cleansings' which were carried out by Nazi methods, and thus to **promise to the invaders**, contrary to all existing international law, **territories which had been occupied** by force. In the last century Africa was divided up in the spirit of such real politics, and after 1918 Europe. Richelieu, Metternich, Palmerston and Bismarck (and also Kissinger) would have played this kind of 'diplomacy' beyond all morality 'better' than the less top-class 'real politicians' of our day.

But the **result** of this unparalleled political drama will probably be **abiding hostility**, revenge at the first opportunity and, if the prospects seem good, a new war. Thus many people all over the world felt that it was allegedly 'realist' diplomacy which in fact led to the greatest political hypocrisy since the glorious European year of 1989. It is scandalous that Croatia, openly protected above all by German diplomacy, was accepted into the Council of Europe in 1995 although President Tudjman, rejected by the majority of his people and contrary to the demand of the Council, did not either co-operate in the arrest of war criminals or allow the elected opposition leader to take up his post as mayor of Zagreb or the Serbian refugees to return. And it is equally scandalous that Milosevic, the war criminal and chief author of the Yugoslavian war, discreetly protected by English and French diplomacy, could have held on to power so long despite the peaceful protests of the people, which went on every day for many weeks, without the Serbian democratic movement so far being helped to make a breakthrough by either the European Community or NATO.

I remember a remark by the Englishman Brian Beetham: 'Hypocrisy – the ultimate sin in the making of foreign policy.' For two reasons: it represents a tremendous disappointment to those concerned, who are deceived, but at the same time an extremely dangerous weakening of the hypocrite himself. So at present no one knows whether Bosnia-Herzegovina, the present artificial product of diplomacy, will not finally fall apart after the departure of NATO troops. For the separation of the three ethnic groups is constantly going on, despite the 1995 Dayton Agreement; the Bosnian Serb state controls about half the territory and the Muslim–Croatian federation the other half. The newly created national institutions (presidency, courts) exist only on paper. Countless refugees are prevented from returning to their homeland. The main war criminals go free. In short, a military conflict could break out again at any time if the hitherto undemocratic authorities in Serbia and Croatia are not replaced by really democratic and tolerant regimes from the previous opposition.

What can be learned from this history of calamities for world politics? That is my question. Or, to put it another way: **How can a new political fiasco** in the Balkans or elsewhere be **avoided**? Here are just a few brief remarks:

1. A diplomacy without any ethical will, a politics of interests beyond any morality, a global politics without a global ethic, always produces new injustices and thus new crises, new conflicts and new wars.

2. When secession is striven for, there is no call for uniform solutions, as have been aimed at first in Yugoslavia and also by Russia, with violence in Chechnya.

3. Nor is the automatic recognition of all too small ethnic groups as sovereign states called for. This must lead to the independence of ever smaller units (one need think only of the Basques, Catalonia, Northern Italy, Scotland, Corsica). If this went on, I was told at UN headquarters, there would soon be around 450 'sovereign' states instead of the 185 UN members there were in 1996 (as compared with the 51 founder states in 1945).

4. Therefore the solution in such cases of conflict is not the 'sovereign' nation state – which in any case is nowadays increasingly giving up many competences – but the widest possible cultural and political autonomy. And in Africa, too, given the numerous migrations, the most flexible boundaries possible, to allow regional collaboration, would be of more use than the most rigid separation (This is called for by the former President of Tanzania, Julius Nyerere.)

5. So instead of uniform or antagonistic solutions, the goal should be a **federal model**, of the kind achieved in the face of similar difficulties in the past century by the United States of America, the Swiss Confederation and Canada, and today by Belgium, Spain, South Africa and others. This is even more urgent in cases of even stronger ethnic mixes, as an alternative to ethnic 'cleansings'.

The federal model means:

- The **greatest possible autonomy** of the different ethnic and religious groups in respect of language, education, business, administration, academic research, media, folklore, traditions, culture and religion generally.
- But: **one** government, **one** army, **one** currency, **one** foreign policy.[24]

However, the critical assimilation of the Yugoslav crisis cannot call a halt at the church. What was the position of the religions? The churches?

(2) **The failure of the churches**: In such a region, will there ever be peace unless the religious dimension of the conflict is seen and taken seriously? Initially the sympathies of many people in Europe were with Croatia (not because it was Catholic, but because it had been attacked), and then above all with the Muslims. But it has not been forgotten, nor is it forgotten, that it was the Catholic Croatian Ustashi state under the protectorate of the German Nazis which killed tens of thousands (some claim hundreds of thousands) of Serbs – without protests from the then Catholic Archbishop of Zagreb, Aloisius Stepinac, or the then Pope Pius XII (who was also very well briefed on this). Both Catholic Croats and Orthodox Serbs have their own long list of offences which they have committed. There are no innocent nations anywhere, far less in the Balkans.

For almost **fifty years both churches had time** to sort out the situation, to acknowledge guilt, to ask for forgiveness, and to prepare for political peace and the reconciliation of the peoples. But what happened? There were individual ecumenical meetings between church leaders, but without serious results. It is no less sad that the first Slavonic Pope, having become a party to the situation with his journey to Zagreb and Sarajevo (in any case they did not want to see him in Orthodox Belgrade and he did not even want to visit the graves of the Ustashi victims), could not prevent new armed conflicts and bloodshed, nor build bridges to peace and reconciliation. The action of the World Council of Churches, which in past decades has preached to the world more than uniting the churches, was certainly well meant but too late when in the middle of the civil war it brought together bishops from both sides. Their ecumenical speeches finally ended in unecumenical accusations.

In the meantime little has changed: regardless of whether one talks with a Serb or a Croat, each speaks of the crime of the other side and is silent about the crime of his own side – like Germans and French earlier.

The others are always to blame! Do the Serbian and Croatian leaderships need yet another war of revenge, contrary to all the opposition in their own country, before they too note that thinking and politics based on revenge never leads to peace but always only to new destruction? And even now, when finally a fragile Dayton Agreement has been reached, is there really no bishop or theologian who could begin an honest dialogue? Self-critical mourning is needed – on all sides. For if peace is only on paper and does not enter the minds of people, far less their hearts, it will not last.

But here a question of principle extends far beyond the Balkans: must these **religions** necessarily stand alongside one another in opposition and dispute? Peace (*shalom, salam, eirene, pax*) is written large in most of their programmes. And their first task at this time should really be to **make peace between one another.** We shall be returning to that very shortly. But first a question must be answered which is both political and ethical: do not both the Gulf War and the war in Yugoslavia show that one cannot avoid **war** even in a new world order?

(d) War for the sake of peace?

One can in fact learn some lessons for a new world order both from the Gulf War and from the war in Yugoslavia:

(1) At the end of the twentieth century **wars are neither 'holy' nor 'just' nor 'clean'.** The time of 'Yahweh's war' and the 'Crusades' is fortunately long past and the *'jihad'* (which in fact does not mean 'holy war' but primarily moral 'effort' for God's cause) in its warlike manifestation should also finally be a thing of the past. In particular the Gulf War, fought and won with high technology, resulted in uncalculable loss of human life, immense destruction of the infrastructure, floods of millions of refugees and an enormous amount of ecological damage (instead of removing the main culprit and 'liberating' the victims), all consequences which make even some supporters of the war ask in retrospect whether it was really 'worth while'.

(2) **Wars are not** *a priori* unavoidable:

(a) *The Gulf War*: American diplomacy (and once again the CIA) had blatantly failed in the lead-up to the crisis: immediately before the Iraqi invasion of Kuwait the US ambassador in Baghdad had personally presented the whole affair as a domestic matter for the Arab world. Moreover the USA, supporting Israel with billions of dollars, had hitherto not achieved a real solution of the Palestinian question, which from the beginning was and remained entangled with the Gulf question, above all because of domestic political considerations, i.e. the American Jews.

(b) *The war in Yugoslavia*: here too, as we saw, better diplomacy on the part of the Western great powers at an early stage could have prevented the war from developing.

(3) An **efficient policy of interests** without an ethic **tends to lead to atrocities!** An examination of consciences after the Gulf War will show that here there is not simply black and white, knave and innocent, good and evil, God and Satan. Demonization of the opponent often served to exonerate the side engaging in it. For everyone has wooed Iraq and equipped it with money, technology and advisers, in a way that has transcended the power blocs: China, the Soviet Union and then above all the West (with the benevolent toleration and co-operation of the USA), in particular France, England, Italy and – by irresponsibly turning a blind eye to the activity of criminal firms – unfortunately Germany as well. Up to 80% of all the weapons in the region have been supplied by the five standing members of the UN Security Council. The same can be said of the war in Yugoslavia, where the chief aggressor Slobodan Milošević was accommodated afresh time and again, and even serious violations of human rights by his opponent Franjo Tudjman were accepted. The withdrawal of the Dutch UN troops for policy reasons from the greatest massacre in Europe since the Second World War in Srebreniza, with 8-10,000 civilians dead has caused people to search their consciences even in the Netherlands. (The scene of their commander drinking champagne with General Mladić, the butcher of Srebreniza, remains stamped on the memory.)

(4) However, an **absolute pacifism** for which peace is the supreme good to which all must be sacrificed is **irresponsible**: the legitimate **right to self-defence** according to Article 51 of the UN Charter is not abrogated even by the Sermon on the Mount: the requirement of non-violence may not be put into practice in a literal fundamentalist way. Pacifism is not enough to keep the peace. For what is called for is not a hollow peace, but peace as the work of justice (as Augustine said, *opus iustitiae pax*), and in some circumstances this means defending those who are attacked and disarming the attackers. What is appropriate here is not an 'ethics of conviction' which is heedless of the consequences, but an ethics of conviction and responsibility which takes all the consequences into account as far as possible. Some 'peace fighters' must be told: mere moral conviction without reason has had, and can again have, catastrophic effects!

(5) Mass murderers and megalomaniac dictators cannot be allowed

the decisive power over a region which is important for the life of the whole world. Stalin (in Finland and the Baltic States) and Hitler (throughout Europe) have demonstrated that **peace at any price is not a responsible policy.** Resistance had to, and has to, be offered also to Saddam Hussein, a man of bloody terror at home and of a ten-year war against his neighbour Iran, with around a million dead. Anyone who fights with hostages, poison gas and oil pollution; anyone who brutally attacks and occupies one state, Kuwait, and threatens another, Israel, with total annihilation by non-conventional weapons, is no partner in negotiations. Limits must be set to him, not least with armed force.[25] And had the previously briefed UN authorities taken a secret warning seriously, it would probably have been possible to avoid the Hutu massacre of at least 500,000 Tutsis (well prepared for by a registration of the Tutsis). Formerly the two lived peacefully together, hence the subsequent panic flight of 2 million Hutus.

(6) As previously in Nuremberg and Tokyo, **war criminals** should be brought before an **international tribunal.**[26] The fact that the UN and NATO troops have so far not arrested the Serb leader Karadzić and General Mladić, both accused of crimes against humanity, must not be blamed on the soldiers, but on those governments who do not want an arrest. Should Hitler, Goering and Himmler perhaps have been allowed to run free after 1945? **Richard Goldstone,** the Chief Prosecutor of the UN tribunal, rightly says: 'The most important challenge for the Yugoslavia tribunal at present is the arrest and hand-over of the accused. It is quite unacceptable for the internal community to set up a court, to give it the right to make orders for arrests which must be carried out in accordance with international law and the Charter of the United Nations – and for these orders not to be implemented. It is important for the credibility and success of the court that these people are called to account.'[27] It is the responsibility of Washington, London, Paris, Rome and Bonn that the UN troops, contrary to the Dayton Agreement, were not instructed to arrest the pair: 'The whole court – the judge, the prosecutors, the administration – feels extremely frustrated by the restrictive policy of these states.'[28] To quote Goldstone again: 'People rightly feel it unjust that the main culprits escape justice and those far below them in the hierarchy are caught and punished. That is unacceptable.' Of course, he too knows that there were all too many perpetrators in former Yugoslavia: 'Therefore one must take the course of bringing the chief culprit before the court, and the others before a Truth Commission.'[29] South Africa has shown the way here with its

'Truth Commission' under the Nobel Peace Prizewinner Archbishop Tutu.

Happily, because of the trial in The Hague, the war crimes were written about in many countries in a way which was still unthinkable a few years ago. That at least can ultimately have a certain deterrent effect on particular political and military leaders, who with their tremendous power over people bear the chief responsibility for countless crimes. But things must not stop at these beginnings of an international jurisdiction: **there is need for a permanent and efficient UN war crimes tribunal.**

(7) Events in ex-Yugoslavia recall **justice in the Federal Republic of Germany**. To begin with it looked as if those chiefly responsible for the injustice in the former German Democratic Republic, beginning with the despot Erich Honecker, the Stasi chief Erich Mielke and their fellow councillors – would get off very lightly, whereas 'junior' guards on the wall, acting under orders, were condemned to two years imprisonment. As a result of the Nazi abomination, the Basic Law of the Federal Republic of Germany covers human rights and deals strictly with infringements of them. As in the USA from the beginning (but not in France), they are a matter for the courts. According to Article 1 of the Basic Law (on the protection of human rights), as 'directly valid law' these 'basic rights' are 'binding' not only on the legislation and force to be used, but specifically also on 'jurisprudence' (para.3). However, the German courts, which on the whole notoriously failed even to deal with the bloody verdicts of Nazi justice, at first virtually ignored this and referred positivistically to the 'retrospective prohibition' (Article 103 section 2 of the Basic Law), according to which a penalty may be imposed only if at the time the act was committed it was specifically punishable under an existing law. So instead of being treated as state organs of the German Democratic Republic, Honecker and Mielke were treated as private persons. An attempt was made to pin the murder of two policemen at the time of the Weimar Republic on the state criminal Mielke, and finally both were released after laboriously long proceedings on the grounds that they were unfit to stand to trial or be imprisoned.

But now, happily, seven years after the collapse of the East German regime, on 24 October 1996, has come a decision by the Federal Constitutional Court, noted beyond Germany, which may be called historic. It does not exact any vengeance, but goes one stage further towards the **justice** which is so missed by many Germans. According to this unanimous decision, the justification put forward for the command to shoot people who only wanted to cross the frontier within Germany, unarmed and posing no danger under generally recognized laws, is inoperative despite an East German regulation to this effect. Why? 'Because of manifest, intolerable offences against the elementary demands of justice and against human rights which are internationally protected'! Here the 'right to life' has priority, and an offence against it 'seems so serious that it violates the convictions about the value and dignity of human beings common to all nations. In such a case the positive law must give way to justice.' For our problem that means:[30]

- Injustice remains injustice, even if it is in the garb of state legislation. Injustice does not become injustice through being ordained by the law but becomes 'legal injustice'.
- The 'convictions about the value and dignity of human beings common to all nations' and 'the elementary demands of justice' have priority over 'positive law'.
- Ethical values like human dignity and justice apply independently of any legal recognition, so that in grave cases a legal norm 'is to be disobeyed *a priori* if it is in manifest, intolerable contradiction with justice'.[31]
- Thus **state legislation presupposes** an ethic common to all human beings, a **world-wide ethic of humanity.** The 'convictions about the value and dignity of human beings common to all nations' of the 'world-wide community of law' are 'normative, and indispensable for human life together; they are part of the unassailable nucleus of the law'.

But of course laws and judgments are not enough to preserve a country from war and crime and to hold a society together. We must go deeper here and ask about a matter of principle.

2. What holds modern society together?

This is a quite general question which today is occupying increasingly wide circles beyond sociologists, philosophers and politicians. This was made clear to me by a congress in Karlsruhe in 1996, and it is certainly not just true of Germany.[32] On a number of points there seems to be agreement in the diagnosis between exponents of different tendencies (conservatives, liberals, socialists, all modern children of the Enlightenment), and of course this diagnosis prompts questions.

(a) Diagnoses of the time

Diagnosis 1: 'The free secular state lives by presuppositions which it cannot itself guarantee without putting its freedom in question.'[33] Modern society needs social and political guidelines. These emerged from **common convictions, attitudes and traditions** which preceded freedom and make use of it as a medium. These resources are not there by nature but need to be cultivated, activated and handed down by upbringing.

There is no disputing this, but **it raises the question**: what is to be done if evidently these common convictions, attitudes and traditions which precede freedom have largely got lost? One can hardly cultivate what no longer exists, and who is to 'activate' what seems to have gone to sleep?

Diagnosis 2: the modern liberal social order has for a long time been able to rely on 'habits of the heart', on a thick **'cushion' of pre-modern systems of meaning and obligation** which today are now **'threadbare'**. Respect for the authority of the state, obedience towards the laws and a work ethic, have long been able to rely on this traditional 'cushion' . But in the meantime the traditional resources of meaning and the ingredients of traditional public spiritedness have come to be exhausted.[34]

This, too, is correct, but **it raises the question**: can citizens themselves 'generate' such resources of meaning? That is asking far too much of them. Human beings cannot invent everything all over again today.[35] So from where is present-day humankind to draw the 'moral resources' and pre-legal conditions of cohesion? On what is it to be able to ground the new social consensus?

Diagnosis 3: there are possibilities for **strengthening the awareness of values,** but for every possibility there are also counter-forces:[36]
– More decentralization and greater closeness to the citizen (but in fact increasing demands from the citizen on state and government).
– Strengthening of community (but increasingly brutal selfishness already evident in the schools).
– Feminization of society (but we are still far from overcoming machismo).
– Building society from the family upwards (but in fact there is an increasing withdrawal of families from society).
– A policy of human rights before export policy (but in fact time and again economic interests predominate).
– Smaller schools (but no funding for more teachers).

These are important perspectives, but **they raise the question**: what about **religion**? Certainly in the congress there was talk of an absence of a consensus and the necessary 'ligatures', but religion appeared at best on the periphery. It was striking that a philosopher in one of his introductory theses felt able to state that society found its cohesion 'through language, through schools and colleges, through an architecture for a public spirit, through art, science and philosophy.'[37] Through philosophy? For a philosopher completely to exclude religion was at any rate surprising and provoked criticism. 'Religion – the missing dimension of philosophy?', one is tempted to ask. Certainly we have 'religion not in the singular but in the plural',[38] just as in my opinion we also have 'philosophy not in the singular but in the plural'. Is it therefore to be able to contribute nothing to the cohesion of society? Just as one may expect something for the cohesion of present-day society from philosophy, which has made undoubted contributions to tolerance, democracy and human rights, so too one may expect something from religion. Those who banish or ignore religion create a vacuum; at any rate they have to say what they have to offer in its place in this time of growing disorientation and pseudo-religiosity, particularly for the many young people who are in search of meaning and orientation in values. So I gladly note the philosopher's postscript to the effect that modern societies as 'binding forces' are not as poor as many think, but 'also not so rich that they can rule out what religions have to offer'.[39]

   Marion Countess Dönhoff, co-editor of *Die Zeit*, whom I quoted in the first sentences of my introduction, spoke more clearly at the congress: 'The exclusive this-worldliness which cuts human beings off from their metaphysical sources; the total positivism which is concerned only with the surface of things and allows the depth-dimension to be forgotten, these cannot represent a lasting meaning for human beings, and therefore lead to frustration.'[40] But before I go more closely into the integrating function of religion, which cannot in the end be replaced by any philosophy or even any ethic, I should quote what I myself said at that congress. As well as being a binding force, religions can in fact have a divisive effect, though they are not the only such factor.

(b) Divisive forces in society

Anyone who sets out to speak on behalf of religion as a political scientist or a theologian is immediately confronted with the objection: 'Religion divides!'[41] That is true. Religion has disseminated two particular divisive forces throughout the world, which are driving societies apart:

(1) **Religious fundamentalism.** Fundamentalism – originally this word

was used for biblicistic Protestantism in America – can present itself in an extremely modern way in some respects (in relation to progress in technology, industry, the media, the transport and financial systems), but at all events wants to hold fast to the 'fundament' (the allegedly inerrant authority of its holy scriptures or one infallible leader) and therefore to its quite specific ancient laws or dogmas.[42]

At present fundamentalism is especially virulent, in a terrifying way, in Muslim countries. As the term 'fundamentalism' is rejected by most Muslims, they prefer to speak of **Islamism**. From Algeria and Egypt, through Israel, Saudi Arabia and Turkey to North America, there is a bloody trail of ever new terrorist attacks to which already tens of thousands of people have fallen victim. Contemptuous of humanity as it is, Islamism in its terrorist form fights not only against Jews and Christians and those of another faith (in Israel, Egypt, Pakistan, the Sudan), but also against its own allegedly 'liberal' Muslims. Yet we should not overlook the fact that alongside the radical and sometimes terrorist Islamists there are also many moderate Islamists who want a (more or less) Islamic state without a totalitarian tinge; indeed, who also want to integrate Western ideas.

The **attitude of the Arab regimes** to Islamism is also so very **diverse** that even from that perspective a total 'clash' between Muslim and Western civilization is highly improbable. So far a real integration of Islamism has not taken place anywhere. Instead, there are different modes of reaction in the various countries with a Muslim stamp:
– Islamism is made the foundation of the state and society by theocratic regimes: in Iran, in the Sudan and in Afghanistan;
– Any Islamism is suppressed by force: in Syria, Iraq and the Lebanon;
– In other countries attempts are made to marginalize Islamism: in Egypt, Tunisia and recently also in Turkey;
– Yet other countries attempt to avoid Islamism by Islamic legitimation of their own regimes: in Saudi Arabia and Morocco.
– Limited assimilations to Islamism have been made by Jordan, Yemen, the Lebanon and Kuwait.

But today **fundamentalism**, a phenomenon with roots which are social and political as well as religious, is not just a phenomenon within Islam. There are variants in Judaism and Christianity, and also within Buddhism and Hinduism. In short, fundamentalism is a **world problem**. No less important than the much-discussed Muslim fundamentalism is a Christian variant which for good reasons does not want to be called 'fundamentalism'.

(2) **Rigorous moralism.** The merciless rigorism of the Roman 'magisterium' confronts societies all over the world in concrete, highly controversial questions like contraception, artificial insemination, abortion, pre-natal diagnosis or euthanasia with an almost fanatical extremism. It is disseminated in particular by the well-funded reactionary secret order Opus Dei, which has been especially encouraged by Karol Wojtyla, already as Archbishop of Krakow and even more as Pope. Although Opus Dei is notorious for its 'secrecy, rigorous inner life (flagellation and hair shirts), the indoctrination of the young, sectarian recruitment, the entanglement of members in financial scandals and the promotion of a traditionalist attitude in the church, tending towards an authoritarian conservatism',[43] even German university professors accept honorary doctorates from the 'Work of God's' own university in Pamplona, in Spain, and moreover promote its cause.[44]

This zealous anti-modernism (the Italians call it 'Woitylismo') wants to split society dualistically into a 'culture of life' and a 'culture of death', to **divide humankind into sponsors of life and conspirators against life.** It therefore sees humankind apocalyptically as being at the crossroads between life and death, blessing and curse. At least according to the most recent papal encyclical *Evangelium vitae* (1995), any woman who takes the pill, any man who uses a condom, belongs to 'the conspiracy against life' and 'the culture of death'.[45] With their 'contraception morality' they are already on the way to the 'pro-abortion culture'.[46] In reality it is the other way round. The women and men who practise contraception want to prevent unwanted pregnancy and, in its wake, abortion, whereas the Pope's attitude, which prohibits even contraception, in fact encourages abortion.

In view of the countless slum children of Nairobi (I have seen them and their everyday suffering without Potemkin-style scenery), to proclaim 'increase and multiply' seems not only to me to be a perversion of the magisterium. No, such teaching splits not only the Catholic Church but humankind as a whole, as has been shown by the World Population Conference in Cairo in 1994 and the World Conference of Women in Beijing in 1995. A coalition of the Roman Curia and a few reactionary Muslim regimes against the 'rest of the world' became evident (and not just to me), and this has substantially damaged respect not only for Christianity and Islam, but for religion in general, not least within the framework of the international organizations.[47]

This is confirmed by the cancellation of the Vatican contribution to UNESCO child aid work (a paltry $2,000 for a state worth $1 billion), the sabotage of UNICEF greetings cards because UNICEF was involved in a UNO brochure about the distribution of contraceptives to refugee women, and the opening speech by the Pope to the UN World Nutrition Summit in Rome on 13 November 1996 in which he publicly chided all those who associate hunger with overpopulation: 'We must reject the sophistic view that to be many condemns us to be poor.' But must not this particular statement have sounded like cynical sophistry in the ears of the professionals present?

(3) **Postmodern arbitrary pluralism.** However, it is no answer to the divisive forces of religion to offer the **insipid soup of indifference** as the 'postmodern' consensus of society. As we know, quite a few people, particularly in the West, and above all those who can afford it, practise a life-style of indifferentism, consumerism and hedonism, and some also shamelessly propagate it in the media.

Am I exaggerating? Must I, who am critical of all moralism, reluctantly also offer examples here of what is such a prominent feature of today's journalism? 'The new enjoyment of vices' ('Excess, lust, greed . . .! Seven prominent women confess their biblical vices'): this is how a new, shallow German women's magazine evidently thought it could gain a large readership, by chance immediately before the National Day of Penitence and Prayer in 1996 (observed in favour of health assurance and the 'holy' holidays that have been abolished). Is that just the gutter press, whose headlines in any case always promise more than they offer? The *Spiegel* had a very realistic lead story on 'The Shameless Society'.[48] Or to give just one example from the literary scene, in which scatological language, cynicism and malice are now quite respectable: in 1991 the once respected jury of the Ingeborg Bachmann Prize (founded by the city of Klagenfurt and Austrian Radio) felt able to award the prize to a Basel journalist for a story in which he presented fantasies of 'fucking baby' – and vigorously defended it against criticism by well-known literary critics.[49]

But many people ask: is freedom of the press and freedom of opinion on everything a good thing? Rights without responsibilities? This is no new prudery, no call for censorship, just food for thought. Or do we need yet more instances to prompt a rethink, like the abhorrent crimes on defenceless children, concealed by the complicity of politicians, journalists and judges, which have recently been committed in Belgium? Do we need to have further child sex rings brought to light as now in Poland (around 100 child sex partners from every possible country on computer lists), or even more shameless, contemptible child prostitution through frivolous sex tourists in the Third World? And – one can hardly believe it – there are in fact constitutional lawyers in Sweden who are publicly expressing outrage at their Queen Silvia because, allegedly going beyond her 'competence', she called for intervention against child pornography . . . But enough of that: these are things which people everywhere can read every day in newspapers and magazines.

The fundamental question is: do perhaps our colourful programmatic or pragmatic libertists and libertinists hold society together, rather than the gloomy Opus Dei clerics? Hardly. At best they atomize it, because they have no sense of public spirit, the common good, or shame, and are out only to satisfy selfish experience and primitive voyeurism. Those who praise 'civilized' hedonism (former 'revolutionaries', now transformed into gourmets)[50] or a banal, empty 'nihilistic ethic' ('ironic attitude', 'being pragmatic and sceptical')[51] involuntarily prove that the Pope and Opus Dei are right. Sociologists like Gerhard Schulze speak of an 'experience society'[52] which has rightly replaced the working society. In another respect one can also talk of **'real politics' in microcosm**; the parallels can hardly be overlooked. The individual selfishly cultivates his interests and seeks to make his everyday life as aesthetically pleasing as possible, and is prepared for commitment only in so far as it serves his needs or gives him pleasure. Here individuality has deteriorated into an unbridled individualism which makes the individual lonely and unhappy and has a destructive effect on society.

It is a welcome sign when one hears, particularly from competent writers, that the experience society is slowly discovering responsibility: 'that the pleasure culture which in the 1980s made us fit for nothing but fun' while 'still chirruping on with false cheerfulness' is showing signs enough that 'the pleasure generation is at its wits' end' and has 'exhausted itself with play': 'One does not have to quote critical statements from the past to detect the mood of weariness with play and exhaustion with pleasure that governs the present and to discover signs of the quest for a new, different earthing. In the pleasure and play of the aesthetic experience all freedoms seem to have been exhausted beyond good and evil. Now the question of the relationship between the aesthetic and the ethical can be put again.'[53]

I am neither a pessimist nor an alarmist, but I can understand why in the face of such fundamentalism, moralism and arbitrary pluralism not a few of our serious contemporaries are asking: where is our society drifting to? Furthermore, serious Europeans are asking themselves '*Quo vadis*' – with or without Euro-Europe?

(c)　Three models of Europe

The prophets of disaster, augurs and pollsters, should be reminded that no one predicted the great **European Revolution** of 1989 – neither astrologers nor political theorists, theologians nor futurologists. But now all over the world those who diagnose the present and analyse the times are asking themselves what is going to happen to Europe and the world. A Christian Europe? Is that still an inspiring idea for the future? What has become of once so proud a slogan? Who today still dreams Novalis' romantic dream of a 'Christianity or Europe'? Has Christianity still a chance in Europe, culturally and spiritually? Or to put the question the other way round: is the Europe of the men of influence, planners and strategists still a Christian Europe? What is the spiritual situation of this continent generally? It is clear that behind such questions are three quite different conceptions of Europe, which are also illuminating for the rest of the world. Which of them has a future?

(1) **Technocratic Europe?** This is the **conception of a functionalist economy and politics** of the kind propagated by some Brussels technocrats and interest groups, like lobbyists in the individual countries. In this conception Europe is primarily a market, organization, economic network. Europe is a giant financial, economic and social sphere which has to be shaped effectively and at the same time given military protection with present-day business techniques, management possibilities and trade union influences. The most recent EC, NATO and CSCE conferences have almost entirely revolved around the Euro and 'security'. The ministers allow the uninfluential European parliament to 'parley' about other aspects.

But there was already a Europe with shared science, poetry, art, culture and spirituality centuries before the destructive nationalisms of the last century and the constructive Euro-politicians and Eurocrats of our century. Cannot a cultural and spiritual concept of Europe be regained? At all events the conception of Europe as a functionalist economy and politics raises so many questions that in principle one can endorse the criticism that the present Pope has constantly made about the spiritual situation of Europe: Europe needs a **spiritual and cultural renewal!** But everything depends on what one understands by this spiritual and cultural renewal.

(2) **The restoration of a Christian Europe?** Already in 1982 John Paul II developed his own conception of Europe at the mediaeval Spanish

pilgrimage place of Santiago di Compostela: the **traditionalist utopia of a 'spiritual unity of Europe'** and the **programme of a 're-evangelization of Europe'** orientated on Poland, which at that time was predominantly Roman Catholic. These papal slogans, along with the most recent moral encyclicals and the Roman Catechism, are now making clear even to Catholic politicians in Poland, Germany and elsewhere what is being asked of all of them: a reactionary conception with which they will perhaps become 'Knights of the Holy Sepulchre', but will certainly not be able to win votes and make a political contribution to the spiritual revival of a renewed Europe.

So this traditionalist conception of Europe raises fundamental questions. For the call for a spiritual and cultural renewal, while intrinsically justified, is accompanied by a penetrating and one-sided denunciation of Western democracy as consumerism, hedonism and materialism. If one listens closely there can be no question of an unambivalent papal affirmation of the modern values of freedom of conscience, parliamentary democracy, pluralism, individuality and tolerance. According to the Roman documents all **freedom of conscience** is clearly **subject to the Roman magisterium,** which is 'infallible' even in questions like contraception and the ordination of women, whereas according to the Second Vatican Council the magisterium should in turn be subordinate to holy scripture (though in fact it controls the interpretation of scripture at will).

But what is the aim of curial policy? That is no secret, but has been declared increasingly clearly: Europe is to be 'renewed' in the mediaeval spirit of anti-modernity, according to the notions of a man who has neither accepted nor assimilated the paradigm shifts of the Reformation or the Enlightenment, but has now lost his own mediaeval Polish Catholic model as a result of the most recent development, probably the greatest tragedy of his life. As critical Poles have also remarked, this spiritual renewal of Europe in fact amounts to a re-Catholicization, or better a **'Re-Romanization'**, in which the fear is of 'Church, Church over all?' (thus a graffito on a wall in Poland). Here those of other faiths and non-believers, Protestants, Orthodox and Jews, doubters and dissenters, are to be marginalized. Nowadays such a vision of the 'restoration of a Christian Europe' seems a nightmare not only to the majority of Poles (the result of the 1996 election was negative for the church despite previous papal appeals in the media), but to most Europeans. At any rate it is not a signpost for the younger generation of women and men who want to be open to the third millennium. But is there a third way?

(3) **Europe with an ethical foundation.** The new postwar Europe was built on ethical impulses which kept coming into play when unity had to be maintained despite all the divergent interests. Spain, Portugal and Greece were certainly not accepted into the European Community for primarily economic reasons but for ethical reasons, and that will be the case with Hungary, Poland and the Czech Republic if they are accepted: also in order to give these nations the chance for development that they have asked for.

However, an analysis of the structural change in politics and society establishes in connection with the present spiritual and religious situation in Europe that:

– We are living in a time of accelerated **secularization,** which need not necessarily mean secularism (godlessness), but does mean secularity (worldliness), a time in which for many people ideological ties have become looser or have been broken.

– We are living in a time of radicalized **individualization,** in which every individual who has 'come of age' claims to have his or her own opinion, to make his or her own decisions and to oppose control by social institutions – state, church, trade unions, other associations of interests.

– We are living in a time of growing ideological **pluralism,** in which even the world religions are increasingly splitting up into tendencies, groups, small faith communities and autonomous institutions, in which a colourful market of religious offers is in full swing and a **patchwork religion** is being practised by millions of people. Evidently demystification, secularization and rationality cannot so easily replace tradition, religion and mystery.

In these circumstances, is it possible to achieve more spiritual cohesion again in Europe? In contrast to the Roman documents, many serious critics of the time see this process of secularization, individualization and pluralization not just as a negative but as an **ambivalent development:** while it presents many risks and dangers, it also offers some opportunities and advantages. Men and women are to act in freedom as responsible persons, though at the same time they will be thrown back upon their own individual destiny. At any rate, in this way the human need for security, for ideal perspectives, for criteria, for points of reference to give them support, has grown rather than decreased. Once again Marion Countess Dönhoff has put both sides clearly: 'Of course pluralistic democracy is unthinkable without the autonomous individual. So there can be no question of retreating from emancipation and secularization; in any case this would be quite impossible. The important thing is to train citizens for greater responsibility and once again to give them a sense of solidarity. In our present-day world with its varied temptations and attractions, the longing for a basic moral orientation, for norms and a binding value system, is very great. Unless we take account of this, then this society will not hold together.'[54]

So for Christians, too, at any rate, it is a matter of unswervingly taking a third way: between a secularistic-technocratic ideology of Europe, which is un-Christian, and a pre-modern hierarchical ideology, which is undemocratic. What is important is a **spiritual concept of a Europe which has a moral foundation**. And therefore the question of what holds modern society together is generally to be answered as follows:

- Modern society cannot be held together in depth by fundamentalism, moralism or arbitrary pluralism, but only by a binding and compelling **ethic**: a basic consensus on common values, criteria and attitudes which combines autonomous self-realization and responsibility in solidarity.
- For **believers** this ethic is rooted in belief in a first and last reality, but it can also be shared in by **non-believers** on the basis of humanity, so that it can embrace quite different social groups and political parties, nations and religions.

However, a society will only be held together by an ethic and achieve a shift towards more reflectiveness, commitment and responsibility if people have the feeling that the **ethical norms and criteria**, particularly if they are put forward by religions and churches,
– should not be chains or fetters, but aids and supports, for constantly rediscovering and realizing a direction and values, an attitude and a meaning in life. It should be a **liberating** ethic;
– should not be the expression of a selfish advocacy of interests by a church apparatus or a religious establishment, but the expression of a basic conviction which is binding on all men and women. It should be a **binding** ethic;
– should not exclude and condemn, but invite and obligate. It should be a **tolerant** ethic.

So this is what is meant by a **global ethic** which also embraces all religions, an ethic of humanity, a **world ethic**. And I want to emphasize here that this should in no way be at the expense of religion. Rather, here – presupposing that religion does not have a repressive or regressive but a liberating and humanizing character – the complementarity of ethics and religion comes into play.

(d) Ethics no substitute for religion

The slogan should not be 'ethics instead of religion'; that would be an Enlightenment form of moralism. Nor should the call in schools be for 'ethical education instead of religious education'; that would be a fundamental misunderstanding of the 'global ethic' project. Nor, however, should there be religion without an ethic, religious education without education in a truly human ethic; without ethical education which has a universal orientation, religion degenerates into dogmatism and sectarianism. Therefore I can imagine that the 'Declaration toward a Global Ethic' of the Parliament of the World's Religions could be an excellent working basis on which religious, ethical and philosophical education, and possibly also other disciplines, could collaborate. But in no way should it be suggested that the Sermon on the Mount should be replaced with the Enlightenment ethic of tolerance, or that the picture of Gotthold Ephraim Lessing, whom I too admire, should be put in schools instead of the sign of the crucified Christ.

So we need to make a distinction between what can be communicated by **ethics** as a purely human ethic on the one hand, and what can ultimately be communicated only by **religion**, in its decisive elements a deeply rooted and at the same time rational trust in God, on the other.[55] It is a delusion to think that modern society will be held together by the Internet and globalized markets, by economic and social modernization. A universal spiritual culture on a technological basis is not in sight. Rather, all over the world a new quest for identity and a reflection on one's own tradition is in process. Here I can only repeat briefly (and schematically) how far religion in particular can help to give support to contemporaries and to hold together modern society:

- No universal ethic, but only religion, can communicate a specific depth dimension, a **comprehensive horizon of interpretation** in the face of the positive (success, joy, happiness, and so on) and the negative (suffering, injustice, guilt, innocence, etc.). Only religion can communicate an ultimate meaning in life even for nihilists who are in despair in the face of the inevitability of death. In other words religion, called the depth memory of humankind, gives an answer to the questions of where we have come from and where we are going.
- No ethic in itself, but only religion, can **guarantee unconditionally** values, norms, motivations and ideals and at the same time make them concrete. Ethical directives are unconditional only on the presupposition of an unconditional. A 'pure' human reason can also pro-

vide a basis for values, norms, motivations and ideals. But, like everything human, they remain conditional. They become unconditional only by being tied to an unconditional, the first and last reality. In other words, religion gives an answer to the ultimate question of why we are responsible and what for.

- No universal ethic, but only religion, can create a **home of spiritual security**, trust and hope through shared rites and symbols, through a picture of history and a vision of hope. In other words, religion gives an answer to the question of an ultimate 'spiritual' community and home.
- No universal ethic, but only religion, can mobilize protest and **resistance against unjust conditions**, even when such protest and resistance **seems to be fruitless**, or frustration has already set in. In other words, religion is an expression of a longing, now already effective and unquenchable within this world, for a 'Wholly Other'.

In short, there is a complementary relationship between religion and ethics, and Christians in particular – like all believers in principle – should not play off religion and ethics against each other. Most conviction will be carried by a religion which obligates people to a humane ethic, and an ethic which is open to the dimension of the transcendent, the religious, indeed which is ultimately supported, motivated and made concrete by religion.

3. Confidence-building measures between the religions

The peoples are still waiting for the new world order which has been promised to them so often. While ideal conditions will not prevail in it, there will be less violence and war, less injustice, hunger and need. But as we saw, after the end of the Cold War new violent conflicts and wars have broken out between peoples and ethnic groups, especially among those whose independence has been violently suppressed. And there is no overlooking the fact that in these conflicts **religions are often misused as a means to an end.** For with a reference to religion it is easier to provide a basis for claims, to sharpen oppositions, to vilify opponents and to close one's own ranks in militant fashion. As the Parliament of the World's Religions stated in 1993 in its Declaration toward a Global Ethic: 'Time and again we see leaders and members of **religions** incite aggression, fanaticism, hate, and xenophobia – even inspire and legitimate violent and bloody conflicts. Religion often is misused for purely power-political goals, including war. We are filled with disgust.'[56]

(a) Religion in the network of states

Of course the role of **religions** in the solution of problems in regional, national and international conflicts must be considered realistically; too much must not be expected of them. The religions must always be seen **in connection with all other social factors,** say against the background of the 'hexagon of civilization'[57] proposed by the prominent Bremen peace researcher **Dieter Senghaas,** as a result of his studies on the process of civilization. Ideally this is made up of six components: the deprivatization of violence (monopoly of violence), constitutionality (a constitutional state), interdependences and control of the emotions, democratic participation, social justice, and a culture of constructive political conflict.

Senghaas also wants to project his components, worked out with the individual nation state as an example, on to the international level. On the basis of four fundamental imperatives which have a good deal in common with the four commitments of the Chicago Declaration (protection from violence, protection of freedom, protection against need and protection against chauvinism), he finally concludes: 'If one wants peace in the sense of a civilization of politics and society at home and on the international level, one must prepare for peace: *Si vis pacem, para pacem!*'[58] The religions can make a not unimportant contribution to this programme, which is based on the *para pacem* maxim – in deliberate contrast to the *para bellum* maxim.

But does not this mean the replacement of the individual states by a **global state** and a global government, as is feared, say, by American Republicans, who are hostile to the UNO? By no means. Senghaas himself rightly points out that such an order of global peace can be realized only by means of a 'quasi-confederative arrangement of regions' (in the sense of 'global governance'), and not by a global state.[59] And against the background of the controversy over the homogeneous model of a world state put forward by the 'globalists' on the one hand and that of individual states put forward by the 'communitarians' on the other (following the work 'On Eternal Peace' written by Immanuel Kant as early as 1795), the Tübingen philosopher **Otfried Höffe** represents the middle line already conceived of by Kant. He calls not just (minimally) for a mere league of nations, nor (maximally) for a universal monarchy, but (as a middle solution) for a **global republic.**[60] Höffe therefore rightly rejects the false alternatives 'either a global state or individual states' and instead meaningfully calls for the 'development of a multi-level concept of the state' so as 'to combine full autonomy at home with limited autonomy abroad and in this way to form the notion of a community of individual states or that of a republic of states, organized by those states, or, more precisely, with a republican constitution'.[61] Thus basing himself on Kant, by whose awareness of the problem Thomas Carson and John Rawls were also inspired, Höffe comes to the conclusion: 'Kant's basic thought proves more plausible not only in relation to contemporary political practice, the United Nations which really exists, but also by comparison with political theory.'[62]

That the United Nations which actually exists (Security Council, General Secretary, General Assembly) urgently needs reform and greater efficiency emerges from all the literature, and above all from Chapter V, 'The Reform of the United Nations', of the 1995 report by the UN Commission on Global Governance,[63] to which we shall be returning in another connection. But another question arises here in the specific context of the religions:

(b) How are Islamism and fundamentalism to be dealt with?

Unfortunately people have so far kept in mind not so much what unites them, as **what divides them:**

– **Jews and Christians** have common roots, but Christians remember above all the rejection of their Christ by 'the' Jews, and Jews understandably remember the centuries of persecution by 'the' Christians all over Europe, and above all the mass annihilation of six million Jews in the Holocaust.

– **Jews and Muslims** lived together well for centuries (in Egypt, Spain and Istanbul), but today they remember above all the dispute over one and the same Holy Land (though it began only in our century).

– Like Jews, **Christians and Muslims** understand themselves as all being children of Abraham (and followers of the 'religion of the Book'), and have much in common in their faiths. But to the present day they remember above all their **five great confrontations:**

The first in the seventh century: the East Roman Christian empire loses the ancestral Christian lands of Palestine, Syria and Egypt through the Islamic conquest;

The second in the eighth century: Islam now also conquers all North Africa and Spain;

The third in the twelfth and thirteenth centuries: the Christian counter-offensive of the Crusades temporarily brings the Holy Land and Jerusalem back under Christian control; there is the Christian *Reconquista* of Spain up to 1492 (the capture of Granada);

The fourth in the fifteenth and sixteenth centuries: the Muslim Turks capture Constantinople (1453) and the Balkans, so that since then there have been peoples here who have been converted to Islam (above all Bosnians);

The fifth in the nineteenth and twentieth centuries: the advance of the Christian European colonial powers which finally comes to dominate Muslim North and East Africa, the Middle and Far East as far as Persia and India, Indonesia and Malaysia. This is a trauma which has left the Muslims restless down to the present day.[64]

In the face of these centuries of controversy we may ask: who would be the greatest statesman, the greatest sage of our time? The one who could make **peace between Jews, Christians and Muslims**, and especially peace between Arabs and Jews, Israelis and Palestinians! Or is such a peace to remain an illusion for ever? In the Balkans there has again been murder, cleansing, rape, burning and destruction; in the Middle East the extremists on both sides have once more gained influence and there is constant shooting and bombing. Must it come to a sixth Israeli-Arab war? Even in Israel, many people are asking: if it was possible to achieve peace between Catholics and Protestants after all the wars, hot and cold, why should not peace also be possible in our time between Jews, Muslims and Christians? And if it was possible to make peace between the two 'ancestral arch-enemies', France and Germany, why should peace between Israelis and Arabs be ruled out?

But – I hear the objection – precisely how is one to deal with Muslim fundamentalism or **Islamism**, which has already been addressed in this book?

– **Islam** is by no means radically fundamentalist. In Islam, too, there are reformers, also including moderate fundamentalists, who do not reject modernization, but total secularization.

– **Christianity** for its part is by no means completely tolerant. There is also fundamentalism in Christianity, of Protestant biblical and Roman Catholic provenance (the Vatican 're-evangelization'). There is also fundamentalism in Judaism (inside and outside Israel).

– Fundamentalism has not only religious but also **economic, political and social roots**. It identifies defects in an often individualistic and libertine modernity which should be taken seriously, even if one rejects the solutions of the fundamentalists.

– Modernization has led to a Westernization and secularization in the Islamic states which has resulted in an **identity crisis** and caused **insecurity** for countless people. These are again looking for points of orientation, values and models, and think that they can find them in their own religion.

– Fundamentalism as a religious phenomenon cannot be conquered in a frontal offensive. It must certainly be approached with a clear democratic and tolerant attitude, but attempts must be made to overcome it with **understanding and empathy,** and this includes above all removing the conditions which have allowed it to arise.

– **Better than** political **polarization,** as in Algeria (where the Islamist victors in the election were suppressed by force), is institutional **integration,** as in Turkey (where the Islamist victors at the election were given the opportunity to form a government).

So **what is to be done** in the face of the fundamentalism in all religions? The fundamentalists should be reminded of the roots of freedom, pluralism, openness to others in their own tradition: in the Hebrew Bible and in the Talmud, in the New Testament and in church tradition, in the Qur'an and the Sunna. Conversely, the **liberalists** should not close themselves to self-criticism: in the face of so much cowardly adaptation to the spirit of the time which cannot say no; in the face of all lack of religious substance, theological depth and ethical commitment in modern liberal religion, which knows no bounds to its tolerance.

But over and above that, here are some positive statements about what the concerns of the religions can be:

* A new overall vision and a new **basic spiritual orientation** which gives identity and security should be striven for and lived out credibly, particularly by all those who are not content with Roman Catholic authoritarianism, Protestant biblicism, Orthodox traditionalism or reactionary trends of Jewish or Muslim origin.
* Despite all difficulties and conflicts, a **dialogue** should be sought with the fundamentalists, and **collaboration** in both the political and social and also the religious and theological spheres should be aimed at.
* However, where fundamentalism is allied with political, military or police power (in some Islamic states, or in the Rushdie case), or even with spiritual power (the Vatican against theologians, women,

bishops), resolute **resistance** to it should be offered (see, for example, the Cologne declaration by 163 professors of theology and the church referendum among millions of Catholics against the authoritarian course adopted by the Vatican – but so far not taken seriously by the intimidated conformist bishops, to the detriment of their own credibility).

Thus in this turbulent transitional period, full of new antagonisms, both ethnic and religious, it is to be hoped that the great religions will find the **way between a modernism without a foundation and a fundamentalism without modernity**, without self-criticism, tolerance and a readiness for dialogue. A way is needed between permissiveness and exclusiveness, between laxity and aggressiveness, which will constantly have to be sought afresh, especially in conflicts.

(c) *What is to be done in regional, national and international conflicts?*

Despite all the failures, religions can make a decisive **contribution to peace,** if they perceive and utilize all the potential for peace that lies within them. There are fundamental motivations in each of the great religions to contribute not only towards personal inner peace but also towards the overcoming of aggression and violence in society. Thus, I repeat, they could blunt hostile conflicts and help to avoid or shorten wars. But peace between the religions and nations is possible only if there is a **basis of trust** between them. However, this does not exist *a priori*. Usually it has to be built up laboriously in the face of prejudices and resistance. Bridges of trust need to be built here, over abysses of ignorance, intolerance and misunderstanding, indeed often over hatred and violence. But precisely what must be done?

This question is not easy to answer, and it is high time to reflect on what today could be **confidence-building measures between the religions.** So here I shall point to practical ways in which the misuse of religions to sharpen conflicts can be opposed. Only in this way can religions contribute towards solving problems instead of themselves being or becoming part of the problem. Here of course I am addressing in particular the **representatives and leaders of the religions.** Taking further the Chicago Declaration toward a Global Ethic one could think of the following measures in conflict situations. Here organizations like the World Conference of the Religions for Peace (WCRP) can also play an important function. All this can only be sketched out schematically here. One could easily write a whole book about it.[65]

(1) History and the present teach us that the **religions** can easily be **misused** to confirm power-political interests and to dramatize hostile stereotypes. Religious justification is said to relieve the conscience in cases of torture, exile, destruction and death. Religions become irreconcilable when they **exaggerate the differences and keep silent about what is held in common.** In this way conflicts can become total, to the point of collective self-destruction.

What can the religions do against this? They should reflect on what they have in common despite all the differences, and what is central to the Golden Rule: What you do not wish done to yourself, do not do to others. In addition there is the power of their spiritual tradition (prayer, meditation), which enables them to become peacemaking communities. Thus they can and should contribute to the **blunting and resolution of conflicts;** they publicly deny themselves when conflicts are exaggerated by religion and intensified by the motive power of religion. Misused religions damage humankind and finally also the religions themselves. The task of the religions is to sharpen the conscience against all politically ideological fanaticism.

(2) Conflicts are often also **foisted on the innocent,** when **streams of refugees** are created in order to destablize the other side, when cities are besieged and starved out, when whole groups of people are taken hostage, areas are rendered uninhabitable and water is made unusable. Sometimes even women and children are deliberately targeted in order to destroy the 'resistance' of the enemy psychologically.

And the religions? They must help to prevent **crimes against humanity and the environment** being committed – as often happens – by members of their own faith with an appeal to religion. They must reinstate their tradition of respect for human dignity and solidarity with all that lives and exists.

(3) **Efforts for peace** are often **undermined** by those who know only the language of violence and therefore incite and perpetuate conflicts with deliberate harassment.

And the religions? They should tenaciously see that **attempts at mediation** are first of all met with a cease-fire, so that **offers of negotiation** can be evaluated calmly and unwillingness for peace can be exposed. They should be ready for reconciliation and prepared time and again to take the first step.

(4) Religious intolerance (like xenophobia, racism and antisemitism)

has not been banished from our societies, despite all the damage that has been done. But anyone who wants to live only among those who are like-minded in religion loses the opportunity to receive enrichment from other religions and to decide self-critically for his or her own tradition, No one who after critical examination is certain of his or her religious heritage must feel **endangered by other trends of faith**. Religions are respected in proportion to the degree of their tolerance and the degree to which they do not sacrifice people to their alleged interests. Anxiety about contact between religions and cultures comes into being not only through **too much** contact but also through **too little**.

So what should the religions do? In particular their representatives and leaders should courageously contradict all who claim to have served their own religion by **ethnic and cultural cleansings**. They should resolutely resist violent cleansings of whole cities and regions. And they should create possibilities for encounter, so that religious multiplicity is not experienced as a threat but as an enrichment.

(5) **Hostile stereotypes** produce enemies and portray the other side as being incapable of peace. This prolongs militant phases.

And the religions? A prime task at this time must be **making peace with one another**. That must be done with every means available today, including the media, and at every level:
– clearing up misunderstandings,
– working through traumatic memories,
– dissolving hostile stereotypes,
– working through guilt complexes, both socially and individually,
– demolishing hatred and destructiveness,
– reflecting on things that are held in common,
– taking concrete initiatives for reconciliation.

Particularly in current conflicts they should persistently ensure that the other side gets **a chance to present itself,** so as to be able to describe the conflict and its resolution from its own perspective.

(6) The **Geneva conventions** may not speak the language of the religions, but they represent the minimum for a **humanization of conflicts**. The rules of humanitarian international law must also be binding on the religions.

And the religions? They have the duty to identify **offences against international law,** even when these come from their own ranks, indeed particularly then.

(7) Attempts are made with money, development aid, power or force to compel people to **change their faith**. But a faith that is not free or has been bought is incompatible with the dignity of human beings and religions.

And the religions? They should oppose such practices and fight against them, especially in their own sphere. The test for religious freedom is the **freedom of others!**

The final conclusion relates to **human rights:**

The religions should not just endorse the Universal Declaration of Human Rights, the implementation of which is often desired more by the ruled than by the rulers. They should provide a basis for it from their own traditions, make it concrete in terms of today's situation and realize it in their own sphere. But at the same time they should give ethical stimuli to humanity beyond the legal level, prompt a perception of **human obligations,** and thus contribute to a universal ethic of humankind. The religions should help to put the following elementary demands into practice.

– The religions should help people in today's pluralistic society to arrive at their own considered **standpoint** and at the same time to practise **tolerance** towards those who think otherwise:

– They should encourage people to be capable and ready to overcome **egoism,** to put forward their own justified claims in a non-violent way, to meet and withstand social confrontations without aggression, and to arouse a sense of **solidarity.** There should be a well-considered use of one's own freedom along with a commitment to fellow human beings.

– The free **practice of all religions** should be guaranteed and made possible. Where adherents of a religion who enjoy freedom of religion in their host country know that this does not happen in the same way in their homeland they should resolutely stand up for equal treatment, instead of one-sidedly only calling for new rights in their host country.

– They should persistently make public objections to **professional discrimination** against religious minorities at home and abroad.

– Dialogue must be sought with the **religious minorities,** simply in order to prevent them from becoming alien islands in an environment which reacts mistrustfully.

– Any kind of **xenophobia** must be opposed as if we were the victims of it; we should **cultivate interest** in the new and good things which other religions have to offer and which could enhance our own culture.

– **Initiatives and publications** should be **promoted** which help people to learn to see themselves through the eyes of others.

– Faith communities should regard it as a primary **educational task** to train their members in the motivations of their faith which further peace, and to enable them to engage in an open encounter with those of another faith: in preparing guidelines, in the development of school books, in concrete co-operation in education, in adult education and in the training of those responsible for teaching.

However, here religious people, and not least Christians, will ask how in such a multi-religious situation it is possible to combine a firm grounding in their own faith with great openness to other religions. And so, having answered the question of 'steadfastness and capacity for dialogue' in principle for all religions in my *Global Responsibility*,[66] here I would like to attempt to answer it specifically for Christians, and in a more theological style.

(d) A personal postscript by a Christian for Christians

In view of the multi-religious situation which I have described, can one still be confident of the Christian cause at all? Confronted with the third millennium, must one not despair of Christianity? Has not Christianity lost plausibility and credibility, at least in the European countries? In six steps I shall attempt to formulate a personal answer which has been worked out laboriously enough in my long life as a theologian:

(1) There is no disputing the fact that more than ever there are **trends away from Christianity**, towards the Eastern religions, towards political and experiential groups of all kinds, or even into the convenient private sphere without any obligations, within the framework of the 'experience society' which seeks ever new experiences, from television through sport to holidays, and finds these least of all in religion. Many people in our still 'Christian' countries associate Christianity – unfortunately with good reason – with an official church which is blind and greedy for power, with authoritarianism and doctrinal dictatorship, with promoting anxiety, sexual complexes and discrimination against women, with repression and refusal to engage in dialogue, and a scornful way of dealing with those who think differently and with opponents. It is depressing: millions have left the church, millions have withdrawn into themselves, and millions – particularly in the new German federal states – have not joined the church. The hierarchs responsible, sometimes confused, sometimes mendacious, prevaricate: it's not so bad. But isn't the **light of Christianity** slowly being **quenched**?

Since all down the years I have warned against this pernicious development as an inconvenient prophet and have suffered punishment for it, I cannot conceal the fact that particularly in the face of the blindness of the Catholic hierarchy in Rome and elsewhere, in the media of some countries, what was once a more or less benevolent indifference to Christianity has turned into aggression, spitefulness and open hostility.

(2) At the same time a great many people, not only in this church, are asking themselves very seriously: where can we find spiritual support in the confusions of our time? What can we really rely on? And many people outside, who can no longer cope with being members of the church, do not simply want to give up Christianity. They want to know what 'Christianity' really means, could mean. They want encouragement: **courage to be a Christian even today.**

The answer to this question can be found in an age-old saying in the Gospels: in the face of all the darkness of the world and the church, Jesus **Christ** stands **as the light of the world'**,[67] 'the light of men',[68] as 'our light': 'The light (of life) shines in the darkness and the darkness has not overcome it.'[69] A myth? Not if one consults serious books rather than trivial and sensational literature. Here is a quite tangible historical figure, but one who stands for more than just 'history'. In company with many others I openly concede that during the long decades of my life as a theologian I personally would hardly have survived so long in the face of so much darkness in the world and the church without this light, which in my fragile humanity has always been for me 'the way, the truth and the life'.[70] Moreover I still stand utterly and completely by what I wrote in *On Being a Christian* more than two decades ago, despite the 'official' defamatory remarks about my Christian faith.[71]

Indeed, one does not have to lapse into a black-and-white dualism or venerate a cheap Qumran-style light-and-darkness simplicity ('children of light' against the 'children of darkness'), to be able to see this Christ, the light for Christians, as still the great hope. This hope also allows us unpretentiously and without self-righteousness to seek the way of discipleship. For because of it I know that one may not tell the history of Christianity, too, simply as a history of knaves and criminals, as a 'criminal history', as is happening today in an increasingly boring series of books. It must be told as it is: as a chiaroscuro history in which the **essence of Christianity** keeps breaking through, despite all the perversions. And this essence of Christianity is not something abstract, general and theoretical. The essence of Christianity has always been this living **historical figure** who for millions of people all over the world has been the orientation, criterion and model for life – for their relations with their fellow men and women, with human society, and finally with God himself: Jesus Christ.

(3) This name has also given hope to countless people on all the continents in modern times, people whose names are not listed in any

church history. They form the faith movement of the countless unknown women and men down the centuries who have orientated themselves on the man from Nazareth, not so much in church history as in the history of Christians. They have learned from this one man that those are blessed who are poor before God, who do not use violence, who hunger and thirst for righteousness, who are merciful, make peace and are persecuted for righteousness' sake. From Christ they have learned what is so lacking in this competitive society of egotists: to notice and to share, to be able to forgive and to repent, to practise mercy and renunciation, and to give help.

Down to the present day it depends on Christians whether Christianity can offer a **spiritual home**, a house of faith, hope and love, truly living by its Christ and allowing itself to be given light, radiance, the Spirit by him. Such Christians constantly show that high ideals can also be lived out in everyday life. Indeed, they show that from the depths of their belief in Christ, suffering and guilt, despair and anxiety, can indeed be overcome. This trusting faith in Christ, who is the light of light, is no mere consolation in a world to come, but a basis for commitment, protest and resistance against unjust conditions here and today, supported and strengthened by hope in God's kingdom.

(4) Many people are now asking whether this Christ is not enough, if he is 'the light of the world', 'our light', if he is 'the way, the truth and the life'. What else do we need? *Solus Christus*! Christ alone is enough – everything else is useless, valueless, uninteresting for faith. Some Protestant theologians have sometimes gone to such an extreme, among them one of the greatest, **Karl Barth**, Think of the grandiose things he wrote in Volume IV/3 of his monumental *Church Dogmatics* on Christ **as the one light, alongside which** there can be **no other lights.** This needs to be taken seriously by all Christians.

But in the course of his long life even Karl Barth had to realize that this exclusivity does not correspond to God's purpose with human beings. Christian exclusivity leads to intolerance. And intolerance is un-Christian, because it goes against the spirit of Jesus Christ. Therefore Karl Barth himself finally quite openly conceded in the last completed volume of his *Dogmatics* that there are also **other lights alongside the one light:** yet other words alongside the one Word of God, yet other truths alongside the one truth of God. So Jesus Christ is not shut up either between the covers of the Bible or within the walls of the church, because as the God of all men and women, God is also active outside the church walls.

(5) In fact it cannot be disputed that according to the Hebrew Bible

and the New Testament, **non-Jews and non-Christians also know the real God**: God is also near to them. And even if for Christians Jesus Christ as the light is the decisive criterion for all talk of God, we cannot avoid seeing that:

– For hundreds of millions of people on this earth in the past and the present Gautama is the '**Buddha**', the 'Enlightened One', and thus the great 'light'.

– For hundreds of millions of Muslims in the past and the present the **Qur'an** is the 'light' which lightens their way, and it has been the Prophet Muhammad, enlightened by the one God, who personally embodies this message of the Qur'an in a convincing way.

I could go on like this and demonstrate that the same is true for all the great world religions.[72] So for Christians the question arises: what is the relation between Jesus Christ as 'our light' and the many other 'lights' which are recognized by other people? Can one reconcile the 'one light' with the other lights? The answer is: Yes, because this compatibility corresponds to the spirit of Jesus Christ. For if we answer this question as Christians, we must look to the Jew **Jesus of Nazareth**, to the particular way in which he behaved, to his orientations in the disputed questions. Jesus of Nazareth did not meditate and philosophize on the religions of the world of his time; he showed no scholarly knowledge of the religions. Rather, he **treated those of another faith** in another way: **he respected them as human beings and left them their dignity**. Indeed, in specific individual examples he showed how one should treat those of another faith. The one who was born of a Hebrew mother was delighted at the faith of a Syro-Phoenician woman and a Roman officer, gave a friendly welcome to the Greeks who sought him, and provoked his Jewish fellow-countrymen by presenting the Samaritan heretic as an unforgettable example of love of neighbour.

So it is crucial that Christians should keep asking themselves the question which for me personally constantly was, and is, the key question (very much on the model of Dostoievsky's 'Grand Inquisitor'). If He returned, what attitude would He adopt to the present world situation? What illumination would He give us? For me there is no doubt about one thing: today He would impress on us the importance of meeting those of other religions, and in these encounters **rediscovering Christian responsibility for the world**.

(6) But in these circumstances is **mission still possible**? That is a question which some committed Christians will ask. Here are some brief indications of my answer:

– Instead of seeing mission ('mission work') as spiritual conquest, we would do better to understand it as **testimony** ('witness work'), and of course that must also be allowed to other religions.

– Instead of being given through the word, it would be better if this testimony were once again (as in the time of early Christianity) given by actions.

– Instead of being given from outside, from abroad, this testimony, for example in India and China, is possible only from within, from the existing communities.

– Instead of through colonialist occupation, this can happen only by understanding inculturation.

– Instead of being given by specialists, it must be given by the whole missionary people of God.

– Instead of being given though confrontation, it must be given through dialogue.

– Instead of being given through various confessions, it must be given through shared ecumenical testimony.

– Instead of being given through increasingly ecclesiastical institutionalization, it must be given through a strengthened solidarity with others and an orientation on a common future.

The **conclusion** to be drawn from all this is that today we all face the tremendous ecumenical challenges of the third millennium. In the present century we have been able to make decisive ecumenical progress within Christianity (unfortunately the lifting of excommunications has not yet been achieved, nor has it yet been possible to achieve eucharistic intercommunion, but it is to be hoped that both will be realized under a new pontificate). Once again we must face the challenges of the interreligious ecumene. In a global society Christians are invited to take shared responsibility with those of other faiths for peace, justice, the preservation of creation and a **renewed ethic**. The fate of the earth is the concern of all human beings, regardless of the religion or world-view to which they adhere.

B. The Global Economy between the Welfare State and Neocapitalism

I

Questions about Globalization

Globalization is the great hope for some and the great terror for others. The fact is that the world economy is in an upheaval: it is growing together and forming a network. Even China and the former Soviet bloc have opened up; the ASEAN states are showing a tremendous economic dynamic which is rapidly also spreading to China. All over the world giant new markets are forming, with offers of goods and labour and possibilities of communication, but at the same time competition is hardening world-wide and there is growing unemployment in the industrial nations. There is no question that **the epoch-making paradigm shift** which has **also** been evident **in the economy** since the First World War and the rise of the new economic great powers, the USA and the USSR, away from a Eurocentric to a **polycentric world economy**, has achieved its **definitive breakthrough** after the collapse of the Soviet block and the globalization processes of the 1990s.

But what will happen when the world economy – not only its flow of capital, but also its labour market – really functions without national frontiers, really becomes global? In the unrestricted competition between companies, regions and centres, who will be the winners and who the losers? Will this not be an 'economized', and thus possibly an unfriendly, undemocratic, indeed inhuman world, into which globalization will catapult us almost overnight in order to achieve higher productivity and profitability?

Here, too, it should be said in advance that of course as an ethicist and a theologian I cannot play the 'arbiter' or teach the economists economics. I do not aim to say anything new to the professionals, but once again to draw their attention to the ethical dimension of the world economy. Nor do I want to moralize as an outsider, but to spell out the problems from within, so as to reinforce those tendencies in the discussion among professionals which go in the direction of new ethical reflection. Infinitely many details must be left out of account here; my concern is with the basic outlines. But I hope that these outlines have an immanent and coherent harmony, so that they also convince economists and, above all, politicians that ethics and the economy cannot be separated.

Moreover it is quite crucial for readers with a background in theology or the church to be introduced to this complex of problems. Theologians are often ignorant about economics, and this ignorance sometimes leads to enthusiastic or naive demands being made of 'the economy'. Here it is important for a theologian to make clear especially to 'his clientele' that one can act with ethical responsibility only by taking the complex economic problems into account. In this way the demand for a global ethic should avoid any artificiality: to some degree it should become clear in terms of its own relevant rationality. So we must guard against apocalyptic scenarios and begin in a matter-of-fact way. What does globalization actually mean?

1. Globalization – a structural revolution in the world economy

According to an OECD definition, the globalization of the economy is that process through which markets and production in different countries become increasingly dependent on one another, because of the dynamic of trade in goods and services, and the movement in capital and technology. Thus the globalization of the **economy** is accompanied by a globalization of **technology**, above all information technology. But our question is: how are we to assess this process of the constantly increasing economic and technological integration of our globe, which is both far-reaching and rapid, not from the economic perspectives of marketing strategies, trade union positions or national interests, but from the perspective of the whole of society, and finally from an **ethical perspective?** I shall attempt step by step to clarify the state of the discussion; here again a certain eclecticism cannot be avoided.

(a) Globalization is unavoidable

Globalization is not a conspiracy of the Americans, the Japanese or some dark powers, but **a result of the technological and economic development of modern Europe.** As a result of the discovery of new ways of trading in the sixteenth century, an international division of labour had already begun with industrialization in the eighteenth century. But as is clear to all the world, the globalization of the economy and trade began in nineteenth-century Europe: on the one hand through the liberalization of foreign trade on the most-favoured nation principle (the British–French Cobden Treaty of 1860), and the gold standard (making possible uniform rules for monetary and financial policy), and on the other hand through the tremendous acceleration in transport with steamships, railways and telegraphs. After a transitional phase of nation-state isolationism following the First World War, globalization ecame firmly established in the world economic system, which was now expanding polycentrically, with air transport, the telephone and the modern financial system. After an interruption by the Second World War it is reaching its almost giddy climax immediately before the turn of the millennium.

Why are people today even speaking of a **structural revolution** in the world economy? The fax, satellite communication, the flow of global data, the WorldWideWeb and the electronic world stock exchanges, along with the immense reduction in the cost of the transport of information, goods and people, show that the transition from the **national economy** to the **global economy** has taken on an unprecedently **hectic tempo** as a result of the worldwide network of economic and technological processes. Market and production, capital and technology, know fewer and fewer boundaries. Not only trade but also companies and their products are becoming increasingly global, and unprecedented competition is achieved in a flash with good offers on the Internet. This contributes to the transparency, intensive competition and therefore turbulence in the markets.

It would be **vain** to attempt to **stop** or even reverse this revolutionary transformation. No new isolationism in the United States, no opposition to a free trade zone in Mexico, no aversion to capitalism in the former Soviet Union, no totalitarian party ideology in China, and no socialist nostalgia in Europe, will make it possible for a nation simply to disengage from this process of globalization, and resume its own course without liberalizing financial markets and abolishing duties. A state which does not join in here will *a priori* be degrading itself to the level of a third-class economic power.

Globalization is felt to be a great new challenge, especially in Europe and North America, where people suddenly see themselves compelled to defend their market positions because of new competition. Globalization therefore involves an internal structural change in the industrial nations, but abroad at the same time **a new economic and political distribution of power throughout our globe,** in which there are no guaranteed rights of possession for any national economy. The developing countries, and especially the industrial threshold countries, also want globalization, so that they themselves can reach the same state of development as the developed nations. And after Japan the Asian 'four tigers' (South Korea, Hong Kong, Taiwan and Singapore) and increasingly also China, indeed almost all the other states in this region of the world, are showing us that because of this development at the beginning of the new millennium, we shall presumably have to reckon with three, to some degree equally important, economic spheres (though internally they will be highly unequal): Europe, North America and East Asia. Possibly South Asia (India), Latin America and Eastern Europe will again grow stronger; in the shade of these economic spheres, Africa remains the great problem continent. But this development of the continents, which in some respects is already very different, indicates that:

(b) Globalization is ambivalent

All of us in the industrial countries enjoy every day the fruits of the globalization of technology: goods, services and capital. Moreover, so much, from faxes to flying, has become cheaper in the course of this development and therefore more affordable to enormous masses of people, and also faster. Human beings can circle the globe within a day, and satellites circle it almost hourly.

It is not just the industrial nations, but also the developing countries, especially the threshold countries, which have completely **new opportunities**. They come on to the world market as suppliers of cheap goods (with often well-trained labour forces) and endanger the old suppliers, among whom jobs are lost. South–East Asia has been able to increase its share in world exports over two decades from 4% to 12%, China by 11% in 1995 alone. Ten years ago the developing countries were earning 34% of the Gross World Product; now it is already 40%.

So should not a **global economy** without frontiers be an advance on the restricted national limited economy, just as formerly the national economy was an advance on the local economy? And should not a transnational, **global knowledge** which draws on persons, equipment and finance from several countries be able to function more cheaply, effectively and meaningfully, for example in major projects in the natural and biological sciences, from space technology to gene research? Should not an international network of **global information**, which makes news and pictures available everywhere on earth almost contemporaneously, be able to help the world-wide democratic movement? Dictators, at any rate, find it increasingly difficult to cut their peoples off from the outside world. The revolutionary economic structural change can no longer be overlooked. Not only labour and production but also science and the media are increasingly detaching themselves from national bases. This new freedom and liberality is creating completely new possibilities, but also completely new difficulties – especially for a previously national economic, social and environmental policy.

For even enthusiastic adherents and advocates of globalization, economists and leading businessmen, can hardly fail to note not only all the positive consequences but also numerous **negative consequences** for employment and the living standard in many of the countries affected, which today are disturbing many people. Here are just a few comments:
– The global networking of the world affects only **certain spheres of life** and not others.
– Though of course it may represent an opportunity for under-developed countries which is not to be scorned, in many cases the exploitation of cheap **labour** in these states has not as yet shown any lasting developmental effect, because of the lack of an accompanying economic policy. Certainly new jobs are created in the export sector, but often so many are lost in traditional sectors that the balance of jobs is disputed among experts.
– The industrialized and politically controlled **agricultural export** policy, say, of the EC, can be helpful, but unfortunately it often destroys the traditional agricultural economy of the developing countries which is focussed on self-sufficiency. There the new investments by the industrial countries have resulted in more consumer goods, but often also in the ruin of local manufacturers.
– The new **financial global players** sometimes seem more influential than the national governments: currency speculators (traders or investors with short-term interests) want to be rational players, and at the same time function as the great egotists, and as the mainstay of the financial market. But their actions are 'controlled' almost by the market itself, and they share the responsibility for dangerous 'stock market jitters' and turbulences in currencies which even national banks as guardians of the international currency system find difficult to cope with. (In 1992 they made a substantial contribution to the departure of the British currency from the European Monetary System, even though it was over-valued.)
– The '**downsizing**' of companies and the '**outsourcing**' of jobs to countries with cheap wages, which is often caused by the relationship between the tariff and the social policies of states, and is accelerated by

the process of globalization, has resulted in the loss of umpteen thousand jobs from the domestic labour force which cannot be taken up by more highly productive enterprises. Of the one billion people worldwide who are unemployed or under-employed (the 1996/1997 labour market report by the International Labour Organization) many millions are in the industrial countries – over four million in Germany alone.

– **Companies active globally** are increasingly avoiding the control of nation states, above all if a policy hostile to industry or disproportionately high taxes are to be expected. Thus they pay increasingly less tax in their European homeland, and along with other factors contribute to the endangering of the social security system, of which in any case too much is being asked. (Although, for example, in 1995 the Deutsche Bank had the second-best result in its history with a profit of 4.2 billion DM, it paid 377 million DM less tax than in the previous year; because of skilful calculations, in 1995 the giant concern Siemens quite legally paid no tax at all in Germany.)

– In some areas the globalization of the economy and technology almost necessarily brings with it **a global extension of ecological problems**: increasing damage to nature, from the pollution of the seas and rivers to the poisoning and warming of the atmosphere, and to the gap in the ozone layer.

– Finally, economic and technological globalization has also resulted in a **globalization of organized crime** (the Mafia).

In view of the ambivalent consequences of this globalization of the economy, technology and ecology, it is not surprising that the **prognoses** and **evaluations** differ widely. Here by way of example are two well-documented analyses which are very different in tendency, method and rhetoric:

– On the one hand there is a study by leading Swiss businessmen and economics professors who recognize 'a **unique opportunity** in the hectic structural change in the world economy': 'New markets are coming into being with a great dynamic of growth. But these opportunities cannot be exploited with a policy of preserving and defending previous positions. There is a need for a radical rethink in business and politics to face the challenge of world-wide competition. There is a need for a change of mentality, and in particular for increased competitiveness, if we are not to experience a drastic decline in prosperity.'[1] Consequently, already in the title the more optimistic 'economic and political agenda' recommends 'Courage for New Departures'.

– On the other hand there is a provocative journalistic book by two editors of *Der Spiegel*, Hans-Peter Martin and Harald Schumann, which with the title 'The Trend Towards Globalization' seeks to draw attention to the '**attack on democracy and prosperity**' which has been launched by globalization. Economists will shake their heads over the lack of precise economic analyses and theoretical syntheses when they read passages like this in the somewhat pessimistic book: 'In economic terms the integration of the world market is highly efficient. But in distributing the wealth which is produced in this way the global economic machine is anything but efficient because there is no state intervention, and the number of losers far exceeds the number of winners. Precisely for this reason the policy of global integration practised so far has no future. The free trade all over the world cannot be maintained without being safeguarded by the welfare state.'[2] The danger is said to be likely to come above all from the anarchical development of the transnational financial markets: 'Another world-wide crash on the stock exchanges is on the cards; those who play billiards on the electronically networked market-place of world finance know that better than anyone else.'[3]

It is not surprising that the response to such publications differs widely, depending on the standpoint of the parties concerned. The study by the leading Swiss businessmen and economics professors, who represent the interests of big businesses with their international orientation, has been vigorously criticized for its neo-liberal prejudice and its lack of social balance. The book by the *Spiegel* journalists, which for the highly-respected environmental expert Ernst Ulrich von Weizsäcker was 'perhaps the most important book of the year',[4] seemed to the long-serving President of the Confederation of German Industry 'interesting and sometimes as attractively written as a pamphlet', but more like the 'proclamation of a Counter-Reformation'.[5]

However, there may be a consensus on one thing: globalization has advantages and disadvantages. And it seems to me that we simply cannot see which will dominate in the future.[6] Hence a third consideration.

(c) Globalization is unpredictable

We may be overloaded with statistics and economic predictions, but what globalization may bring not only in **intended main effects** but also in **unintended side effects** cannot be predicted exactly today. The longer-term the prognosis, the riskier it is. As 'conditional forecasts', long-term economic prognoses are doubtless 'more precise' than longer-term conditional weather forecasts (if economists will forgive me the bold comparison), but they depend entirely on the stability of the social conditions which are their frameworks, and the overall political situation. The economists tell us that the economy is an open process: business activity is the result of constant human action and not of a single human plan.

So we can hardly exclude completely the possibility that '**chaos theory**' has something to tell the economists, as it does the meteorologists: small disturbances of the system, hardly noted at first, can in time lead to dramatic changes. One example is the dramatic financial crisis in Mexico in January 1995, completely unexpected except to critical observers of world currency policy. This could easily have led to a crisis of the whole world financial system; only through international credits amounting to more than $50 billion could it be coped with at the last moment. But the stock-market augurs know that the next financial crisis will certainly come, and it is by no means certain that it can be coped with so easily. At any rate, the forecasters are working more than ever with many 'if-then's and now are abandoning most of the econometric models which were so popular in the 1960s and 1970s. However, in practice 'conditional forecasts' (relating to limited context) are of only limited help.

This damps down exaggerated optimism over the globalization of the economy: it will certainly go on, but **unforeseeable political and economic developments** could completely throw overboard all the expectations which are thought to be plausible. Even before the intensified globalization, for example the oil shock in 1973 had made all the economic extrapolations, calculated with an infinitely great amount of statistical material, so much waste paper. No economist today dares to predict with certainty which countries and branches of the economy will be successful in the long run and which will not, which companies will survive in the long term and which will not. Nor does any economist dare even to make longer-term forecasts about the dollar, let alone the world currency: not to mention the Euro, the economic and political risk of the century, which is not being discussed at all thoroughly. For those economists with a mathematical turn of mind: on 29 December 1989 the Japanese Nikkei index was at a record height of 38,915.87. At that time all the world reckoned it would go on rising. Seven years later, on 10 January 1997, it stood at 17,303.65, only 44.46% of its peak, and many fear yet a further fall. All in all this is a dramatic loss in national wealth, dangerous to the Japanese banking system, to the economy as a whole and also to the government.[7] Hardly anyone today is saying that the Dow or the Dax are excessively high; rather, analysts are giving us reasons why the Dow and Dax can rise still higher in 1997. But can the opposite be ruled out?

Of course individual events in the process of globalization can be calculated; nevertheless the overall development cannot be forecasted. 'In a comparatively small sector like welfare contributions, many developments are possible, indeed almost probable, despite qualifications,' comments one of the most knowledgeable and experienced economists in Germany, Professor Norbert Kloten of Tübingen, 'but the mass of conceivable developments in a national economy or even the world economy can no longer be surveyed and certainly cannot be forecast.'[8]

So what are we to make of projections which on the basis of globalization even announce an economic boom for the next thirty years, and forecast that in the year 2025, between two and three billion people in the Third World will have made the transition from poverty to the level of the middle class? Are we to believe those **optimists** who already see international economic superhighways on the horizon, which are to integrate the national economies into global economies in a hitherto unprecedented way? Or are we to believe the **pessimists,** who in addition to the possibility of the nuclear pollution of great areas or other ecological catastrophes also think a new crash in the world financial system ('Black Friday') possible, and who doubt whether this process of globalization will really improve the destiny of humankind when so much unemployment and personal and family misfortune are already tied up with it? And who has the certainty that in the industrial countries the trends towards free trade, a reduction in state budget deficits, the deregulation of the markets, harmony between the former enemies in the Cold War and collaboration with the rising powers of Asia – all presuppositions for a moderate optimism – will last?

Such fundamental uncertainties mean that we will do well not simply to leave the whole process of globalization to itself. For:

(d) Globalization can be controlled

Globalization is **not a natural phenomenon** like an approaching weather front, in the face of which one is powerless. And since even the 'invisible hand of divine providence' never ruled out human failure, we can look with scepticism upon the still-widespread economic dogma of the 'invisible hand of competition' which is supposed to rule out world economic crises. Self-critical economists at any rate will agree that the market can fail as a regulatory instrument, so there is a need for politics and the order that it brings.

Certainly, national governments, national banks and economic communities like the European Community still have considerable room for manoeuvre. But, if even the best-known international currency speculator, George Soros,[9] is now calling urgently for **international market regulations** 'against excessive speculation' which moves hundreds of billions of dollars a day to and fro, then economists, too, ought to make more practical proposals about the direction and control of markets, which are 'possessed with greed and anxiety' and therefore do not react rationally, but 'emotionally'. 'Whenever the politicians and heads of banks concerned have worked together, they have been able to impose their will on the market.' But hitherto regulations have always come into being only 'after collapses'. Or is it really inconceivable that the globalized world financial system, after record index level upon record index level, could collapse in a chain reaction because of a natural catastrophe or a political earthquake?

Be this as it may: should the supreme criterion in the present process of globalization prove to be the maximization of profit, and should that alone prevail, we must be prepared for **serious social conflicts and crises.** The present strength of capital and the weakness of the trade unions should not mislead us here. For we **cannot** assume that society as a whole would accept a lapse into nineteenth-century liberalism and **pure capitalism without putting up any resistance.** It is well known that economic tensions can cause social tensions, and these in turn cause social conflicts. We might recall that American society reacted in this way at the beginning of the present century under President Theodore Roosevelt: public control of big-business interests, state regulation, anti-trust laws and labour legislation (the 'square deal'); and again after the Wall Street crash of 1929 and the subsequent Great Depression, under President Franklin D.Roosevelt, against '*laissez-faire*' by the construction of the welfare state (the 'new deal'). Thus in our day, too, a one-sided demolition of the welfare state ('no deal'?) would sooner or later lead to a backlash against the market economy and the social order that it supports.

Whereas some journalists and theologians like **apocalyptic language,** some economists and businessmen like **euphemistic language.** We must see clearly the growing poverty and anxiety which so often underlies such fine-sounding words as 'outsourcing' and 'downsizing' (a word which was used in the 1970s of smaller automobiles and has also been used of people only since the 1980s). And regardless of whether someone in 1980 hears 'You're fired'; in 1985, 'You're laid off'; in 1990, 'You're downsized'; or in 1995 perhaps 'You're rightsized', for the person concerned in the end it all adds up to the same misery.

We should note that all these phenomena are not necessary natural processes (as Marx thought) but are also **developments** which can be **guided** (within certain limits); the questions at issue here are not only economic questions but also **highly political** and ultimately also **ethical questions**, affecting the **whole of society**. Moreover some business decisions turn less on globalization in itself than on the question whether profit, i.e. the maximizing of gain, should be the sole purpose of a company.

However, the very phenomenon of economic globalization makes it clear that **there must also be a globalization in ethics**. How can a world with contradictory ethical norms and orders become peaceful and just? There is need for reflection on a minimum of specific ethical values, basic attitudes and standards which are binding on all nations and all classes, on employers and employees. Just as there is a need for a new global regulatory framework for the financial markets (like the Bretton Woods Agreement in its time), so that where there are restrictions those affected do not simply flee to other markets, so there is also a need globally for **a basic ethical consensus**, to guarantee a life together on our globe which is to some degree peaceful. This basically follows from Part A of this book on world politics, but the argument will be developed here in Part B on the world economy in a similarly inductive way. This introductory chapter results in the following programme.

- The globalization of business and technology calls for global direction through a global policy.
- Global business, technology and politics need a global ethic as their foundation.
- **Global politics and a global economy call for a global ethic.**

All this will be thought through first at the macrolevel of the national and international economy, then at the mesolevel of business, and finally at the microlevel of persons. But before we address the basic question of a global plan for the economy, we must first subject two opposed economic political models to critical examination: on the one hand the Swedish model of a welfare state and on the other the American model of neocapitalism.

2. The welfare state in crisis

The socialist state-planned economy has also been abandoned in the countries of the former Second World, and in principle even in China. Like the English Labour Party, so too the German trade unions have given up their demand for the nationalization of the key industries and controlled investment. All reasonable defenders of the welfare systems, particularly as they have developed on the European continent, now concede that the welfare state is in crisis. This is not only because of globalization but because in its present dimensions it has simply become too expensive in the face of diminishing growth and the excessive ageing of the population. According to numerous economic opinions and reports, in addition to the fight against inflation the need for **reorganization** is **urgent:** the state budget deficit and the state contribution need to be drastically reduced; the social security systems need to be examined; taxes and social security contributions need to be lowered; and regulations which hinder the national and global development of the economy need to be abolished.

For anyone who has any doubt whether the reorganization measures mentioned above are needed or are right, here is one example of a supposed welfare paradise, Sweden.

(a) The Swedish model

For Sweden under the Social Democrat Prime Ministers Tage Erlander (1946–1969) and Olof Palme (1969–76, 1982–86), I refer to a precise analysis by the long-serving Swedish finance minister, now President of the Swedish National Bank, Professor **Kjell Olof Feldt** ('What happened to the Swedish Welfare Paradise?').[10] Professor Feldt helped to build up the 'huge, generous and expensive Welfare State' on the principles of solidarity and equality. What is true of Sweden is also to a lesser degree of Germany, France, Italy and smaller European states.

Sweden created a welfare state which looked after its citizens 'from the cradle to the grave', and for twenty to thirty years such a state also functioned splendidly in Norway and Denmark, with an almost unique mixture of economic growth, full employment and a stable currency. The general level of education was and is remarkably high. More and more tasks like child and infant care, which formerly had been performed within the family, were financed by public means, and an increasing number of women aimed to go out to work. However, an ever greater involvement of the state in industrial production was needed to maintain employment; some amazing parallels to the socialist East Germany emerged here.

This process went well until in Sweden, too (which unlike Norway has no oil resources), economic growth declined, unemployment increased and the national economy could no longer finance the welfare state to the same extent. Why? According to Kjell Olof Feldt, 'our citizens no longer were able and willing to carry the tax burden required to keep the Welfare State going'.[11] It had been overlooked that a very large part of the population had to be gainfully employed and thereby create a sufficiently large volume of income for the state to tax. This became less and less possible. For on the one hand economic growth declined considerably, while on the other state expenditure increased terrifyingly:

– because of the ageing of the Swedish population;
– because people took advantage of the social system;
– because of absenteeism from work and early retirement;
– because of an explosion in state-subsidized housing;
– because of the enlargement of the welfare state which was going on regardless.

The **results** of this development were fatal: the state contribution had increased from 40% of the Gross National Product in 1970 to 71% in 1994 and at the same time the tax element had risen from 40% to 55% of the GNP. Nevertheless the state deficit grew to 13% of the GNP. However, even the Social Democrat government under Ingvar Carlsson was not prepared to put on the emergency brakes: Finance Minister Feldt resigned in 1990 in a dispute with the Prime Minister. Catastrophe came: in 1994 the GNP had declined by 5%, while unemployment had risen by 12%, and in addition there was a giant budget deficit and a national debt which now amounted to around 85% of the GNP.

Things could not go on like this. In the following two to three years the government and parliament tried to **correct the course of the Swedish ship** in the areas of economic and employment policy: unemployment benefits were cut by 10%, in cases of sickness there was no continuation of wages on the first day, while on the second the amount was often only 75%, and the pensionable age was raised to 66. Yet in 1996 the unemployment level was still almost 14%. A further aggravating factor was that the Social Democrat party, which (apart from the period 1976–82) had been ruling for sixty-four years, was shaken by a whole series of unprecedented smaller **scandals** involving local and national politicians. The popular Deputy Prime Minister and candidate for Prime Minster had to resign because of misuse of her state credit card and similar offences.

In the wake of this development, the Swedish model society, for a long-time admired for its self-confidence, honesty, generosity and high ethical standards, is now proving to be considerably less sure of itself, mistrustful, and perhaps also more severe. European normality is setting in: as in Germany, France, Italy and other European countries, now too in Sweden a **correction of course** is proving **difficult**. There are more and more holes in the budget, debt crises and unemployment; and drastic cuts are leading to increasing civil protests and threatening demonstrations by the trade unions. No one wants to give up the standards they have now achieved; no one wants to do without anything, unfortunately not even those who govern. So what is to be done?

(b) Not dismantling the welfare state, but restructuring it

On the basis of this development, what are we to think of the welfare state in Europe and America (in so far as it has also been built up there since Franklin D. Roosevelt's 'New Deal')? At least in Europe the consensus may be that those who govern can no longer look after all the aspects of welfare that seem to be important, from the beginning to the end of this earthly life; they must implement restrictions. And to prevent a further mess in state finances, while the **welfare state must not be abolished**, it must be **reconstructed**.

Anyone who wants not only to see, discuss and expound the problems but also to solve them must progress to action with insight and courage:

– In the long run the state cannot give out more than its citizens are capable and willing to pay in taxes; excessive taxes lead to massive tax evasion and black labour.

– If the borrowing by the state comes to exceed the surplus income from the growth of the economy, new indebtedness on the part of the state becomes unavoidable. Constantly rising new indebtedness leads to the destruction of state finances and finally to *de facto* state bankruptcy.

– The overblown state needs to be slimmed down; over-large parliaments need to be reduced; an often ponderous and extravagant state administration needs to be purged. Nowadays this is disputed only by died-in-the-wool bureaucrats or traditionalist Marxists. For many people the welfare state has become an impenetrable bureaucratic monster.

– In the long run no one can close their eyes to the sobering insight that a job may not cost more than it earns, and that in a time of heightened global competitive struggle, unproductive jobs will be abolished more quickly than before in order to reduce labour costs. There is a connection between the level of wages and the level of employment.

– In the age of globalization a redistribution machine which kills achievement and rewards laziness is not a suitable instrument for a basic structural reform; those who work must clearly earn more than those who do not.

– Higher welfare payments by the state to the citizens will not in themselves in the long run guarantee a higher standard of living and social peace; this has to be achieved by corresponding economic growth, more jobs and higher real income. Even in oil-producing countries like Norway and Venezuela people are now coming to terms with the fact that oil, their source of finance, will run out in the foreseeable future.

Much is said today in economics about the realization of 'five Is': ideas, impulses, innovations, initiatives and investments. But it is certainly not enough to understand these to mean simply a lowering of state benefits, a speeding up of procedures, increased efficiency in administration, a form of business tax which encourages competition, a reduction in incidental labour costs, and an abolition of bans on new technology. In their proposals and plans for reform, politicians and managers may have failed to note sufficiently that the **ethical dimension** always also needs to be addressed in such a reconstruction of the social state:

- If it is impossible for the state in the long run to see to the fulfilment of all human needs from the cradle to the grave, individuals must **claim less** for themselves. But to restrain oneself, to give up something more or less voluntarily, to practise solidarity, entails eminently **ethical questions**.
- Whether such **self-restraint**, which must also include an ecologically meaningful utilization of natural resources, has only a political, a purely humanistic or a religious foundation is of secondary importance. However, philosophies and religions which have in their programmes not only self-realization and self-fulfilment but also self-restraint and moderation, responsibility and solidarity, can provide motivation here.

- Yet self-restraint and solidarity cannot be expected only of part of the population, possibly even the weaker members; in one way or another self-restraint and solidarity are **required of all**, employees and employers, rulers and ruled, and primarily of those who have the greatest scope to practise them.
- Where there are scandalous offences against ethical standards, particularly by political and business leaders, they can have a negative impact on the whole economic and political system.

In view of the failure of the Swedish model, the question arises whether the American model of recent years, which is manifestly more successful, does not represent an alternative worth aiming at.

3. Neocapitalism – not the solution either

Even the champions of the deregulated slim economy and the slim state, who are to be found particularly in the USA and in England, will have to recognize that:

– The claim that the **invisible hand of the market** *a priori* functions for the well-being of all citizens and guarantees constant progress is just as much a myth, refuted by reality, as the claim that socialism will bring the paradise of prosperity for everyone.

– Wherever the **policy of free trade** is no longer a principle of action, to be used with discrimination, and becomes an absolute dogma and an end in itself, to which all other economic and social perspectives are to be subordinated, it must take into account the likelihood of opposition from powerful sources.

– The more **jobs are abolished or exported** (whether or not with economic or political justification), the more confidence in economic security and stable purchasing power will also be shattered. Savings in research and development are often made at the cost of opportunities for innovation.

– Those who **slim down only for short-term gain** endanger future opportunities for growth and completely neglect the loyalty factor, which is based on confidence in the employer and long years of collaboration. In services industries the staff are the greatest management assets.

– When productivity and profitability are rising, **workers** must not be underpaid but must have **their due share in the increased productivity** instead of possibly even being made redundant because of their success.

(a) The American model

If Sweden is the prime example of the crisis of the welfare state, the **United States** under Presidents Ronald Reagan (1981–1989) and George Bush (1989–1993) is the prime example of the problems of neocapitalism. Now between the middle of the 1960s and the end of the 1970s, because of the extraordinary increase in social expenditure (though it was still far from being enough) and the financing of the Vietnam war, there had been a corresponding expansion of the budget and a considerable public deficit, driven even higher by Reagan's tax reform. Of course it was understandable that the Republican administration reacted against the welfare state bureaucracy and the high taxation, and followed a new course in the economy and the labour market. And it cannot be disputed that in the USA, in contrast to Europe, many new jobs were created (38 million since the beginning of the 1970s, almost 11 million under President Clinton) and that today the official unemployment figures are just under 5%, not even half as high as in Europe. But do these successes justify the new ultra-liberal economic model?

This section does not seek to give a sweeping verdict on the American economy or economic policy,[12] but to propose corrections to the neocapitalist US economic model, which has been followed by many European economies. It is this model that according to Newt Gingrich, the now morally tainted Speaker of the Republican majority in the House of Representatives and author of the 'Contract with America', is to realize the vision of a **post-welfare state America**. 'The Europeans tend to exaggerate the American achievements,' says **Lester C. Thurow**, Professor of Economics and Management at the Massachusetts Institute of Technology. On the one hand many who are in fact unemployed no longer register officially. On the other hand the creation of new jobs has demanded a 'high price': 'Since the beginning of the 1970s, the real wages for workers who have no supervisory function (those who have no one under them, say eighty per cent of the whole labour force) have dropped at a rate of less than one per cent a year. In the same period all the wage increases in America have gone to the top twenty per cent of the labour force. As a result there is the greatest gap in income between the top fifth and the bottom fifth of the population since statistics began. In 1995 average family income rose in real terms for the first time since 1989, but it is still below the level of the late 1970s.'[13]

Many economists, in Europe too, argue that this is inevitable. But many American voices also warn[14] that the **horrendous differences in**

income are now out of all proportion in a population where on the one hand the poor are deprived of help and the middle class is stagnating, while on the other hand the super-rich are relieved of taxation and given unprecedented prosperity. No other industrial nation has such a disequilibrium in incomes. In the past fifteen years three-fifths of all American households have had to accept a real drop in income, while the income of the top fifth has increased by 28% and that of the top 1% even by 91%! This 1%, which in the middle of the 1970s controlled 18% of private property, now controls an incredible 40%![15] The dramatic increase in child poverty in the 'richest land in the world' (from 3.5 million to 6.1 million between 1979 and 1994) may be ominous for future developments. Every fourth American child under six years of age now lives in poverty, a higher rate than in any other great Western democracy.[16]

Such scandalous conditions cry out for correction. In the long run it is quite intolerable for the rich to grow increasingly rich and for the same 'global managers' who dismiss umpteen thousand workers (and sometimes, as in Germany, through colossal errors of judgment and megalomaniac projects, lose billions without taking any personal responsibility) to keep increasing their **income**, which is in any case **excessively high.** In the US it rose by an average of 23% in 1995 alone. The average income of the chief executives of the biggest companies amounts to $4.37 million a year (on average around $18,000 each working day). There is often not the slightest connection between success measured by profit and turnover and the rewarding of key personnel (according to an investigation of 2,000 quoted companies in the USA); often the best paid managers come from the least successful companies. Does this mean the highest remuneration for the biggest flops?

If in connection with this development we look not only at the financial balance sheet of particular companies and their chief executives but also at the overall **social balance sheet of the country**, we can hardly fail to notice that in the USA around 50% more people (around three million a year) are affected by **redundancy** than are affected by violent crime (two million). Even if the duration of unemployment may be shorter and the chances of finding another job greater than in Europe, this unsettles wide areas of the population a great deal. For to make blue-collar and white-collar employees redundant, with the financial and psychological upheaval which that brings, of course also infects family, friends and communities with sorrow, anxiety and anger that they are threatened with becoming 'surplus people'. Even in the civil service and the academic world people nowadays are not certain that sooner or later they will not receive a pink slip. Since 1980, almost three-quarters of all households in the USA have had experience of redundancies, and in a third of all households, one member of the family has lost his or her job.[17]

To give just two **examples**: between 1982 and 1992 General Electric made around 25% of the workforce redundant: 100,000 employees. At the beginning of 1996 AT & T made as many as 40,000 redundancies, which were shamelessly announced by the chief executive, Robert Allen, who in 1995 earned about $16 million in salary and share options. The public indignation about this particular case marked a certain turning point, at least in the rhetoric of management and its advisers. Instead of droning out the number of redundancies and blandly calling for sacrifice for the sake of the survival of the company, now they put the need for growth first, though they may remark in passing that unfortunately this will also result in some redundancies.

But increasingly doubts are spreading about the company policy of 'downsizing' or 're-engineering'. The loss of jobs often results in a loss of team spirit, uprooted families and a loss of confidence in business and government. A steady wave of redundancies, wages stagnating in real terms and an increasing drop in income are factors which **endanger social peace**. The business world seems to have stood many things on their heads, when top executives and shareholders profit from the high productivity of workers while the workers themselves have to expect redundancies. The downsizing effect on the incomes of the American middle class is alarming trade unions and consumer organizations. Though the unemployment figures are certainly lower than those in Europe, more and more Americans are sinking below the median level of all incomes. Around one-seventh of the population (about 35 million!) are counted as officially poor; because their chances are also getting worse in the decentralized and highly unequal American educational system, the social decline of a growing proportion of the population threatens to continue. Divisive tendencies in society are increasing dangerously and resulting in increased social tensions, as is indicated not least by the high crime figures; for compared with Germany, as a proportion of the population more than eight times as many people are in prison in the USA.[18]

However, the outcome of discussions about the future social policy of the USA is uncertain. Thus Americans, too, are increasingly asking whether **the victory of the rich in the class struggle** can be the last word. **Richard N. Goodwin**, economic adviser to Presidents Kennedy and

Johnson, and himself a member of the top class, felt it necessary to state recently: 'Today all of us who can read know that we Americans are in the greatest phase of the redistribution of income upwards since the great depression. Political power is firmly in the hands of monetary power, in a symbiotic relationship which continues to encourage inequality and injustice.' He remarked that the two great parties are also part of this process and that the 1996 presidential election would not change anything: 'But it is improbable that this will be a lasting victory. Concern over the flagrant violation of democratic fairness has already led to unrest which will become all the stronger, the more clearly the Americans see the signs of economic injustice.' His conclusion was: 'The desperate feeling of being deceived which is the basis for the political fragmentation in America is not governed by ideology . . . Even a relatively mild economic decline could be enough to change public life in America.'[19]

If we look at **Great Britain**, Margaret Thatcher (1979–1990) rightly limited the excessive influence of the trade unions, privatized state concerns, abolished subsidies, cut back the often inflated welfare state and especially the health service, and shaped the tax system in a way that favoured business. Nevertheless Great Britain is not a model for the world, because as a whole, in social terms Thatcher's measures were completely unbalanced. The state contribution certainly dropped to 41% in 1989, whereas in Germany at present it is 50%, but at the same time a new poverty spread (15% of British are poor); and the gap is increasing between poor and rich. According to a 1996 report by the UN Development Programme, the distribution of income in Great Britain is more unbalanced than in any other Western country, as the poorest two-fifths have less share in the national prosperity than in any other industrialized country apart from Russia. In some areas the infrastructure is disintegrating, and a third of British young people are leaving school without any qualifications. The employment situation improved only in the short term. And on the whole, although deregulation attracted much foreign investment, it did not lead to any lasting revival of the economy and the labour market.[20]

The **social costs** of British competitiveness are too high, and the **financial scandals** in the shadow of Thatcherite liberalism are too numerous. A wise American observer has remarked that if Heathrow Airport, London, with its hundreds of departures and arrivals world-wide every day, were as unsafe as the City of London with its 520 banks and 170 securities houses from 75 different countries (in contrast to Wall Street, not supervised by an independent commission), then after the scandals there involving millions (the Lloyd's insurance debacle, the Maxwell pension fund fiasco, the worldwide BCCI fraud, the collapse of Barings Bank, the Sumimoto copper futures scandal and the Deutsche Morgan Grenfell manipulations of funds), it would presumably soon have to close.

When Ronald Reagan as presidential candidate proposed simultaneously to reduce taxes, develop the greatest arms programme in times of peace, and at the same time abolish the state debt, his Republican rival George Bush rightly called these 'Reaganomics' **'Voodoo Economics'**. But when Bush himself became President, he continued precisely the same economic policy. Thus the greatest creditor state in the world became the greatest debtor state, with a deficit in 1988 at the end of 'Reaganomics' amounting to $2,079,000 million. In 1993 it had already grown to a gigantic $4,353,000 million; only now is it being slowly reduced by President Clinton under massive pressure from a Congress dominated by the Republicans; and this along the same lines as are being attempted in some EC countries, which are similarly deeply in debt. But how many party friends of Reagan, who rightly simplified the taxation system to a substantial degree, were able to enrich themselves in many ways at this time? High dividends from the armament and transportation industries, large profits on the stock exchange and at the same time lower taxes – what more could one want?

What President Reagan introduced to the USA has been called a 'plutocratic revolution'. In so doing he had no more armed the Soviet Union to death than the Pope had preached it to death. At an earlier point the USSR had already manoeuvred itself into a fatally dangerous economic and social situation, because of its own intrinsic contradictions, and it finally destroyed itself. An alternative argument could be that Reagan armed his own country sick through an unprecedented state deficit (and the Pope preached his own church empty), lulling it with highly expensive projects into partly grotesque illusions like 'Star Wars'. By contrast, racial integration has been neglected and has largely failed.[21] But a few further reflections are in place.

(b) Only the profit motive?

The neocapitalist economy of America, hatched by particular management gurus and business schools, and propagated by journalists and hosts of consulting firms, has two main features. First, at every level of economic, social and political development it presents completely **unregulated free trade** as **unqualifiedly positive:** in the longer term, it is said, it will bring a better life to all groups and countries involved, whether rich or poor. Secondly, the **only appropriate criterion** for entrepreneurial decisions is said to be the **profit** from the share capital invested. Any concern for the well-being of employees, the state of the local community and the situation of the nation, any 'company responsibility' and any concerns for social benefits therefore merely disturb the immanent rationality of the market.

No one disputes that we can learn something from the American economic model. But seen as a whole, how is this **neocapitalist economy** to be judged at the business level? Successful in many ways in the short term, in the longer term it tends to be:

– **Obscurantist:** all over the world there are companies which treat their staff fairly and generously and yet (precisely for that reason) make profits and employ additional workers. 'Slimming down' does not in itself mean profit, but can result in a drop in turnover; indeed irrational redundancies can lead to corporate starvation (too few qualified workers with high productivity), which does not help anyone: first slim, then sick. On the basis of the most recent figures the Americans **Dwight L.Gertz** and **Joao P.A.Baptista** have pointed out that 'years of downsizing have left companies leaner but not necessarily richer. The result is that **growth** is the six-letter word on the minds of senior executives and the perceived solution to most of their long-term concerns.'[22] After investigating various successful companies from the giant retailer Sears to the computer firm Hewlett-Packard, Gertz and Baptista argue that even if there is no panacea for all firms and subsidiaries, the most effective course of action involves careful analysis of customers, the development of innovative products, and the optimization of selling methods.

– **Anti-social:** such a capitalist business policy destroys those bonds on which a society depends for its continued existence. The social costs of applied economics on the basis of pure capitalism have become clear. Labour morale and productivity can suffer: 'It is easy to believe that an organization whose employees are systematically reduced in number will have low morale. The people left behind generally remain at their posts with a sense of impending doom, knowing that they could be the next to go and that no one's job is truly safe . . .Many of those who remain end picking up part of the work left behind by furloughed colleagues – often with no added pay . . . In an age when knowledge, know-how and human ingenuity are more important than than capital and physical labour, it doesn't pay to demoralize workers.'[23] Indeed even the American system could not get by without a **minimum of social community**, better professional training and national health care. No economy can flourish in the long term without a minimal social consensus.[24]

– **Illusory**: in the longer term it is not the consumption of luxuries which is decisive for the quality of the state of a economy but a better infrastructure, greater security, an intact environment, and above all 'human capital', a better-trained labour force. It is here that investments should be made. The mood of financiers and stock markets in these 1990s have been compared with that in the 'Roaring Twenties', where people also made tremendous profits, despite all the symptoms of crisis, and kept up their expensive lifestyles until the profits and expensive lifestyles came to an end with the great stock market crash of 1929. George Soros is not alone in his fear.

So can the American model be an example for the world? The political scientist **Zbigniew Brzezinski**, former Security Adviser to President Carter (he dedicated his book to 'Jimmy Carter, whose message of human rights is still valid'), calls for a transformation of American power 'into a leadership that commands moral legitimacy'.[25] Brzezinski mentions '**the twenty basic dilemmas requiring some need of redress**', the last ten of which require 'attitudinal shifts' before an improvement can occur. Here, only briefly, are his headings: they would represent almost a catalogue of the vices of American neo-Darwinism, did not non-economic factors also play an essential part in them, and did they not in some respects also apply to Europe:

1. Indebtedness.
2. Trade deficit.
3. Low savings and investments.
4. Industrial noncompetitiveness.
5. Low productivity growth rates.
6. Inadequate health care.
7. Poor-quality secondary education.
8. Deteriorating social infrastructure and widespread urban decay.
9. A greedy wealthy class.
10. A truly parasitic obsession with litigation.
11. A deepening race and poverty problem.
12. Widespread crime and violence.

13. The spread of a massive drug culture.
14. The inbreeding of social helplessness.
15. The profusion of sexual licence.
16. The massive propagation of moral corruption by the visual media.
17. A decline in civic consciousness.
18. The emergence of potentially divisive multiculturalism.
19. The emerging gridlock in the political system.
20. An increasingly pervasive sense of spiritual emptiness.

No one will dispute that many of these negative developments affect not only the economic, political and social dimension but also the truly **ethical dimension** of human life and human society. One can read in European business magazines that the 'immoral 80s' in the USA could return again at the end of the millennium under an increasingly Reagan-like president. And one recalls the very realistic depictions in novels or films like Tom Wolfe's bestseller *Bonfire of the Vanities* or Oliver Stone's *Wall Street* with the yuppie Gekko, alias Michael Douglas. And one asks oneself: is the unrestrained greed for money and glamour, brilliance and glitter from the 1980s also to govern the beginning of the new millennium? Will its patron perhaps be the greatest economic criminal of the 1980s, Michael Milken, who robbed countless people of their money with cheap, profitable and high-risk junk bonds and himself made billions in the process? Now, in contrast to the film, after a couple of years in prison he can celebrate a splendid come-back (however, revealingly without a toupee) to give seminars at a Californian university on financial strategies. Is this to be the perspective for the economy of the new millennium? Critical reflections need to be made here.

- The highest rates of crime, imprisonment, divorce, teenage mothers, drug trading, poverty (especially child poverty) among all the industrial states on the one hand and the lowest electoral turn-out on the other show the present **weaknesses** of American society. Is it not evident how easily **freedom and individualism** can turn into an uncontrolled society?
- Personal freedom and the entrepreneurial spirit, great freedom of opinion and assembly, top universities, and the development of minority rights, low taxation and much voluntary commitment in the social and the church sphere are the great traditional **strengths** of the United States. So cannot this country in particular correct its

economic and social **course,** as it already did at the beginning of the century and in the 1930s? A 'coming American Renaissance'?[26]

Here the question is put not only to the economy but also to the economists, who are responsible for much in the economy.

What Global Plan for Economic Policy?

Beyond question, different economic, political and social-philosophical plans for an economic order underlie different measures in economic policy. For decades there has been an ongoing discussion about this among economists and I must enter into it here (as I entered earlier into discussion among political scientists) because of the consequences for a global ethic. However, I shall not lose myself in the details of economics, which are infinitely complex. My modest aim is to make clear what global plan of economic policy best corresponds to the overall view presented here, which is governed by ethics. In the face of the market economy which has been establishing itself all over the world with tremendous speed during the last decade, critical reflection is particularly urgent. What kind of market economy should be established? That is the question.

1. Pure market economy?

Anyone who wants to join in the discussion here should be aware that the **old liberalism** ('palaeoliberalism') of the early nineteenth century, which recognized the self-interest of the individual as the motive force in business and society, propagated the free play of economic forces with the minimum possible state intervention as its basic principle. This was realized particularly in Great Britain, which was the leading economic power: in commerce (according to the original principle of the French physiocrat, *laissez faire*), and also involving the principle of international free trade and the freedom of the seas. However, this economic liberalism already fell into discredit in the nineteenth century, with the 'social question' and then with the First World War, for which it bore some of the responsibility. Indeed, with the economic crisis (the Great Depression) at the beginning of the 1930s, it collapsed. Since then economists have tended to distance themselves from 'Manchester liberalism' – originally a battle slogan of the conservative Disraeli against his opponent from Manchester, Richard Cobden, who was liberal in trading policy and socially committed. Originally Manchester liberalism had tremendous industrial successes (in Manchester itself as early as 1789 the first steam engine for spinning cotton, then industrial canals and railways and in 1889 the first industrial park in Great Britain), but it soon resulted in social misery (in Manchester with a thirty-twofold rise in population from 17,000 in 1760 to 544,000 in 1901), which became politically unacceptable.

In the second half of the nineteenth century, particularly under stimuli from utopian socialism, as an alternative the **socialist planned economy** was called for, but it was developed only after the Russian October Revolution. Initially it had primarily political success: among the employees concerned, with their political and social organizations, and the intellectuals who were in solidarity with them. At the end of the twentieth century we have now seen its epoch-making collapse, already long in the making, from the Elbe to the Yellow Sea, and it has been refuted in both theory and practice. Since then there has no longer been a dispute between two extremely different schemes in social philosophy and economic policy, the market economy or the planned economy. The market economy has won, and all leading economies are now 'neoliberal'.

The discussion today turns on the question which market economy will be realized. For the apparently clear general term 'neoliberal' conceals two very different approaches to economic policy.[1] We shall be analysing them in the following sections:
– A **market economy (with no adjective)** or a **pure market economy** ('no ifs and buts') as developed theoretically by the economists von Mises, von Hayek and Milton Friedman, who can be called **ultra-liberals** (arguing for neocapitalism), which the politicians of Reaganomic and Thatcherism have attempted to put into practice;
– A **market economy with social obligations** or a **social market economy**, which was worked out in theory by the economists Eucken, Böhm-Bawerk, Müller-Armack, Rüstow and Röpke, who with a similar abbreviation can be called **social order liberals** (arguing that a state framework should order the economy) and achieved in exemplary fashion shortly after the Second World War by Ludwig Erhard.

Before we turn to the social market economy and Ludwig Erhard, we need to make an ethical examination of ultraliberalism and its main representatives today.

(a) Economic ultra-liberalism: Milton Friedman

Some of the advocates of economic liberalism would reply that it is intrinsically moral. But doubts arise: certain **parallels** make themselves felt between the **political realism** and its management of power that we looked at in Part I (A II) and **economic liberalism** and its management of the market. Is this pure chance? Also at the University of Chicago, where the political scientist Hans Morgenthau had put the concept of the interest of the sovereign state at the centre of his theory of power, and at the same time, **Milton Friedman** developed his equally 'realist' market theory. This makes the interest of the free individual the basis of all order within and outside the economy:
– in political science the analysis of the mechanisms of power politics: competition and (as an ideal) the balance of political forces;
– in economic theory the analysis of the mechanisms of the market: competition and (as an ideal) the free competition of economic forces.

As in the case of Morgenthau's political theory, the **origins of ultraliberal economic theory** lie **in Europe**, again in the German-speaking area. For after the 1920s, when classical economic liberalism had lost all its influence in Great Britain, the land in which it had originated, and in a few years had been almost completely replaced in a kind of paradigm shift (the 'Keynesian revolution'), decisive further developments in liberal economic theory took place, above all in the 'Vienna School' founded by Carl Menger (1840–1921). There it was primarily the Austrian national economist **Ludwig von Mises** (1881–1973: he was born in Lemberg, and after teaching for twenty years in Vienna first emigrated to Geneva in 1938 and then in 1940 to New York) who, as the representative of 'Austrian economics' (the 'marginal utility' school) in America, subjected any planned economy and all state interventionism to radical scientific criticism.[2]

However, his pupil **Friedrich August von Hayek** (1899–1992) was even more influential. Born in Vienna, where he gained his doctorates, in 1931 Hayek moved to the University of London and the London School of Economics, and in 1938 became a British citizen. From 1950 to 1962 he was also Professor of Social and Moral Science at the University of Chicago; only after his retirement, now highly esteemed, did he accept a chair at Freiburg in Breisgau, where he died at the age of ninety-three. Hayek, who as early as 1944 in his work *The Road to Serfdom* (ironically dedicated to 'the socialists in all parties')[3] had presented the piecemeal reforms and manipulations of the state economy in the Weimar Republic as the way to the economic depression (1929–1933), domestic political disaster and totalitarian take-over of power by Hitler, was and remained convinced that any state direction and control of the free market could only have negative consequences for the economy: inflation, unemployment, recession or even depression. He had no objection to wages, like prices, rising and falling on demand, a grim notion for any trade union. Hayek was deeply individualistic in his whole approach, orientated on moral autonomy and consequently on an 'atomistic' view of society. His **allergy to the word 'social'**, which he saw as an opening for anti-liberal ideas, turned into open repudiation when his friends in Germany gave the term market economy the attribute 'social'.

No wonder that in England Friedrich von Hayek had become the most vigorous critic of the man who was then the most influential economist and advocate of the welfare state, **John Maynard Keynes** (1883–1946). As we heard, Keynes had resigned as leader of the British Treasury delegation at the Versailles Peace conference in 1919 because of the Allied demands for reparations which were nonsensical for the German national economy, and in 1920 had called for a revision of the Versailles Treaty.[4] Later, again as adviser to the British government (he was made a peer a few years before his death in 1946), he had proclaimed *The End of* Laissez-Faire (1926), three years before the world economic crisis.[5] In so doing he had put in question the central dogma of the classic liberal national economy, according to which the level of prices, wages and interest which would be arrived at in free competition would automatically lead to full employment. According to Keynes's macroeconomic theory of the economic cycle, the economic situation, which runs in cycles, can be guided in a controlled way by variations in state expenditure and taxation, so that in a recession, growth and employment are guaranteed by increased expenditure ('deficit spending'). In this 'rational economic policy', the state plays a central role alongside private households and businesses.[6] This legitimation of state indebtedness on the basis of economic policy had powerful effects. Only in time did people find out in practice on the one hand how little politicians were prepared to reduce state expenditure and cut debts again in a boom, and on the other hand the extent of the lack of available information, so that the policy could not guarantee to fine-tune the economic cycle effectively.

However it was **Hayek** who in 1974 won the Nobel Prize for Economics. This prize did not yet exist in Keynes's lifetime, and before Hayek, two Keynesians (the American P.A.Samuelson and the British J.R.Hicks) received it. There was evidently no wish to give it to a representative of the most successful post-war economics, the social market economy. Meanwhile the times had changed again: in the 1970s, because of an over-heated economic situation, the problem of inflation increasingly came to the fore, so that the limits of state deficit financing and the burden of interest became clear. Hayek and the neoliberals seemed to have the better prescriptions for countering this economic ill. Particularly in the last few years, several monographs have been devoted to Hayek's significant work.

The rise of ultraliberalism to become the dominant economic political theory of the 1970s and above all of the 1980s could no longer be overlooked. Consequently, only two years after Hayek, the Nobel Price for Economics was awarded to another equally ultraliberal economist from the University of Chicago for his historical and theoretical contributions and his account of the complexity of the policy of monetary stabilization: **Milton Friedman**. Friedman was born in New York in 1912 and had been teaching in Chicago since 1946. As early as 1950 he had called for a reordering of the international currency system with flexible rates of exchange, only half a decade after the historic Bretton Woods Agreement of 1944, which resulted in fixed exchange rates and the foundation of the World Monetary Fund and the World Bank. For a long time the tendency had been to ridicule this radical ultraliberal as an extremely conservative commentator on economics. At any rate he did not become President Kennedy's economic adviser; that post went to the progressive-liberal **John Kenneth Galbraith** (born 1908), of Harvard University. Unlike Friedman, Galbraith emphasized the disproportion between private extravagance and public poverty (an inadequate infrastructure, no state projects) as the main social evil and therefore wanted to cut back private consumption in favour of state activities. He called for vigorous state intervention in cities which were becoming impoverished, in bad schools and in a polluted environment.[7]

However, under President Nixon and even more under President Reagan, whom he advised (as he did Prime Minister Thatcher and the Chilean state president Pinochet), Friedman became politically the most influential economic theorist of the last quarter of the twentieth cenutry. As such he even had some influence on German economic theory, which tends to distance itself from the 'extreme' Friedman. This will become evident in a later chapter about the 'social responsibility' of businesses. Some economists, who since the 1960s have been dreaming that with the help of mathematics they could soon make economics resemble the exact sciences of physics and chemistry in its capacity to explain and predict, have possibly not even noticed how they have in fact moved from the social to the pure market economy.[8] That makes a further matter-of fact examination of their basic positions all the more urgent.

(b) A free market and restrictions on the state

Friedman's ultraliberal approach, which is meant to guarantee prosperity, can be described with three principles which in our day are also shared by an increasing number of economists outside America:

(1) **Freedom** (individualism). Freedom in the sense of the absence of all compulsion is the supreme principle for the ordering of public life, as Friedman programmatically stated in his fundamental work *Capitalism and Freedom* (1962): 'As liberals we take the freedom of the individual, or perhaps the family, as our ultimate goal in judging social arrangements.'[9] The people themselves know best what they should do. The subjects of the economy should therefore be allowed **to pursue their economic interests freely,** whether they do so in a selfish or generous, foolish or wise way. Normally the autonomous individual acts rationally and seeks to satisfy his interests, and the more he can do this, the greater is his motivation and innovation. Hence:

(2) **Free market** (capitalism). Here the subjects of the economy interact, and the more unhindered the exchange of different goods (from property and labour through industrial production to the movement of capital) is, the better for the individual. As human beings normally act rationally in pursuit of their own advantage, their action can be predicted sufficiently if they are not manipulated by any monopoly. **All economic processes are then controlled by competition,** so to speak behind the backs of those involved in them, presupposing that competition remains as unhindered and as functional as possible. Prosperity does not grow through state intervention but with the division of labour and the size of the markets, so that a liberalized exchange of goods and production factors is to be aimed at world-wide. Hence the further demand:

(3) **Restrictions on the state.** Interventions by the state necessarily lead to the concentration of state power ('big government') and sooner or later to the failure of the state, as can be seen time and again. Because of a lack of information and control (it often comes too late and remains too ineffective), state policies aimed at bringing stability to the economic situation tend to lead more to instability than to stability. The more rational solution is to give private ownership a freedom for action which is limited as little as possible by the state. And the state? Let it see to

national defence and internal order, guarantee the personal protection of its citizens, and create a stable framework for undisturbed economic development. If that happens, **self-regulating market forces** always lead in the long term to an equilibrium, provided that the regulating function of price is not hindered by manipulations with taxes and credit squeezes. Homes, schools, hospitals and airports are thus better built by the private sphere, and social insurances, health and education are better left to the self-regulation of the market economy.

Constant economic growth makes it possible to satisfy needs more and more through the mechanisms of the market economy, and leads not only to individual freedom but in the longer term also to social justice, so that the excesses of Manchester liberalism can be avoided. However, one asks oneself, doesn't ethics come off rather badly in this economic system? By no means, Friedman thinks.

(c) Domestication of ethics by the economy

Against the background of this neoliberal, individualistic, capitalistic and anti-state conception of the economy one can understand that, when confronted with the increasing failure of the welfare state, particularly in the United States and in Great Britain, both Ronald Reagan's and Margaret Thatcher's economic programme took over four neoliberal elements: 1. lower rates of taxation; 2. lower state contributions; 3. a free market instead of state regulation of industry; and 4. the stable and controlled growth of the amount of money in circulation ('monetarism'), already a special concern of Friedman and taken up by some central banks. However, Friedman's view was that both governments had basically taken only the fourth point seriously, and in particular had scorned the bitter 'medicine' of lower state expenditure.[10] Others criticize this policy more fundamentally, arguing that given the ongoing employment problems in the industrial nations, Keynes was right in his central thesis of the limited effectiveness of interest-rate and wage mechanisms: Friedman's recommendations simply could not be implemented politically.

However, it is not for us to come to a decision in this dispute over positions. We are interested primarily in the overall ethical problem. What kind of a role do **ethical principles** pay in this capitalistic economic system?[11] In simply prescribing a free market and restrictions on the state as a panacea for all the problems of productivity, distribution and energy, inflation and unemployment (which will not be discussed here), Friedman is basically reducing the whole ethic of the economy to a demand for and promotion of the **freedom of the individual**. But he understands this as **arbitrary freedom**: in fact the unlimited freedom of the stronger, even at the expense of the weaker. The individual may indeed have higher ethical principles, but there is no principle for the interaction of individuals with one another, other than the widest possible freedom. According to Friedman: 'There are thus two sets of values that a liberal will emphasize – the values that are relevant to relations among people, which is the context in which he assigns first priority to freedom; and the values that are relevant to the indivdiual in the exercise of his freedom, which is the realm of individual ethics and philosophy.'[12] According to Friedman, society and the state have nothing to prescribe for the individual. Whether the individual perceives his freedom generously and courageously, or selfishly, is irrelevant, as long as he respects the freedom of the other.

But are there not **obligations towards the nation**? Friedman's answer is that the free man should not ask what his country can do for him, nor should he ask (as President Kennedy required) what he can do for his country. He should only ask himself: 'What can I and my compatriots do through government to help us discharge our individual responsibilities, to achieve our several goals and purposes, and above all, to protect our freedom?'[13] Since the individual is the primary unit in this economic theory and his freedom is paramount, in principle the function of the government can consist only in making possible an unforced transaction between individuals.

But ultimately is there no **specific responsibility for society**? In 1970 Friedman provocatively made his answer the title of an article in the *New York Times* Magazine: 'The Social Responsibility of Business Is to Increase Its Profits.'[14] The ethic of business is reduced to the '**moral obligation**' to **increase profits**! Those are clear words. Basically morality is reduced to business, of which it is then said: the business of business is business. Here of course the relevant laws are to be observed, but no one should speak of a so-called 'social responsibility' which would relate to such diffuse collective goals as the 'common good' or social justice. In Friedman's economic theory, which in fact only knows a collection of individuals doing business rationally, understood atomistically and ultimately united only by their obligation to freedom, the idea of a *bonum commune*, a common good, or even of a 'public interest', has no place. And how many of the financial jugglers, takeover specialists and stock market speculators have also practised this 'morality'?

As a reader one rubs one's eyes: morality = increasing profits? So is there no longer to be any tension in principle between profit and morality, self-interest and ethics? Not in Friedman's view. Why? In this ultraliberal economy **morality** seems to be completely and utterly instrumentalized. Contracts are to be honoured, the best possible quality is to be offered, since that pays: it creates confidence and reduces the cost of information and advertising. As the obligation to increase profit for the purpose of individual (and therefore in sum also collective) prosperity, morality is an **instrument for the shrewd, long-term preservation of the interest of individuals** in a society based on the division of labour. And as for economics or economic theory, this is *a priori* brilliantly justified in moral terms: it presents itself as a general theory of human behaviour from an economic perspective, which of course also includes the questions of morality in its investigation. In other words, ethics becomes the economic theory of morality, the handmaid of the market. The conclusion is clear: this liberal economics aims at no more and no less than the **domestication of ethics by economics.**

We now understand why for its advocates the ultraliberal economy is intrinsically moral, just as – without attribute or adjective – it is already intrinsically social. Here is a perplexingly simply solution to the ethical problem. But this now raises some doubts on the other side. First of all the question:

(d) The liberal market economy – simply a law of nature?

Certainly the **market** is rightly called one of the oldest of human social inventions, chronologically even earlier than any of the inventions which restrict the power of the state (these were surveyed in the first part). But the term **market economy** already represents a conceptual extension which points to a decisive change in the evaluation of the economy in society. However, many neoliberal economists present the modern market economy which established itself at the beginning of modernity, in connection with the rise of the great nation states, as the most natural thing in the world. They have it developing quite 'naturally': as though in the course of social modernization the local markets extended to become greater markets automatically and without conflict.

But this is certainly not the case historically: this economic process was a paradigm shift of epoch-making proportions. For in the Middle Ages and even in the period of the Reformation, as E.Salin has pointed out, economic thought was 'practical theology', which in principle from a moral perspective called for a 'fair price' and a 'fair wage'. However, in long-distance trade (for example in connection with the Crusades) essential financial instruments had already been created which are still used today. Then in the seventeenth and eighteenth centuries the economy became a part-system of society, and economic thinking became 'practical politics'. This led to an independent scientific discipline with the name 'political economy' or, in the German-speaking world, 'national economy'. Thus the modern market economy by no means developed automatically but was imposed politically, and indeed against resistance. It was of course imposed by the interested side and not without certain costs, as we shall be seeing in more detail.

It was the Hungarian-American economist Karl Polanyi (1886–1964), from 1957 at Columbia University, New York, who in 1944 made a thorough investigation of this 'great transformation' and gave an impressive description of it.[15] The history of the modern liberalization of the economy was long and complex. The foundations for it were already laid in the flourishing business towns of the later Middle Ages. Here a few great merchants, who increasingly also came to dominate politics, managed to withdraw the long-distance trade which they controlled from the domination of the landed aristocracy, and step by step also to open up the strongly regulated internal markets of the cities to it. That led in due course to the separation of urban society from the feudal state, which formed the foundation for the later separation of business from the state without which the modern liberal economy would have been impossible.

The development for which the foundations were laid at such an early stage was carried through in the second half of the eighteenth century: against the 'mercantile' policy of state privilege and monopolies, subsidies and import restrictions introduced and dominated by the absolutist regimes in the seventeenth century. What became established was the modern extended competitive market, liberated from state regulations and self-regulating, which proved economically more efficient, especially in the great expanding nation states. After the French Revolution, in connection with the industrialization which made a massive beginning in the nineteenth century, the definitive steps were taken towards the greatest possible liberalization of the economy and its movement of goods.

The products of agriculture and the crafts were already being marketed as goods or commodities, and in the transition to modern times so too was **money** (as capital and interest), and then to an even greater extent mass-produced industrial products. Finally, in the nineteenth century, at the height of modernization, **nature** was increasingly treated as a commodity for rapidly advancing industrialization, under the title 'property'; so, at the same time, were **people**, under the title 'labour force'. Thus alongside the markets in the original local sense, not only did the institution of the large-scale capital market develop, but also a 'property market' and a 'labour market'.

This was indeed an epoch-making transformation: the **autonomous economy** and in its wake the **classical national economy** became possible only **by detaching the economic system from the overall structure of the rest of life.** The foundation was laid for this at the birth of the industrial age by the well-travelled Enlightenment Scottish moral philosopher and economist **Adam Smith** (1723–1790), with his three volume *Inquiry into the Nature and Causes of the Wealth of Nations*, published in 1776, very vividly written and also intended for lay readers.[16] In this brilliant synthesis, which combines some known principles and surveys the consequences of them for economic policy, the main source of the prosperity of the nations is presented as being, not the accumulation of money and foreign trade, as practised by the 'mercantilists'; nor land and agriculture, as practised by the 'physiocrats'; but labour and the industrial division of labour.

All the basic statements of classical liberal economic theory as it was further developed by D.Ricardo, J.B.Say and J.S.Mill and has been reinterpreted for our time by the neoliberals already appear in Smith's great work: self-interest properly understood and the individual pursuit of profit as the basic motive force of economic development; capital which gives prosperity and independence to the citizen quite apart from land-owning; the economic freedom which prepares the ground for individual freedom; the market economy which is not to be disturbed by any state interventions and which leads to the greatest possible prosperity of state and society; free trade, which makes possible the large market needed for widespread distribution of labour and allows domestic monopolies to be controlled; free competition as the 'invisible hand' which frequently transforms self-interest into social action. All this was substantiated and made concrete by Adam Smith with his description of the market laws of supply and demand and by a theory of capital and interest, price and the value of labour.

However, Smith, perhaps the most successful author in the history of economics, was by no means a 'Manchester Liberal' *avant la lettre*. In the controversy between the ruling Tories under Disraeli and the socially-concerned Liberals in Manchester under Richard Cobden he would have taken the side of the latter. But he did not rule out political interventions in the economy *a priori*. He also recognized state financing of defence and internal order. And above all he saw the national economy in the wider **framework of a moral philosophy** which he had already developed two decades earlier: in his two-volume *Theory of Moral Sentiments* (1759),[17] which is built up on three elementary virtues, namely prudence, justice and benevolence. To put it simply: the motivations (especially economic motivations) stemming from self-interest are to be controlled by prudence, and the interplay of economic actions is to be balanced out by justice. But the basis of all moral judgment and also of moral self-examination must be benevolence.

The classical and neoliberal economists in the years following Smith pay hardly any attention to this embedding of the national economy in the ethical context. In so doing they merely reflect what had already happened in the economy. Polanyi put it like this: in the end the economy is 'no longer embedded in social relations, but social relations are embedded in the economic system'.[18] Some critical **questions** therefore arise which need to be addressed to Adam Smith and the classical national economy, but also to neoliberal economic theory:

- Is there really such an idea (earlier attributed to divine providence but now handed on in secular form) as a **'natural' harmony or 'spontaneous' order** existing on earth which despite occasional disruptions directs our being and the whole of society for the best, and on which in the last resort the economic system can also rely?
- Does the **'invisible hand'** of competition really function in such a way as to combine highly egotistical self-interests, compensate for distortions in society, and thus finally also 'maximize' the common good?
- Does not this 'invisible hand' sometimes show such marked signs of paralysis that with good reason people and even economists call for deep state **interventions** in the economy and society, in order to harmonize the market process with the common good and to avoid social conflicts which are politically destabilizing?
- So alongside the **failure of the state,** which is discussed so much today, is there not also and already a manifest **failure of the market,** and is not an economic theory which is constructed without the state (individual freedom as freedom from the state) as defective as a

theory of the state which does not take adequate account of the
economy?

• Is there not a need for a new awareness in economics, too, that the
economy has to do not only with money and commodities but also
with **living people,** who in their thought and action by no means
allow themselves to be limited to the self-interested *homo
economicus?*

Thus it is quite understandable that for all the recognition of the great
achievements of classical national economy in both theory and practice,
among the economists of our century, the question is still asked whether
there is not an alternative approach to the old-liberal and ultraliberal
economic policy which does not *a priori* identify the social element with
the economic element, but understands the social element as an ethical
requirement of the economy. In other words, not a pure market
economy again, but a social market economy?

2. Social market economy

In the modern economy there are no miracles, only strictly **economic
rationality.** And yet an economic 'miracle' happened, acknowledged all
over the world, just after the Second World War: it was a miracle which
transcends that economic rationality which is orientated only on
market-related exchange value. It had to do with the practical reason of
human beings who always take into account in real life not only the
exchange value that can be calculated but also the multi-dimensional
intrinsic value which cannot, instead of externalizing it. What I am
referring to is of course the proverbial 'German economic miracle' –
achieved in a Germany lying in rubble and ashes. Amazingly this did not
have a socialist orientation, though in all the countries round about – in
England, France and Italy – there was a massive move towards
socialism, and large concerns were 'nationalized' which are now being
privatized again. Nor did it simply have a capitalist orientation, though
'capital' (initially after the currency reform a per capita allowance of
only 40 DM for each individual German) played a by no means small
role. Rather, from the start it recognized a **social obligation,** not for
sentimental reasons, as Milton Friedman could possibly have assumed,
but on the basis of a quite rationally formed economic 'order' which
without any moralism is nevertheless bound up with fundamental
ethical values, norms and goals.

(a) Social liberalism: Ludwig Erhard

It started with the 'first conception for financial and economic policy after the post-war period', a memorandum prepared in March 1944 on the problem of the transformation of the German war economy into a peace economy. I find the story of this memorandum, which my revered Tübingen colleague and neighbour, the Nestor of German political science, Theodor Eschenburg, has told me more than once, quite unforgettable. At the end of the war in Berlin, a forty-seven-year-old economist, still quite slim, asked him for reasons of security to guard in his office a thick briefcase containing that memorandum, which he constantly carried around with him, even on the tram.[19]

The person who made the request was none other than **Ludwig Erhard** (1897–1977), who like Henry Kissinger came from Fürth. Severely wounded in the First World War, in the 1920s he had done his doctorate in Frankfurt under Franz Oppenheimer, the distinguished Jewish sociologist, national economist and advocate of a 'third way' between capitalism and socialism, on 'The Essence and Content of Unit Value'. As an economist, in 1931/32 he had been brave enough to express sharp criticism in public of both the deflationary policy of the Chancellor, Heinrich Brüning, and the *Principles of German Economic Policy* produced by Hjalmar Schacht, who helped Hitler to come to power. (He called it a 'rape of thought, especially economic thought, for the purposes of a political career'.) From the beginning he opposed the Hitler regime, refused to join the party and now, after the war, working for the Western forces of occupation, was able to help in the preparations for implementing the currency reform, and laying the foundation for a free economic policy in the face of all resistance in the Economic Council and the public. The *'Leitsätze-Gesetz'* accepted by the Economic Council on 17 and 18 June 1948, establishing basic principles, which abolished most of the controls and price-fixing, was decisive for the economic reform, and thus supported the currency reform of 20 June 1948.[20]

This Ludwig Erhard, whose ethically motivated memorandum of 1944 already proposed a consolidation of debt through a 'just distribution of burdens' of the consequences of the war in the hitherto unknown form of an 'equalization of burdens', on the principles of social justice and in accordance with economic policy. Moreover, no one else deserves the historical credit for having **combined the currency reform** (prepared for by American experts and implemented by the Allies) with an **economic reform** which decisively and successfully shaped the economic policy of the Federal Republic of Germany.[21] It was not the currency reform in itself but the lifting of price controls which was Erhard's personal decision. (His insubordination for the sake of the currency reform was finally accepted by General Lucius Clay.) 'This "stroke of liberation" marked the real birth of the market economy in the occupied zones of West Germany ... Both the currency reform and the economic reform, with their basic decisions about the political order, shaped the German idea of the structure of a market economy.'[22]

It seems to me that Erhard's achievement can be evaluated even better since the German reunification of 1989/1990. In 1948/1949 he achieved what the later illusory reunification policy, which required no sacrifice for the sake of solidarity ('no increase in taxation') and was largely felt in the East to be ultraliberal (the free play of forces), criminally neglected to do. In 1989/1990 no economist had made theoretical preparations for the new situation, as Erhard had in his day, despite the spirit of the time; no 'national economist with the stature of a statesman', as recently called for by H.Giersch, had been appointed by the Chancellor). With 'scientifically based boldness' (as Eschenburg put it), Erhard and others presented a **plan** for the historically unprecedented situation in war-shattered and hungry Germany, with a few clear aims and a concrete **programme,** on the basis of an **overall conception** at first sketched out only in rough outline. This went beyond a planned economy and unrestrained capitalism, and called for a few elementary but coherent and ultimately successful measures. All in all it was a reform built up 'from below', and not enforced 'from above' with public measures.

The full shop windows on the day after the currency reform have been called the 'key experience of the market economy'. Doggedly convinced of the correctness of his policy, in the face of very real difficulties, Erhard was not even deterred from his lifting of controls on consumer prices by a twenty-four hour general strike, called by the trade unions in November 1949. Contrary to the 'socialist spirit' in the British Labour government and in other European countries, in the Social Democrat Party and on the left wing of the Christian Democrat Union, shortly after the proclamation of the Basic Law in May 1949, at a party conference in the British Zone in July 1949, he had put the CDU on course for a market economy with a passionate speech, and his 'Düsseldorf Theses'. Here for the first time he had used the term '**socially committed market economy**', and with this programme made an essential contribution to the great victory of the CDU in the first elections for the Bundestag in August 1949.

For fourteen long years, between 1949 and 1963, Ludwig Erhard (with a picture of his liberal-social teacher Oppenheimer in his office) worked as Minister for Economic Affairs, fighting extremely successfully against unemployment and currency crises. He served in the governments under Chancellor Konrad Adenauer, who did not want him and yet needed him as a vote-winner. The 'stout man with the cigar' (subsequently equalled as Minister for Economic Affairs only by the economics professor Karl Schiller), was also a gifted propagandist of his economic political conception without any academic jargon; indeed he was quite rightly recognized even by his opponents as 'the father of the German economic miracle'. This was the time when the prime requirement for the Federal Minister for Economic Affairs was not a particular party card (Erhard became a member of the CDU only in 1963, immediately before he himself became Chancellor), but academic status, a professional judgment and political integrity. A man of integrity through and through, he had become the symbol of that **market economy** which (in contrast to his original comrade-in-arms, Hayek, and any pure market economy) programmatically carries with it **the attribute 'social' as an ethical obligation.** And he was right when, looking back, he thought that no later government and no later parliament would have had the nerve to introduce and keep the system of the social market economy.[23]

Of course Ludwig Erhard, who was more significant as a political economist than as an economic theorist and administrator, did not stand alone. The basic features of this plan for the economy had already been laid down in the 1930s, above all by the representatives of the **Freiburg School** and its **'regulated liberalism'**, which was very different from the later Chicago School. Unlike American neoliberalism, this social liberalism, only loosely orientated on the Christian *ordo*, with its **theory of an order,** called for a strong state capable of establishing an ordered framework for free competition whilst at the same time pursuing a **policy of order** to maintain competition. The founder of the Freiburg school was **Walter Eucken**, who made a distinction between 'constitutive' principles of economic policy (like guaranteeing the free fixing of prices and a stable currency) and 'regulative principles' (like an active competitive policy).[24]

The aspects of social justice and equality of opportunity were emphasized by the sociological neoliberals even more than by Eucken: these were **Alfred Müller-Armack** and the two German emigrés **Alexander Rüstow** (Istanbul and then Heidelberg)[25] and **Wilhelm**

Röpke, who in his special position between the schools was probably the most important figure for Erhard. In 1933 Röpke was dismissed from his post and from 1937 to 1960 he taught in Geneva (in my youth his writings like *Civitas Humana* of 1944[26] were visibly present even in smaller bookshops). It was Röpke who, in thorough investigations of the social and cultural foundations of the economic order, put particular emphasis on the interdependence of society, the state and the economy. Today all those who feel indebted to the schemes of these economists, who are increasingly lumped together, are called 'order liberals'.

It was the Cologne professor of economics **Alfred Müller-Armack** (1901–1978)[27] above all who helped this economic theory to break through. More than Erhard he developed the concept of the social market economy and, together with him, as his right hand man in the Ministry for Economic Affairs, implemented it in the building up of the Federal Republic of Germany. As early as 1946 Müller-Armack had given a convincing account of this conception of a politics of order in his work *Market Control and Market Economy* (dismissing the Nazi controlled economy), where he gave it the title 'social market economy'.[28] It is the 'significance of the social market economy that it **combines the principle of freedom in the market with that of social equilibrium'.**[29]

The successes of this conception were soon evident. The economy flourished out of all proportion; millions of those damaged by the war, the exiles and the refugees, could be integrated; exports increased; and finally the convertibility of twelve European currencies was achieved (1958). With rising growth rates the constantly rising social obligations could also be fulfilled without too much difficulty.

(b) Free market and social equilibrium

Social or **order** liberalism differs decisively from ultraliberalism. It, too, stands for a free and functional **competition** which of itself already guarantees a by no means small degree of fairness in distribution. But at the same time it requires the state to create the **legal framework** for this, to prevent any kind of monopolistic and group-egotistic expansion of power from becoming a burden on other groups in society. A **consistent policy of ordering** is meant to safeguard competition by legal regulations, to consolidate economic development, to work against fluctuations in the economic situation (to this degree its advocates agree with Keynes), and at the same time to protect the rights of those who have a weak position in the market. Only in this way would **the freedom of** individuals (the concern of the neoliberals) **and social justice** (the concern of the socialists) be realized. All in all, this is an approach with a strongly ethical motivation and foundation.

Thus after the Second World War, in the face of all the negative experiences of both the economic crisis of world capitalism and Stalinist Communism, a way was found in economic policy and theory between West and East, capitalism and socialism, freedom and unfreedom.[30] Both the Nazi and the socialist control of the economy and the purely liberal market economy were regarded as 'intrinsically worn out'; the quite deliberate concern was to realize a **'new third form' as a 'synthesis in economic policy'**.[31] This produced a distinctive profile, quite distinct also from Anglo–Saxon liberalism, which at that time was not yet very strong:

(1) A **model** (the idea of order, the style of thinking) that seeks to be merely a basic conception for social and economic policy and which can be constantly filled out afresh: not only the free market or capitalism, as in Anglo–Saxon liberalism, but the social (not capitalist) market economy.

(2) A **plan** which describes the main aims: pursuing not just the economic freedom of the individual, but also social justice and the requirements of the common good.

(3) A **programme** which makes concrete the model and plan for the whole of the particular situation: not only confidence in the self-regulating powers of the market and competition, contrary to the 'socialist spirit of the age' after 1945, but at the same time the function of the state in creating social balance and order.

Beyond doubt the social market economy had **more realist presuppositions** than ultraliberalism, which professed itself to be so realist. After all the fearful experiences of twentieth-century Europe it was no longer possible to maintain the ultraliberal idea that a natural harmony of interests had to be the model for economic and social life. **Conflicts, not harmony** are the realistic starting point for the social market economy; to this degree there was agreement with Marxism. But at the same time there was a concern not to rake up the old 'class struggle' between labour and capital all over again: new ways were sought towards a political consensus between employers and employees. In this sense, for a long time the model of the social market economy has functioned as a **peace formula** in Germany, in contrast to other lands, where strikes have been the order of the day (the 'English disease').

A positive effect of this was that here ideas of **Protestant social ethics** were combined with those of **Catholic social teaching,** the foundations for which were laid in the papal encyclicals *Rerum Novarum* (1891) and *Quadragesimo anno*.[32] These had been thought through above all by advocates of the concept of solidarity as put forward by Heinrich Pesch, Oswald von Nell-Breuning and Gustav Gundlach (which placed itself between individualism and collectivism).[33] Long before any 'communitarianism', two basic principles of social philosophy and social policy (apart from that of personality) were taken over from this:

– **The principle of solidarity**, which in the face of particular interests calls for political and social balance and the furthering of the common good;

– **The principle of subsidarity** as a principle of responsibility, according to which what the individual can do on their own initiative should not be done by the community, and what the smaller community can do of itself should not be done by the larger community or the state. (In another respect, through the preamble of the 1992 Maastricht Treaty, the principle of subsidiarity has now become a key maxim to indicate the responsibility of the citizen in the European Union.)

(c) Times of crisis

How an economic and social-political concept can lead to an inflation of the state apparatus, and a welfare state which is meant to look after everything, but can no longer be paid for, has not only been demonstrated by the example of Social Democrat Sweden, but is also becoming increasingly evident in Germany, the prime example of the social market economy. Here economists cannot agree whether the way in which things have gone wrong is intrinsic to the concept or has been caused by wrong political moves. Partly against Ludwig Erhard's intentions here, too, at any rate, there was a **blind trust** in:

– perpetual prosperity,
– a social policy with no limits,
– unbounded possibilities for the welfare state.

   The **crisis** was already manifesting itself clearly in the last period of Erhard's own involvement in government. By 1965 the formerly proud financial reserves of the federation had been completely exhausted, and for the first time in the history of the Federal Republic, state income had fallen behind expenditure. And even Erhard's own party supporters do not dispute that his three years as Chancellor (1963–66) ended in fiasco, though finally diplomatic relations were entered into with Israel and there was a 'loosening' of policy towards the East.

However, there continues to be a dispute as to why 'the most successful minister of the Federal Republic' became 'its most unfortunate Chancellor'.[34] Was Erhard, the unpolitical politician, the innocent who did not know how to use power and, unable to make up his mind, gave his government no clear aims and his party no leadership, himself to blame for this tragedy? Or was it caused by the deviousness, jealousy and malice of the old Adenauer; the dispute between the 'Atlantics' all orientated on America and the 'Gaullists' who were friendly to France; Erhard's journey to the USA, which was so disappointing (because President Johnson refused to postpone the repayment of around 2.4 billion DM); the structural crisis in the Ruhr; the first election which Erhard lost (in North Rhineland/Westphalia); or finally the departure of the Free Democrats from the government coalition as a result of the federal budget, which for the first time was completely overstretched? Be this as it may, in 1996 one can only smile that in 1966 the deficit in the budget was only a billion instead of the almost incalculable dozens of billions today, and that the number of unemployed stood at half a million, not four million as it does today. If only we had the problems of Ludwig Erhard!

Thirty years after Erhard's resignation as Chancellor on 30 November 1966, some politicians, national economists and journalists are asking in connection with the present[35] whether something had not gone wrong long before, and whether Erhard, who was said to have the right 'stop signs' in his head (what works and what does not work in the economy!), was not right in many things after all. For example,

– when he fought bitterly to the end against the automatic adjustment of **pensions** to gross wages (covered by investment instead of capital), carried through by the CDU social politicians together with Adenauer and the SPD in 1957, as being inflationary and in the long run impossible to finance (it was repealed in 1978);

– when, sceptical about the **popularist democracy** of vote-catching concessions and subsidies which had already begun with Adenauer, he did not understand the social market economy to mean as much welfare as possible, but primarily stable currency and a competition which functions without monopolies;

– when he wanted to achieve state **welfare**, of which he was basically in favour, not through an unstructured expansion of subsidies and the distribution of ever new social benefits (in fact practised by all parties!) but by training and supporting free and responsible citizens?

But in the pampered economic wonderland of 1966 people saw the drop in the growth rate, and the increase in inflation and unemployment, as a catastrophe which matched the social-psychological explanation of the economic situation given by Adolf Jöhr.[36] The situation and the mood did not coincide, and the mood was worse than the situation. The anxiety over the crisis produced a longing for a great coalition of Christian Democrats and Social Democrats. The real historical background was that the **restoration policy** of the Adenauer era in politics and society, and even in church and university spheres, which was associated with the social market economy, avoided any confrontation with the Nazi past. It could only superficially wipe away the 'brown spots' which kept appearing all over the place (on many senior politicians, commentators, judges and doctors). To the young generation of intellectuals, who took the achievement of rebuilding for granted, the political structures seemed increasingly rigid and encrusted. In particular, the party establishment seemed to them to be worn out and incapable of innovation. So, beginning at the Berlin Free University, an **extra-parliamentary opposition** was formed. It was sparked off by college political questions ('University of Professors') but in 1968 issued in the world-wide protest movement of students and intellectuals, starting from America, where it was motivated by the race question and the Vietnam war. This now had all the social questions in view.

The ideology of this protest movement in the Federal Republic of Germany was eclectic: alongside bourgeois liberal and Freudian ideas (sexual liberation) it had taken up above all Marxist (and anarchist) elements. (Its main theoretician was Herbert Marcuse.) After two decades of a social market economy it was a professed **neo-Marxism** which shocked many people and in West Germany reached its climax in 1968, following the protests against the Shah's visit (1967) and against the Springer publishing empire, with a nationwide campaign against the Emergency Laws that paralysed the universities. The protest had become fundamental opposition to the social and political system, and at the end of the 1960s, instead of being enthusiastic about political reformers like John F. Kennedy, people were enthusiastic about Lenin, Mao, Che Guevara, Ho Chi Minh and so on. But in this new 'class struggle' the revolutionary focal point was not the clash between capital and labour, as with Karl Marx, but that between the authoritarian apparatus of the state and the autonomous individual spontaneously articulating his or her needs. However, and here was a second difference from classical Marxism, this programme did not arouse the enthusiasm of the workforce for the revolution.[37]

The result of this protest movement of students and intellectuals was ambivalent. It rightly led to the removal of many encrusted structures in university, state and society, along with long outdated tabus, and helped the **self-experience society**, which replaced the previous strict achievement society, to break through. But despite many valuable stimuli it did not create any generally convincing future model for the economy and society. After the acceptance by the Bundestag in 1968 of the Emergency Laws for peace abroad and at home (including the right to resist), though they were never to be used in the following three decades, the protest movement again concentrated more on university problems. In the course of the 1970s it split into many groups (the terrorist Baader-Meinhof group was notorious) before finally breaking up. But the problems of the social market economy were not solved by the Social Democratic governments under Willy Brandt and Helmut Schmidt (1969–1982) either; and they are still unresolved today.

(d) The new challenges: ecology and ethics

New problems call for new solutions. The overall framework for the economy and society had already changed fundamentally in 1966. While the 'social market economy' could remain the key idea and model of society, the approach with its prime aims of economic freedom and social justice needed to be expanded. And the economic programme, which implemented the model and plan for new economic, social and political conditions, needed thorough change and transformation. That was inconvenient; it called for a radical rethink and was probably too much for the great heroes of the economic, social and political reconstructions, a tremendous achievement. The fathers of the system had brought up no sons. There were grandsons, but they had to wait for the moment to seize power. However, already at an early stage the new forces in society and politics indicated the direction of the new development and were able to mark out the outline of new basic conditions. Two challenges had become clear:

(1) **The ecological challenge.** When the first **Greens** emerged in the 1970s in connection with the extra-parliamentary opposition, making **ecology** the centre of their programme and calling for a fundamental transformation of industrial society, at first the established parties kept their distance. The result was that in 1980 a separate political 'Green' party formed, and its basic values – 'ecological, social, grass-roots democratic, non-violent' – also spread with greater or lesser success to other European industrial nations. The Greens are an expression of the

paradigm shift from modernity to a postmodernity which is **no longer** prepared simply to allow **nature as a 'commodity'** to be marketed, exploited and destroyed everywhere.

Nowadays people far beyond the Green Party have realized that land, water and air are the central foundations of humankind and that their existence and quality are being threatened world-wide. So today even the established parties are asking:

- Should not the programme of the social market economy be **reorientated on ecological goals**? In this way it would become an economic and social order with not only social but ecological commitments, taking seriously the problems of the burdening and endangering of the environment, from agriculture through transport to nuclear energy, and aiming at a socially and environmentally friendly means of production.

(2) **The ethical challenge.** When in the 1970s the question of the meaning of life, of self-determination and emancipation, along with new criteria for trade, was raised not only by the Greens but by **the women's movement, the peace movement and the alternative movement,** and by countless very different civic initiatives and lifestyle groups, here again the established parties, confronted with novel expressions and public activity by these new social movements, held their ground. But towards the end of the twentieth century these movements, too, have found a place in all established parties. They, too, are an expression of that paradigm shift from modernity to a postmodernity which is **no longer** prepared to have **people** themselves primarily branded and treated as a 'work force' and in this way as 'commodities'.

Today far beyond the organized new social movements it has been realized that people are more than a workforce: that their dignity, their rights and duties must be defined in a new way, and that a new social consensus is necessary. Therefore today the established parties, too, are posing the second question:

- Doesn't the **ethical basis** of the social market economy need to be **rethought** programmatically? Unless this happens, an **ecological-social market economy with an ethical foundation** will remain an economic and political model which has only an instrumental character and will not rise to become an independent basic value of society. Accordingly, politics should not just conform to the market, but should also have in view the interests of all those concerned (and not just those of the owners of capital), weighing them up on all sides, so that the market mechanisms will have to meet particular political and ethical values and criteria.

(3) **Moral appeal instead of practical politics?** It was already a paradox that in attempting in his domestic policy to keep group interests in due proportion, 'the father of the social market economy', of all people, should have been 'humiliated, hounded and finished off' without 'a trace of fairness and noblesse'.[38] Erhard's passionate **call for moderation,** addressed to trade unions, workers and consumers generally, to hold back prices and stop inflation, was ridiculed on all sides as 'massaging souls'. So was he wrong in his conviction that people should be moved not only by laws but also by an insight into what is good for them and for society, the common good? Is no one really prepared to do anything voluntarily, but only under compulsion, as Erhard finally stated with resignation?

No, the decisive thing is that just as charitable actions cannot replace practical foreign policy (as in the case of Yugoslavia), so moral appeals cannot replace practical domestic policy. **No appeals** to moderation (then) or to thrift (today) **can replace political action.** To be specific, what is needed is expenditure reduced in proportion to the loss of income from taxation, balanced out with as much social justice as possible. To seek to achieve a balanced budget, stable prices and full employment through 'morality' alone is political moralism; and no cut-back in the welfare state will obviate certain social hardships. But calls for soberness, savings, solidarity in the face of exaggerated demands will make most sense in times of an overheated economy and times of recession and possible depression if they are first of all addressed to those in government (for example in the case of inflated parliaments and bureaucracies, and exorbitant expense allowances and tax privileges). In these circumstances concrete results cannot be achieved just by constant state intervention; it is also necessary to make an impact on the minds and sense of responsibility of adult citizens.

But what should be the grounds for such appeals against selfishness and consumerism if they seek to be more than massaging of souls? Should the arguments simply be pragmatic, like the fact that rising prices and demands will result in constantly rising inflation? Competition is the nature of the market economy, and according to classic economic theory the motive force of competition is self-interest: to produce and consume as much as possible so as to be able to produce and consume even more. Maximizing of production and consumption, profit and enjoyment? Doesn't that necessarily mean excess? Here in fact an ethical problem arises to which we shall have to return at the microlevel of the personal:

- Why not be an egotist? Why be moderate? What is moderation? What is the standard for human beings? And what is the standard for society?

But all these discussions about the social market economy have so far been carried on in the **national** context of Germany (with an eye to Europe). As a result of the globalization of the economy and technology, the market economy, too, as we saw, has in the shortest time assumed hardly imaginable **global** dimensions, so that the ecological and ethical challenges must also be seen as global challenges. So far the theoreticians and practitioners of the social market economy have hardly done justice to them.

3. A global market economy requires a global ethic

After the collapse of the Communist system in the great European Revolution of 1989, a **globalization of the economy and technology** has intensified all over the world, which is increasingly **avoiding control by a global policy** and which **lacks the foundation of a global ethic**. However, slowly an international system of order is developing, even if it is doing no more than introduce many exceptions to the principles of the market economy (political intervention, social cushioning, ecological precautions). All this is hardly sufficient. Is an ever wider deregulation and privatization to be the key to almost all problems? Despite the positive effects of the dynamic of the economy, which is taking its own course in an unprecedented way, no account is being taken of its social and ecological costs to both the present generation and those to come. This tendency must be contradicted in theory and opposed in practice. Therefore:

(a) No economic imperialism

We should reflect that the classic European theoreticians of the economy and society (not only Plato, Aristotle and Thomas Aquinas, but also the founder of modern economics and moral philosophy, Adam Smith) do not put forward any narrow economistic view, but see the economy and politics always embedded in an overall social and ethical context. At a very early stage in our century, however, so significant an American economist as **Kenneth E.Boulding** had to warn against an 'economic imperialism' in the sciences. And many people think that in the meantime, despite all the warnings, this has also extended to practice.

The term 'economic imperialism' has been taken up by another economist, **Peter Ulrich**, the first full Professor of Business Ethics in the German speaking world, at the St Gallen Hochschule.[39] Ulrich has thought through the ethical problems of business in a more knowledgeable, clear-sighted and detailed way than many others in recent times, in critical reflection on the normative foundation of the concept of economic rationality and with proposals for a comprehensive business ethic. Others are thinking in the same direction, like the economist **Ingomar Hauchler** of the University of Bremen, with his theses that global development can be controlled. Many of these theses have been substantiated empirically with facts, analyses and prognoses of 'Global Trends 1996' by a research team within the framework of the 'Foundation for Development and Peace'.[40] Some arguments for an ethically committed economy and against liberal economism can also be found among American writers on business ethics, especially **Warren R.Copeland**[41] and **J.Philip Wogaman**.[42] I myself found a good deal of support when I spoke on 'Globalization Needs a Global Ethic" at the First International Congress of Business, Economics and Ethics in Tokyo in July 1996.

The central social and political question which arises for us from the discussion so far is: what should dominate human society? Here the quite fundamental emphasis must be that the **economy must not dominate everything**. According to Ulrich, particularly if in the age of globalization 'the unfettered, strangely anonymous dynamic of the rationalization of the economic system seems increasingly to be forcing its own (and arbitrary) logic on politics', there is an urgent need for business ethics to make a 'basic criticism of the political and economic spirit of the age': 'a fundamental criticism of the political **economism** which is spreading, i.e. an attempt to express the ethical and rational claim of democratic politics as such in the categories of economic rationality'.[43] As Hauchler puts it: 'But economic globalization lacks political support which would ensure the subordination of economic achievement to human and social goals.'[44]

Underlying what in Ulrich sounds somewhat abstract and theoretical to those who are not economists, is a problem which is highly relevant in practice. For the economic sciences, is *homo sapiens* really identical with *homo oeconomicus*, that maximizer of his own self-interest, who allegedly is a subject exclusively interested in himself and disinterested in others, who according to this economic theory normally acts selfishly (indeed must act in this way for the theory to be correct)? And in market societies, do people primarily work only for income? Even economists will say that *homo oeconomicus* is a model and not a real person (economists sometimes talk of a *homunculus oeconomicus*). But precisely at that point questions arise. Cannot people also act differently in the economic sphere from what the possessive selfishness presupposed by economism requires? In their working lives do not people pursue a multitude of aims, not least to employ and develop their capacities, as well as to conquer spheres in which they can make decisions? It would certainly puzzle even economists if anyone 'spoke of the price of love, affection or mutual respect as if it were a sum of money'.[45]

As we saw, radical individualism is the presupposition of ultraliberalism: human society is seen entirely from the perspective of the individual, whose characteristic is freedom. But over against such a strictly individualistic foundation for all social action, present-day cultural anthropology and developmental psychology in particular confirm the old classical insight of Aristotle that right from the beginning the human being is essentially a *zoon politikon*, an *animal sociale*: a **social being**, who can achieve personal individuality and identity only through that constant social interaction and integration without which a small child cannot even learn to speak and behave in a human way. Many economists will agree with this.

Even the **relationships involving exchanges** from which economic theory begins do not originally have an economic motivation.[46] Not every exchange is a market exchange, nor is it done for economic purposes. Already among primitive peoples, as today among children and in rural societies, presents and gifts are exchanged not primarily in strategies of economic utility (market exchange) but as communication, as a sign of mutual feeling and readiness for peace ('social exchange'). They express an **'ethic of mutuality'**, which is 'the cultural anthropological foundation on which the bourgeois-liberal concept of the socialization of private autonomous individuals is first – and so to speak parasitically – formed, through exchange agreements'.[47] So as a counterpoint to all the *'terribles simplificateurs'* of an ultraliberal economy, I would state:

- Human beings do not just act in accordance with economically rational maxims.
- Their achievements are not just governed by material interests and their drive is not just one to exchange.
- Not all human needs can be satisfied by what the economy produces.
- It is no use each person pursuing his own interests.
- People (including economists) everywhere and increasingly need more than just the market economy for well-being, a good life in society and happiness.

It is therefore clear that **democracy** also must not be understood **too reductively in economic terms** (and Ulrich demonstrates this, also referring back to the discursive ethic of Karl-Otto Apel and Jürgen Habermas). It is not just a continuation of private business with political means, on the basis of a social contract which is advantageous to all (*à la* Thomas Hobbes), in which while each should come off better, given the existing situation over possessions and power this is simply presupposed uncritically as a given. Rather, on the presupposition of self-interested economic action, democracy is **to be understood ethically**: as a social contract (in Kant's sense) which is fair to all, grounded in a basic consensus on universal human rights and responsibilities. While not everyone *a priori* comes off better in it, everyone is in principle recognized as a person and a subject with a legal status. On this basis a rational politics will not one-sidedly strive for the greatest possible freedom for the individual citizen (in which those with lesser opportunities come off worse), but at the same time strive for **just social conditions** even if this is difficult. And what follows from all this for the market economy?

(b) *The market economy in the service of humankind*

Everyone knows that there is more to human life than business. But in practice, too, the fact must be taken seriously that the **market economy** is not an end in itself; it must **serve people's needs** and not subject them totally to the logic of the market. The world market, too, is there for people and not vice versa. And as far as politics is concerned, the market economy should supplement democracy, not replace it or reshape it. This danger is more real than ever under the conditions of globalization.

To put this in sociological terms: the **economy** (and thus the market), is only a **sub-system** of society, alongside and with other sub-systems like law, politics, science, culture and religion. The principle of economic rationality is a justified one, as we shall go on to see in more detail, but it must not be absolutized: it is always justified only in relative terms. But in economic ultraliberalism there is a **danger,** which can now be formulated more clearly, **that the sub-system of the market economy will in fact be elevated to become a total system,** so that law, politics, science, culture and religion are not only analysed with economic instruments (which is justified), but are in practice subjected to the economy, domesticated by it and depotentiated.

However, a domesticated and depotentiated ethic puts at risk its very own values and criteria; it serves only as a pretext and remains inefficient. And at the same time, as is already proving to be the case in many areas and regions, a **total market economy** has **devastating consequences:**

the **law,** instead of being grounded in universal human dignity, human rights and human responsibilities, can be formulated and manipulated in accordance with economic 'constraints' and group interests;

politics capitulates to the market and the lobbying of pressure groups, and global speculation can shake national currencies;

science delivers itself over to economic interests, and forfeits its function of achieving the most objective and critical control possible;

culture deteriorates into being a contributor to the market, and art declines into commerce;

ethics is ultimately sacrificed to power and profit, and is replaced by what 'brings success' and 'gives pleasure'; and finally

even **religion,** offered as a commodity on the supermarket of ideas along with much that is para-religious or pseudo-religious, is mixed at will into a syncretistic cocktail for the convenient stilling of a religious thirst which sometimes overtakes even *homo oeconomicus.*

What is true of politics is also true of the economy: time and again, with all their legitimate arguments (for example critical references to 'opportunity costs'), economists present **de facto** pressures as **axiomatic.** In that case fundamental alternatives seem to be excluded in practice. But what is often presented to us by experts as 'autonomy' or as quasi-natural economic 'constraints' need not *a priori* be accepted, or subsequently legitimated, by democratically elected representatives of politics (far less by ethicists). Here some **elementary critical insights** which anyone can confirm by personal experience must come into play:

- Not everything in the economy need be as it is; not everything which in fact happens may be regarded as a norm.
- Not everything that functions, functions well; not everything that is efficient is also legitimate.

- Not everything that seems economically rational leads to the common good. What is a means and an instrument (market and competition) should not become the supreme value and goal of the economy (this remains the common good).

In the face of what Jürgen Moltmann has called a 'religion of the market' there is a need for demythologizing: even the 'invisible hand' of competition, left completely to itself, by no means leads quasi-providentially to the well-being of all and to the greatest possible social harmony.

(c) The primacy of ethics over economics and politics

The interests, constraints and calculations of economic rationality must in no way overwhelm the fundamental demands of ethical reason and of the great religious traditions. **Social Darwinism**, according to which only the fittest will survive in the struggle for existence, must **not** prevail within a globalized world economy. Rather, **each individual and group must be treated humanely.** That is an obligation on all agents of the economy, particularly in a free and democratic society, which cannot be denied in the name of 'economic freedom' (though the charge of 'social dumping' on Third World countries by Europe and America is often levelled, not for primarily humane but for primary egotistical motives).

In order to counter the increasing economizing of the world in which we live, it is of the utmost importance to reflect critically on its foundations, first of all looking behind the **normative premises of the economic positions**, whether these are explicit presuppositions or only diffuse background assumptions. Here first of all we must reflect that the economy and the state exist for the sake of human beings, so that both state and economic institutions must not be shaped solely by power, but must always have to **do justice to human dignity.**

Not only in the political but also in the economic sphere it should be noted that specifically in Germany, after the exploitation of human beings by other human beings in the time of National Socialism (often justified with the claim that 'the common good comes before individual advantage'), the concept of human dignity was put at the head of the Basic Law of the Federal Republic, although previously it had had no constitutional position. All the consequences of the thorough reflections over past decades by constitutional lawyers (I am writing this a few days after the death of my Tübingen colleague Günter Dürig, who was a significant commentator on the German Basic Law) have not been noted sufficiently by many later economists, who are glad to leave such questions to lawyers, philosophers and theologians. Conditions un-worthy of humanity cannot be accepted, and **humane conditions** must be aimed at, infinitely difficult though this may be in many cases. In principle the following two premises must be thought through again by economists in connection with practice:

- First, the **primacy of politics over the economy**: the economy must not function only in the service of the allegedly rational strategic self-assertion of *homo oeconomicus*; rather, it must be at the service of higher ethical and political goals, expressed in measures of a political order.
- At the same time the **primacy of ethics over the economy and politics**: fundamental though the economy and politics may be, they are individual dimensions of the all-embracing world of human life which (as I already demonstrated at length in the first part) must be subjected to ethical and humane criteria for the sake of human beings. So neither the economy nor politics comes first, but human dignity, which must be unassailable in all things: basic human rights and basic human responsibilities, and therefore ethics, must be formulated for the economy in an appropriate ethic.

The **practical implications** of this ethic, which also needs to be reflected on by economists, are:
– '**Constraints**' are not to be accepted as if they were quasi-natural, but are to be investigated critically.
– '**Autonomies**' which regularly lead to ethical dilemmas are not to be respected as unchangeable natural laws but seen as market mechanisms which can be changed and corrected by political means through a reform of the conditions which form their context.
– Even in the economic sphere, '**the normative power of facts**' is not to be sanctioned by the simple recognition of the existing balance of power. This has to be restrained by institutional measures to control corporate power, by changing structures for ordering power throughout society, and an ethic which runs counter to the facts.

Precisely because the economy in our day has to be adapted to global conditions, human dignity must not suffer harm, nor must human society fall apart. However, it has become increasingly clear in the previous sections that the counter-model to the widely-prevalent economic system cannot be '**a new state interventionism**', which would only result in new bureaucracy and economic inefficiency and, like the state-planned economies which have been disavowed, result in contempt for ecology and social oppression. It must be 'a **global market economy** which is **politically obligated to humane and social goals**, which does justice to future needs and risks, and reckons with the natural foundations of life'.[48] What significance the principles formulated at the macrolevel of an ethic for the economy have for the mesolevel of a business ethic and the microlevel of an individual ethic will need to be considered in the following chapters (B III and B IV). First, here are some tasks at the macrolevel.

(d) The tasks of a global economy

In the face of the globalization and deregulation of the markets and the principle of economic competition, which is increasingly dominating international relations, there must also be explicit reflection beyond the national level on the global dimensions of a truly social and ecological market economy. As I stated right at the beginning of this second part, globalization calls for a global ethic; **world politics and the world economy call for a world ethic.** Now the world economy has largely become independent, and at present no world policy is capable of directing its global development effectively. Furthermore, when ultraliberals also propagate an economic 'competitive framework' at a global level, they put in question the primacy of politics over the economy, and at the same time the primacy of ethics over the economy and politics. Is this not the programme for a struggle of all against all, or at least of each economic block against the rest? And in addition, is there not a danger that despite all the mechanisms to safeguard it, an uncontrolled world economy will finally lead to world chaos through another world economic crisis? In the face of possible catastrophes, verbal 'assurances' by economists are no real assurances for those concerned.

Everything that has been described so far in this book is therefore based on the 'postulate of a **global, competitive, social and environmental order** which ensures that the global markets, too, are incorporated into the ethical and political framework of a global "vital policy"'.[49] By this, Peter Ulrich certainly does not mean a craze for global regulation of the kind that is sometimes demonstrated by the Brussels Eurocrats, to the annoyance of citizens, but an **ethically defined global framework** which imposes reasonable and uniform rules on competition and shapes it in a way which is compatible with society, the environment and humanity. However, this is not to be confused with a world planned economy: 'As global markets escape national political control, liberal thinking in terms of an ordered economy points to the inescapability of the institutionalization of international conditions of competition. In this view anyone who wants global competition must, to be consistent, also want a global framework for the markets, one which creates primarily ethical criteria so that the dynamic of the world economy is compatible with humanity, society, the environment and the future.'[50] The leading economic powers (the USA, the EC and Japan) should take the lead and later also involve the Asian threshold countries.

This would be accepted by Ingomar Hauchler, who, as we saw, explicitly rejects any new state intervention. What he has emphasized as the **central tasks of a global policy**, on the basis of detailed data, statistics and analyses by his team,[51] accord with this. His findings should be taken seriously by economists and politicians on 'the right', although they come from the 'left-wing' Bremen economics faculty. As one who is not an economist and who here must refrain both from stating facts and from making detailed evaluations of judgments, I would like to commend these proposals to economists for fair discussion, in the hope that politics may yet come before the economy in the longer term.

(1) The creation of an international **competitive order**. Free competition is endangered by the transnational concerns operating worldwide and their strategic alliances; small and medium-sized businesses get squeezed out; many developing countries are excluded. If competition is to function globally, then it needs the security of law and a competitive order which is set by politics. What was created within the industrial states in a long historical process needs also to be aimed at, *mutatis mutandis,* in a new era for the globalized economy.

(2) A stronger link between the international **flow of financing** and the real economic goals of growth and employment. Money has lost its neutral function, in which it is tied to goods and services, and has become independent. Flows of money and capital which are completely uncontrolled create autonomous movements of interest rates and exchange rates which in the globalized market can lead to the distortion of prices and local conditions, and to a destabilization of the world financial system.

(3) Social security as a protection against the growing **structural discarding** which the globalized economy has intensified. So far in the globalized economy there are no points at which the free market forces can be accompanied by systems of basic social securities and basic rights as these have been established in the industrialized countries in a process

full of conflict (thus making possible social peace as well as the necessary mass purchasing power).

(4) A balance between the drastic **economic and social differences among the regions of the world.** The social asymmetry is being accentuated, not only between individuals, but also between states and regions, and here above all at the expense of most of the developing countries. Many countries in Asia and particularly in Africa have either completely lost any link with the world economy and high technology, or display economic development only in isolated centres. The economic strength of many developing countries often lags far behind that of individual transnational concerns acting freely. These often appear to be the real subjects of the dynamic of the global economy, and some states seem only to be objects.

(5) Internalization of the **mounting social and ecological** costs which accrue from economic globalization. The fixation on present needs and the free play of resources absolutizes material growth at the expense of other spheres of life, and the safeguarding of the future. Current economic calculations take no account of the social and ecological costs of the dynamic of the economy but 'externalizes' them; this despite the fact that, say, in the form of unemployment and damage to the environment they are putting an ever greater burden on productive-capacity and so are leading the national economies into ever greater debt. Often businesses shift social and ecological costs on to the state, and the industrial countries shift them on to the developing countries (horizontal externalizing). However, a world-wide establishment of the Western economic model (one need think only of India or China) could destroy the natural basis of the economy. Given rapidly growing populations, scarcity of resources and damage to the environment, in the longer term poverty and migration could result in bloody wars for survival.

(6) A legalized international order which puts a stop to the **excessive consumption of non-renewable resources.** Present-day prices in no way reflect future scarcities and needs. In contrast to economic production, the environment and resources cannot be increased at will. No further increase in productivity through the most modern technology can compensate in the long term for the loss of non-renewable resources. Problems for the present (scarcity of resources, state indebtedness) must not simply be transferred to future generations (vertical externalizing).

Can a global competitive, social and environmental order which binds the global markets within the ethical and political framework of a global policy be achieved at all? There is no doubt that some economists are opposed to excessive regulation, in particular of the international financial and capital markets. They say that controls on financial activities would be counter-productive, and that it is enough to prepare a trustworthy framework of economic and monetary policy.[52] But can economic explanations, be they ever so learned, dispel the fears of many people today as they have most recently been expressed in discussion papers for the ongoing consultation process of the churches in Germany on the economic and social situation? After all, short-term currency and financial transactions in particular have developed a life of their own with no social reference, and thus have contributed to destabilization and crisis in the economies of the Western nations. A new monetary regime with fixed exchange rates, as proposed in the report of the Bretton Woods Commission, would in itself be a great help.[53] In addition, the establishment of public agencies to control the flow of capital, or even a single World Central Bank, are being discussed.

As for a **global** framework for the markets, at the beginning of the twenty-first century the nations, which are often far from being 'united nations' , are perhaps at the stage at which they were over a **national** framework in Europe and North America at the beginning of the twentieth century (the first law relating to bank notes was enacted only in 1844, in England under Peel). As we have already seen, national economic regulations which were to some degree effective were produced in the industrial countries only after 1929 and the complete collapse of the world economy; indeed in part only after the Second World War. And if these national economic regulations are now in crisis as a result of globalization, because the nation state is increasingly losing its role as the omnipotent ordering power, capable of solving all problems, and no new currency agreement along the lines of Bretton Woods is in sight, one asks oneself whether it will take another **world economic crisis** before people seriously concern themselves with a comprehensive **world economic order**. For anyone who is not an economist, a cursory glance at the globalized financial markets on which several hundred billion dollars are traded every day (only a fraction of this in trade in commodities) can give the impression in the 1990s of being another dance round the volcanoes, as in the 1920s ('the roaring twenties'), with excessively high share prices and a highly irrational hunt for records on the stock exchange. Will it really take a bigger stock exchange crash than in October 1987 (I watched it as a visiting professor at Rice University in Houston) for people to pay attention and recognize the need for a global regulation of the markets (without dirigist state intervention)?

The slightest remark, for example by the President of the American Federal Bank, Allan Greenspan, at the beginning of December 1996, that an 'irrational exuberance' had led to an overvaluation of the financial markets was enough to drive the nervous investors on the high-flying stock markets of Asia, Europe and America into a spin, and panic selling. This also shows that crises in globalization do not *a priori* balance out, but perhaps get progressively worse. So one feels confirmation that the chaos theory is also applicable to the economy. And even among economists and experts in international law, who might exclude the possibility today of a return of the world economic crisis and the collapse of the economic order of 1929-1933, there is anxiety that 'the process of internationalization will set in motion a development which confronts the national economies with heightened risks of stability, accompanied by a reduction in the possibilities of state action': 'Whereas tectonic tremors remain limited locally, today even small misfortunes on local financial markets send their waves far beyond the epicentre of the disaster. Furthermore, unfavourable circumstances easily develop such waves into storm floods.'[54] In the banking sector, the great **bank scandals** of the 1980s and 1990s (Herstatt Bank, Banco Ambrosiano, BCCI and Barings) resulted in the first attempts 'to regulate the processes which underlie the very process of globalization' and in 'measures to regulate the international finance markets'. The fear of 'floods' on the international finance market 'might in the future lead to the strongest pressure for the creation of an international financial order'. Yet we are still a long way from 'a financial order for the international community'.[55] However, there are clear signs of a new world political order.

III

Responsible Economics

When I wrote my book *Global Responsibility* in 1990 there were no documents by world organizations on a global ethic to which I could refer. Certainly there were declarations on human rights, above all the United Nations Declaration of 1948, but none on human responsibilities. Yet only three years after the appearance of *Global Responsibility*, the Parliament of the World's Religions proclaimed the Declaration toward a Global Ethic, which I have already mentioned at length. And now, six years later, there are already three further important international documents which not only state human rights but explicitly speak of human responsibilities; indeed, they programmatically call for a global ethic and even attempt to make it concrete.

1. An ethically motivated policy for world order

Of course an international financial order would have to be seen within the framework of a comprehensive **world economic order** if it were to be efficient and lasting. I have already shown that moral appeals at best have a limited effect here unless they are combined with political action. In fact the global social and ecological responsibilities of businesses would have to be redefined and appropriate action called for. On the other hand, political action towards a world economic order cannot possibly be carried through in the face of all the special interests and collective egotisms of the nations concerned without ethical motivations. In this connection the significance of international commissions, declarations and proclamations can easily be underestimated.

(a) Are declarations and proclamations useless?

Of course there are countless declarations which are useless, one-sidedly partisan or even eccentric. And indeed one need not sign everything that is presented or sent to one for signature. But perhaps there are some important declarations and proclamations relating to the whole of humankind which deserve the support of all; not signing them amounts to disowning all those who are committing themselves to justice, solidarity, peace and human dignity, on the front lines of the world, often at great sacrifice. Just think:

– Would the **Geneva Convention** of 1864 and the founding of the **Red Cross** (also the Red Crescent), which is beneficially active today in 150 countries on earth, have come about without the unselfish ethical will of Henry Dunant (honoured with the very first Nobel Peace Prize in 1901), and the small Geneva committee which wanted to mitigate the suffering of war, encourage the humane treatment and exchange of prisoners, and create safety zones? As the famous Zurich international lawyer and President of the International Red Cross, Max Huber, whom I have already quoted, remarks: 'The notion of help for the wounded and sick without discrimination which is embodied in the Geneva Convention . . . and the development of this principle into a system of moral values supported by the world organization of the Red Cross can be regarded as the first practical attempt at an international ethic.'[1]

– Would the **League of Nations** ever have been founded after the First World War without the ethical will of certain statesmen to prevent a new great war and to make possible a peaceful resolution of conflicts of interests by settling disputes? It may not have been successful in its time, as we know, but it also had an influence as a prototype for the future. 'It was the First World War with its fearful consequences which deterred the world from its materialistic belief in progress and made it possible for so utopian a project as Wilson's plan for a League of Nations to be introduced into practical politics. Under the slogan, "Never another war!" there was a moral revolt against war.' Thus, again, Max Huber.[2]

– Would the founding of the **United Nations** after the second great genocide, that of the Second World War, have come about without the renewed ethical will finally to arrive at a peaceful understanding among the nations and at the same time, through the re-establishment of the International Court of Justice and the International Labour Organization, to deepen and improve collaboration among the nations for the well-being of humankind? The establishment of the special organs of the United Nations Organization also derives above all from ethical interests: UNICEF (aid for the children of the world), the High Commission for Refugees and other subordinate organs, and even more the special international organizations associated with UNO: the Organization for Education, Science and Culture (UNESCO), for food and agriculture (FAO), the World Health Organization (WHO) and others. 'The development of UNO, namely the creation of UNESCO and other organizations, outside and inside UNO, are further signs of how alive ethical and humane ideas are in the international world.' Thus, once, again Huber.[3]

– Would the proclamation of the United Nations' Universal **Declaration of Human Rights** ever have come about without the ethical will of so many champions of human rights, who after the atrocities of the Nazi regime wanted unconditionally to ensure more humanity, freedom and justice? 'Through the Declaration on Human Rights . . . the United Nations gave expression to the correct view that only through a spiritual and moral homogeneity of the nations united in an alliance for the preservation of peace and justice can inner substance be given. The **human rights** proclaimed by UNO form a system of political and social order. What is right for a political organization is of fundamental significance for an ethical system as described by an international ethic.' Thus, for the last time, Max Huber.[4]

Of course everyone knows the **objections** of the sceptics and the pessimists who say:

– The actions of the Red Cross are often only a drop in the ocean;

– The League of Nations manifestly failed and could not prevent the Second World War;

– The United Nations has failed in numerous instances: it did not bring peace to Somalia but left it in the lurch; it did not put a stop to the murders and deaths in Rwanda; it did not remove the dictatorships in the Gulf despite the spectacular victory of American military power: the despot in Iraq did not fall, there is no democracy in Kuwait, no improvement in the situation of the Kurds and Shi'ites and no peace in the region;

– Even now the Declaration on Human Rights does not prevent the constant violation of human rights in China, Tibet and Myanmar, in Indonesia, Israel, Palestine and Bosnia (not to mention other states).

All this is true and sometimes makes pessimism seem justified. But there is also **the other side** of reality:

– What would the world be without the tremendous dedication of the often heroic helpers of the **Red Cross** in every possible crisis area on earth, from Kigali to Lima?

– What would the world be without the ethical idea of the **League of Nations** which was maintained despite the ideologies of Fascism, Nazism and Communism, so inimical to peace, and which manifested its power again in the Atlantic Charter of August 1941, and then in the creation of UNO?

– What would the world be without the **United Nations**, this association of states to ensure world peace and to further international collaboration, at whose tribune in New York so much aggression by greater or lesser powers is vented, bloody conflicts are avoided from the start, and others can finally be settled?

– What would the world be without the **Charter of Human Rights**, to which civil rights movements all over the world have been able to, and still can, refer? What would the world be without the Helsinki Declaration of the 1975 Conference for Security and Collaboration in Europe, on the basis of which in 1976 the Soviet civil rights movement was formed by A. Amalrik, W. Bukovsky, A. Ginsburg, L. Kopelev, A. Sacharov and A. Sozhenitsyn; and also the brave Polish Workers' Defence Committee and the trade union organization Solidarity, along with all the other civil rights movements in the Communist sphere, which ultimately were able to celebrate a moral and political victory over the totalitarian policy and military dictatorships of the Communist states that was totally unexpected by most people?

The very history of the **charter** (Latin parchment, document), from the *Magna Carta Libertatum* of 1215 to the United Nations Charter and Charter 77 of the Czechoslovak civil rights movement, shows abundantly clearly to all sceptics that:

• The ethical and political will tends strongly towards written **documentation** and its public **proclamation** which seals the ethical and political will.
• Written documentation and public proclamation then help to **realize the ethical-political will** which is the presupposition of its origin, and works as a motive force for its realization.

So let no one today repeat the foolish judgment that in any case declarations and proclamations are no use, as I go on to discuss three important international documents, all of which in this time of globalization have addressed the need for, and urgency of, a global ethic.

(b) Human rights and human obligations: The International Commission on Global Governance

The report by **The Commission or Global Governance** appointed by UNO bears the title *Our Global Neighbourhood.*[5] The term 'global governance' can be misunderstood, as indicating a 'global government'; such a thing is neither realistic nor worth striving far. It would be all too remote from the citizens of the world, nor could it be legitimated democratically. Moreover a world government is already firmly ruled out by the co-chairmen of the distinguished twenty-five member commission, the former Swedish Prime Minister Ingvar Carlsson and the former Commonwealth General Secretary Shridath Ramphal, in their introduction: 'We are not proposing movement towards world government'; this could lead to 'an even less democratic world than we have', indeed to 'one more accommodating to power'. But on the other hand the goal is not a 'world without systems or rules'; this would be 'a chaotic world' and 'it would pose equal or even greater danger'.[6] So the challenge is 'to strike the balance in such a way that the management of global affairs is responsive to the interests of all people in a sustainable future, that it is guided by basic human values, and that it makes global organization conform to the reality of global diversity.'[7] Indeed, the growing number of people who are committed to a global ethic will find themselves supported by this report: 'This is a time for the international community to be bold, to explore new ideas, to develop new visions and to demonstrate commitment to values in devising new governance arrangements.'[8]

The phenomenon of **globalization** in all its dimensions forms the starting point for this analysis of 'a new world' which takes several hundred pages: 'Never before has change come so rapidly, on such a global scale, and with such global visibility.'[9] This is true:
– of the **military** transformations and the total change in the strategic setting: a new arms race, the arms trade, the rise in civil conflict, widespread violence;
– of the **economic** trends, in which the economic rise of several developing countries is distracting attention from the still rising number of the poorest of all;
– of the **social and environmental** change, in which people are beginning to assert their right to participate in their own governance; this urgently calls for an enlightened leadership which represents all countries and peoples and not just the most powerful.

After this analysis of the situation in the first chapter of the report, there follow a wealth of analyses, reflections and proposals on the great **problem areas** of a policy for world governance today:
– the advancement of global security (avoiding, recognizing and settling crises),
– the management of economic interdependence,

– the strengthening of the rule of law world-wide (international law),
– the reform of the United Nations.[10]

What is surprising here from the perspective of a global ethic is that before all these problem areas, immediately after the analysis of the situation, in a whole chapter the question of 'values for the Global Neighbourhood' is raised and in view of the increased neighbourhood tensions in all spheres, a '**neighbourhood ethic**' is called for. Why? Without a global ethic the frictions and tensions in life together in the one world would multiply: 'Without leadership (a courageous leadership infused with that ethic at all levels of society) even the best-designed institutions and strategies will fail.'[11] There is then the terse comment that '**global values must be the cornerstone of global governance**'.[12] And anyone who asks doubtfully whether enough of today's political leaders are steeped in this ethic is given hope by the remark that 'many people world-wide, particularly the young, are more willing to respond to these issues than their governments, for whom the short term in the context of political expediency tends to take preference'.[13]

But let us leave aside speculation as to which politicians in particular will stand out in respect for the '**ethical dimension of the world political order**'.[14] More important is the question how it can be made concrete. And here, too, it is amazing that that this document gives the **Golden Rule** as the main basic principle: 'People should treat others as they would themselves wish to be treated.'[15] On this foundation the basic values of respect for life, freedom, justice, mutual respect, readiness to help, and integrity are developed: 'All these values derive in one way or another from the principle, which is in accord with religious teaching around the world, that people should treat others as they would themselves wish to be treated.'[16]

And the report goes very much further in explicitly requiring 'these values to be expressed in the form of a **global civic ethic** with specific rights and responsibilities', in which 'all citizens, as individuals and as members of different private groups and associations, should accept the obligation to recognize and help protect the rights of others'. This ethic should be incorporated into the developing 'fabric of international norms'.[17] For such a global ethic 'would help humanize the impersonal workings of bureaucracies and markets and constrain the competitive and self-serving instincts of individuals and groups'.[18] Indeed, without this global ethic the new wider global civil society which is coming into being could 'become unfocused and even unruly'.[19]

It would be hard to think of a finer confirmation of the global ethic project than these statements by the commission. Finally, the commission even makes an explicit request. The authors were presumably unaware that, as I remarked earlier, it had already been made in a discussion in the Revolutionary Parliament of 1789 in Paris, but could not be met at that time: 'Rights need to be joined with responsibilities.'[20] For the 'tendency to emphasize rights while forgetting responsibilities' has 'deleterious consequences'.[21] 'We therefore urge the international community to unite **in support of a global ethic of common rights and shared responsibilities.** In our view, such an ethic – reinforcing the fundamental rights that are already part of the fabric of international norms, would provide the **moral foundation for constructing a more effective system of global governance.**'[22]

It cannot be repeated often enough that all human beings have rights, **human rights:** the right to a secure life, equitable treatment, an opportunity to earn a fair living and provide for their own welfare, the definition and preservation of their differences through peaceful means, participation in governance at all levels, free and fair petition for redress of gross injustices, equal access to information and to the global commons.

But hardly ever has it been stated in an official international document that concrete responsibilities, **human responsibilities,** are associated with human rights: 'At the same time, all people share a responsibility to:
– contribute to the common good;
– consider the impact of their actions on the security and welfare of others;
– promote equity, including gender equity;
– protect the interests of future generations by pursuing sustainable development and safeguarding the global commons;
– preserve humanity's cultural and intellectual heritage;
– be active participants in governance; and
– work to eliminate corruption.'[23]

Moreover it is remarkable that this fundamental section of the UN Commission Report on a civil ethic ends with a very concrete hope, that 'over time, these principles could be embodied in a more binding international document – a **global charter of Civil Society** – that could provide a basis for all to agree on rules that should govern the global neighbourhood'.[24]

On the basis of the commission's report it is also possible to give a clearer answer to the question '**Who can realize a policy of global governance?**'[25] Of course the **nation states** remain the chief agents in international politics, but they are no longer the only ones. Today there are already several **global economic organizations** which function to keep order in economic matters: the World Trade Organization (WTO, the successor to GATT) and, irreplaceable despite many failures, the International Monetary Fund and the International Bank for Reconstruction and Development (World Bank), the necessary reform of which is being worked on at present. Happily the WTO recently for the first time laid down globally binding conditions for the regulation of foreign investments, international services and aspects of the protection of cultural properties relevant to trade, and most recently of all (Singapore, December 1996) the abolition of trade restrictions on computer and communication technologies. However, in the case of corruption it was possible to agree only on further studies.

In time, what has already begun here needs to be co-ordinated to form a comprehensive world economic order with social standards, which in its turn should be part of the comprehensive global governance that is being striven for.[26] However, and this is the view of the commission, this will only come about through a 'wide-ranging dynamic and complex process of interactive investigation' in which many more agents are involved: in addition to nation states as the main agents, together with the **business world** of the powerful transnational concerns, the global network of the **media world**, and also the increasingly international network of the movement of **non-governmental organizations**, which represent the germs of a still weak but globally orientated 'international civil society' with a vision of global citizenship.[27]

(c) Development, not just economic growth: The World Commission on Culture and Development

The equally extensive report by the World Commission on Culture and Development which was published in collaboration with the UN and UNESCO under the title *Our Creative Diversity* is just as important as the report on global governance.[28]

What does **development** mean for the commission? Not just economic growth, as is traditionally understood, occasionally qualified by a wide distribution of the profits of growth. No, in a more comprehensive view (following the lines of UNESCO and many previous thinkers), development is seen as the process which furthers the actual freedom of human beings, who need it for aiming at that to which they attribute value. In this perspective **poverty** arises not only through a lack of basic goods and necessary services, but also through a lack of opportunities to choose a more satisfying, more valuable life.

And what does **culture** mean for the commission? Culture is understood quite generally as 'ways of living together', which have different consequences, depending on the understanding of development. If development is simply identified with economic growth, culture has no intrinsic value but is simply a means to further and sustain economic growth. But is not economic growth, desirable though it may be, only a means and not the goal and purpose of human life? The cultural dimensions of human life are possibly more important than economic growth. For example, education as an essential dimension of cultural development certainly also furthers economic growth, but it has an intrinsic value. That means that culture cannot in any way be reduced to an aid towards furthering economic growth, but in addition to that should bring meaning into our life. Thus culture is given a twofold role: it is related to the particular values and goals of different spheres of life (also including the economic sector), but its role is in no way reduced simply to an instrumental function; rather, it forms the common foundation on which the different values and goals are based. Thus in this perspective development also embraces cultural growth, the furthering of respect for all cultures and the principle of cultural freedom.

In such a report the 'commitment to pluralism' is on the one hand the natural presupposition, but on the other it is also the constant task: it is a matter of a creative difference which constantly has to be developed anew. The new feature of this document, however, is a chapter which, even before the remarks on pluralism, stresses what human beings hold in common rather than their differences: '**A New Global Ethics**', an **ethic of humankind**, a **world ethic**. Important questions are answered in this connection:

(1) **Why** a global ethic? Because **collaboration** between people of different cultures and interests can be made **easier** and their **conflicts diminished and limited** if all peoples and groups 'see themselves bound and motivated by **shared commitments**'.[29] Hence the call for a global ethic: 'So it is imperative to look for a core of shared ethical values and principles.'[30] The Commission on Culture and Development emphasizes the agreement between its concern and the efforts of the UN Commission on Global Governance, and states: 'The idea is that the

values and principles of a global ethic should be common points of contact which offer a minimal **moral stimulus** which the world must observe in its manifold efforts to **overcome** the **global problems** mentioned.'[31] To this degree today there is a whole 'culture in search of a global ethics'.[32] Such a search is already in itself a cultural activity *par excellence*. Questions like 'Who are we? How do we relate to one another and to humankind? How do we behave to one another and to humankind as such? What is our meaning?', stand at the centre of culture.

(2) What are the **sources** of such a global ethic? The formulation of a global ethic must draw its content from 'the cultural resources, the insights, emotional experiences, historical memories and spiritual orientations of the peoples'.[33] Despite all the differences between cultures, there are some themes which appear in almost all cultural traditions and which could serve as the inspiration for a global ethic.

The first of these sources are the **great cultural traditions**, especially 'the idea of human vulnerability and the attendant ethical impulse to alleviate suffering where such is possible, and to provide security to each individual'.[34] This seems to be more of a Buddhist formulation of the starting point, but the suffering human being also stands at the centre of other religions. And in this report, too, at the same time reference is made above all to the Golden Rule, which has found expression in the traditions of Confucianism, Taoism, Hinduism, Buddhism and Zoroastrianism, Judaism, Christianity and Islam, and is also implicit in the practices of other faiths. It points to the equal moral worth of all human beings.

Alongside the elements from the great cultural traditions, this Commission also cites elements of an ethic which derive from '**global civic culture**' and which are similarly to be incorporated into a new global ethic. It is concerned with the following five ethical 'pillars':[35]

– Human rights and responsibilities;
– Democracy and the elements of a civil society;
– Protection of minorities;
– An obligation to the peaceful resolution of conflicts and fair negotiations;
– Equal treatment of the generations (intergenerational equity).

This report by the Commission on Culture and Development, too, is a document which points towards the future, and we cannot be grateful enough to the members for it. If I raise questions here, it is not so much as a criticism of what has been achieved but in order to take things further.

(3) **Questions**. Happily, this document too speaks of human rights and human responsibilities or duties. On other points (democracy) it deals more with political postulates than with ethical principles. At all events, though, this document confirms our early insight that a universal ethic for humankind can **only partially be derived from the human rights which are proclaimed.** For this Commission, too, cannot avoid the recognition that in some non-Western societies human rights are perceived very differently. In South Asia, for example, some human rights activists have had to recognize: 1. that many rights would be regarded only in the context of religion, the family or other institutions; 2. that people would always talk about their responsibilities before the question of their human rights; 3. that the human rights as expressed in the UN Declaration are either unknown or very far removed from their own experience.

Would it not have been a good thing if the World Commission with its welcome plea for a global ethic had also spoken more energetically and substantively about the great religious and ethical traditions of human-kind? Is this for fear of the very word 'religion', or for fear **of the reality of the religions**? I know a famous French sociologist who (unlike, say, my friend Alfred Grosser, who calls himself an agnostic) would want the very word religion to be avoided in international documents. Dogmatic lay people and dogmatic clergy – the extremes meet here! – then easily confirm each other's prejudices. However, if it has an empirical rather than a dogmatic basis, this restraint towards the reality of religion is understandable in the light of the **fatal role** which some religions have played in more recent history and, as we saw, still played at the most recent UN conferences in connection with human rights, democracy and world peace.

But should we not also, whether we are religious or agnostic, see the **constructive role** of religion to which I have already referred in the context of world politics? Has not the newest era of all, the postmodern era of human history, from Eastern Europe to Latin America and from South Africa to the Philippines, shown that religions can have not only a destructive but also a constructive influence? Indeed that they can release a quite tremendous dynamic to liberate people from totalitarian systems, to protect human dignity, to establish human rights, and to preserve world peace?

So, very much along the lines of *Global Responsibility* and the Chicago Declaration, in the future the **incomparable resources of the world religions** should be used constructively for establishing and implement-

ing a global ethic. This should happen above all for the following three
reasons:

1. Despite all manifestations of decadence, over the millennia the
religions have kept demonstrating their indestructible, inexhaustible
spiritual power.

2. The religions can speak much more concretely (for example with
parables, images and models) of elementary human responsibilities than
some more recent ethical doctrines.

3. The great leading religious figures of humankind have lived out an
ethic in an exemplary way: no general, no statesman and no philosopher
has maintained down the millennia the spiritual authority and radiance
of Buddha or Confucius, Jesus Christ or Muhammad.

I have nothing against philosophical and political arguments for a
global ethic: all constructive philosophical and political ideas, notions
and arguments help to realize a global ethic which presupposes the
coalition of believers and non-believers. That is why I always speak of
religious and ethical traditions. But in a 'postmodern' age we should
discard that neglect of the religions so characteristic of modernity in
favour of a realistic assessment. That has happened most recently of all
in a third international document which can support the two other
documents, while introducing a greater degree of concreteness and
differentiation.

(d) Humanity in concrete: The InterAction Council

I have already reported this statement by the InterAction Council, which
consists of former Presidents and Prime Ministers under the chairman
ship of the former German Chancellor Helmut Schmidt, in connection
with world politics (see A IV above). Under the title **In Search of Global
Ethical Standards,** taking up the Chicago Declaration of the Parliament
of the World's Religions, it calls for 'a minimal basic consensus relating
to binding values, irrevocable standards and moral attitudes which can
be affirmed by all religions despite their dogmatic differences and can
also be supported by non-believers'.[36]

(1) This body of experienced statesmen formulates the **nucleus of the
global ethic** even more precisely, fundamentally and concretely by
establishing as a basic principle a **prime imperative of humanity** (in
concrete situations sadly anything but a matter of course) which not
only expresses the humane impulses of the world religions in words
referring to humanity, but also takes up what has been presented since

the time of Kant in purely philosophical terms as a categorical imperative: that **every human being must be treated humanely**. Associated with this is the Golden Rule, which is now increasingly establishing itself in the human consciousness. It is to apply not only in politics but also in economics: 'What you do not wish done to yourself, do not do to others.'

As we have already seen, the InterAction Council has taken over these two principles from the **Declaration toward a Global Ethic by the World's Parliament of Religions**, and at the same time it has emphatically referred to the Declaration's four irrevocable directives: commitment to a culture of non-violence, solidarity, tolerance and equal rights. In the first part of this book I quoted literally from this Chicago Declaration for politicians (but of course not only for them) the commitment to a culture of tolerance and a life of truthfulness. It is certainly appropriate for me now to quote for businessmen and women (and of course not only for them) the commitment to solidarity and a just economic order. This adopts a clear standpoint not only over against totalitarian state socialism but also against unbridled capitalism, in favour of a market economy which has a social and an ecological orientation.

(2) **Commitment to a just economic order**: Numberless men and women of all regions and religions strive to live their lives in solidarity with one another and to work for authentic fulfilment of their vocations. Nevertheless, all over the world we find endless hunger, deficiency, and need. Not only individuals, but especially unjust institutions and structures are responsible for these tragedies. Millions of people are without work; millions are exploited by poor wages, forced to the edges of society, with their possibilities for the future destroyed. In many lands the gap between the poor and the rich, between the powerful and the powerless is immense. We live in a world in which totalitarian state socialism as well as unbridled capitalism have hollowed out and destroyed many ethical and spiritual values. A materialistic mentality breeds greed for unlimited profit and a grasping for endless plunder. These demands claim more and more of the community's resources without obliging the individual to contribute more. The cancerous social evil of corruption thrives in the developing countries and in the developed countries alike.

A. In the great ancient religious and ethical traditions of humankind we find the directive: **You shall not steal!** Or in positive terms: **Deal honestly and fairly!** Let us reflect anew on the consequences of this ancient directive. No one has the right to rob or dispossess in any way whatsoever any other person or the commonweal. Further, no one has the right to use her or his possessions without concern for the needs of society and Earth.

B. Where extreme poverty reigns, helplessness and despair spread, and theft occurs again and again for the sake of survival. Where power and wealth are accumulated ruthlessly, feelings of envy, resentment, and deadly hatred and rebellion inevitably well up in the disdavantaged and marginalized. This leads to a vicious circle of violence and counter-violence. Let no one be deceived: There is no global peace without global justice!

C. Young people must learn at home and in school that property, limited though it may be, carries with it an obligation, and that its uses should at the same time serve the common good. Only thus can a **just economic order** be built up.

D. If the plight of the poorest billions of humans on this planet, particularly women and children, is to be improved, the world economy must be structured more justly. Individual good deeds, and assistance projects, indispensable though they be, are insufficient. The participation of all states and the authority of international organizations are needed to build just economic institutions.

A solution which can be supported by all sides must be sought for the debt crisis and the poverty of the dissolving Second World, and even more the Third World. Of course conflicts of interest are unavoidable. In the developed countries, a distinction must be made between necessary and limitless consumption, between socially beneficial and non-beneficial uses of property, between justified and unjustified uses of natural resources, and between a profit-only and a socially beneficial and ecologically oriented market economy. Even the developing nations must search their national consciences.

Wherever those ruling threaten to repress those ruled, wherever institutions threaten persons, and wherever might oppresses right, we have an obligation to resist – whenever possible non-violently.

E. To be authentically human in the spirit of our great religious and ethical traditions means the following:

- We must utilize economic and political power for **service to humanity** instead of misusing it in ruthless battles for domination. We must develop a spirit of compassion with those who suffer, with special care for the children, the aged, the poor, the disabled, the refugees, and the lonely.

- We must cultivate **mutual respect** and consideration, so as to reach a reasonable balance of interests, instead of thinking only of unlimited power and unavoidable competitive struggles.
- We must value a **sense of moderation and modesty** instead of an unquenchable greed for money, prestige, and consumption! In greed humans lose their 'souls', their freedom, their composure, their inner peace, and thus that which makes them human.[37]

2. Outlines of a new paradigm of an ethic for the economy

At a time when the economy has in fact completed the epoch-making paradigm shift to a world economy which is no longer Eurocentric but polycentric, and now must adapt rationally to global conditions, we need a new paradigm of an ethic for the economy which combines economic rationality with a basic ethical orientation. I have already referred to several European and American works on such an ethic,[38] and doubtless in the very near future we shall be able to expect works with a new integrating ethic which see themselves as offering critical reflection on the rational business ethic which is at the heart of it.[39]

(a) Constants and variables

Already in the context of politics I made a distinction between ideals and realities, and we must also note this distinction in connection with the economy. Ethical norms for the economy, too, did not simply fall from heaven as fixed solutions, nor can they be derived from an immutable human nature. They emerged at a very early stage on the basis of particular needs and emergencies, for example the need to protect property against any exploitation and cheating, and include the basic norm which, as we have seen, still persists in the different religious and ethical traditions, 'You shall not steal (lie, cheat).' Here we have an ethical **constant,** or, as the Chicago Declaration puts it, one of the 'four **broad guidelines** for human behaviour which are found in most of the religions of the world': an '**irrevocable directive**'.[40]

However, this irrevocable character does not apply in the same way to more special (or detailed) norms like the prohibition against interest in the Bible (and also in the Qur'an) as it does to the basic norms.[41] We now know that this prohibition found general recognition in Judaism only after a long period of practice, refinement and testing, and was finally put under the legitimating and protective authority of the covenant God Yahweh, though only for Jews dealing with Jews.[42] But it is evident precisely in this prohibition against levying interest that norms which were already observed at an early stage had to be adapted in changed times; indeed in some circumstances they even had to be diluted and finally abandoned. So we cannot overlook the fact that particularly in business, specific ethical norms not only differ between nations or groups but can also change with the economic context. They often have a variety of areas of validity and a variety of periods of validity. So these are ethical **variables**.

Let us clarify this issue in the sphere of economics. The specific biblical prohibition against profiting from a loan (the Latin *usura* can be translated as 'interest' or 'usury') comes from a period of an almost pure natural economy, where most people had to pledge goods they needed every day only in times of distress. For Christians to profit from such credit enforced by need amounted to a violation of Christian love of neighbour. Moreover the prohibition was constantly repeated by the churches in relation to dealings between Christians (not with Jews!). But at the latest from the middle of the sixteenth century, with the rise of the modern monetary economy, loans increasingly took on a significance of their own, as they had long since ceased to be primary credit for survival, and moderate interest could hardly any longer be regarded as unjust profit. So the prohibition against interest lost its original sense and was tacitly abandoned by the churches, though only after a long period of toing and froing. Where no interest is required, there are usually other obligations, which can be more binding and perhaps also more unpleasant than going to the bank.

The same can be said about the specific moral commandment on the **fair price** (*iustum pretium*). It was established in the Middle Ages to protect the purchaser from being exploited by the authority through taxes, but in time it led to prices being kept artificially high, to the disadvantage of the consumer. The new competitive economy, which arose in the eighteenth century (brilliantly analysed, as we saw, by Adam Smith), was able to provide people with cheaper goods through the 'invisible hand' of free competition and to protect them better from exploitation than the moral commandment to observe the price prescribed by the state.

Nevertheless, despite all the changes in specific or detailed norms directed against the constantly changing forms of exploitation and cheating by others, the elementary basic ethical norm of 'not stealing' was applied in constantly new moral and legal formulations. All this means that a **concrete ethic** is a structure of **constants and variables**. And since Kant, modern ethics has been seeking a course of action between Scylla and Charybdis:

– Those who see only moral constants everywhere will arrive at a rigid moral dogmatism or fundamentalism which is alien to the world.

– Those who think they can see only variables in ethics succumb to an erosive relativism or scepticism. In the following basic reflections on an ethic for the economy, corresponding to those on a political ethic (A II, 1), I shall try to avoid both dangers.

(b) No ethic of conviction based on idealistic views about economics

To reduce the problems of an ethic for the economy to the **alternative of God or money** is a grotesque over-simplification. Indeed there is no question

that according to a Christian (Jewish or Muslim) view, not money but God rules, or should rule, the world;

that all Christians have to decide whether, be they large savers or small savers, they pin their hearts on God or mammon: whether money is a necessary 'means of payment and life' for them, or is their idol;[43]

that all Christians are called by the message of Jesus at any rate to a modest simplicity, a generous readiness to help, and to inner detachment from possessions ('poverty of the Spirit'), in short:

that economic values cannot and may not head the scale of values for Christians.

But at the same time there is no question,

that although Jesus was himself poor and took sides with the poor, he did not preach a goulash communism ('first guzzle, then morality!') or a prosperous society, but 'God's kingdom and then everything else';[44]

that he did not call on his followers to dispossess the rich, take vengeance on the exploiters and renounce possessions generally;

that various of his disciples owned houses and, like Jesus himself, were dependent in their itinerant life on the support of those among his followers, especially women followers, who had possessions.[45]

For today, this means that in spite of all their resolute commitment to oppose unjust and inhuman conditions Christians (especially theologians and bishops) should not appear to be economically naive enthusiasts who in a religious way gloss over poverty and sweepingly discredit riches. Still less, of course, should they be pious fanatics, whose zeal only conceals a lack of competence in economics, who all too often preach water to the world and themselves drink wine and eat smoked salmon. Voluntarily chosen poverty is a charismatic form of life for individuals or groups, inspired and legitimated by the gospel, but, as the history of the Franciscan order shows, it was not easy to realize even in the Middle Ages, far less in the modern world.

Even genuine idealists must understand that while an idealistic demand like lending without interest (or at very low interest) with an appeal to the biblical prohibition against usury could be highly meaningful within the family circle, among neighbours and church communities, or even for some social actions, for development projects, or for charitable or ecological plans, it cannot be a universally valid economic solution (as is being vainly attempted in the Islamic sphere). Why not? Because, as we have heard, the economic background has completely changed. In principle such an ethic of conviction lacks economic competence in today's globalized world. For:

- An **ethic of conviction based on idealistic views about economics**, for which a purely moral motivation and good purpose (justice, love, truth) is enough, but which pays little attention to given economic laws, and the possibility of implementing the purpose in a highly complex economic system, is of no use for a new world economic order.[46] Such an ethic of conviction tends, in principle at least, in specific cases to discredit the profit motive as being *a priori* immoral.
- It also has to be said that to make **moral demands devoid of any economic reality** a general principle, and not to take note of the laws of the economy, is not morality but **moralism**. Pursuing one's own interests and seeking a profit is legitimate if it does not violate higher goods.

'Well meant' is also the opposite of good in economics. Such a simplistic ethics of conviction is, on closer inspection, not ethics but romanticism, more or less pious day-dreaming. Particularly in an age of globalization it is true that good motives do not in themselves guarantee good business. The art of doing business successfully includes an assessment not only of the effects intended (say an increase in production), but also the side-effects which are in no way intended but are often very serious (for example the reaction of the trade unions, the pollution of the environment). Those who want only to act well without heed to the possibly bad consequences and side-effects, are acting irresponsibly, even culpably, even if in cases of failure they like to blame others or the circumstances. A false idealism has so often led socially-concerned and charitable undertakings astray. The important thing in doing business responsibly and successfully is not just the motive but also the results.

(c) No realist ethic of the economy devoid of conviction

To reduce the whole problem of economics and morality to the **alternative of profit or conviction** is an equally naive over-simplification. An ethic of success with no convictions is not an ethic, even if it is commended by consultants, but a technique, an egotistic technique of behaviour. It can lead to crass libertinism and unrestrained capitalism. But neither big banks nor international concerns and international organizations, neither the higher institutional level of a policy of order nor the subordinate level of business policy, stand above morality. Why? Ethics, because it is categorical and not hypothetical, universal and not particular, knows **no ethic-free zones or levels**, which seem to be presupposed by some economists who accept ethical and political frameworks for the national sphere but reject them for the international sphere.

- The **mere ethics of success of 'real' economists**, for whom profit 'sanctifies' all means (in 'emergencies' even immoral means like breaches of faith, lies and deceit), and also all aims (even unrestrained greed), is therefore of no use for a new world economic order. Here the profit motive, which is morally justified, is elevated to become a dogmatic 'profit principle' or even a 'principle of maximizing profit'.
- Against this it has to be said that dogmatically to put forward **economic views devoid of any ethical norms** is not economics but economic reductionism, **economism**. In no way can the primacy which is due to ethics be granted to success. Perception of one's own interests and any business activity must be ethically responsible, even if in the specific instance of the pressure of competition this may be asking too much.

At all events, in principle 'business needs a firm moral basis; it is not a moral-free area. Economic activity always also has moral dimensions. It would be disastrous to overlook that.' These are the comments of the Göttingen economist **Helmut Hesse**, who is certainly representative of many in his discipline, in his programmatic article on 'Economy and Morality': 'Of course, people who live together have an unchanged interest in being protected from economic exploitation by others, who, to use the words of the Bonhoeffer circle, are possessed by the demon "avarice" and by ambition. Moral norms must be established against such people.'⁴⁷ Of course, the economist adds, if the economy is subject to constant changes, ever-new ways open up for greed and ambition. Therefore the relevant moral norms must also change. 'However, in essence they are always about the same thing. Wherever selfishness, greed and ambition put others at a disadvantage or even result in their exploitation, the way to them must be blocked. Where morality is too weak for this, it must be supplemented by ordered competition. Moreover in that case the moral norms must be embodied in state laws and be imposed by the authorities.'⁴⁸ In short: 'Moral norms in economic life change, and have to change. But in the end their aim remains the same, namely to preserve human beings from exploitation and cheating by others.'⁴⁹ Even a theologian could not put it more clearly than that.

(d) An ethically responsible way of engaging in business

The reason for engaging in business is to guarantee the foundations of human life. But is perhaps the 'maximizing of profit' necessary for human survival? On the basis of everything that has been developed in this section, it can be stated that while the **profit motive** is ethically justified on the understanding that higher values are preserved, precisely because of this **the maximizing of profit** can in no way be justified ethically as an economic principle. For why must (financial) gain be maximized, if social or ecological costs are as well?

- The only ethic that is of use for a new world economic order is a **responsible ethic of realist economists with idealist horizons.** Such an ethic also presupposes ideals and values in doing business, but asks realistically about the foreseeable consequences of economic decisions, particularly if they are negative, and also takes responsibility for them.
- A responsible way of doing business in the postmodern period is convincingly **to combine business strategies with ethical judgment.**
- This new paradigm of a business ethic becomes concrete by testing business dealings – even though profit is legitimate – to see whether they violate higher goods or values, whether they are **compatible with society, the environment and the future.** Because such a reasoned examination of ethical justification is difficult in each individual instance, some political ordinances are necessary.

I must leave the various ways of interpreting the profit principle in business ethics to the professionals: profit and loss have the priority here. **Peter Ulrich**, an expert in business ethics and a pioneer in his attempt to clarify the relationship between business ethics and the 'profit principle' (a 'basic ethical problem which has yet to be resolved'), makes the programmatic demand that ethics should not merely have corrective 'external limits' for senior management, but should also integrate a **'basis for business'** as an integrative concept.

'Whereas the tension between ethics and the aim to achieve success is thought of horizontally on one level in corrective business ethics (and accordingly can only be resolved by a compromise), in an integrative approach it is turned as it were by ninety degrees to the vertical. Now ethics is conceived of as the intrinsic basis of any legitimate, responsible and practically meaningful strategy of success in business. Or, to put it in a less metaphorical way: the integrative approach understands the normative presuppositions as constituting a way of doing business which produces economic success and at the same time is reasonably practical.'[50]

So the issue is that of the primacy of ethics over the systemic logic of the market economy. Here it is hardly relevant whether the decision-makers concerned are members of a smaller or larger group. At all events the primacy of ethics applies not only, as is claimed by some representatives of the 'economic theory of morality', which I have already rejected, in the limited circumstances of small groups (family, village community), but by analogy also applies at the level of the anonymous wider society. (In fact at all levels of decision this still consists of small groups and individuals.) Such a division also neglects the whole spectrum of intermediary institutions which fulfil a mediating function between the private sphere and social megastructures (professional organizations, industrial associations, trade unions).[51]

Of course 'morality in a large group . . . cannot be understood as a seamless extension of small group morality'.[52] But **'large group morality'** cannot simply be opposed in the abstract to **'small group morality'**: not only because in real life large groups and small groups are interwoven and the same persons in their different roles are often members of both, but above all because 'large group morality' may not simply be detached from the irrevocable ethical constants which apply universally and unconditionally. Otherwise the primacy of ethics over economics is put in question. For example, any kind of 'legal' export of technology and weapons by German firms for the production of rockets or poison gas by dictators like Saddam Hussein or Muammar Gadaffi could be justified morally (as is done by such economic moral theologians),[53] simply by putting the blame for the immorality on the legislator. 'If what we have done is immoral, then there is something wrong with our laws.'[54] Such an 'institutional ethic' intended for large groups through their organizations in the market economy scorns all genuine business ethics. This requires the businessmen concerned (and their companies) to make their political influence felt in order to establish economically meaningful and ethically responsible frameworks.

Perhaps one should recommend these economic moral theoreticians of an all too convenient voluntary large group morality to study the '**Lopez Group**', a small group which allowed itself to be lured away in somewhat unattractive circumstances, and is supposed to have taken important business documents and plans by the caseful. In the persons of these 'warriors' those moral economists could study the effects of a lack of 'small group' morality on the morality of a global big business like Volkswagen and its dispute with the big business General Motors, and finally on the stock market. I do not know whether the former top VW manager José Ignacio Lopez, who is said to be closely connected with Opus Dei and is accused of industrial espionage, has read works of moral economics. But undoubtedly he could have justified what he did by the argument that a small group morality could not be applied to his large group and that specific imperatives like 'You shall not steal' or 'You shall not lie', manifestly intended only for small groups, at best applied to village communities in his Basque homeland. So we are waiting for the hour when, if things go as they should, another small group (the judges in Darmstadt, the jury in Detroit?) passes legal judgment on the large group morality of the small Lopez group. For meanwhile, as was to be expected, on the sure basis of small-group morality, the two large groups of VW and GM have finally arrived at an out-of-court settlement in favour of the large groups (including the shareholders), in which the moral and financial loser is clear. And what one can learn generally for large groups from the case of the small group is that just as the globalized financial markets need stricter insider rules, so the big businesses which act globally require stricter ethical rules of conduct if they want to stand up to the public criticism of mature citizens and survive in a sphere in which competition has become harder.

What is left of morality? That is sometimes the question today from people who are beginning to doubt the system of the market economy.

Of course top executives in business are not *a priori* less moral than others, but they often have to make decisions in particularly difficult situations, where business success should be achieved within a framework of ethical principles, as will be demonstrated in a later chapter. However, as a transition to the basic question of ethics and 'sustainable development', let me quote the answer of a top executive to the question 'Does increasing competition still leave room for ethical action?' His answer is: 'Of course competition still leaves room for ethical action. That's anything but a luxury; it's a compelling presupposition for success. The more exposed a business is, the more sensitive the climate in which it operates. And in that I include not only our customers, our employees and our partners, but also our competitors. In some situations, to abandon ethical principles may bring short-term advantages, but in the longer term the opposite is the case.' Thus Bernd Pischetsrieder, Chairman of BMW.[55]

3. Sustainable development and a global ethic

How urgent and indispensable ethical reflection is for a constructive policy for the world order also emerges from the fact that apparently obvious demands, like that for a long-term, 'durable' or '**sustainable**' **development** are by no means a matter of course, or even evident to the general public. The 1995 **World Summit for Social Development** in Copenhagen affirmed this demand fully, but the members were better on agreeing a programme of what they would like than on agreeing a concrete policy. Not only the industrial countries but also the developing countries did not want to commit themselves to concrete measures to remove the causes of environmental destruction, migration and war. Not only are specific political structures lacking here, but above all the ethical and political will, and this needs a motivation. Moreover, developmental theorists and politicians also speak of a **motivation problem**. To put the question in concrete terms: why should things not be worse for the generation after us, if that is the way in which things are going? Why should things go even better for them, as is sometimes desired? These are the questions not only of sceptics, cynics and nihilists, but also of economists, pragmatists and realists.

(a) Provisions for the future: on what basis?

First let us make the question theoretically clear. We shall do this in two stages, since the demand for sustainable social development needs to be distinguished from the demand for provisions for the future. What can be proved here with rational arguments? Here, in fact, some scepticism is now called for.

(1) **Pure reason cannot prove** the demand for a **sustainable** development. By 'sustainable' is to be understood 'a development in which the natural foundations remain preserved in such a way that the living conditions of the present generation are also still an option for coming generations'.[56] Or, to put it simply: things must not be essentially worse for subsequent generations than they are for us. But why?

It is bad that apparently no scientific reasons can be given which with a quasi-automatic logic show compellingly that a policy of sustainability must necessarily be practised. Even advocates of a sustainable development have recognized that this is an **ethical decision**: the need to select particular elements of the environment and particular living conditions which are worth preserving cannot be proved either in purely economic or purely ecological terms. This is a matter of cultural self-understanding: it is not a matter for an individual science but one of ethics and politics. It is true that the social sciences can clarify and interpret the process of selection which is necessary here, as is shown by the impressive preparatory document for the UN Social Summit. But, and this is unfortunately shown by the ultimately disappointing result of this summit, the result itself must be arrived at 'ethically and politically'. In a sentence: sustainability is 'neither an economic nor an ecological concept, nor even a scientific concept, but an ethical demand'.[57] Now if this is the case, the question arises as to the **basis for this ethical demand**. Grappling with it is above all the task of philosophy and theology.

(2) **Nor can pure reason substantiate** the demand for **provisions for the future**. This principle says: we should act in such a way that things not only do not get worse for subsequent generations than they are for us. But again we have the question, Why? For many people this is a sympathetic principle, but perhaps, at least for economists, one which goes too far and is therefore unrealistic.

One thing at any rate cannot be disputed: it depends absolutely and utterly on our ethical motivation whether we decide that things should go as well for the generation of our children as it does for us, or worse or better. Here it is not enough to argue using pure, theoretical reason. For this insight (which we owe to Jürgen Habermas) has become established in philosophy: that **reason is subject to interests**.

Now this means that the question whether I should concern myself here and now with the fate of future generations can hardly be decided by pure reason. Don't I already have enough anxieties, so that I can be quite indifferent about what happens to later generations? Arbitrary pluralists can 'argue' like this: Why should I worry about devastated landscapes, elsewhere? What is the problem about the disappearance of species, as long as my garden blossoms and my dog remains alive? Why worry about changes in the climate, which will make the oceans rise only in the year 2000 plus x? And why shouldn't I really think that the main thing is for me to live well and do what gives me pleasure? This is completely in accord with today's psychological and psychotherapeutic 'correctness': everything depends on one's own fulfilment. At a recent lecture in Tübingen, an expert on the German and French scene, Alfred Grosser, remarked that political and social involvement is put on the front pages of the newspapers and 'Do what you want and have your fling!' on the last. Why bother about others, least of all those still to be born?

But now to speak seriously to the serious: it is in fact a deeply ethical basic decision whether I think at all about the fate not only of our children but of future generations generally, not to mention whether I work so that things go better for future generations than for mine, or at least no worse. So ethics is more than weighing up interests in the specific instance. Ethics aims at a commitment to others which is both unconditional and universal. And of course, given divergent interests and the pressure of facts, this must be reflected on critically. For ethics, too, cannot be had without conflict. Ethical decisions are often subject to great tensions, especially if they are governed by deep religious convictions. Therefore we must now turn to religion.

(3) **Religion can fail** in the face of the demand for **sustainability and provisions for the future.** That already became clear at the 1992 UN Conference for the Environment and Development in Rio de Janeiro. This environmental summit approved an agenda for sustainable development, and an agreement on the climate which points towards the future. But what use is this if so far not a single state is ready to translate the decision passed there, quite unanimously, into practical policy? Here what is lacking towards implementation is not just an internationally binding regime but the ethical and political will to act (and the 1995 Berlin **Conference on the Climate** confirms this). Here the religions play an important, if not always happy, role. Obviously a consensus on ecological problems, particularly among the developing countries,

could not be aimed at through an appeal to purposive rationality alone, because ideological and religious factors kept coming into play.

The same was also true of the 1994 UN **World Population Conference** in Cairo. Here, with much expenditure of science and rhetoric, it was made clear that one of the greatest dangers posed to a worthwhile survival of the human race is the excessive population growth, above all in the poor countries. The world population will rise to 9.4 billion by the year 2050 ('World Population Prospects: The 1996 Revision'), and already in many places it cannot find schools, jobs or even enough to eat. In some countries trends are evidently in the other direction: slowing growth rates. The essential cause of this is seen in the fact that already more couples than had been assumed use contraceptives. Compared with this, the rise in mortality rates through wars and AIDS, the reduction in life-expectation, the fight against poverty, and better offers of education, are secondary causes. But we have already seen in connection with fundamentalism and moralism that here the religious opposites come very close to each other, particularly over the question of the population explosion and contraception. Fundamentalists of Christian and Islamic provenance irresponsibly did all they could in Cairo to establish their own sexual morality and to give free rein to uncontrolled development of the population.

So when we speak of an ethical foundation to the demand for sustainability and provisions for the future, unfortunately we must expect that not only is pure reason insufficient, but that religion, too, can fail, because reason is disowned by particular religious interest groups and power blocks. Especially when one commits oneself to a universal human ethic supported by the religions, one has to take a clear stand against the **religious moralism which knows no limits to its competence.** A church or religion must not (as most recently even at the 1996 UN **Nutrition Conference** in Rome) play down the significance of the ongoing growth in the population: at present every nine months the population of the world is growing by 80 million, the population of Germany!

(b) Aim and criterion: human beings in an environment worth living in

But now for a positive question. What could be the ethical maxim for a sustainable development? On the threshold of the third millennium the cardinal ethical question arises more urgently than ever: **on what basic conditions** can we survive; survive **as human beings on a habitable earth** and give our individual and social life a humane form?[58] On what presuppositions can human civilizations survive in the third millennium? What basic principle are the chief figures in politics, the economy, science and also the religions to follow to make a sustainable development possible? On what presuppositions can the individual achieve a happy and fulfilled existence?

First, here is a quite general and fundamentally ethical answer:

A **'biocentric' conception** which wants to attribute a right to existence not only to plants and animals but also to ecological systems and biological species seems as little suited to give help in a practical decision as a **'holistic conception'** which also wants to protect inanimate nature for its own sake. We may agree with Dieter Birnbacher's criticism of these two positions (although of course they represent important concerns). On the maxim 'Everyone should take everything into consideration' he rightly remarks: 'If everything is worth protecting, there are no criteria which can justify interventions in nature.'[59]

However, no **'anthropocentric' conception** in the traditional and exclusive sense, which ignores the suffering of animals and neglects the environment, should be put forward either. What we need is an **integral humane conception**: humanity in a **cosmic context**, as this has been emphasized from of old, more in Indian and Chinese spirituality than in the Christian West. Instead of the exploitative domination of nature by human beings we need an incorporation of human beings into nature.

What the fundamental goal and criterion of ethical action in a global economy and a global ecology has to be has already become clear in the context of global politics: it has to be **the human being in the midst of an environment worth living in.** Human beings must expend their human potential in a different way from before to ensure the most humane society possible and an intact, habitable, environment capable of functioning and corresponding to human values, and therefore worth living in. For the possibilities of their humanity which can be activated are greater than the state in which they actually exist. To this degree Hans Jonas's realistic principle of responsibility and Ernst Bloch's 'utopian' principle of hope belong together.

No matter what economic and ecological projects are planned for a better human future, the basic ethical principle must be that human beings may **never** be made **mere means** (since Kant this is a formulation of the categorical imperative). They must remain the ultimate end, always the **goal and criterion.** Money and capital are means, as work is a means. Any assessment of the consequences of technology has to note that science, technology and industry are means. They, too, are in no way intrinsically 'value-free', 'neutral'. Rather, in each individual instance they should be judged and used in terms of how far they help human beings as individuals and a genre to develop in an environment worth living in.

Today it is easy to agree about this in theory. The problem is how to realize it in practice. 'Everyone wants, but no one does anything', is the pointed remark of those who know anything about the situation. 'There is a great awareness of the environment, but little action which takes account of the environment.'[60]

(c) The problem of motivation

With specific rules, a rational ethic can commend quite specific **attitudes** and **life-styles**: self-restraint, a capacity for peace, fair distribution, the furtherance of life. It can also offer particular **rules of priority and safety** for estimating benefits when weighing up the consequences of technology: rules for solving problems, for the burden of proof, for the common good, for urgency, for the ecology, for reversibility.[61]

All these rules offer pointers towards discriminating rational action, but they do not give an answer to the question of moral **motivation**. This question arises particularly acutely in connection with a long-term responsibility for coming generations and for nature: 'So far the **problem of motivation** is largely unresolved.'[62] Why? According to the experts, in psychological terms almost everything tells **against** the practicability of responsibility for the future: the impossibility of **compensation** for ethically motivated provisions by corresponding benefits, the **anonymity** of the future, and finally the **uncertainty** of our prognoses. In these circumstances the question becomes acute: from where are we to get the motivation for an ethic of the future, for long- term responsibility towards later generations, for long-term responsibility towards nature?

Such a motivation first of all presupposes a change of consciousness. The important thing is 'to develop an **awareness of one's own chronological position in the chain of generations** and to develop a feeling of community which goes beyond the generations, if not with the whole of humankind, at least with a limited cultural, national or regional group'. From such a change of consciousness it is possible to gain a twofold attitude, namely 'a retrospective attitude of gratitude and a recognition of one's responsibility to make provisions for the future'.[63] Any help in motivation that philosophy and theology in particular can provide is welcome here.

So the Tübingen philosopher **Otfried Höffe** has constructively worked out '**components for an ecological global ethic**'.[64] His view is that ij particular on the basis of modern developments, the sciences are proving to be 'morally open', even 'prone to morality'. It is not so much that mistakes have increased as the possibilities of going wrong; not so much a lack of conscience as moral fallibility. In the face of the scientific and technological illusions of omnipotence on the one hand, and excessive anxiety as a consequence of a radical pessimism about technology on the other, Höffe calls for a rehabilitation of the classical virtues which have been suppressed by autonomous morality (the four 'cardinal virtues'). He also seeks a further development of the classical ethic of virtue. As the components of a new ecological global ethic he specifically calls for two ecological virtues:

> **serenity** (against the hybris of science which overestimates itself); and
> **level-headedness** (against the immoderation of technology and economic rationality).[65]

According to Höffe, these demands made by an ecological global ethic are addressed directly to a legal and state order, and to individuals only through the medium of this order. However, one may think that these demands are also addressed quite directly to individuals and that it is precisely here that the **religions** have their special motivating function, which is not to be neglected. To this degree the Declaration toward a Global Ethic made by the Parliament of the World's Religions could deepen this philosophical approach. As for sustainable development, the religions in particular most of all have a sense of what the developmental specialist calls the '**chain of generations**', and particularly of the dimensions that he calls for: retrospective **gratitude** and **expectation** and **provision** for the future.

The question of the **unconditional** and **universal nature** of such an ethic is also easier to answer, as I already explained, in the context of global politics. For basic ethical questions also arise in connection with the global economy. Provided that one suffers no risk oneself, why should not a dictator tyrannize his people and even require them to suffer sanctions imposed by the international community (in 'Orthodox' Serbia, in 'Muslim' Iraq)? Why should not a group cut down a tropical rain forest, a nation begin a war over supposed oil or gold resources, if it is in its own interest and there is no authority which stands unconditionally and for all, including those who rule states? Why should they all act in a different way?

In his work on an ethic of responsibility **Hans Jonas** has rightly asked an even more radical question in connection with the apocalyptic potential of nuclear or genetic technology, and one with which ethics had not previously been confronted: whether and why in the future there should be a humanity, why its genetic heritage should be respected, indeed why there should be life at all. That he has ventured on this root question indicates that Jonas is a truly radical thinker. Here he openly concedes that there is a philosophical need to provide a rational foundation even for the **prime imperative of an ethic of survival**: 'that there be a mankind',[66] that for statesmen there should be 'the prohibition of a *va-banque* gamble with mankind' and of a desire for an 'end' – possibly deserved – to mankind.[67] In view of Adolf Hitler's feverish fantasies before his suicide of the 'deserved' destruction of the whole German people (who were not worthy of him) or in view of the possibilities for Saddam Hussein in the possession of nuclear weapons against Israel or a greater nuclear war, such reflections are truly not far-fetched.

Here the philosopher Jonas openly concedes the **limits of philosophy**, even if he does not want to accept them as a philosopher: that 'mankind has no right to suicide'.[68] 'To underpin this proposition theoretically is by no means easy and without religion perhaps impossible.'[69] The '**unconditional** duty for man to exist'[70] and thus 'the duty arising from procreation is far harder to prove, and if at all, then surely not from the same principle . . . Thus here we are dealing with a duty which is not a counterpart of another right – unless it be the right of God the creator God over against his creatures, to whom, with the bestowal of existence, he has entrusted the continuation of his work.'[71] I can only agree with Hans Jonas when he says 'that religious belief has answers here which philosophy must still seek, and must do so with uncertain prospects of success'.[72] However, it also has to be conceded to him that 'faith thus can very well supply the foundation for ethics, but it is not there on command.'[73]

But now it is time, in the next two chapters (as already in the questions of politics, now in those for economics), to go beyond global perspectives to yet greater concreteness and closeness to life:
– from the **macrolevel**: the questions of the morality of the economic system as such;
– through the **mesolevel**: the questions of the policy and strategy of the organizations or businesses involved in the economy;
– to the **microlevel**: the questions of the morality of individuals and above all business executives.

IV

Ethic, Business and Managers

In 1971 **Klaus Schwab**, a professor of economic policy who had just returned from the USA at the age of thirty-three, arranged the first annual meeting of business leaders in Davos, later to become the World Economic Forum, and at the same time formulated as a 'model for business' what was to become even more topical in the 1990s in the face of globalization: that 'all the groups mentioned in alphabetical order here have a direct interest in the success of a business' (here I quote him word for word):[1]

– The **shareholders and lenders** expect not only a safe investment but also appropriate interest on the capital invested.

– The **customers** expect a good product at a favourable price. For machinery, service is also particularly important. It does not just begin with the delivery of the machine, but at the first plannning of the product, because here already the producer must already be concerned with the problems of the purchaser.

– The **suppliers** expect the business to be capable of paying them. Furthermore, they have an interest that the competitiveness of the purchaser should be maintained in the long term, and grow further.

– The **employees** expect not only appropriate financial remuneration for their contribution, but also recognition and encouragement. The best results can only be achieved when employees are convinced of the significance of their work and individuals are given possibilities of developing it.

– The **national economy, the state and society** expect the business to contribute in a variety of ways to the improvement of the common good (jobs, taxes, etc.).

The model must take these expectations, needs and interests into account. – Thus Klaus Schwab.

1. Principles of a business ethic

Already at the third Davos management forum in 1973, a 'code of good ethical behaviour for executives' was presented. This saw it as its task 'to serve customers, workers, backers and society' and to 'balance their conflicting interests'. It culminates in the concluding remark that profit is 'a necessary means but not the end' of any business enterprise.[2] Now it is certainly not a coincidence that a vehement attack on this approach followed, with an explicit reference to Milton Friedman. It came from a professor of business theory, **Horst Steinmann**, who read out of the text a rejection of 'institutional measures to control power', an 'ideological justification and capitulation to environmental interests' and a 'repudiation of demands for reform'. However, none of this is to be found in the Davos manifesto; nor can it even be attributed to the Corporate Social Responsibility movement which may have influenced this manifesto as a principal factor, but certainly not as the sole one. Would Horst Steinmann, who in the meantime has done very good work in business ethics, still construe 'a break-up of bourgeois liberal ideas of order' from the idea of the 'social responsibility of businesses' and discover a 'contradiction to the idea of democracy'[3] in it? Or was this perhaps a sin of his youth? Be this as it may, twenty years later one can read in the same author that 'ethical considerations' must 'systematically be put before the profit principle, not only at the level of order but also at that of business'.[4]

In the time of Reaganomics some economists thought that morality had lost its 'controlling power'. That is certainly not completely wrong, in that businesses and national economies have come to depend very closely on one another, and the economic interactions have become complicated and anonymous. But on the other hand, particularly in the 1990s, economists find themselves confronted with an unexpected **return of morality** in public discussion, in particular in the national economy and the business world. I shall now go on to mention two indications of the new significance of ethics in business.

(a) Not just for shareholders but for all involved

Two statements provide evidence for the 'global ethic project' that co-operation is quite possible both between different religions and between believers and non-believers, in questions of business ethics:
– **The Interfaith Declaration. A Code of Ethics on International Business for Christians, Muslims and Jews.** It was worked out under the

patronage of Prince Philip, Duke of Edinburgh; Hassan bin Talal, Crown Prince of Jordan; and Sir Evelyn de Rothschild in 1988 (at Windsor) and 1993 (in Amman).[5]

– **Principles For Business. The Caux Round Table.** The Caux Round Table was founded by Frederik Philips (former President of Philips Electronics) and Olivier Giscard d'Estaing (Vice President of INSEAD) in 1986. It was taken further by Ryuzaburo Kaku (Chairman of Canon Inc), and concluded with the considerable involvement of leading business representatives from Europe, Japan and the USA.[6]

The Caux Declaration begins from the fact of globalization: 'The mobility of employment, capital, products and technology is making business increasingly global in its transactions and its effects.'[7] Yet at the same time it states that **companies have responsibilities over and above earning profits,** and that they cannot just rely on the 'magic' of the market for solving problems: 'Laws and market forces are necessary but insufficient guides for conduct. Responsibility for the policies and actions of business and respect for the dignity and interests of its stakeholders are fundamental. Shared values including a commitment to shared prosperity, are as important for a global community as for communities of smaller scale.' Therefore the Declaration speaks of the 'necessity for moral values in business decision making. Without them, stable business relationships and a sustainable world community are impossible.'

It is significant that both declarations in no way see the task of the business only as earning profits for the **shareholders,** but in responsibility for all **stakeholders** who have a stake in the business. The Caux Declaration finds this point so fundamental that it makes it the first general principle: 'The Responsibilities of Businesses: Beyond Shareholders towards Stakeholders'.[8] The profit motive is seen as fully justified but not sufficient: 'Businesses have a role to play in improving the lives of all their customers, employees and shareholders by sharing with them the wealth they have created.'[9]

It is therefore consistent that both declarations should have more or less detailed sections on the responsibilities of business to all six parties: towards employees, customers, suppliers and financiers, the community (local and national governments), and finally also the owners/ shareholders/investors (in the Interfaith Declaration put in last place, in the Caux Declaration in third place).

Both declarations agree on the responsibilities of businesses towards their **employees.** The Caux Declaration states: 'We believe in the dignity

of every employee and in taking employee interests taken seriously. We therefore have a responsibility to:
– provide jobs and compensation that improve workers' living conditions . . .
– engage in good faith negotiations when conflict arises . . .
– promote in the business itself the employment of differently abled people in places of work where they can be genuinely useful';
– and finally, in addition to all the obligations of employers to provide information and communication, health care and further training, in particular to 'be sensitive to the serious unemployment problems frequently associated with business decisions, and work with governments, employee groups, other agencies and each other in addressing these disclocations'.[10]

The Interfaith Declaration emphasizes: 'Employees make a unique contribution to an organization; it follows that in their policies businesses shall, where appropriate, take notice of trade union positions'; businesses should show 'a respect for the individual (whether male or female) in their beliefs, their family responsibility and their need to grow as human beings. It will provide equal opportunities in training and promotion for all members of the organization. It will not discriminate in its policies on grounds of race, skin colour, creed or gender.'[11]

But it would take us too far were I to go on to report on the ethical responsibilities of businesses to the other five groups involved. Rather, what is important for a global ethic at a time of globalization is what underlies the individual ethical requirements. Both declarations are quite clear about this.

(b) Basic values and basic attitudes

It is highly illuminating that in the preface to the Caux declaration both a 'Western' and an 'Eastern' basic value are to be found which happily supplement each other:
– not only 'human dignity' and the sacredness of the value of each individual, who must always remain an end, and not simply be a means for other purposes;
– but also the Japanese concept of 'kyosei', which means living and working together for the common good, enabling co-operation and mutual prosperity to co-exist with healthy and fair competition.[12]

The Interfaith Declaration makes the necessary distinction beween various levels in an ethical approach to business: the intrinsic morality

of the economic system in itself, then the policy and strategy of the organizations concerned, and finally the behaviour of individual employees in the context of their work. At the same time reference is made to the different legal frameworks, depending on the country in which business is conducted. However, mention may be made of some of the key concepts or **basic values** which have great significance in **Judaism, Christianity and Islam,** and for which numerous texts from the sacred scriptures of these three Abrahamic religions can be cited:
– **Justice:** fairness, exercising authority in maintenance of right;
– **Mutual respect:** love and consideration for others;
– **Stewardship:** human beings are only 'stewards', 'trustees' of natural resources;
– **Honesty:** truthfulness and reliability in all human relationships, in short integrity.

The Caux Declaration, in which respect for the law and for national and international rules is inculcated, also stresses that one 'must get beyond the letter of the law to a **spirit of trust**':[13] honesty, boldness, truth, keeping promises and transparency, all of which contribute not only to the credibility and stability of a business but also to the smooth efficiency of business transactions.

It should also be mentioned that the Caux Declaration openly addresses the particularly tricky point of the **'avoidance of illicit operations'.** 'A business should not participate in or condone bribery, money laundering, or other corrupt practices: indeed, it should seek co-operation with others to eliminate them. It should not trade in arms or other materials used for terrorist activities, drug traffic or other organized crime.'[14]

A question which must be raised is: are only Western values and criteria appealed to here? The strong Japanese involvement in the Caux paper already makes this seem doubtful. But the question plays a role which extends to official statements by Chinese and Indonesian statesmen.

(c) Asian versus Western values

It is easy to understand why today Asians, who are open to the West, while affirming modernization, **are sceptical about the Western system of values.** There was an outcry from half the American press (the other half was wisely self-critical) when a young American vandal who had maliciously damaged automobiles and other objects was subjected in Singapore to the caning customary there (though not always enforced).

Singapore took its revenge with concrete figures: in the United States, where the population has increased by 41% since 1960, crimes of violence have increased by 560%, divorces by 300%, single mothers by 419% and children who grow up with one parent by 300%.[15] Singapore really has no intention of being infected by this Western 'morality'. We have heard similar tones from Japan, and in America the former President's drug representative W.J.Bennett, attacking the decline in values, wrote a *Book of Virtues* which presents a 'reasonable mean between *carte blanche* for vandals and torture'.[16] Moreover it promptly became a bestseller, a sign that responsibility, honesty, loyalty, courage, sympathy, friendship, tenacity and self-discipline are being more sought after in the West as well.

However, we are not concerned here with individual virtues, but with the basic question whether the peoples of Asia will adopted **limitless individualism** (which pays no heed to the community) and **unbridled freedom** (with the associated phenomena of Western decadence), or whether, as the wise diplomat and Director of the Institute of Policy Studies in Singapore, Tommy Koh, remarks, they should not maintain and encourage 'the ten values which support the strength and success of East Asia', by attaching importance to strong families, intensive education, hard work, savings, moderation and national teamwork.[17] Already in my dialogue with Julia Ching, an expert on Chinese religion from the University of Toronto,[18] I drew attention to the researches of the French sinologist Léon Vandermersch. In his study of the 'new sinified world',[19] Vandermersch investigates the economic, political and cultural dimensions of the peoples who are bound together by the Chinese writing system or ideograms. These are the same everywhere (though they are read differently), and express meanings and reflect common basic attitudes and values that reproduce the more than two-thousand-year-old Confucian tradition. We need not decide here whether this is also a reason why the cultures of East Asia have been able to advance so amazingly in recent decades by comparison, say, with the Islamic countries. Singapore, at any rate, adopted Confucian ethics in school teaching material in 1984, and similar efforts are also being made in other countries of the Far East. At all events, it is certain that the West has every reason to treat specifically Asian values with modesty and respect, despite all its reservations about a Confucian patriarchalism.[20]

Now does this mean on the other hand that Asian values may be cited **against human rights,** as was done by the Chinese Communists (and other autocratic Asian governments) at the Second World Conference

on Human Rights in Vienna in 1993? Human rights emerged in the
Enlightenment Christian philosophical tradition of the West and also
in Asia (one can ask why). Because religion is the 'missing dimension of
statesmanship', none of the Western diplomats and politicians at that
Vienna conference was evidently knowledgeable enough to point out
to the Chinese delegation that for example the concept of *'jen'*, the
'humanum', is very much a central concept of the Chinese tradition. In
the present situation a great many human rights can be grounded in it
which have considerable resonance all over Asia and Africa. In the long
run these cannot be suppressed by force. How effective it would have
been had a Western speaker pointed out that Confucius had already
stated that a government could most easily dispense with the military,
if need be also with food, but least of all with that trust which the
people puts in it.[21]

Of course the rulers in Asia and elsewhere are often less interested in
human rights than are those whom they rule. But in today's age of
mass communication the fact can no longer be overlooked that from
China, Tibet, Myanmar and Thailand through East Timor, West Irian
in Indonesia and the Philippines to Kenya and the Congo, human
rights express a deep longing of the ruled in the face of the rulers. And
the 'dissidents' are no tiny minority, as one can sometimes read even in
Western newspapers, but for many dictators a terrifying if oppressed
power. There is no question that, given freedom of speech, those
millions whom the bold Nobel Peace Prize-winner Aung San Suu Kyi
was able to mobilize through free elections in Burma could also be
activated in China by a man like Wei Jingsheng.[22]

However, the 'global ethic project' differs from the Western human
rights movement in so far as it does not attempt simply to disseminate
human rights deriving from Western natural-law thinking all over the
world, but rather the values, criteria and attitudes of the ethnic and
religious traditions peculiar to each people, in order to make fruitful
use of them for human responsibilities and human rights. As I have
described, the Chicago Declaration of the Parliament of the World's
Religions also came into being in an attempt to extract from the
traditions of the various great religions what is common to the
religions today and can also be supported by non-religious people. The
opposition of Asian values to Western values is relativized by the
common foundation of human responsibilities and human rights in
each particular tradition. However, we are now moving from these
questions of principle to the more practical questions of today's
industrial societies.

(d) Inconvenient questions, practical suggestions

Are economics, politics and society at all prepared at all for this epoch-making postmodern paradigm shift of globalization now taking place, which in its way is as far-reaching as the change from a mediaeval agricultural economy to modern industrial society? It is important above all to find **a new status for the state, labour and capital.** 'The globalized economy must not become synonymous with a freewheeling market economy, a train without brakes, which wreaks havoc,' remarks Professor Klaus Schwab, the President of the Davos World Economic Forum. The 'human costs of globalization' have reached 'a level at which the whole social structure of the democracies will be put to the test in an unprecedented way'. 'The social responsibilities of businesses (and governments) remain as important as ever. What is on the agenda is the need to redefine them and to weight them.'[23]

All sides have to make their contribution to a **new social consensus.** Nowadays many statesmen, too, see that there must be a fair **balance of burdens.** As the German Federal President Roman Herzog remarks, with an eye to the often blind and selfish functionaries of the different interest groups: 'My experience shows that when people see that a real problem is being addressed and there are not just mischievous cuts, they contribute much that their representatives in the association hierarchies, the parties and even in the media do not understand. People may say that I have illusions, but I still believe that the population is ready to accept cuts as long as it feels that they are needed and the cards are put on the table.'[24]

Thus here first of all some inconvenient but also unavoidable questions arise on all sides. I shall not offer any recipes, but present questions for discussion which are prompted by the problems above all of the Swedish and the American economic models (B I) and the discussion of neocapitalism and the social market economy (B II). To discuss them in the spirit of an ethical responsible way of doing business (B III) might perhaps open up ways out of the present crisis.

(1) Experiences with the American model raise the question: do we not need a **new responsibility for businesses?** 'Globalization is an irreversible process. One of its greatest challenges has not yet been resolved: unemployment. It would be out of the question for companies to be concerned only with their own surplus value and to leave the negative consequences of their restructurings to the world at large.'

Thus the Swiss Federal President Pascal Delamuraz.[25] The following thoughts seem to me to be worth considering:

– In principle '**lean production and management**' (USA) and **social responsibility** (EC) must be achieved together.

– Specifically, we must get out of the vicious circle in which only the slimming down of companies and the mass redundancies connected with this lead to improved profits and thus to higher share values, so that now redundancies are often identified with gains on the stock market. The efforts of business must be concentrated on creating **new jobs with new tasks** instead of just saving 'superfluous' jobs.

– More success might be achieved if, rather than making workers redundant for short-term gain and in order to **consolidate a company, the level of training among the work force** were improved ('upgrading') with a view to a longer-term increase in productivity and possible recruitment for an expanded market.

– Just as the share of income from dependent work must not drop arbitrarily, so too **the share of income from business activity must not rise arbitrarily.**

– More precise **rules relating to the responsibility of the chairmen and directors of companies** need to be aimed at, in order to protect the shareholders and the employees. Bad business decisions and misman-agement, which in individual cases result in the loss of millions or billions and threaten the very existence of a company, must also have tangible consequences for the chairmen and boards responsible.

– Not only the top executives but all employees should share in the return, the success and the resources of a company. **Participation and profit-sharing** can increase identification with work and the company and can also strengthen motivation to personal responsibility, an awareness of costs and better performance.

– A good atmosphere at the workplace and **social peace** are also 'productive factors'.

Against the advocates of a pure capitalism who are miles away from a social market economy, it must be pointed out clearly that an **economic doctrine and praxis which aim only at profit** and do not take the slightest notice of either the workforce or the citizens who are also affected, and which rather *a priori* accept monstrous differences in income and unimaginable suffering and poverty must be said clearly to be not only unrealistic and anti-social, but also downright **immoral.** Truly, 'What is the use of globalization if it is no more than a vehicle for cynics who want to avoid the norms of the law and morality?' That is a remark by no less a person than the Director General of the International Monetary

Fund, Michel Camedessus.[26] And since some advocates of this pure capitalism still claim to be believing Christians, Jews or adherents of other religions, they should be referred to the powerful thousand-year-old tradition which, beginning with the prophets of Israel, the philosophers of Greece, the Jesus of the New Testament and the Qur'an, down the centuries to the present, has sharply required a **morality of social justice** from the greedy, the ambitious and the exploiters: justice and fairness to the poor, the helpless and the exploited.[27]

(2) Experiences with the Swedish model in particular make us ask: do we not also need a **new responsibility on the part of employees?** As we have seen, the global structural change has led to **mass unemployment,** which represents a tremendous existential burden for hundreds of millions of people. But cannot this central problem of our time be solved not just by creating new jobs but by **obliging those unwilling to work** to look seriously for jobs, or helping them to create their own independent jobs? The unemployed must not earn as much as the employed (or even more, through the black economy); the net income from work must clearly be higher than the income provided by the state for those out of work; and badly paid work is better than no work at all and therefore can be asked of people.

But can such **new flexibility and differentiation of wages** be achieved? This would mean quite a significant change both for individuals and for trade union policy. It would mean 'the willingness of large groups in our societies to take jobs which pay less well than today', and thus to accept 'larger inequalities'. That at any rate is the comment by the Social Democrat economic policy expert Kjell Olof Feldt on the Swedish model, contrary to his own party ideology.[28] A discussion is going on here. Some people are suggesting that there could be more extensive and intensive work, if labour in the industrial nations as a whole were to be made cheaper, so that it regained its competitiveness, and consumers were not required to pay high prices, so that their purchasing power diminished again, to the detriment of the economic boom. Specifically this could mean less absenteeism and more flexibility in the working week (in Japan the working year is 2200 hours and in Germany 1250).

(3) Experiences with both the Swedish and the American models raise the question whether we do not need a **slimmed-down state.** The state must certainly not be made into merely a night-watchman state again, as the ultraliberals may want, but perhaps it will have to concentrate more

on the core areas of defence, internal security, law and order and also education. However, a **basic provision** must be made for **all** citizens in the areas of health care, education with equal opportunities and social and old age welfare, so that real poverty continues to be excluded.

But wouldn't this result in a **diminution of claims on the state?** Mustn't claim and achievement stand in a reasonable relationship? Many people say that those who achieve less should also receive less; and those who have a special wish (in respect of health care, social security) should pay for it themselves. In this connection the following proposals are being discussed:

– The **state contribution** (in the German federation, the states and local communities) must be **reduced** and space made for the private sector.

– In times of financial need **large-scale projects costing billions**, the need for which is doubted even by many professionals (Eurofighter, Transrapid, Expo etc.), should be abandoned.

– **Subsidies running into billions** should be **reduced** and the burden on the state budget should be substantially lightened;

– **Taxes,** which are often far too high, should **be lowered**; tax legislation which only experts can understand must be simplified, and tax allowances and possibilities of writing off tax which are often misused must be abolished.

– **Businesses** which pay less and less tax at home should not still be rewarded with high state subsidies, but should be 'obliged' to make a relevant social contribution at home.

– Once again, more **responsibility and independence** should be required of the individual.

However, all these are not patent recipes, but basic reflections over which there is much argument. They have been put forward by members of very different political and social interest groups. All this aims on the one hand to relieve the state of a burden and on the other to increase not only the responsibility but also the economic scope of the individual. So these proposals are aimed at a consolidation of the budget, not through piecemeal financial measures (which are also common outside Germany) and unplanned cuts, but by a **fair middle-term concept of consolidation** which affects not only the large low- and middle-income group, but also the employers, their expenditure and their privileges; then tax allowances for the rich; and not least subsidies of all kinds.

If the morass of state subsidies is drained and both taxes and payments are tangibly lowered, will not **individuals** once again be able to, indeed have to, decide how to utilize their financial resources? I can decide for myself what I buy and what I do not buy, whether I save or spend. This brings us from the mesolevel of businesses to the microlevel of persons, and here especially executives.

2. Ethics – a challenge for managers

There are more managers than is generally assumed who are the opposite of hardliners, thinking only of profit and shareholder value. There are managers who attempt, rather, to live out a high ethic, even in the harsh reality of business. One of them always carries around an already yellowed slip of paper with the admonition of Mahatma Gandhi on it, 'The Seven Deadly Sins in Today's World':

Wealth without work,
Enjoyment without conscience,
Knowledge without character,
Business without morality,
Science without humanity,
Religion without sacrifice and
politics without principles.

(a) Where does strong management come from?

Here are three cases to reflect on:

Why in a particular branch have two great multinational concerns not merged, whereas two others have? Because the man behind the decision had the conviction, which was ultimately grounded in ethics and religion, that expansion and concentration of the power of the companies were not in themselves sufficient justification for a merger: it was not necessary economically and would be at the expense of people in their various positions.

Why in a world-famous German company was a financial director quietly dismissed from the board for irregularities? Because one individual against all the rest did not agree to a cover-up on account of his ethical convictions. Long afterwards, he was thanked by his colleagues for his unyielding attitude – and subsequently recognized as an extremely wise policy-maker.

A concern known all over the world was entangled in several bribery scandals, and a number of its employees had to accept responsibility for paying bribes, while the chairman, directors and managers distanced themselves from such manipulations. A rival firm has so far remained free of all such accusations. Why? Because in the second international concern it was part of the business philosophy that any employee with a management function had to sign a paper entitled 'legality'. This stated that the company applied the principle of strict legality 'to all actions, measures, contracts, etc. of this group and its workers', regardless of any opportunistic considerations. Specifically it stated: 'Every employee is personally responsible for observing the laws in his sphere of work.' So this was a legality grounded in morality.

It is quite clear that today much is expected of **executives** in business, administration and politics. They must show that they are not only capable of analysis but can also take decisions and implement them. Thorough training and long experience are needed to achieve this. Executives have to set clear goals for themselves and others, employ workers and resources effectively, be able to grasp complex situations in a very short time, and make the right decisions in them. In a word, **strong management** is required.

By contrast, **weak management** ('nobodies in pinstripe suits'), whether in private business or public administration, in a firm or a ministry, has a depressing, demoralizing and destabilizing effect down to the last employee, whereas strong management provides motivation and inspiration. Think of all the far-sightedness, steadfastness and dynamism that is called for. Can management be learned? In principle, yes. Think of all the books that are written and journals published, all the seminars that are held and courses taken to train first-class management and keep retraining it. Modern management consultants rightly require executives to communicate rather than to inform, to co-operate rather to delegate, to lead rather than to control. A holistic training and perspective is called for which incorporates a person's own feelings, intuition and creativity; humanity has to be learned, along with communication, co-operative partnership and social competence.

However, there should be a consensus that all this, that strong and effective management, has to do not only with actions and strategies but also with **attitude, character and personality**: leadership through personality, with the head **and** the heart. Hence the question: don't attitude, character and personality at the same time have to do with **integrity, morality and ethos**? Not just with ethics = teaching, but with **ethos = attitude, inner moral attitude?** And doesn't this have to do with values, patterns of interpretation and criteria for action, and thus quite often, directly or indirectly, also with religious convictions, religious upbringing, positive or negative religious experiences?

(b) No business culture without personality culture

Business culture, always important but nowadays of stategic relevance, ultimately consists in the totality of the decisive attitudes, values, criteria, norms and behavioural patterns of management and employees in a business.

A business consists primarily of people, and therefore business culture presupposes a **personality culture.** Hence my very direct questions:

– Is it not necessary, first, for **executives themselves** to be aware of their own moral and religious attitudes, and thus to understand the moral and religious aspects of leadership more clearly? So the question is: who, what, how are you – as a human being, a person, a character?

– Secondly, is it not important for **employees,** too, not only to see management from the outside as directors, executives, managers, supervisors and so on, but also to learn something of what moves their heads and hearts, what determines their invisible and yet very influential 'ethos'? The question here is, 'Where do we stand in your attitude?'

– Thirdly, in a time when the credibility of public institutions and representatives has suffered a great deal (at a time of satiation with politics, politicians and parties), must it not once again be made clearer to the **public** what the supreme values, generally binding moral criteria, norms, normative authorities are, to which our leading figures feel bound in business, administration, politics and in education and science? So the question is a personal one: What are your fundamental convictions? What is unconditional, categorical for you, without any ifs and buts?

Since all professionals, including politicians and business executives, want to present a good **image** to themselves and to the public, it is worth knowing that in **America** a questionnaire[29] about the ethical standards or honesty of particular professional groups circulated among business students in the middle of the 1980s produced the following results: clergy 67%, chemists 65%, doctors 58%, dentists 56%, college professors 54%, engineers 54%, police 47%, bank staff 37%, television reporters/commentators 33%, journalists 31%, newspaper reporters 29%, lawyers 27%, leading businessmen 23%.

Does this perhaps apply only to America? In **Germany,** in 1993 the Allensbach Public Opinion Research Institute,[30] which enjoys a very high reputation, obtained the following answers to a question as to which profession enjoys the highest respect: doctors 81%, clergy 40%, lawyers 36%, college professors 33%, diplomats 32%, writers 28%, chemists 27%, businessmen 26%, engineers 26%, nuclear physicists 25%, schoolteachers 24%, directors of large firms 22%, journalists 17%, student chaplains 15%, officers 9%, politicians 9%, booksellers 9%, trade union leaders 8%.

But aren't the questions raised above perhaps all superfluous? Are executives solely and exclusively concerned with the statistics of success? Is their own career more important even than the well-being of the firm? As a well-known business consultant announced: in order to remain in the 'fast lane of life', certainly one must 'always believe in something, but it doesn't much matter what', 'everything is right, everything is wrong' . . .[31]

(c) Business consultancy: Machiavelli for managers?

Back in 1967 a book appeared in Britain with the title *Management and Machiavelli*; the German publisher gave it the provocative sub-title 'The art of keeping on top in our organized world'.[32] If we look more closely at this bestseller, it is easy to see that the author does not want to argue for Machiavellianism in management, but only for Machiavelli's method 'of grasping a contemporary problem and then investigating it in a practical way with reference to the experience of others who faced a similar problem in the past'.[33]

Be this as it may, the link between management and Machiavelli was made, and in some circles **Machiavellianism in management** became respectable. I shall merely illustrate briefly here what the St Gallen specialist on Machiavelli, Alois Riklin, documents at length:[34]

– According to a test game at an elite American university (one is reminded of the diplomacy games which were so popular among Kissinger's students) a good Machiavellian is someone who rejects statements like 'One should only act if one is certain that one's action is morally unobjectionable' and accepts statements like 'The essential difference between criminals and other people is that the criminals are stupid enough to get found out.'

– There is a Machiavelli course for rising managers at a well-known American Graduate School of Business and Public Administration with the aim of recognizing Machiavellianism among others, and also being able to practise it oneself.

– The advertisement for a course in a German managers' magazine runs: 'Managers' Machiavelli, seminar on success for managers, the theory and practice of power in business life.' The slogan is: 'Guaranteed effective. Almost moral-free. Use at your own danger. No refunds.' And

there are rules like: Lies are occasionally necessary, sometimes practicable. But lie only when it is worth it.
– Then at Cornell University, as a counter-movement, there has been an
interdisciplinary investigation into selfishness and solidarity in student
attitudes. It found that economists did much worse in tests on fairness
and social behaviour than the students of any other discipline.
– Riklin's comment: 'What a tremendous difference between the
patriotic common sense of Machiavelli and the egotistical career mania
of the Machiavelli courses for managers!'[35]

However, more important than these Machiavelli courses which,
while symptomatic, are isolated, is the effect of the occasions organized
by some business consultants infected by Machiavellianism which
doubtless confirm among 'ordinary people' the view that **many
businesses show a lack of ethical responsibility**; that most firms
unscrupulously pursue their profit at the expense of the environment or
the safety and health of consumers, untroubled about society as a whole.
Those who know the scene even think that since the time of
Reaganomics and Thatcherism a new style of profit-orientated, go-
ahead young men (in this case, happily few women) who do not always
act morally ('Yuppies') is climbing the top levels of American and
European business. An attitude of **opportunism** is said to be widespread
generally: on the one hand there is an orientation on material success,
and on the other a readiness to use even dishonest means to achieve
success and to affirm rules of life which point in a similar direction.[36]
Indeed, it is often possible to detect a tendency towards the opportunist
separation of legality and morality, a high degree of individualistic
orientation and a less than average readiness for practical commitment
to third parties. The existence of universal criteria is denied by such
opportunists, and the ethical distinction between good and evil is often
termed 'a mere matter of feelings'.

Unfortunately this tendency is to be found in particular among some
of the **business consultants** who are so influential behind the scenes,
though they often only popularize the ideas of academics and journalists
at management levels and adjust their views to the trends. It seems
suspicious that to generate sales, an 'adviser on personal development
and manager training' by the name of **Reinhard K. Sprenger** has
reminted the title of the famous book by the German American
philosopher Hans Jonas, *The Imperative of Responsibility*, into *The
Imperative of Self-Responsibility*.[37] And it is even more suspicious
when, for his 'philosophy' of self-responsibility ('commitment'), he
refers to a remark of Martin Heidegger, which Heidegger is supposed to

have 'made to his students at the end of the 1920s': 'We must see clearly that at the present time we have no support from an objective generally binding knowledge or power; the only support which remains for us today is attitude.'³⁸ The author does not seem to be aware that statements like these (in reality from the famous/notorious speech which Heidegger gave as Rector in 1933, immediately after Hitler's seizure of power) made it possible for Heidegger and his students, who objectively had no 'support', to 'find support' in the 'attitude' of National Socialism. Anyone who propagates 'attitude' as mere form must not be surprised if one day it comes to be given content by ideology.

However, it is most suspicious of all when in 1995 this same business consultant – doubtless having given his readers much helpful advice, makes his remarks on the 'principle of self-responsibility' (the 'central idea which shapes business') lead up to a no less fatal epitome of the '**credibility**' of management: in a business with self-responsibility 'you are credible as management only on one condition: not because that it is morally good or is recognized by others, but because you have **chosen** it. For no other reason.'³⁹ Is this cynicism or stupidity? According to such a subjective definition of credibility beyond good and evil it seems that any law-breaker, financial cheat, drug dealer or Mafia boss can claim credibility: because he has '**chosen**' it, 'for no other reason'!

In all this there is one consolation: most recently some self-criticism has become evident even within the guild of the 'supermen' and 'saviours' of business in a disastrous time. In his *Consulting Report*,⁴⁰ the business consultant **Jörg Staute** analyses the many arrogant business advisers who, with empty talk and manipulated statistics, are masters of the art of self-presentation but, constantly surfing on the fashionable waves of management literature, and despite juicy fees (in Germany alone these supposedly amount to 15 billion D M per year), in practice produce little that is helpful. The book ends with the statement: 'There is less substance than is often assumed behind the great consulting bluff.'⁴¹ Here of course ethical questions often come up, but even in this self-critical book, the ethic of business consultants nowhere becomes a topic; indeed, key words like morality, ethics do not appear in the wretched index. However, there are of course many serious business consultants to whom this criticism does not apply.

But contrary to my expectations, the question of ethics is also not a topic in the most recent book by the American management guru **Peter F. Drucker**, whom I much admire; with his Japanese colleague **Isao Nakauchi** he makes some interesting points in the section 'toward a new personality' but does not move on to state clear ethical requirements.⁴²

The contribution to the discussion by **Joanne B. Ciulla**, Professor of Leadership and Ethics at the Jepson School of Leadership Studies in the University of Richmond, is quite different. Basing herself on the observation that in the past ten years there has been a strong and increasing interest in questions of business ethics (documented by the numerous 'business ethics conferences and forums all over the world, from Moscow to Caracas'), she comes to the conclusion: 'It was no longer good enough for a business leader to be ethical; he or she had to make sure that moral values were inculcated into the organization.'[43] But do business leaders normally also do this?

(d) Financial and political scandals

There is no overlooking the fact that **where values and clear standards have been dismissed,** and where a religious orientation can no longer command a majority, **the Kantian ethic of duty and orientation on a common good unfortunately does not get very far.** Be this as it may, anyone who at a university has kept coming into contact with young people, and still does, could report at length the doubts, particularly among the most intelligent of our young generation, about the credibility of our leaders. These are purely subjective impressions. In a representative opinion poll[44] among Germans between fourteen and twenty-nine as to which organizations and personalities they thought credible, the following figures emerged: Greenpeace 64%, Amnesty International 50%, trade unions 17%, churches 15%, business 8%, political parties 5%.

Older observers of the contemporary scene sometimes get the impression that in the banking world and credit system, as in economics and politics, whereas formerly petty offences were more usual, nowadays offences have become possible to a degree which people formerly, two, three decades ago, would have thought impossible in our civilized countries. Never before in the history of German business, it is claimed, 'have so many top managers been convicted of fraud, corruption, self-enrichment and status-seeking at the expense of their firms and shareholders as in recent years'.[45] It is not only due to the influence of the mass media, which are often ignorant, malicious and one-sided, that businessmen and politicians are increasingly represented in films and literature as greedy, self-seeking persons.

One thing at any rate is clear: **the credibility of the institutions, their representatives and experts, has declined.** And the **protest potential** of alternative movements, civil initiatives, groups, sub-cultures and also the 'potential for opting out' has increased, as has the resultant **pressure for legitimation** on the institutions and their representatives. So too have mass protests. And unfortunately this applies to the representatives of politics, as well as those of business and the trade unions (not to mention the representatives of the church and the Vatican Bank). In fact nowadays those who have long been accustomed to taking the public statements of these representatives at their word cannot do other than put a sceptical question mark against any public statement.

Obviously today's financial and political scandals are not just fortuitous; they are not just individual failures and mistakes, but part of the **'system' and 'method'**. This compromises the great majority of respectable people. Blatant abuses are often officially tolerated, concealed and excused for years, and quite often the political parties bear a special responsibility. It would be worth making a closer investigation of the degree to which the great bank, stock exchange and corruption scandals first utilized the same mechanisms, secondly showed a similar character, and thirdly had similarly devastating results. Here I mean above all a discrediting of the political and business elite who so often forfeit all credibility by their trivialization of actual dangers, by helpless or deceitful reactions, and finally by disarming assertions of innocence.

However, happily we do not have to wait for counter-measures to the great many scandals. I was able to discover current developments and trends in questions of business ethics not only through reports in the media but above all also at first hand through personal conversations and hard information about business ethics at the Tokyo Conference, **The First World Congress of Business, Economics and Ethics** in July 1996. In addition to the individual ethos of top management and its responsibility for a business ethic, especially in the USA, which generally dominates the market for management innovations, for some years (after a whole series of serious scandals) a tendency has become evident for business to seek to influence the behaviour of employees and begin to prevent offences which damage business through **ethical programmes** aimed at establishing codes of behaviour and wider values. With the US Sentencing Guidelines established in 1991, a clever system of incentives at the legislative level is ensuring that: first, businesses are being required to set up ethical programmes; and secondly, if they scorn or offend against ethical guidelines they are faced with significant penal measures and sanctions.[46]

These ethical measures are also being accompanied and supported by the way in which numerous **business schools** have made the dimension of business ethics a firm element of their teaching programmes. By way of example I might refer to the ethics programme of the Harvard Business School in Boston, which was initiated as early as the end of the 1980s by Thomas R. Piper; then to the Graduate School of Business under the direction of Kenneth Goodpaster at the University of St Thomas, Minnesota; and finally to the Council for Ethics in Economics in Columbus, Ohio, with Paul M. Minus as the Director of the International Conferences for Business Leaders. At almost the same time a network of business ethics has formed in Europe, the European Business Ethics Network (EBEN), which has as members such prominent experts in business ethics as Horst Steinmann, Peter Ulrich and Henk van Luijk.

Individual defects and institutional failings in the realm of ethics, the disappearance of values, criteria and finally also the credibility of people in leading positions in business on the one hand, and the way in which scandals will not go away on the other, direct our attention to the heart of these problems and make us ask directly:

3. Has ethics a chance in business?

In view of the many crises and scandals, one cannot avoid the impression that the god to whom tribute is paid in the most different shapes and forms is the great god of modernity *par excellence*, the god progress, the god **success**! That means **efficiency** instead of transcendence; **profit, career, prestige and success at any price** instead of openness to another dimension.

(a) Beyond good and evil?

In all the well-known scandals, from Germany and Italy to America and Japan, the obvious presupposition was that **success** sanctifies, **justifies all means**. For success one may lie, steal, bribe, break promises, whatever. If the matter unintentionally becomes notorious, then first of all in one disputes everything and where possible goes over to the counter-attack. The media which uncover the scandal are normally to blame for it (and here unfortunately the media all too often go for the principle of success and an increase in circulation). As for the guilty ones, only what can be demonstrated without providing openings for legal action is then given out, bit by bit. Then a terrifying degree of blindness to reality manifests itself, an extreme loss of confidence and a complete lack of the culture of public shame and repentance. Finally, should all honourable declarations and words prove false, it can happen that someone as a last resort commits suicide or, as in the case of Calvi, the church and Vatican banker, is done away with; Calvi was found hanged under a bridge on the Thames near to the London Opus Dei bank. No, even the early prophet of contemporary nihilism, Friedrich Nietzsche, did not imagine 'beyond good and evil' and the new 'superman', without religion and morality and committed only the 'will to power', as being so primitive, banal, trivial.

But wait. Fortunately this is not the whole picture. Surprisingly, the questionnaire among leading business figures quoted above also shows **trends in the opposite direction.** Many people still believe in God, the true God, and even more appeal to their conscience, though in concrete terms the contours of this authority remain vague. In general, Christianity (as opposed to the church) is seen in a positive light, though the content of Christianity, for example the commandment to love, evidently has little influence on management decisions. And if at the same time the biblical revelation or the social teaching of the church plays hardly any role in this group, conversely many executives regard openness to transcendence as an important element in moral decisions.

Yes, one has to choose, doubtless time and again, and executives often find that their decisions are a difficult **choice between** what is required by **business** within the sphere of calculating success and what their **conscience** prescribes. Various empirical investigations into business ethics[47] have time and again brought out the following ways of thinking:
– Those who are asked, regard their own ethical standards more optimistically than those of their colleagues.
– Ethical codes of behaviour are welcomed, but are regarded as ineffective by themselves; but also
– Responsibility towards customers is put above responsibility towards the shareholders.

In the matter of establishing ethical standards in business, a considerable number of the executives questioned look to **help from outside:** improved legislation, harsher punishment, external audits, greater watchfulness on the part of consumers and the media. But even more executives put their trust in **solutions from within:** an improved ethical training and above all an improved business culture.

Negative and positive aspects, taken together, show a **tension in relation to religion** on the part of many executives.[48] They are convinced that 'people' need religion, that Christianity should be preserved at least 'for the others', 'for the people'. But they themselves often believe that they can do without such a religious connection. Ethical conflicts between one's profession and religion, commerce and Christian faith, profit and confession, politics and ethics, are hardly perceived in these terms. Such perception is most likely when particular people with whom one is confronted are affected by commercial decisions, say in the harsh competitive struggle, in mass redundancies, in competition, or when because of professional dedication the executive's own marriage is destroyed and the family breaks up. By contrast, it is more difficult to perceive the conflict when more wide-ranging, more impersonal, more complex and more abstract situations have to be considered: say in business relationships with the developing countries or in dealing with nature.

All this shows that the question of ethics or religion cannot easily be settled in the sphere of business executives. In many ways it seems to be **latent and diffuse**. But people all too rarely give an account of themselves – either of their public status or their private attitude. However, it would help to reflect consciously on the ethical and the religious question. In principle, what is an appropriate ethic for present-day executives (and not just for them)?

(b) The chances of doing business morally

Throughout this second part, which is about the world economy, between welfare state and neocapitalism (considered globally, nationally and locally), it has become clear that no uncritical economism was to be presented here, nor any moralism alien to the subject: no ethic imposed upon economics, but **an ethic arising out of economic processes**. Economics and ethics are not mutually exclusive, no matter how often this is asserted.

But particularly in the age of globalization the problem is becoming acute: 'Competition is getting harder. Has ethics still a chance in business?' I was asked this at the German Management Congress in Munich in 1994. My answer was that **a moral way of doing business has more chances**. Only those who themselves have an ethic can give clear **orientation** to others, which is what strong **leadership** requires. They can give this orientation by pointing to all the values to which there must be an obligation, presenting aims, observing standards consistently, and adopting a quite specific attitude in practice. Or, as the businessman whom I quoted in the introduction said: a business may be run in the style of a large family, a strictly rational organization or a monarchical hierarchy,[49] but the decisive presupposition for survival and long-term success is integrity. One must always be able to rely on the firm, never have the wool pulled over one's eyes, never be lied to, never be hauled over the coals, but always be treated and served with respect and honesty.[50]

In the long term an immoral way of doing business does not pay. Why?

(1) Sooner or later a **conflict with the criminal law** threatens even those who think that they can always get by unscathed.

(2) Where offences are repeated there is always a cry for **legal regulation**, which is commonly complained about by business and is now complained about by the banks.

(3) Lenders do not like giving **credit** to those who are not credit-worthy, and credit is often decided (according to a Swiss banker) according to the following criteria: first, **character** and then 2. Capacity, 3. Collateral, 4. Capital, 5. Conditions.

(4) All firms are dependent on more than merely financial credit: they need **credit in** the sense of **credibility**, and in many respects:
– for members of the business and those who are being trained, who want to work in a reputable firm;
– for those who live nearby and the local community on whose good will any firm is dependent;
– for the financiers, the suppliers and the customers, none of whom trusts those who have no moral credit;
– for the wider public, who in the long run will not tolerate a bad image for any firm (not even A T & T and Shell).

(5) Laws have only external sanctions, but an ethic has an internal sanction: a **bad conscience** cannot simply be suppressed, but makes itself felt, even if only in dreams and disturbed sleep. One hears that there are more neurotics at the top than is generally assumed.

So at the meso- and microlevels too, ethics is not just a matter of 'moral appeals'. In business, too, the **pressure of suffering** often finally becomes the **pressure to reform,** and this becomes **a political force.** But can one change well-established ways of behaving? Yes, we have already seen that a change of consciousness is possible in the middle and long term. And instead of constantly just discussing and identifying problems, after mature consideration we as individuals should do better in our own world, smaller or greater. After all, ethical decisions are in the first place matters for the individual. For example, it is a quite personal ethical decision on the part of the banker who is already being asked too much of by his existing directorships, whether he refuses to take on yet more, or in the face of many scandals and deficient control structures protects himself against criticism by bland statements.

In view on the one hand of the corruption which is spreading like a cancer even in countries where officials, judges and the medical profession used largely to have integrity, and on the other of the increase in organized crime and juvenile criminality – defensive measures against corruption and organized crime are being strengthened everywhere – , the question of the foundation for basic values and attitudes is being raised more clearly than before. It is being raised in a new way especially in the market economy. Why should I unconditionally observe certain rules, moral standards, ethical norms?

(c) From creed to cash: the 'Singapore dream'

Ethics should not just apply hypothetically (if it corresponds with my interests), but categorically (as Kant stated it), unconditionally. But what is the foundation for the **unconditional validity** of particular basic ethical values and attitudes? For the authors of the Interfaith Declaration they clearly come from the religion concerned, be this Jewish, Christian or Muslim. But the Caux Declaration evidently presupposes that the basic values and attitudes which it calls for are also accessible to non-believers and doubters, agnostics and atheists. This cannot be disputed. But on the other hand a purely secular argument for particular values and attitudes easily gets into trouble over finding a foundation.

Thus people say, 'I must see how I get on in my profession, career, business, and get established; only I can help myself there.' The answer to that is that such an attitude will easily undermine any sense of responsibility and in the long run any sense of the law. But again there is the objection: why shouldn't I pursue my career and my business heedlessly and use my elbow? Make way for the bold! The answer is: if **the maximum** is always **the optimum,** and earning money (capitalism) and enjoying life (hedonism) have become the highest value, not only the harmony and stability of a community are threatened, but also the individual's sense of life and identity. Indeed democracy is endangered by a libertinism which is the modern way of taking to excess that *'liberté'* which originally helped democracy to break through.

However, there is increasing agreement that a society without rules, norms of behaviour, moral maxims, indeed a minimum of binding values, inner attitudes and binding criteria, cannot survive. Slowly our secular contemporaries are also recognizing that modernization brings not only an unavoidable secularization, but also a by no means unavoidable ideological secularism, in which all that is transcendent, trans-empirical, authoritative, indeed **unconditionally normative,** seems to have been **banished from life** and subsequently replaced by helplessness and an oppressive spiritual void. Is each his own measure?

But how is the individual or group to be given **criteria if man himself is 'the measure of all things':** not just under ethical obligation, as in the original Greek sense of the saying, but without any ties, as in the modern libertinistic or nihilistic sense? Since human beings cannot stand this emptiness *(horror vacui)*, the spiritual vacuum already prognosticated by Nietzsche is being filled by substitute values: by something relative, if only money, which now becomes the **pseudo-absolute,** the idol, in place of the true absolute. Everything is voluntarily sacrificed to it, often with meaningless pomp and luxury to satisfy personal vanity, often even personal integrity and identity; but above all solidarity. This is a freedom without equality and brotherhood.

Can human standards ultimately be given an irrefutable foundation if man wants to be completely his own measure and recognizes no norms, **no normative authority which transcends humanity**? Does it make people happier if they know neither standards nor purpose and then, because they want to set their hearts on something, prescribe for themselves a modern pseudo-religion, of the kind expressed in the 'Singapore dream' (and to be truthful, it is not just dreamed there):

- Instead of the age old **five Cs of true religion,** Creed, Cult, Code, Conduct, Community,
- the mundane **five Cs of pseudo-religion:** Cash, Credit Card, Car, Condominium, Country Club?

Will not such unconcealed materialism and egotism in time lead even in that Asian country which so far is most free from corruption to an equally unfair, polarized, split society of the privileged and the unprivileged, despite tremendous election results for the ruling party? The most recent controversy in Singapore over certain privileges of those in power suggests this. But these questions not only arise for the remote future; they also press in on us in the immediate present.

(d) Strong leadership with a basic ethical and religious attitude

Enlightenment in the name of a **religion,** which is not about restoration but renewal, is one of the great tasks of our time. While prosperity, progress, consumption, satisfaction or power are not bad in themselves, people may possibly damage themselves and others if they absolutize these so that they become the supreme value, the purpose and aim of life to which they are ready to subordinate, indeed to sacrifice, everything else. No, nothing 'earthly' should be denigrated here in a moralistic way, but **simply put in the overall context of human life:**

- against an ultimate horizon of meaning,
- in accordance with a scale of values,
- in accordance with basic norms, non-negotiable standards, which are unconditionally valid.

And what about religion itself? For all its failure in individual instances, it can be a help towards such an ultimate discovery of meaning, towards the preservation of personal identity, and towards legitimating a fundamentally correct action and making it concrete. This has already been shown in connection with politics: unless all the signs are deceptive, despite all the secularization, seen globally we are in the middle of a process of the **rediscovery** of that factor which for all too understandable reasons has been increasingly forced out, ignored and often violently suppressed in the paradigm of modernity: the rediscovery of **religion**. That is true above all if we do not remain imprisoned in the Eurocentric perspective but look to the Middle and Far East, to North and Latin America and to Africa. Here perhaps is the clearest symptom of a transition from modernity to post-socialist and post-capitalist postmodernity.

Of course, as we have seen repeatedly, there are **no patent religious solutions** for coping with the problems of today's world and the difficulties that are bound up with them; there is no religious substitute for a understanding of economics, professional knowledge and common sense. But it is also true that, as we saw in the first part of this book, religion can be of help in rediscovering a basic social consensus about **ultimate values**, without which modern pluralism will have a destructive effect.

Religion has an indirect effect, as it were **from the ground up,** through individuals, but it also extends to questions of the day and matters of technical detail. It does so by bringing into play basic convictions, basic attitudes, basic values, and by providing ultimate foundations, motivations and norms for concrete behaviour and decisions. To this degree economics and religion cannot be separated any more than can politics and religion, but have to be related to each other constructively. And for executives this means that economic political leadership and ethical religious leadership are interdependent, even if the decision about personal religion always remains with the individual.

Be this as it may, to be a '**great business personality**' today more than ever it is not enough to have a capital of millions upon millions, or hundreds of connections, or dozens of directorships. No, to be a 'great business personality', in addition to all analytical competence, power to make decisions and a will to implement them, one needs a view of reality as a whole which goes beyond technical knowledge and professional competence, a sense of basic human questions and ethical convictions which are deeply rooted and have been well thought out.

Conclusion

I hope that I have succeeded, as promised, in taking the global ethic project further and demonstrating a realistic vision, pointing towards the future in a global perspective which makes clearer the outlines of a more peaceful, just and humane world.

No one knows better than a person who with some difficulty has laboured through all the countless problems, just how many details are lacking in providing a basis for this work, shaping it and making the necessary distinctions. But it is more important for the decisive features to have been clarified. Both in the sphere of politics and in that of economics we need a new **sense of responsibility**:

– a responsible **politics** which seeks to achieve the precarious balance between ideals and realities which has to be rediscovered over and over again;

– a responsible **economics** which can combine economic strategies with ethical convictions.

The change of consciousness needed here is a task for the new millennium. And it is for the young generation to realize decisively the sketch for the future presented here. As Victor Hugo says, the future has many names:

> For the weak it is the unattainable.
> For the fearful it is the unknown.
> For the bold it is the opportunity.

Notes

Wanted – A Vision

1. M.Gräfin Dönhoff, 'Zehn Thesen', *Die Zeit*, 24 November 1995.
2. Cf. R. Würth, *Erfolgsgeheimnis Führungskultur. Bilanz eines Unterneh-mers*, Frankfurt 1995, 67.

A. I *The Old Real Politics Again?*

1. Cf. J. Kocka, *Vereinigungskrise. Zur Geschichte der Gegenwart*, Göttin-gen 1995.
2. For this development cf. H. Küng, *Christianity. Its Essence and History*, London and New York 1995, Chapter C V, 2: The new political constellation in Europe.
3. Cf. H. Kissinger, *Diplomacy*, New York 1994, 67, 58.
4. Cf. ibid., 19.
5. Cf. H. Kissinger, *A World Restored. Castlereagh, Metternich and the Restoration of Peace, 1812–1822*, New York 1957.
6. H. Kissinger, *American Foreign Policy*, New York 1969.
7. S.Schama, 'Die Spiele grosser Männer', *taz*, 17 February 1995.
8. Cf. Kissinger, *Diplomacy* (n.3), 833.
9. Cf. ibid., 834.
10. M. Howard, 'The World According to Henry. From Metternich to Me', *Foreign Affairs* 73, 1994, 132–40.
11. Cf. Kissinger, *Diplomacy* (n.3), 39.
12. Cf. ibid., 40.
13. Cf. ibid., 47.
14. Ibid.
15. Cf. ibid., 45.
16. Ibid.
17. Ibid.
18. Cf. ibid., 48.
19. Howard, 'The World According to Henry' (n.10), 139.
20. Cf. Kissinger, *Diplomacy* (n.3), 46.
21. Quoted ibid., 32.

22. Cf. ibid., 23 and 46.

23. Cf. S.M.Hersh, *The Price of Power. Kissinger in the Nixon White House*, New York 1983; W. Isaacson, *Kissinger. A Biography*, New York 1992.

24. Cf. A. Lewis, '20,492 Reasons Kissinger Was Wrong', *New York Times/International Herald Tribune*, 7 May 1994.

25. W. Isaacson, 'How the World Works', *Time Magazine*, 2 May 1994.

26. Isaacson, *Kissinger* (n.23), 766.

27. Ibid., 767.

28. The relatively unanimous French research into Richelieu – from G. Hanotaux's six volumes (1893–1947) to M.Carmona (1982/83) and C.Jouhaud (1991) – presents Richelieu as the great secular statesman and promoter of reasons of state. It has recently been corrected in some points by Anglo-Saxon scholars, cf. J.Bergin and L.Brockliss (eds.), *Richelieu and his Age*, Oxford 1992.

29. Cf Bergin's critical remarks in *Richelieu and his Age* (n.28), 6f., on H.Weber's account of Richelieu's foreign policy (45–69).

30. The basic work on reasons of state remains F Meinecke, *Die Idee der Staatsräson in der neueren Geschichte*, Munich 1924, ³1929.

31. H. Münkler, *Machiavelli. Die Begründung des politischen Denkens der Neuzeit aus der Krise der Republik Florenz*, Frankfurt 1982, 283 and 281. As well as this historically based study, A. Riklin, *Die Führungslehre von Niccolò Machiavelli*, Bern 1996, offers a compact discussion with Machiavelli in terms of present-day politics.

32. Kissinger, *Diplomacy* (n.3), 63, 62.

33. Küng, *Christianity* (n.2), Chapter C IV, 5, 'The defeat of the third force'.

34. S. Schama, 'Die Spiele grosser Männer' (n.7), particularly criticizes this lack in Kissinger's account. For the present state of research into Grotius see H. Bull, B.Kingsbury and A. Roberts, *Hugo Grotius and International Relations*, Oxford 1990.

35. Cf. Kissinger, *Diplomacy* (n.3), 64 (his emphasis).

36. Cf. ibid., 59.

37. Cf. ibid., 61.

38. Cf. ibid., 62.

39. Cf. ibid., 67.

40. L.von Rochau, *Grundsätze der Realpolitik. Angewendet auf die staatlichen Zustände Deutschlands*, Part I, Stuttgart 1853 and Part II, Heidelberg 1869; new edition with an introduction by H.-U. Wehler, Frankfurt 1972.

41. A. Doering-Manteuffel, *Die deutsche Frage und das europäische Staatensystem 1815–1871*, Munich 1993, 39.

42. T. Nipperdey, *Deutsche Geschichte 1866–1918, II: Machtstaat vor der Demokratie*, Munich 1992, ³1995, 425.

43. L. Gall, *Bismarck. Der weisse Revolutionär*, Frankfurt 1980, 450.

44. Doering-Manteuffel, *Die deutsche Frage* (n.41), 51.

45. Kissinger, *Diplomacy* (n.3), 136.
46. Cf. the biographies of Bismarck by A.J.P.Taylor (1955), O.Pflanzer (1963), L.Gall (1980), E.Crankshaw (1981), E.Engelberg (1985/90).
47. Quoted in the large-scale study by H.-U. Wehler, *Deutsche Gesellschafts-geschichte, III: Von der 'Deutschen Doppelrevolution' bis zum Beginn des Ersten Weltkrieges 1849–1914*, Munich 1995, 999.
48. Quotation ibid., 854.
49. Cf. ibid., 1291.

A. II No Moralizing Ideal Politics

1. Cf. H. Kissinger, *Diplomacy*, New York 1994, 226. Cf. T.Kuhn, *The Structure of Scientific Revolutions*, Chicago 1962.
2. The 'Fourteen Points' are included in *Documents of American History*, ed. Henry Steele Commager, New York ^{5}1949, 317–19.
3. Kissinger, *Diplomacy* (n.1), 51.
4. Ibid., 808.
5. Cf. R. Niebuhr, *Moral Man and Immoral Society. A Study in Ethics and Politics*, New York 1932.
6. For the nationalistic ideology of Reagan (and the 'New Religious Right') in a Christian garb cf. the work of the Swedish theologian K.O.U.Lejon, *Reagan, Religion and Politics. The Revitalization of 'a Nation under God' during the 80s*, Lund 1988.
7. Cf. H. J. Morgenthau, *Politics among Nations. The Struggle for Power and Peace*, New York ^{3}1961.
8. Ibid., 3.
9. Ibid., 4.
10. But see the fine obituary of his 'teacher' and 'friend' by H. Kissinger, 'Hans Morgenthau. A gentle analyst of power', *The New Republic*, 2 August 1980.
11. The discussion volume edited by K. W Thompson, *Community, Diversity, and a New World Order*, Lanham/Md. 1994, is illuminating. Professor Thompson of the University of Virginia, a former assistant to Morgenthau and also known today as editor of the rich composite volumes on the last American presidencies, had introduced himself with a work inedebted above all to Morgenthau, Niebuhr und Kennan, *Political Realism and the Crisis of World Politics. An American Approach to Foreign Politics*, Princeton 1960. But twenty years later he made the question of morality in foreign policy the topic of a study of his own, *Morality and Foreign Policy*, Baton Rouge 1980. I found much stimulation for my discussion of Hans Morgenthau in the interdisciplinary seminar on 'Global Politics and Global Ethics' arranged with Professor Volker Rinberger of the Tübingen Institute of Political Science.
12. Cf. the dissertation by C. Frei, *Hans J. Morgenthau. Eine intellektuelle*

Biographie, Bern 1993, ²1994, produced at the Wirtschaftshochschule, St Gallen.

13. Cf. especially R. Niebuhr, *The Nature and Destiny of Man. A Christian Interpretation*, I–II, New York 1941.

14. Cf. Frei, *Hans J. Morgenthau* (n.12), 101.

15. Quoted from ibid., 117.

16. Cf. ibid., 117.

17. Cf. ibid., especially ch.5.

18. Nietzsche's development and thought world is described at length and subjected to careful criticism in H. Küng, *Does God Exist? An Answer for Today*, London and New York 1984, Part D: Nihilism – Consequence of Atheism.

19. Kissinger, 'Hans Morgenthau' (n.10), 13.

20. For this other side of Morgenthau see also Frei, *Hans J. Morgenthau* (n.12), especially chs. 6 und 7. G. Russell, *Hans J.Morgenthau and the Ethics of American Statecraft*, Baton Rouge 1990, works out the distinction between Morgenthau's realistic political theory (which accepts moral principles) and the European theory of 'reasons of state', but only on the basis of Morgenthau's later writings. But cf. already R. L. Shinn, *Realism and Ethics in Political Philosophy*, in K. W Thompson and R.J. Myers (ed.), *Truth and Tragedy. A Tribute to H. J.Morgenthau*, Washington/DC 1977, New Brunswick ²1984, 95–103.

21. H.J.Morgenthau, Diary, 31 May 1930, quoted in Frei, *Hans J.Morgenthau* (n.12), 153.

22. Id., *La réalité des normes; en particulier des normes du droit international*, Paris 1934.

23. Cf. also H. J. Morgenthau, *In Defense of the National Interest*, New York 1951, which followed soon afterwards.

24. Id., *Politics* (n.7), 10.

25. Cf. ibid., 11, and also for the following quotations.

26. Cf. id., 'Another "Great Debate". The National Interest of the United States', in id., *Politics in the Twentieth Century, I: The Decline of Democratic Politics*, Chicago 1962, 110.

27. Id., *The Purpose of American Politics*, New York 1960, 223.

28. Id., *A New Foreign Policy for the United States*, New York 1969, 176.

29. Cf. E. H. Carr, *The Twenty Years' Crisis 1919–1939. An Introduction to the Study of International Relations*, London 1939, ²1946.

30. Cf. ibid., 224.

31. Cf. ibid., 235f.

32. Cf. ibid., 236.

33. Cf. H. Morgenthau, 'The Surrender to the Immanence of Power: E. H. Carr', in id., *Politics in the Twentieth Century, III: The Restoration of American Politics*, Chicago 1962, 43.

34. Cf. M.Weber, *Wirtschaft und Gesellschaft. Grundriss der verstehenden*

Soziologie, ed. M. Weber, Tübingen 1921, here quoted from the fifth edition revised by J.Winkelmann, Tübingen 1972, 28f.

35. A. Riklin, 'Politische Ethik', in H. Kramer (ed.), *Politische Theorie und Ideengeschichte im Gespräch*, Vienna 1995, 81–104: 87.
36. Outstanding among Morgenthau's former critics are M. Kaplan (1957), S. Hoffmann (1959/1965) und R. Rosecrance (1963). I am grateful to the Bremen peace researcher Dieter Senghaas for suggestions about the discussion of international political theory since Hans Morgenthau.
37. Cf. K.N.Waltz, *Theory of International Politics*, Reading/Mass 1979.
38. Cf. R.O.Keohane (ed.), *Neorealism and its Critics*, New York 1986.
39. Cf. ibid., 24.
40. Cf. ibid., 340.
41. Cf. R.O.Keohane and J.S. Nye, *Power and Interdependence. World Politics in Transition*, Cambridge/Mass 1977, second edition, with a postscript, 1989.
42. Cf. R.G.Gilpin, 'The Richness of the Tradition of Political Realism', in: Keohane, *Neorealism* (n.38), 301–21.
43. Cf. ibid., 319.
44. Cf. id., *War and Change in World Politics*, Cambridge 1981; id., *The Political Economy of International Relations*, Princeton 1987.
45. Cf. id., 'The Richness' (n.38), 320.
46. Cf. ibid.,321.
47. I am grateful to the Marburg social ethicist Stephan Pfürtner for this reference.

A. III Responsible Politics

1. Cf. J N. Rosenau, *Turbulence in World Politics. A Theory of Change and Continuity*, Princeton/NJ 1990.
2. Cf. the excellent article by J.C.Garnett, 'The National Interest Revisited', in K. W Thompson (ed.), *Community, Diversity, and a New World Order*, Lanham, Md 1994, 87–110. Part IV, the debate between R.De Vries and K. W.Thompson, is particularly illuminating.
3. Ibid.,106.
4. Ibid.
5. Ibid., 107.
6. Cf. R.Falk, *On Humane Governance. Toward a New Global Politics. The World Order Models Project Report of the Global Civilization Initiative*, Cambridge 1995.
7. H. Kissinger, *Diplomacy*, New York 1994, 831.
8. Ibid., 834.
9. Cf. M. Weber, *Politik als Beruf*, Tübingen 1919, in id., *Gesammelte Politische Schriften*, Tübingen 1958, here quoted from the third edition revised by J.Winkelmann, Tübingen 1971, 505–60, esp. 551.

10. Cf. ibid., 559.
11. Cf. H. Jonas, *The Imperative of Responsibility: In Search of an Ethics for the Technological Age*, Chicago 1985.
12. Cf. C.F.v.Weiszäcker, *Der Garten des Menschlichen. Beiträge zur geschichtlichen Anthropologie*, Munich 1977, especially the chapter on power, 253–93.
13. Cf. E.U.v.Weizsäcker, *Erdpolitik. Ökologische Realpolitik an der Schwelle zum Jahrhundert der Umwelt*, Darmstadt 1989, third edition updated after the Rio de Janeiro summit, 1992.
14. A.Gore, *Earth in the Balance. Ecology and Human Spirit*, New York 1992. Also important in this context is *The Earth Charter Consultation Process*. There is a report on it in S.C.Rockefeller, 'Global Ethics, International Law, and The Earth Charter', in *Earth Ethics. Evolving Values for an Earth Community* 3/4, 1996, 1–7.
15. Cf. W Schluchter, *Religion und Lebensführung I: Studien zu Max Webers Kultur- und Werttheorie*, Frankfurt 1988, 195–200.
16. Cf. M.Weber, *Politik als Beruf* (n.9), 546.
17. Cf. K.R.Popper, *In Search of a Better World. Lectures and Essays from Thirty Years*, London 1992, 249f. (his emphasis).
18. A. Riklin, 'Politische Ethik', in: H. Kramer (ed.), *Politische Theorie und Ideengeschichte im Gespräch*, Vienna 1995, 81–104: 101f.
19. N.Machiavelli, *Il Principe* (written in 1513 and published in Rome in 1532, five years after his death); English translation *The Prince*, Oxford Classics 1984, 59.
20. Ibid.
21. M. Weber, *Politik als Beruf* (n.6), 507.
22. Cf. E. Bahr, *Zu meiner Zeit*, Munich 1996, 447.
23. For the basic problems of the foundation and significance of ethical norms with a full bibliography cf. H. Küng, *On Being a Christian*, New York and London 1974, Chapter D II, 1: Norms of the human.
24. Cf. Ex.34.28; Deut.4.13; 10.4.
25. Cf. Ex.20.2–17; Deut. 5.6–21.
26. Cf. H.Küng, *Christianity. Its Essence and History*, London and New York 1995, 52–55.
27. Z. Brzezinski, *Out of Control. Global Turmoil on the Eve of the 21st Century*, New York 1993, 221.
28. Cf. *International Herald Tribune*, 28 October 1996.
29. The figures in this section are those of L. Källén (Chairman of the Swedish Ericsson Corporation in Washington), 'Business and Lobbying the American Scene', in *The Report. SOMFY International Symposium Enlightenment in Stockholm 15–19 May 1996*, 27–31.
30. Interview, '"Wie nütze ich mir?", Wahlkampfberater Phil Noble über die Kunst, dem politischen Gegner nachhaltig zu schaden', in *Focus* 24/1996.
31. All the figures on the 1996 American election are taken from the *New York*

Times (cf. *International Herald Tribune*, 19/20 October, 20/27/28 December 1996). Cf. also H. E. Alexander and E.Corrado, *Financing the 1992 Election*, New York 1995.

32. Cf. the election results in the *International Herald Tribune*, 7 November 1996.
33. This is the proposal of the German Federal President R. Herzog, 'Die Rechte des Menschen', in *Die Zeit*, 6 September 1996.
34. A very informative survey of the different aspects of the sanctions are given by the twenty authors in the *Zeitschrift für ökumenische Begegnung und internationale Zusammenarbeit, Der Überblick* 2/ 1996; see especially the articles by the North American experts on sanctions, D.Cortright and M. Doxey, who have written important books on the subject.

A. I V A Global Ethic as a Foundation for Global Society

1. There is a bibliography on A.MacIntyre, R. Rorty, M. Foucault and R.Bubner in H. Küng, *Global Responsibility*, London and New York 1991, 148–9.
2. There is a bibliography on J.-F. Lyotard und W.Welsch in ibid., 144.
3. Cf. M.Walzer, *Spheres of Justice. A Defense of Pluralism and Equality*, New York 1983.
4. Cf. id. *Thick and Thin. Moral Argument at Home and Abroad*, Notre Dame/Ind. 1994, 1.
5. Ibid., 1f. (my emphasis). The quotations which follow appear on pp. 2f.
6. Cf. J. Rawls, A *Theory of Justice*, Cambridge/Mass. 1971. However, Rawls has substantially relativized his earlier reflections on the theory of justice and introduced them into the sphere of international relations.
7. Cf. id., 'The Law of Peoples', in S.Shute and S.Hurley (eds.), *On Human Rights*, New York 1993, 41–82. Cf. the critical discussion in F. R.Tesón, 'The Rawlsian Theory of International Law', *Ethics and International Affairs* 9, 1995, 79–99.
8. Cf. J. Habermas, *Theory of Communicative Action* I–II, Oxford 1986, 1989; id., *Moral Consciousness and Communicative Action*, Oxford 1990; id., *The New Conservatism*, Oxford 1990; id., *Philosophical Discourse of Modernity*, Oxford 1990.
9. Thus in his most recent volume of articles, *Die Einbeziehung des Anderen. Studien zur politischen Theorie*, Frankfurt 1996, Part 1, on 'How Rational is the Authority of the Ought?'.
10. Walzer, *Thick and Thin* (n.4), 4.
11. Ibid., 7.
12. Ibid., 9.
13. Ibid.
14. Ibid., 10.
15. Cf. the radio broadcast by the Director of the Max Planck Institute for the

History of Human Rights in Europe, Frankfurt am Main, D. Simon, 'Der Richter als Ersatzkaiser' (I am quoting from the mansucript).

16. Cf. the information in Z. Brzszinski, *Out of Control. Global Turmoil on the Eve of the 21st Century,* New York 1993, 105.

17. Cf. G. Keil and H. Kress, 'Pflicht', *Theologische Realenzyklopädie* XXVI, Berlin 1996, 438–49.

18. Cf. M. Huber, 'Prolegomena und Probleme eines internationalen Ethos', *Die Friedens-Warte* 53, 1955/56, 4, 305–29; the following quotations are on 305f. and 328f. Professor Dieter Senghaas recently drew my attention to this important article by Max Huber in which, happily, the term 'global ethic' (*Weltethos*) already appears (329). It (still) seemed impossible to Huber to get beyond the multiplicity, variety and contrast in the existing religions and ideologies and to bring them together in a 'global ethic'; in his view a 'global legal organization' could be achieved more easily than a global ethic. Huber also points out: 'Law can be broken like iron when it is not itself ethic. But ethic is like a diamond'(329). To this it may be replied, from a present-day perspective: while diamonds may differ in size, form and brilliance, they have similar internal structures. Today we know that despite all the differences between the religions, there are basic common factors particularly in their ethics, and thus it has proved possible to arrive at a global ethic.

In his *Interiorisierung der Transzendenz. Zum Problem Identität oder Reziprozität von Heilsethos und Weltethos* (1972), reprinted in his collected articles *Zur Theologie der Ethik. Das Weltethos im theologischen Diskurs,* Freiburg 1995, 131–50, the Tübingen moral theologian A.Auer, highly regarded for his Christian 'worldly piety' and autonomous morality, used the term in a completely different way – not in an interreligious humanistic context, but within the context of Christian theology, opposing it to an 'ethic of salvation'. So the claim in the foreword by his pupils to the volume of Auer's articles that the term 'global ethic', which I coined in analogy to global politics, global economy, global financial system and so on to denote a universal human ethic of the various religions, derives from Auer is both historically and substantively incorrect.

19. Cf. H. Küng and K.-J. Kuschel (eds.), *A Global Ethic. The Declaration of the Parliament of the World's Religions,* London and New York 1993.

20. Those involved were Pierre Trudeau (Canada), Miguel de la Madrid (Mexico) und Andries van Agt (The Netherlands). The following experts from the different religions took part: Mughram Al-Ghamdi (Saudi-Arabia), Michio Araki (Japan), Shanti Aram (India), Thomas Axworthy (Canada), Abdoljavad Falaturi (Iran), Ananda Grero (Sri Lanka), Kim Kyong-Dong (South Korea), Cardinal Franz König (Austria), Hans Küng (Germany), Peter Landesmann (Austria), Liu Xiao-feng (Hong Kong), L. M. Singhvi (India), Marjorie Suchocki (USA).

21. In addition to those already mentioned, the following were present in Vancouver: Oscar Arias Sanchez (Costa Rica), Malcolm Fraser (Australia), Kurt Furgler (Switzerland), Valéry Giscard d'Estaing (France), Kenneth D.Kaunda (Zambia), Kiichi Miyazawa (Japan), Abdel Salem Al-Majali (Jordan), José Sarney (Brazil), Kalevi Sorsa (Finland), Ola Ullsten (Sweden).
22. InterAction Council, *In Search of Global Ethical Standards*, Vancouver, Canada 1996, No. 2.
23. Ibid. No. 2.
24. Ibid., No. 9.
25. Ibid., No. 8.
26. Ibid., No. 9.
27. Ibid., No. 10.
28. Ibid., No. 11.
29. Ibid., No. 12.
30. Ibid., No. 13.
31. VgI. Küng and Kuschel (eds.), *A Global Ethic* (n.19), 18.
32. Cf. ibid., 22f.

A. V World Peace – A Challenge for the World Religions

1. Cf. H.Küng, *Christianity and the World Religions. Paths of Dialogue with Islam, Hinduism, and Buddhism* (with J.van Ess, H. von Stietencron and H. Bechert), London and New York 1986, reissued 1993, Epilogue.
2. UNESCO Colloquium, 'World Religions, Human Rights and World Peace', Paris, 8–10 February 1989.
3. Cf. S.P.Huntington, 'The Clash of Civilizations?', *Foreign Affairs* 72, 1993, no. 3, 22–49. There are first critical comments on this in H.Küng, *Christianity. Its Essence and History*, London and New York 1995, Chapter C V,9: Tasks for an analysis of postmodernity: A war of civilizations?
4. Huntington, 'The Clash of Civilizations?' (n.3), 39.
5. Cf. id., *The Clash of Civilizations*, New York 1996.
6. Cf. the critical comments on Huntington by F.Ajami, R.L.Bartley, L.Binyan, J.J.Kirkpatrick und K. Mahbubani in *Foreign Affairs* 72, 1993, no.4 (Sept./Oct.) und Huntington's 'Response' in no.5 (Nov./Dec.), 186–94. I have explained at length elsewhere why in the last two cases I distinguish not so much between basically different civilizations as between different paradigms (constellations in space and time) of one and the same Christianity.
7. Huntington, 'Response' (n.6), 191f. and 194.
8. Id., 'The Clash of Civilizations?' (n.3), 22.
9. Ibid., 25.
10. Id., *The Clash of Civilizations* (n.5), 318.

11. Ibid., 312.
12. Ibid., 321.
13. Ibid., 312–18.
14. Ibid., 320.
15. Ibid., 321.
16. Cf. D.Johnston and C.Sampson (eds.), *Religion.The Missing Dimension of Statecraft*, Oxford 1994.
17. Ibid., IX.
18. F.Luttwak, 'The Missing Dimension', in ibid., 8–19: 13.
19. Ibid., 14f.
20. Ibid., 16.
21. S.Burnett, 'Implications for the Foreign Policy Community', in Johnston and Sampson (eds.), *Religion* (n.16), 285–305: 293.
22. Cf. the thorough analysis of these two paradigms in Küng, *Christianity* (n.3), Chapter C II: The Ecumenical Hellenistic Paradigm of Christian Antiquity, and C III: The Roman Catholic Paradigm of the Middle Ages.
24. Quotation in Rosenfeld, 'How America Might Have Helped Avert the Slaughter', in *Washington Post/International Herald Tribune*, 13 March 1995.
24. Cf. the 'Basel Charter for the Federalistic Resolution of Conflicts', printed in *Neue Zürche Zeitung*, 4 October 1995. The Charter was worked out by more than eighty scientists and politicians at the international conference 'Federalism versus Ethnicity' held in Basel from 27 to 29 September 1995.
25. This is the legitimate concern of A. Glucksmann, *De Gaulle où es-tu?*, Paris 1995, Chapter IX, The Murderous Identity.
26. Cf. R. Huhle (ed.), *Von Nürnberg nach Den Haag: Menschenrechtsverbrechen vor Gericht. Zur Aktualität des Nürnberger Prozesses*, Hamburg 1996.
27. Cf. R. Goldstone, 'Über Frustration und Glaubwürdigkeit in Den Haag. Der Chefankläger des Uno-Kriegsverbrechertribunals zieht Bilanz', interview in *Neue Zürche Zeitung*, 20/21 July 1996.
28. Ibid.
29. Ibid.
30. The following quotations also come from the written opinion given by the Second Senate of the Federal Constitutional Court on 24 October 1996 (Manuscript, 52–5).
31. Through Article 20 para. 4 of the Basic Law the right to resist has gained constitutional status, but is only to be exercised in a subsidiary way: 'Germans have the right to resist anyone who ventures to do away with this (constitutional) ordinance; all Germans have the right to resist if they have no other expedient.' I am grateful to my colleagues Professor Jürgen Baumann and Ferdinand Kirchhof in the Law Faculty at Tübingen for the clarification of important points in this section.

32. This topic was discussed at the congress convened at Karlsruhe by the Prime Minister of Baden-Württemberg, Erwin Teufel, 'What holds modern society together? Individualism, responsibility and community in the twenty-first century', 6/7 April 1995. The contributions quoted below are published in E. Teufel (ed.), *Was hält die moderne Gesellschaft zusammen?*, Frankfurt 1996.

33. Thus the Federal constitutional judge E.-W Böckenförde, 'Fundamente der Freiheit', ibid., 89–99: 89. Böckenförde formulated the thesis quoted above as long as thirty years ago; it can hardly be said to have been fully accepted.

34. Thus the sociologist H. Dubiel, 'Von welchen Ressourcen leben wir? Erfolge und Grenzen der Aufklärung', ibid., 79–88.

35. This statement was made in the discussion by the Christian Democrat H. Geissler. See his contribution 'Die integrative Kraft der Grundwerte', ibid., 100–8.

36. That is how the director of Deutschland Radio, E.Elitz, summed up the discussion which I documented in my own contribution, 'Die Verantwortung der Religionen und der Kirchen', ibid., 286–93.

37. Thus the Tübingen philosopher O.Höffe, 'Individuum und Gemeinsinn – Thesen zu einer Sozialethik des 21. Jahrhunderts', ibid., 15–37: 24.

38. Cf. ibid., and the postscript to the written version of the lecture, in which the comments on religion were much expanded, 35f.

39. Ibid., 35.

40. Thus in the contribution to the congress by Gräfin Dönhoff, 'Verantwortung für das Ganze', ibid., 43–4: 43.

41. This happened to the markedly Roman Catholic political theorist H.Maier in the discussion, at the hands of the 1968 revolutionary D.Cohn-Bendit, who is now a protagonist of hedonism. Cf. H.Maier, 'Der unsichtbare Staat', ibid., 50–2, and D. Cohn-Bendit, 'Gelassenheit, Konsens und Streit', ibid., 38–42.

42. Cf. Küng, *Christianity* (n.3), C IV, 10: The two faces of fundamentalism, 635–49.

43. 'Opus Dei', *Brockhaus Enzyklopädie*, Vol. XVI, Mannheim [19]1991, 230. There is serious insider information on Opus Dei (in the most recent editions) in: P. Hertel, *Geheimnisse des Opus Dei. Verschlusssachen, Hintergründe, Strategien*, Freiburg 1995; id., *'Ich verspreche euch den Himmel.' Geistlicher Anspruch, gesellschaftliche Ziele und kirchliche Bedeutung des Opus Dei*, Düsseldorf 1991; R. Hutchison, *Their Kingdom Come*, New York 1996; R.Javier, *Im Bann des Opus Dei. Familien in der Zerreissprobe*, Zurich 1995; M. Tapia, *Tras el umbral*, 1992; K. Steigleder, *Das Opus Dei, eine Innenansicht*, Munich 1996.

44. In addition to the Munich Catholic dogmatic theologian L. Scheffczyk, who decades ago wrote a pamphlet against the theology of his former Tübingen colleague, the Munich philosopher Robert Spaemann has now

thought that he has to write against a global ethic. '*Si tacuisses, philosophus mansisses!*' ('Had you kept silent, you would have remained a philosopher!'). This comment on Spaemann's defamatory article 'Welt-ethos als "Projekt"' in the journal *Merkur* (9/10, 1996) may be sufficient for those who know the scene. The fact that this man, who has been given an honorary doctorate and made visiting professor in Spain by Opus Dei, and has been personally singled out by the Opus Dei prelate Alvaro del Portillo (bishop since 1990), defends in his article the fatal nominations of bishops by Rome, the unbiblical obligation to celibacy, the ban on the ordination of women and suchlike perhaps affects his philosophical honour but does not absolutely destroy it. And there may be personal factors that I do not know about behind his tirades against ethical commissions. But the fact that this philosopher makes public to all the world not only his ignorance in matters of inter-religious dialogue but also his jealous emotions and his resentment against the Enlightenment (indeed at both the beginning and end of his article he pathetically confesses that in the face of the 'Global Ethic Project' he has 'simply lost his cool head') makes one now doubt whether he is philosophically *compos mentis* – which will certainly do him no harm with Opus Dei.

As for my own position, I would simply note that so far I have experienced such confused, blinkered, total falsification of my intentions, statements and aims only in reactionary Roman Catholic pamphlets like the Swiss *Timor Domini* (popularly known as *Tumor Domini*, in analogy to the Spanish *Octopus Dei*). Even the true statements in this article with its tortured, wounded arguments go wrong because of the context and do not deserve a serious refutation: in any case my position in this book is clear. That this philosopher who at the centre of his article talks about a 'suspicion of nihilism' which clings to me, a Catholic theologian who has kept faith with his church despite all the adverse circumstances, does not augur well for his state of mind. As he himself says, this suspicion clearly rests on a 'prejudice', though later he 'tries to justify' it. At all events I cannot be expected to follow such a muddlehead, who on all sides denounces the 'rational middle way' (Aristotle and Thomas would turn in their graves), up the tree of absurdities which he himself has planted: 'transformation of ethics into a project, instrumentalization of ethics, institutionalization of ethics'. Any unprejudiced reader will recognize that this article is full of resentment about me, and as far as my cause is concerned, reduces itself to absurdity. The moral invective and the defamation of my Christian faith show a degree of hatred which also terrifies me for pastoral reasons. What have I done to this man? *Habeat sibi*, they would have said in Rome. My parting wish for his next trip to Pamplona is that '*el caballero de la trista figura*' may continue to find '*molinos di viento*' (windmills) to fight against there.

45. Pope John Paul II, Encyclical *Evangelium vitae*, English text *The Gospel of Life*, London 1995, nos.17; 19/28.

46. Ibid., no.13.
47. So I am told by the manager of the Global Ethic Foundation, S.Schlensog, in connection with the International Round Table 'Evaluation of the UN World Conferences 1990–1996 from the Perspective of Development Policy: A Comparison of their Goals, Results, and Implementation Strategies', Berlin, 29 October to 1 November 1996.
48. Cf. *Der Spiegel*, no. 2, 1993, lead story.
49. Thus H. Karasek, 'Verbrechen der Phantasie', in *Der Spiegel* No. 28, 1991. Starting from this case, my Tübingen colleague K.-J. Kuschel has made some detailed critical comments on the question of aesthetics and ethics in, 'Ästhetik ohne Ethik? Analysen zur Gegenwartsliteratur', in W. Wolbert (ed.), *Moral in einer Kultur der Massenmedien*, Freiburg 1994, 51–75.
50. Thus D.Cohn-Bendit in his contribution to the congress.
51. Thus, in solitary *Weltschmerz* and with a fixation on death, referring to a completely one-sided interpretation of European decadence from Baudelaire to Cioran, the German scholar K. H. Bohrer, 'Möglichkeiten einer nihilistischen Ethik' (a radio broadcast on SWF Baden-Baden, 8 December 1996). Bohrer, the editor of the journal *Merkur*, mentioned above, would have been the right person to whom to attach Spaemann's 'suspicion of nihilism' (n.44).
52. Cf. the major study by G.Schulze, *Die Erlebnisgesellschaft. Kultursoziologie der Gegenwart*, Frankfurt 1992, which offers a perceptive analysis on the basis of excellent empirical evidence.
53. Thus the new magazine editor of *Die Zeit*, S.Löffler, 'Die Spass-Generation hat sich müde gespielt', *Die Zeit*, 29 November 1996, here taking up Hermann Hesse's criticism of the 'magazine age'. See W.Jens and H. Küng, *Anwälte der Humanität. T. Mann, H. Hesse, H. Böll*, Munich 1989, ²1993, 210–15: 'Die Vision eines postmodernen Zeitalters', and 'Ein postmodernes Ethos'.
54. Cf. M.Gräfin Dönhoff, 'Verantwortung für das Ganze' (n.40), 44.
55. For the difference between fundamental trust and trust in God cf. H. Küng, *Does God Exist? An Answer for Today*, London and New York 1984, Chapters E: Yes to Reality – Alternative to Nihilism, and F. Yes to God – Alternative to Atheism.
56. Cf. H. Küng and K.-J. Kuschel (eds.), *A Global Ethic. The Declaration of the Parliament of the World's Religions*, London and New York 1993, 17.
57. Cf. D.Senghaas, *Wohin driftet die Welt? Über die Zukunft friedlicher Koexistenz*, Frankfurt 1994; especially the chapters 'Die Welt im Lichte des zivilisatorischen Hexagons' and 'Weltinnenpolitik: Ansätze für ein Konzept'.
58. Ibid., 48.
59. Cf. id., 'Dimensionen einer Weltfriedensordnung', forthcoming in *Jahrbuch Politisches Denken*, 1997.
60. O.Höffe (ed.), *Immanuel Kant. Zum ewigen Frieden*, Berlin 1995.

61. Id., 'Ausblick: Die Vereinten Nationen im Lichte Kants', in id. (ed.), *Immanuel Kant* (n.60), 245–72: 266.

62. Ibid., 266.

63. *The Commission on Global Governance, Our Global Neighbourhood*, Oxford 1995.

64. Cf. H. Küng, *Islam* (in preparation).

65. The following thoughts are based on a conversation with Dr K.Lefring-hausen (Bonn) and Pastor F.Brendle (Stuttgart) of the World Conference of the Religions for Peace (WCRP), who worked out a first draft which I then revised and subsequently discussed with various local groups of the German section of the WCRP. It was expanded on that basis by Prof. Dr J. Lähnemann (Erlangen/Nuremberg). I am grateful to all these. I would also like to thank Professors H.-K. Beckmann (Erlangen/Nuremberg), W. Kralewski (Tübingen) und D. Senghaas (Bremen) for valuable suggestions which have found their way into the text.

66. Cf. H. Küng, *Global Responsibility*, London and New York 1991, Chapter B V: Capacity for Dialogue and Steadfastness are not Opposites.

67. Job 8.12.

68. Job 1.4.

69. Job 1.5.

70. John 14.6.

71. After two decades I would not want to make the slightest deletion from my Book *On Being a Christian*, in which all this is developed in detail..

72. Cf. Küng, *Christianity and the World Religions* (n.1).

B. I *Questions about Globalization*

1. D.de Pury, H.Hauser and B. Schmid (eds.), *Mut zum Aufbruch. Eine wirtschaftspolitische Agenda für die Schweiz*, Zurich 1995, 13.

2. H.-P.Martin and H.Schumann, *Die Globalisierungsfalle. Der Angriff auf Demokratie und Wohlstand*, Hamburg 1996, 317.

3. Ibid.

4. E.U.von Weizsäcker, 'Im Turbokapitalismus herrschen die Gesetze des Dschungels', *Süddeutsche Zeitung*, 14 October 1996.

5. See the commentary on the book by T.Necker, President of the Bundesverband der Deutschen Industrie.

6. H.G.Preusse, *Handelspessimismus – alt und neu*, Tübingen 1991 shows that 'the mere extension of insights from the past into the future . . . usually proves irrelevant'; moreover, despite the modern 'pessimism over trade', Preusse optimistically gives 'forces directed towards a further free development of trade and production on a global scale . . . relatively good chances of establishing themselves in a long-term perspective' (211).

7. Cf. the figures given in the *New York Times/International Herald Tribune*, 11/12 January 1997.

8. N. Kloten, lecture given on 17 June 1995 in Reutlingen (manuscript).

9. G. Soros, '"Ich bin kein Spieler". Super-Spekulant George Soros über Milliardengier und seine Angst vor einem Crash des Weltfinanzsystems', in *Der Spiegel* 24/1996.

10. Cf. K.O.Feldt, 'What Happened to the Swedish Welfare Paradise?', in *The Report. SOMFY International Symposium Enlightenment in Stockholm 15–19 May 1996*, 66–72: 66.

11. Cf. ibid., 67.

12. For this it is necessary to consult major publications with contributions by many specialists, like M.Feldstein (ed.), *American Economic Policy in the 1980s*, Chicago 1994, or C.-L.Holtfrerich (ed.), *Interactions in the World Economy. Perspectives From International Economic History*, New York 1989.

13. L.C.Thurow, 'Die Illusion vom Jobwunder', *Die Zeit*, 25 Oktober 1996.

14. As well as a number of leading columnists (E.J.Dionne Jr, J.Hoagland, A.Lewis, W.Pfaff), among most recent major publications see especially J. K.Galbraith, A *Journey Through Economic Time. A Firsthand View*, Boston 1994; D.C.Korten, *When Corporations Rule the World*, San Francisco 1995.

15. These last figures are given under the title 'Social Unrest to Come' by the Professor for Business Administration at the University of Southern California, W.Bennis, in a commentary in the *Los Angeles Times/ International Herald Tribune*, 27 February 1996.

16. Thus according to the study by Columbia University, *One in Four*, New York 1996; cf. *International Herald Tribune*, 17 December 1996.

17. How far jobs are also being 'evacuated' in Europe is shown by the Swedish–Swiss concern ABB: 54,000 jobs have been abolished in Europe and 46,000 new ones created in Asia.

18. I have taken this last information from the admirable report produced by the Commission for Questions Relating to the Future, set up by the Free States of Bavaria and Saxony, *Erwerbstätigkeit und Arbeitslosigkeit in Deutschland. Entwicklung, Ursachen und Massnahmen*, I, Bonn 1996. It contains a comparison with other countries which industrialized earlier; the information on the USA, Sweden and Great Britain, 128–41, is of particular importance to us.

19. R.N.Goodwin, 'Die Reichen gewinnen den Klassenkampf. Warum die soziale Gerechtigkeit in Amerika auf der Strecke bleibt', *Die Zeit*, 2 August 1996.

20. This is the finding of the Bavaria/Saxony Commission (n.18), 138–41.

21. Cf. T.Wicker, *Tragic Failure. Racial Integration in America*, New York 1996.

22. D. L. Gertz – J. P. A. Baptista, *Grow to be Great*, New York 1995, 3.

23. Ibid., 19.

24. Even the father of the 'slimming' mania, S. Roach, now thinks that it has

gone too far: 'downsizing' and 'compression' of wages are ultimately the 'recipe for industrial suicide', and a 'backlash' from those concerned can be expected (cf. the report in *Süddeutsche Zeitung*, 18/19 May 1996).

25. Z. Brzezinski, *Out of Control. Global Turmoil on the Eve of the 21st Century*, New York 1993, 103; following quotations 103–7.

26. See the optimistic book by the US Government and World Bank adviser M. Moynihan, *The Coming American Renaissance. How to Benefit From America's Economic Resurgence*, New York 1996.

B. II *What Global Plan for Economic Policy?*

1. In clarifying the often confusing terminology I have been much helped by J.Starbatty, 'Soziale Marktwirtschaft als Forschungsgegenstand: Ein Literaturbericht', forthcoming 1997 in the *Festschrift* for the centenary of Ludwig Erhard's birth.

2. Cf. especially L.von Mises, *Nationalökonomie. Theorie des Handelns und Wirtschaftens*, Geneva 1940.

3. Cf. F.A. von Hayek, *The Road to Serfdom*, London 1944, ³1976.

4. Cf. J. M. Keynes, *The Economic Consequences of the Peace*, London 1919, 1971; id., *A Revision of the Treaty. Being a Sequel to the Economic Consequences of the Peace*, London 1922, 1971.

5. Cf. id., *The End of* Laissez-Faire, Cambridge 1926.

6. Cf. id., *The General Theory of Employment, Interest and Money*, London 1936, 1973.

7. Cf. J. K. Galbraith, *The Affluent Society*, London 1958, second revised edition Harmondsworth 1977; id., *A Journey Through Economic Time. A Firsthand View*, Boston 1994.

8. 'As far as possible – but that would be another topic – a change in this direction would be progress for economic research, the currently predominant orientation of which is formal and mathematical. At the same time it could prove that works like those in particular of Röpke, Rüstow und Müller-Armack with their anthropological stamp could prove highly modern' (Starbatty, 'Soziale Marktwirtschaft' [n.1], 7).

9. M. Friedman, *Capitalism and Freedom*, Chicago 1962, 12.

10. Id., 'Das ganze Sozialsystem ist falsch', conversation in *Der Spiegel* 3, 1982.

11. Cf. W R.Copland, *Economic Justice. The Social Ethics of US Economic Policy*, Nashville 1988.

12. Friedman, *Capitalism* (n.9), 12.

13. Ibid., 2.

14. Id., 'The Social Responsibility of Business Is to Increase Its Profits', in *New York Times Magazine*, 13 September 1970, reprinted in T.Donaldson and P H. Werhane (eds.), *Ethical Issues in Business. A Philosophical Approach*, Englewood Cliffs ³1988, 217–23.

15. Cf. K.Polanyi, *The Great Transformation*, New York 1944.
16. A. Smith, *An Inquiry into the Nature and Causes of the Wealth of Nations* (London 1776), Oxford 1976.
17. Id., *The Theory of Moral Sentiments* (London 1759), Oxford 1976.
18. Polanyi, *The Great Transformation* (n.15), 88f.
19. Cf. T.Eschenburg, 'Aus persönlichem Erleben: Zur Kurzfassung der Denkschrift 1943/44', in L.Erhard, *Kriegsfinanzierung und Schuldenkonsolidierung. Faksimiledruck der Denkschrift von 1943/44*, Frankfurt 1977, XV–XXI.
20. Cf. K. Hildebrand, 'Erhard', in *Staatslexikon*, Freiburg [7]1986, 354–7. Cf. N. Pieper, 'Was würde Erhard heute tun', *Die Zeit*, 24 May 1996.
21. Of course the centenary of the birth of Ludwig Erhard, already a myth in his lifetime, and with an influence that spans the parties even today, has led to attempts at denigration and to posturing. But the biography by the Mainz economic historian, V.Hentschel, *Ludwig Erhard. Ein Politikerleben*, Munich 1996, which is publicized as a 'farewell to the Erhard myth', carries little weight against the assent, indeed the veneration of so many of the politicians, businessmen and economist in the professional world of that time and the statement by the neoliberal F.A von Hayek, who was not otherwise in sympathy with the social market economy, that he had met wiser economists than Erhard, but only rarely anyone who was endowed with such an 'instinct for what was economically right'. Quoted in the review by N. Pieper, *Die Zeit*, 8 November 1996. Pieper criticizes as 'the greatest defect' of Hentschel's book 'the fundamental prejudice of the author towards the subject of his research'. And in fact one has only to compare say Hentschel's account of the 1943/44 memorandum or of Erhard's relationship to the resistance fighter Carl Goerdeler, who was later executed, with Ludwig Erhard's own memoirs (L. Erhard, *Kriegsfinanzierung*, VII–XIII). With so much manifest partisanship, even the sympathetic reader loses the desire to read on. Maliciousness in scholarship is even more offensive than it is in journalism.
22. N. Kloten, ' "Was zu bedenken ist" – Bemerkungen zum Referat von Rainer Klump: Wege zur Sozialen Marktwirtschaft – Die Entwicklung ordnungsphilosophischer Konzeptionen in Deutschland vor der Währungsreform', in E. W Streissler (ed.), *Studien zur Entwicklung der ökonomischen Theorie*, XVI, Berlin 1997 (forthcoming).
23. Cf. L. Erhard, *Wohlstand für alle*, Düsseldorf 1957.
24. Cf. W. Eucken, *Grundsätze der Wirtschaftspolitik*, ed F. Eucken and K.P.Hensel, Berlin 1952, Tubingen [6]1990. Also important is the pioneering work by E Böhm, *Die Ordnung der Wirtschaft als geschichtliche Aufgabe und rechtsschöpferische Leistung*, Stuttgart 1937.
25. Cf. A. Rüstow, *Das Versagen des Wirtschaftsliberalismus*, [no place of publication given] 1945, [2]1950; id., *Zwischen Kapitalismus und Kommunismus*, Godesberg 1949.

26. Cf. W Röpke, *Civitas Humana. Grundfragen der Gesellschafts- und Wirtschaftsreform*, Zurich 1944; id., *Jenseits von Angebot und Nachfrage*, Zurich 1958.

27. Cf. J. Starbatty, 'Müller-Armack', *Staatslexikon*, III, Freiburg 1987, 1238–40.

28. A. Müller-Armack, *Wirtschaftslenkung und Marktwirtschaft*, Hamburg 1947, especially Part II: Soziale Marktwirtschaft.

29. Id., *Wirtschaftsordnung und Wirtschaftspolitik. Studien und Konzepte zur Sozialen Marktwirtschaft und zur Europäischen Integration*, Freiburg 1966, Bern ²1976, 243 (my emphasis).

30. Cf. R. Blum, 'Soziale Marktwirtschaft', in *Staatslexikon* IV, Freiburg 1988, 1240–50; N. Kloten, 'Marktwirtschaft', in ibid., III (n.27), 1017–23.

31. Cf. Müller-Armack, *Wirtschaftslenkung*, 87f. (my emphasis).

32. There is a good survey in A. Rauscher, 'Sozialenzykliken', *Staatslexikon*, IV (n.30), 1250–7.

33. I am grateful to the social ethicist Gustav Gundlach SJ, who taught me during my studies in Rome from 1948 to 1955, to the moderate 'social circle' in the German College, and to an expert in Soviet Marxism, Gustav A. Wetter SJ., whose study circle I was also allowed to lead for a year, for my early introduction to the problems of social philosophy and social policy.

34. There is a precise and fair account of the current state of discussion, written with critical sympathy, in P.Carstens, 'Der gescheiterte Volkskanzler. Vor dreissig Jahren stürzte Erhard', *Frankfurter Allgemeine Zeitung*, 30 November 1996.

35. Cf. Pieper, 'Was würde Erhard heute tun?' (n.20).

36. That social and psychological elements (limited transparency, uncertainty, mood) play a major role in shifts in the economic situation was worked out by W.A.Jöhr, *Theoretische Grundlagen der Wirtschaftspolitik, II: Die Konjunkturschwankungen*, Tübingen 1952, 372–460. The distinguished Swiss economist dedicates this book of almost 700 pages to his wife Martita Jöhr, who stimulated him to reflect on the social and psychological aspects of the economic process. For years Martita Jöhr has shared the intentions of my work and has been interested in the idea of a global ethic, and therefore in 1996 she made possible the establishment of the Global Ethic Foundation of Switzerland by a generous bequest.

37. Cf. from a contemporary perspective the critical discussion with the ideologists of the 1968 movement in W.A..Jöhr, *Der Auftrag der Nationalökonomie. Ausgewählte Schriften*,Tübingen 1990, 416–95.

38. Carstens, 'Der gescheiterte Volkskanzler' (n.34).

39. Cf. P.Ulrich, *Transformation der ökonomischen Vernunft. Fortschrittsperspektiven der modernen Industriegesellschaft*, Bern ³1993.

40. Cf. I.Hauchler (ed.), *Globale Trends 1996. Fakten – Analysen – Prognosen*, Frankfurt 1995, here 10–32: id., *Weltordnungspolitik – Chance oder Utopie? Thesen an Steuerbarkeit globaler Entwicklung.*

41. Cf. W. R. Copeland, *Economic Justice. The Social Ethics of US Economic Policy*, Nashville 1988.

42. Cf. J.P.Wogaman, *Economics and Ethics. A Christian Inquiry*, London 1986.

43. P.Ulrich, 'Demokratie und Markt. Zur Kritik der Ökonomisierung der Politik', in *Jahrbuch für christliche Sozialwissenschaften* 36, 1995, 74–95: 75f. In this article, which I shall follow, there is a reference to a sign of the reversal of the relationship between democratic politics and the market economy in the ancestor of the Chicago School, L. von Mises (*Nationalökonomie. Theorie des Handelns und Wirtschaftens*, Geneva 1940, 260), and a criticism of 'professional advocates of philosophical ethics, social, legal and political philosophy', who 'often in an amazingly uncritical way succumb to the analytical charms of the economic approach and nowadays in part tend to base themselves more on an economic theory of democracy (A. Downs), justice (O.Höffe), indeed even morality (K. Homann and I. Pies), than on their own categories of practical reason, to be developed in reflection, though some professional philosophers, in keeping with the spirit of the time, are evidently disillusioned about their normative power' (79).

44. Cf. Hauchler, *Weltordnungspolitik* (n.40), 16.

45. Cf. C. Watrin, 'Geld – Massstab für alles?', in H.Hesse and O.Issing (eds.), *Geld und Moral*, Munich 1994, 167–78: 178.

46. Cf. R. E. Lane, *The Market Experience*, Cambridge 1991.

47. Ulrich, 'Demokratie und Markt' (n.43), 90.

48. Hauchler, *Weltordnungspolitik* (n.40), 20f. (my emphases).

49. Ulrich, 'Demokratie und Markt', 94.

50. Ibid.

51. Hauchler, *Weltordnungspolitik* (n.40), 21f.: summary 21; argument 16–20.

52. Thus A. Schüller, 'Gefährden internationale Kapitalmärkte Stabilitat und Wohlstand? Ein Plädoyer gegen die Forderung nach verscharfter Finanzmarkt-Regulierung', *Neue Zürche Zeitung*, 28/29 December 1996. G. Soros, 'Die kapitalistische Bedrohung', *Die Zeit*, 17 January 1997, differs; cf. id., *Soros on Soros*, New York 1995, esp.ch.5.

53. Cf. N. Kloten, Die "Bretton Woods Commission": Zur Zukunft der Internationalen Währungsordnung', in W. Zohlnhöfer (ed.), *Zukunftsprobleme der Weltwirtschaftsordnung*, Berlin 1996, 133–70.

54. H.-D. Assmann, *Globalisierung der Finanzmärkte: Auf dem Weg zu einer Internationalen Finanzordnung? Symposion 'Das Recht vor der Herausforderung eines neuen Jahrhunderts: Erwartungen in Japan und Deutschland', Schloss Hohentübingen, 25–27. Juli 1996* (manuscript).

55. Ibid.

B. III Responsible Economics

1. M. Huber, 'Prolegomena und Probleme eines internationalen Ethos', *Die Friedens-Warte* 53, 1955/56, no. 4, 312.
2. Ibid.
3. Ibid., 313.
4. Ibid., 324f.
5. The Commission on Global Governance, *Our Global Neighbourhood*, Oxford 1995; this commission stems from an initiative by the former German Federal Chancellor Willy Brandt and was established in 1992 with the support of the General Secretary of the United Nations, Boutros Boutros Ghali. Its co-chairmen are Ingvar Carlsson (Sweden) and Shridath Ramphal (Guyana); other members are Ali Alatas (Indonesia), Abdlatif Al-Hamad (Kuwait), Oscar Arias (Costa Rica), Anna Balletbo i Puig (Spain), Kurt Biedenkopf (Germany), Allan Boesak (South Africa), Manuel Camacho Solis (Mexico), Bernard Chidzero (Zimbabwe), Barber Conable (United States of America), Jacques Delors (France), Jiri Dienstbier (Czech Republik), Enrique Iglesias (Uruguay), Frank Judd (Great Britain), Hong-koo Lee (Republic of Korea), Wangari Maathai (Kenya), Sadako Ogata (Japan), Olara Otunnu (Uganda), I.G.Patel (India), Celina Vargas do Amaral Peixoto (Brazil), Jan Pronk (The Netherlands), Qian Jiadong (China), Marie-Angélique Savané (Senegal), Adele Simmons (United States of America), Maurice Strong (Canada), Brian Urquhart (Great Britain), Yuli Vorontsov (Russia). The general secretary is Hans Dahlgren.
6. Ibid., xvif. (emphases in the following mostly mine).
7. Ibid., xvii.
8. Ibid.
9. Ibid. , 7.
10. This follows in Chapters III to VI of the Commission report.
11. Ibid., 46.
12. Ibid., 47.
13. Ibid.
14. Ibid., 49.
15. Ibid., 49.
16. Ibid., 55f.
17. Ibid., 55.
18. Ibid., 55.
19. Ibid., 56.
20. Ibid.
21. Ibid.
22. Ibid.
23. Ibid.
24. Ibid., 57.
25. Cf. in what follows the heavily systematized and concentrated abbreviated

version of the Commission's report in D. Messner and F. Nuscheler, 'Global Governance. Herausforderungen an die deutsche Politik an der Schwelle zum 21. Jahrhundert', in *Policy Paper* 2, produced by the Foundation for Development and Peace, Bonn 1996.

26. For the problem of social standards, which are meant to ensure that competitive disadvantages follow from the failure to respect social human rights, see H. Sautter, 'Sozialklauseln für den Welthandel – wirtschaftsethisch betrachtet', *Hamburger Jahrbuch für Wirtschafts- und Gesellschaftspolitik* 40, 1995, 227-45.

27. Messner and Nuscheler, 'Global Governance' (n.25), 5 and 2.

28. *Report of the World Commission on Culture and Development, Our Creative Diversity*, Paris 1995. Chairman: Javier Pérez de Cuéllar (Peru). Honorary members: Crown Prince El Hassan Bin Talal (Jordan), Aung San Suu Kyi (Burma), Claude Lévi-Strauss (France), Ilya Prigogine (Belgium), Derek Walcott (Santa Lucia), Elie Wiesel (United States of America). Members: Lourdes Arizpe (Mexico), Yoro Fall (Senegal), Kurt Furgler (Switzerland), Celso Furtado (Brazil), Niki Goulandris (Greece), Keith Griffin (Great Britain), Mahbub ul Haq (Pakistan), Elizabeth Jelin (Argentina), Angeline Kamba (Zimbabwe), Ole-Henrik Magga (Norway), Nikita Mikhalkov (Russia), Chie Na-kane (Japan), Leila Takla (Egypt). Executive Secretary: Yudhishthir Raj Isar (India).

29. Ibid., 34.

30. Ibid.

31. Ibid., 35.

32. Ibid.

33. Ibid.

34. Ibid., 36.

35. Ibid., 40-6.

36. InterAction Council, *In Search of Global Ethical Standards*, Vancouver, Canada 1996, No. 13.

37. H. Küng and K.-J. Kuschel, *A Global Ethic. The Declaration of the Parliament of the World's Religions*, London and New York 1993, 26-9.

38. An indication of the speed of the development in the 1990s is the important book by the Professor for Business Ethics at Georgetown University, Washington DC, T.Donaldson, *The Ethics of International Business*, Oxford 1989. Announced as the first book on the 'moral nature of international business', it indeed deals at length with the moral foundations, rights, obligations and decision-making processes of the 'multinationals', but does not once use the word 'globalization' – immediately before the revolutionary developments of 1989!

39. One has been announced by P. Ulrich, *Integrative Wirtschaftsethik. Grundlagen einer lebensdienlichen Ökonomie*, Bern 1997.

40. Cf. Küng and Kuschel, *A Global Ethic* (n.37), 24.

41. From a historical perspective see K. E. Born, 'Die ethische Beurteilung des

Geldwesens im Wandel der Geschichte', in H. Hesse and O.Issing (eds.), *Geld und Moral*, Munich 1994, 1–20.

42. Cf. Deut.23.20.

43. Cf. Matt. 6,24.

44. Cf. Matt. 6.33.

45. Cf. Luke 8.1–3; Mark 15.40f. par.

46. Cf. H. Tietmeyer, 'Zur Ethik wirtschaftspolitischen Handelns', in Hesse and Issing (eds.), *Geld und Moral* (n.41), 115–23. In his contribution the President of the German Federal Bank not unjustly criticizes in various ways the objections made from the side of the church to 'ethically responsible and necessary decisions of economic or social policy' (118). Hyped abroad by those ignorant of economics as the 'high priest of the DM' (to use P.Bourdieu's phrase), and often attacked vigorously as a representative of the financial policy of the Federal Bank, Hans Tietmeyer appeals in the face of his critics to the 'role of guardian and adviser' over financial stability prescribed by legislation for the Federal Bank. Cf. id., 'Der Stabilität verpflichtet', *Frankfurter Allgemeine Zeitung*, 28 December 1996.

47. Cf. H.Hesse, *Wirtschaft und Moral*, Bursfelder Universitätsreden 6, Gottingen 1987, 10.

48. Ibid., 11.

49. Ibid

50. P. Ulrich, 'Unternehmensethik und "Gewinnprinzip": Versuch der Klärung eines unerledigten wirtschaftsethischen Grundproblems', in H. G. Nutzinger (ed.), *Wirtschaftsethische Perspektiven III. Unternehmensethik, Verteilungsprobleme, methodische Ansätze*, Berlin 1996, 137–69: 166. In this article Ulrich distinguishes his integrative business ethic from instrumentalized, charitable and corrective business ethics (presented in the form of ideal models). For the present state of the fluid discussion see the relevant contributions in H. Steinmann and A. Löhr (eds.), *Unternehmensethik*, second revised and expanded edition Stuttgart 1991.

51. P.L. Berger, 'Demokratie und geistige Orientierung. Sinnvermittlung in der Zivilgesellschaft', in W. Weidenfeld (ed.), *Demokratie am Wendepunkt. Die demokratische Frage als Projekt des 21. Jahrhunderts*, Berlin 1996, 450–68.

52. Cf. K. Homann, 'Wettbewerb und Moral', *Jahrbuch für Christliche Sozialwissenschaften* 31, 1990, 34–56: 55. For criticism of Homann's position cf also P. Rottländer, 'Ordnungsethik statt Handlungsethik? Bemerkungen zum wirtschaftlichen Programm der neuen Institutionenökonomik', *Orientierung* 60, 1996, 165–71.

53. Cf. G. Engel, 'Wirtschaftsethik als ökonomische Theorie der Moral. Ein Überblick', in *Diskussionsbeiträge aus dem volkswirtschaftlichen Seminar der Universität Göttingen* 52, April 1991 (manuscript), 43f.

54. Ibid., 44.

55. B. Pischetsrieder, 'Antwort auf eine Umfrage', *Rheinischer Merkur*, 20 December 1996.
56. O. Renn, 'Ökologisch denken – sozial handeln: Zur Realisierbarkeit einer nachhaltigen Entwicklung und die Rolle der Kultur- und Sozialwissenschaften', in H.G.Kastenholz, K.H.Erdmann and M.Wolff (eds.), *Nachhaltige Entwicklung. Zukunftschancen für Mensch und Umwelt*, Berlin 1996, 79–117, quoted from the manuscript of the speech.
57. Ibid., quoted from the manuscript of the speech.
58. How much not only economics and politics but also questions of ecology, demography, agriculture and the revolution in industry, communication and finance have become questions about survival on the threshold of the twenty-first century is shown in global and regional perspectives by the American historian P. Kennedy, *Preparing for the Twenty-First Century*, New York 1993.
59. D. Birnbacher and C. Schicha, 'Vorsorge statt Nachhaltigkeit – Ethische Grundlagen der Zukunftsverantwortung', in Kastenholz, Erdmann and Wolff (eds.), *Nachhaltige Entwicklung* (n.56), 141–56: 145.
60. O. Renn, 'Ökologisch denken' (n.56), quoted from the manuscript of the speech.
61. Here I am using formulations by the Tübingen ethicist Dietmar Mieth. Cf. his article 'Theological and Ethical Reflections on Bioethics', in *Concilium* 203, 1989, 26–38 (the whole issue is devoted to the topic of 'Ethics in the Natural Sciences').
62. Birnbacher and Schicha, 'Vorsorge' (n.59), 154.
63. Ibid.
64. Cf. O.Höffe, *Moral als Preis der Moderne. Ein Versuch über Wissenschaft, Technik und Umwelt*, Franklurt 1993, 151–71.
65. Ibid., 155–67.
66. H. Jonas, *The Imperative of Responsibility. In Search of an Ethics for the Technological Age*, Chicago 1985, 43.
67. Ibid.
68. Ibid., 36.
69. Ibid., 12.
70. Ibid., 37.
71. Ibid., 40.
72. Ibid., 45.
73. Ibid.

B. IV Ethic, Business and Managers

1. K. Schwab and H. Kroos, *Moderne Unternehmensführung im Maschinenbau*, Frankfurt 1971, 21.
2. Cf. H.Steinmann, 'Zur Lehre der "Gesellschaftlichen Verantwortung der Unternehmensführung". Zugleich elne Kritik des Davoser Manifests', in

Wirtschaftswissenschaftliches Studium 10, October 1973, 467–73 and 500. The version printed on 472f. is identical with the final version of the Davos Manifesto.

3. Thus Steinmann, 'Zur Lehre' (n.2); similarly, again with reference to M.Friedman, the economist G.Engel, 'Wirtschaftsethik als ökonomische Theorie der Moral. Ein Überblick', in *Diskussionsbeiträge aus dem volkswirtschaftlichen Seminar der Universität Göttingen* 52, April 1991 (manuscript).

4. H. Steinmann and A. Löhr, *Grundlagen der Unternehmensethik*, second revised and enlarged edition, Stuttgart 1991, 97.

5. *An Interfaith Declaration, A Code of Ethics on International Business for Christians, Muslims and Jews*, London 1993.

6. Caux Round Table, *Principles For Business*, The Hague 1994. The preparation for this was done by the Minnesota Center for Corporate Responsibility, Minneapolis/USA.

7. Id., Preamble (subsequent quotations also come from this).

8. Id., *Principles* (n.6), Section 2.

9. Ibid. These responsiblities are the basis for everything else: obligations towards the foreign countries in which these firms are active, and to the world community generally, respect for the environment, support for multilateral trade.

10. Id., *Principles* (n.6), Section 3.

11. *An Interfaith Declaration, A Code of Ethics* (n.5), 16.

12. Caux Round Table, *Principles* (n.6), Introduction.

13. Ibid., Section 2.

14. Ibid.

15. Cf. the reservations of the Deputy Foreign Minister of Singapore, K.Mahbubani, in his response to Huntington's 'Clash of Civilizations?', in *Foreign Affairs* 72, 1993, no.4, 14.

16. Cf. W J. Bennett, *The Book of Virtues. A Treasury of Great Moral Stories*, New York 1994.

17. Cf. T. Koh, 'The 10 Values That Undergird East Asian Strength and Success', *International Herald Tribune*, 12 December 1993.

18. Cf. H. Küng and J. Ching, *Christianity and Chinese Religions*, New York and London 1989, reissued 1993.

19. Cf. L. Vandermeersch, *Le nouveau monde sinisé*, Paris 1986.

20. Cf. Küng and Ching, *Christianity and Chinese Religions* (n.18), Ching's remarks on Confucianism today, 81-91.

21. Cf. Confucius, *Analects* XII,7.

22. Han Minzhu (ed.), *Cries for Democracy. Writings and Speeches from 1989 Chinese Democracy Movement*, Princeton, NJ 1990.

23. K. Schwab and C. Smadja, 'Start Taking the Backlash Against Globalization Seriously', in *International Herald Tribune*, 1 February 1996.

24. Federal President R. Herzog, *Focus* 52/1996.

25. Cf. the article 'Globalisierung verändert die Arbeitswelt. Das St. Galler Management-Symposium zeigt die Problematik des Wachstums auf', *Süddeutsche Zeitung*, 24 May 1996.

26. M. Camedessus, report on the conference 'Economic Growth for What Kind of Future?', Rome, 30 November – 2 December 1995.

27. Cf. the almost 1000-page volume edited by M. Stackhouse, D.P.McCann and S.J.Roels, *On Moral Business. Classical and Contemporary Resources for Ethics in Economic Life*, Grand Rapids, Mich. 1996.

28. Cf. K.O.Feldt, 'What happened to the Swedish Welfare Paradise?', in *The Report. SOMFY International Symposium Enlightenment in Stockholm 15–19. Mai 1996*, S. 66–72: 71.

29. I am grateful for this information to K.Leisinger, the Basel Professor for the Sociology of Development and head of the Novartis Foundation for Sustainable Development. Cf. his forthcoming book *Unternehmensethik. Globale Verantwortung und modernes Management* (Munich 1997).

30. Cf. ibid., 19f.

31. Cf. G.Gerken, interview in *Stern*, 10 November 1988.

32. Cf. A. Jay, *Management and Machiavelli*, London 1967.

33. Ibid., 36.

34. Cf. A. Riklin, *Die Führungslehre von Niccolò Machiavelli*, Bern 1996, 10–21: 'Renaissance des Machiavellismus'.

35. Ibid., 84.

36. Cf. F X. Kaufmann, W.Kerber and P.M.Zulehner, *Ethos und Religion bei Fuhrungskräften. Eine Studie im Auftrag des Arbeitskreises für Führungs-kräfte in der Wirtschaft (München)*, Munich 1986, above all Part IV: 'Bewusstseins-Anpassung: Religiöse Indifferenz und Opportunismus'.

37. R.K.Sprenger, *Das Prinzip Selbstverantwortung. Wege zur Motivation*, Frankfurt 1995.

38. Ibid., 38.

39. Ibid., 242.

40. Cf. J. Staute, *Der Consulting-Report. Vom Versagen der Manager zum Reibach der Berater*, Frankfurt 1996.

41. Ibid., 235.

42. Cf. P.F.Drucker and I. Nakauchi, *The Time of Challenges/The Time of Reinventing*, Tokyo 1996.

43. J. B. Ciulla, 'Business Leadership and Moral Imagination in the Twenty-First Century', in Andrew R.Cecil (ed.), *Moral Values: The Challenge of the Twenty-First Century*, Dallas,Tex. 1996, 155f. Cf. also T.R.Piper, M.C.Gentile and S. D.Parks, *Can Ethics be Taught? Perspectives, Challenges, and Approaches at Harvard Business School*, Boston 1993. W.D.Hitt, who also emphasizes the ethical dimension in a variety of publications on management consultancy, has very recently written a book on a global ethic: *A Global Ethic. The Leadership Challenge*, Columbus/Ohio 1996. R.E.Allinson, *Global Disasters. Inquiries into Management Ethics*, Hong

Kong 1996, analyses moral responsibility in business in the light of the serious business catastrophes of the past decade.

44. Cf. the Emnid Institute study, in *Der Spiegel* 38/1994.

45. Cf. the book by two economic journalists, F.Bräuninger and M.Hasenbeck, *Die Abzocker. Selbstbedienung in Politik und Wirtschaft*, Düsseldorf 1994,14: 'the deeper causes are a universal loss of values, the lack of moral principles and suitable models' (368).

46. Cf. M.Frechen, 'Geschenke sind tabu', *Die Zeit*, 6 October 1995.

47. Cf. T.M. Jones and F.H.Gautschi, 'Will the Ethics of Business Change? A Survey of Future Executives', *Journal of Business Ethics* 7, 1988, 232f.

48. Cf. W Kerber, 'Bewusstseins-Orientierung: Zur Begründung ethischer Normen in einer säkularisierten Gesellschaft', in Kaufmann, Kerber and Zulehner, *Ethos und Religion* (n.36), 121–214: 182.

49. Cf. the interesting typology of understandings of business responsibility (instrumentalist, paternalist, legalist, idealist...) in P.Ulrich and U.Thidemann, *Ethik und Erfolg. Unternehmensethische Denkmuster von Fuhrungskräften – eine empirische Studie*, Bern 1992.

50. The author of *The End of History and the Last Man*, F.Fukuyama, discusses the signifiance of trust – distinguishing between 'low-trust societies' and 'high-trust societies' – in his extensive study *Trust. The Social Virtues and the Creation of Prosperity*, New York 1995. For a basic treatment of trust see H.Sautter, *Was glaubt der 'homo oeconomicus'?*, Marburg 1994.

A Word of Thanks

Global politics, global economy, global ethic: if I wanted to thank all those throughout the world who have helped me over five decades through meetings, conversations and books, on visits, congresses, meetings of experts and guest seminars, to understand this world, its politics and economics, I would need to fill all too many pages.

So I shall limit myself to expressing my thanks to those so to speak representative colleagues who within the University of Tübingen have been an inestimable help for this book through their active participation in our interdisciplinary colloquia and seminars and through a great deal of personal contact: Professors Otto Bachof (Public Law), Theodor Eschenburg (Political Science), Norbert Kloten (Economic Theory), Gerd Kohlhepp (Economic Geography), Volker Rottberger (Political Science); then from outside Tübingen Professors Peter Ulrich (Business Ethics, St Gallen) and Hermann Sautter (National Economy, Göttingen). In addition to my colleagues Norbert Kloten and Peter Ulrich who read the whole manuscript, Professors Anselm Doering-Manteuffel (Modern History) and Alois Riklin (Political Science) read Part A and Professors Heinz Gert Preusse and Joachim Starbatty (both Economic Policy) Part B, all despite pressure of work. They have unselfishly helped me to correct and sharpen my views at some points in this minefield of politics and economics. It should go without saying that I bear sole responsibility for the final text of this book.

Since I always first write out my books two or three times by hand, line by line, before I dictate them, I am more dependent than others on a secretary. And when I am writing such a complex book of this, with the vision of the whole before my eyes, from beginning to end, each section needs constant expansion and correction. Before the computer age every page had to be typed out afresh between six and twelve times. Now it is no longer possible to determine how many thousands of corrections have been entered into the computer. So I am grateful to my personal secretary Inge Baumann for her endless patience. As successor to

Eleonore Henn, who has often helped her out, she has worked herself splendidly into her many tasks; and I am also grateful to Annette Stuber-Rousselle.

My colleague Karl-Josef Kuschel now has his own chair in the theology of culture and inter-religious dialogue: I am grateful to him for the trouble he has taken in reading through the finished chapters. Time and again the manuscript has been read by Frau Marianne Saur to make sure that it is understandable. But many corrections have come from the younger members of our team, Johannes Frühbauer and Michel Hofmann; the latter had the burden of getting hold of the considerable number of books and checking the notes. The design and production has again been in the experienced hands of Stephan Schlensog, Manager of the Global Ethic Foundation. I am grateful to all these for their intense and highly committed collaboration.

I must also mention that this time I have asked a tremendous amount of Piper Verlag. The problems of world politics and economics, which burst all bounds, called for a much larger and longer book than I expected. So I am grateful for all their understanding and for the smooth collaboration of the publisher, Viktor Niemann; the Lektor, Ulrich Wank; and the Production Manager, Hanns Polanetz.

I am particularly grateful to the Robert Bosch Jubilee Foundation and the Daimler Benz Fund in the persons of Dr Markus Bierich and Dr Paul A.Stein. With this book the project 'No world peace without peace among the religions' which they have encouraged reaches its formal conclusion. The volume on *Islam* must wait, but since a third of it is already written, it will be finished in due course.

I have dedicated this book to Count and Countess von der Groben. The Global Ethic Foundation which they have made possible was a gift from heaven, since it enables me to continue my scholarly tasks without a break after my retirement.

When I look back on this whole event, one of my favourite sayings from the Bible comes to my lips: 'What do you have that you have not received?' (I Corinthians 4.7).

Translator's Note

This book has posed more translation difficulties than usual. German often has one word which does duty for two or three English ones (e.g. *Pflicht* = duty, responsibility, obligation; *Wirtschaft* = both business and economy). Moreover, the differences between German and Anglo-Saxon discussions of politics and economics go deeper than mere terminology and it is virtually impossible to translate one climate of thought into another. Thirdly, the structure of the book, its chapter headings and sub-headings impose their own constraints, in particular in the contrast between 'real' and 'ideal'. *Realpolitik* has established itself in English untranslated, and 'real politics' doesn't sound quite right; however, *Idealpolitik*, the contrast with which is integral to the first part of the book, just doesn't appear at all in Anglo-Saxon political discussion. I have done my best to struggle with the situation, and ask readers to forgive any oddnesses and infelicities.

I am especially grateful to Professor Ronald Preston for reading through the whole translation; his expertise in the two areas with which the book is concerned have vastly improved it, and saved me from some errors. However, any remaining are my own. I am also grateful to Professor Don Smith of Grinnell College, Iowa, for supplying the original texts of a number of references to American books which were inaccessible here.

John Bowden

Index